Globalization and Labour–Management Relations

Globalization and Labour–Management Relations

Dynamics of Change

C.S. VENKATA RATNAM

Los Angeles | London | New Delhi
Singapore | Washington DC | Melbourne

Copyright © C.S. Venkata Ratnam, 2001

All rights reserved. No part of this book may be reproduced or utilized in any form or by any means, electronic or mechanical, including photocopying, recording or by any information storage or retrieval system, without permission in writing from the publisher.

First published in 2001 by

SAGE Publications India Pvt Ltd
B1/I-1 Mohan Cooperative Industrial Area
Mathura Road, New Delhi 110 044, India
www.sagepub.in

SAGE Publications Inc
2455 Teller Road
Thousand Oaks, California 91320, USA

SAGE Publications Ltd
1 Oliver's Yard, 55 City Road
London EC1Y 1SP, United Kingdom

SAGE Publications Asia-Pacific Pte Ltd
3 Church Street
#10-04 Samsung Hub
Singapore 049483

Published by Vivek Mehra for SAGE Publications India Pvt Ltd, typeset in 10.3 pt Garamond by Innovative Processors, New Delhi.

Library of Congress Cataloging-in-Publication Data

Venkata Ratnam, C.S.
 Globalization and labour-management relations: dynamics of change/ C.S. Venkata Ratnam.
   p. cm.
 Includes bibliographical references and index.
 1. Industrial relations—India. 2. Globalization. 3. India—Economic policy—1980 I. Title.

HD8686.5.V44   2000   331'.0954—dc21   00-055386

ISBN: 978-07-619-9490-9 (PB)

SAGE Team: Uma Garud, R.A.M. Brown and Santosh Rawat

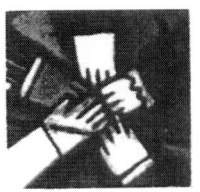

Contents

	Preface	7
One	A Historical Analysis of Industrial Relations in India	13
Two	Labour–Management Relations and the World in Transition	76
Three	Economic Development and Industrial Relations: The Case of South and South-East Asia	105
Four	The Economic and Social Dimensions of Structural Adjustment Reforms	132
Five	Competitive Labour Policies and Labour Laws in Indian States	180
Six	Social Dialogue and the Reform Process	208
Seven	The Labour Adjustment Process	239
Eight	Aligning Labour Policy with Economic Policies and Industrialization Strategies	254
Nine	Judicial Activism	267
Ten	India and International Labour Standards	281
Eleven	New Paradigms in Employment Relations	302
	Author Index	337
	Subject Index	340
	About the Author	343

Preface

In the period following the Second World War, most of humanity has broken free from the clutches of colonialism and won political freedom. Since the end of the Cold War in the late 1980s almost all the countries in the world, which pursued the path of centrally planned socialist or communist regimes, have shifted to a market economy, albeit on a negative vote. Military dictatorships have propped up intermittently in some countries, but these have usually come to be shunned. At the dawn of the new millennium, however, over a third of the world's population still suffers from illiteracy, poverty and unemployment and India is home to the largest proportion of this third.

At the time of Independence in 1947, India was one of the few major economic powers in the Asia Pacific region, next only to China. India chose to pursue the path of a socialist republic and embarked on a planned mixed economy. During the late 1960s and early 1970s India became more inward looking and began to pursue policies of self-reliance based on an import substitution industrialization policy. This was the period when several of the miracle economies of Asia embarked on an export-oriented industrialization policy. Most other countries even in South Asia began to open up their economies willy-nilly by the early 1980s, but India opened its economy and cautiously pursued the policies of structural adjustment based on the 'Washington consensus' and dictated by the Bretten Wood twins—the World Bank and the International Monetary Fund—in the wake of a crisis precipitated by the Gulf War and the collapse of the former Soviet Union. During the decade of the 1990s India completed its first generation economic reforms. On the eve of the new millennium it began its tryst with second generation economic reforms. In the first 50 years of its political independence, India missed the opportunities of industrialization in the old economy. But the knowledge economy of the new millennium holds out the promise for an information technology leap in the service sector, which could make up for the technological lag in the manufacturing sector. While the workers and the trade unions were skeptical about the impact of the 'new economic regime', the initial euphoria too amongst the industrialists about economic reforms of the 1990s gradually became subdued. The skeptics were apprehensive about the revival of the ghost of the East India Company. Domestic industry was, in some sectors, finding it difficult to compete even in domestic markets, let alone in export markets, and increase their market access in the developed world. Hitherto labour had been protected in the labour markets and capital in the product markets. Now both feel less protected or even unprotected. The consumer, who received a raw deal in the protectionist regime, is beginning to realize the advantages of a buyer's market, with considerable choice in select fast moving consumer goods segments. Critical areas of the economy such as key inputs and infrastructure continue to be plagued with inadequate and erratic supply, low quality, and increasing price. The proponents of the reforms, however, are sanguine about India's potential to take on the world in the new economy.

India has everything—abundant resources and a growing market—yet, its economic growth has been more or less nullified by the population growth. Overactivity in regulation and controls and underactivity in economic and social development has also deprived India from realizing its true potential.

There are many explanations about what ails the Indian economy. From the perspective of labour and labour–management relations, the arguments so far have lacked a balanced perspective. The pro-labour proponents look at labour markets and harp on poverty, unemployment and falling real wages and the share of labour in the GDP. The pro-industry proponents wax eloquent on the need to cut costs and improve competitiveness. The need of the hour is to harmonize the concerns of both labour and product markets and look at the issue not in terms of equity vs efficiency, but in terms of the promotion of equity and efficiency.

The Finance Minister, Mr Yashwant Sinha has, in his budget speech on 28th February 2001, proposed certain investor-friendly labour law reforms. He has promised to waive prior approvals for lay-off, closure and retrenchment in companies employing less than 1,000 (as against 100 at present) and amend the Contract Labour Act to permit the engagement of contract labour. Similar proposals from Maharashtra and Punjab, made earlier this year, await central government clearance. Both Andhra Pradesh and Kerala took initiatives in the year 2000 to come out with a new vision on labour policy; while the former has rationalized labour inspection, the latter has promised action on skills training, mobilizing workers' funds and strengthening tripartite boards for different, major occupations. While intentions matter, the process of making labour law changes in this country has never been easy. The disinvestment of the Bharat Aluminum Company Limited mirrors the approach and attitude of the central government. By putting the cabinet decision to vote, the government is sending a clear signal that it is more serious this time than ever before.

Mere changes in labour laws and hasty, though delayed, privatization efforts are not adequate and sufficient. There is need for a significant stepping up of investments in the spheres of social and physical infrastructure. On the social infrastructure front, there is little hope as yet, including in the budget for the year 2001-2002. Concerning physical infrastructure, however, the initiative of the Prime Minister in persuading the chief ministers of different states to agree to a minimum agenda on power sector reforms raises hopes, Mamta Banerjee's election-oriented Railway Budget notwithstanding.

The manifest trends in the Indian economy have begun to ring alarm bells over jobless growth. The organized labour with relatively decent working and living conditions, which even some leftist trade unions have termed the labour aristocracy, has become thinner. Economic growth is accompanied by growing imbalances among individuals and states and regions. There is growing concern about the society being the servant of the market and the perverse impact of competition on social relations. Elsewhere in the world doubts have been raised by Roderick about whether social disintegration is the price we have to pay for economic integration. Even economists in the World Bank and the International Monetary Fund have begun to pay attention to the social and labour impact of economic liberalization and stress support for providing credible systems of compensation and social safety nets for those affected. Five years since the Copenhagen Social Summit of 1995, the goal of full, productive and freely chosen employment continues to be a mirage. The Asian Crises has made many ponder on whether capital has become too productive and wonder whether globalization has gone too far.

Against this background this volume seeks to reflect on the emerging pressures and tensions in the industrial relations system in the country in the wake of economic liberalization. Chapter 1 provides a historical analysis of the industrial relations system in India. Chapter 2 is intended to look at the developments in India within the context of changes occurring in the industrial relations system in different countries in an era of globalization. Chapter 3 addresses itself to the question of whether, why and how policies of economic development need to be aligned with the industrial relations policy. It contrasts the changes in the policies pursued in South Asia during the early and advanced stages of import substitution with those pursued in South-East Asia during the early and advanced stages of export orientation. In the past, few countries followed export orientation policies. Now almost all countries are pursuing them. Therefore the policies, which worked in the past, may not prove to be adequate and sufficient in the present context. Even so, there are quite a few lessons to be learnt from the experiences of the South-East Asian countries, particularly the emphasis on developing sound labour–management relations instead of merely preoccupying oneself with dispute resolution.

Chapter 4 assesses the social and economic impact of economic liberalization in India. It looks at the contextual factors as well as the role of politics and governance. Labour being in the concurrent list of the Constitution under Article 246, there has been a trend in select states to pursue competitive labour policies. Chapter 5 briefly reviews and analyses the scope for and the limitations of such measures and the tensions that industrial relations issues can produce in centre–state relations. Chapter 6 studies the promise, performance and pitfalls of tripartite social dialogue in the reform process. It examines the role of the special tripartite committee, tripartite industrial committees and the link between tripartism and bipartism. The need for expanding the scope of the social dialogue to minimize social exclusion and widen the basis for social dialogue for greater social cohesion is stressed. A few suggestions have also been made to strengthen the social dialogue in India.

Chapter 7 looks at the labour adjustment process with a view to examining the causes for and the choices in dealing with human resource obsolescence caused by external and internal factors in the wake of social, economic, technological and structural changes in the economy and enterprises. Chapter 8 identifies the key elements of the current debate for aligning labour law with economic and industrial relations policies. This assumes significance in the context of the setting up of the second National Commission on Labour. The chapter provides a useful contrast between the terms of the first and the second commission. While the first commission terms focused mainly on the labour market, the second commission has been asked to focus on product market developments insofar as organized labour is concerned and recommend the suitable rationalization of labour laws. It has also been asked to suggest an umbrella-type legislation for the unorganized labour. This chapter also considers the recent clash between the rights of labour with those of consumers and citizens and reviews a few important judgments. The need for greater harmony between the executive, legislature and judiciary is stressed. Chapter 9 examines the recent trends towards judicial activism. It also examines the tensions between consumer rights and the rights of workers and employers. Chapter 10 delves into the contemporary discussion on international trade and social clause within the context of India's record and contribution to the promotion of international labour standards. It is argued that while the World Trade Organization and the International Labour Organization may have their limitations in ensuring compliance, social labelling and social boycotts by industry associations and interest groups in civil society have greater, immediate and effective say and control on the matter. Finally, Chapter 11 attempts to identify, in very broad terms, the new paradigms in employment relations with references to changes in the world of work, work organization, workplace and workforce. It is argued that the Indian scene will continue to be diverse and it is difficult to have a unified approach to deal with the unskilled and semi-skilled blue collar workers in agriculture and traditional manufacturing on the one hand and the skilled, knowledge workers in the service and high-tech industries on the other. Thus while control continues to be the dominant mode of management philosophy in some sectors, obtaining the consensus and commitment of the workforce becomes imperative, not a choice, in other sectors. With the growing emphasis on creativity and innovativeness, organizations will emphasize heterogeneity over homogeneity and growing diversity will eventually call for pluralistic values. Competitive pressures will force labour and management to bridge their differences and come together. Cooperation at the workplace to expand the proverbial pie and conflict at the bargaining table for a better share for both would, hopefully promote cooperation in labour management relations. And, increasingly labour and management will have to pay greater attention to balance the needs of the family with those of industry as 'work becomes home and home becomes work'.

The various chapters in this book are based on papers presented at various seminars and conferences held in India and abroad, some of which have been published earlier. They are included here after having been updated and re-written to ensure consistency and continuity, and to avoid repetition. It is hoped that this book will assist in a better understanding of the issues and aspects raised and discussed.

C.S. Venkata Ratnam

ONE

A Historical Analysis of Industrial Relations in India

A BRIEF OVERVIEW OF THE ECONOMY

India's was predominantly an agricultural economy till Independence in 1947. Even after Independence, the emphasis was on agriculture in the First Five-Year Plan (1951–56). With the Second Five-Year Plan (1956–61) there was a marked shift towards heavy industrialization. (The resultant structural change in the Indian economy can be seen in Table 1.1) The share of agriculture in the gross domestic product (GDP) declined from about 56 per cent in 1950–51 to less than 30 per cent in 1998–99 while the share of industry rose from 15.6 per cent to 25 per cent and of the services sector, from 29 per cent to 45 per cent during the corresponding period. It must be said to India's credit that it produces a wide variety of industrial and consumer goods and that, over the years, the dependence of the performance of the industrial sector on the agriculture sector has reduced considerably. India also has not felt the crunch of recession or the adverse effects of business cycles. Its middle class has grown to over 250 million, a vast enough market, even as over 220 million continue to live below the poverty line.

The industrialization strategies and industrial policies followed in India from Independence to the mid-1980s aimed at development

TABLE 1.1 Gross Domestic Product at Factor Cost by Industry of Origin

Year	Agricultural	Manufacturing, Construction, Electricity, Gas and Water Supply	Transport, Communication and Trade	Banking, Insurance, Real Estate, etc.	Public Administration, Defence and Other Services	GDP Factor Cost
1950-51 (Old series 1980-81 prices)	24,204 (56.45)	6,451 (15.06)	4,718 (11.00)	3,870 (9.03)	3,628 (8.46)	42,871 (100.00)
1960-61	32,793	11,790	7,945	5,185	5,191	62,904
1970-71	41,385	20,209	12,884	7,258	8,692	90,426
1980-81	48,536	29,828	20,437	10,791	12,835	122,427
1990-91	69,860	59,493	37,744	21,700	23,456	21,253
1998-99 (New series, 1993-94 prices)	315,415 (29.16)	267,269 (24.71)	230,556 (21.31)	130,671 (12.08)	13,793 (12.75)	10,81,834 (100.00)

Source: Government of India, Economic Survey 1999-2000.

and a faster growth rate, but emphasized regulation rather than development. To protect the domestic industry from foreign competition and to promote self-reliance, import substitution was encouraged as a state policy. But import substitution and export promotion were not viewed as two sides of the same coin. Instead, a plethora of controls led to the erection of entry and exit barriers. It also resulted in pygmies being treated as giants, a denying of the economies of scale to Indian enterprises, tariff and other restrictions on imports and exports, distortions in pricing of inputs and outputs, and a sheltered market and protective regime based on political patronage. The end result was the creation of preemptive capacities to minimize or avert competition, gross underutilization of capacities, profiteering by trading in licences and quotas (for state-controlled raw material, etc.) and collusion rather than competition. Thus, too much government in business and industry, and vice versa, eventually proved detrimental and counter-productive to the conduct of state affairs as also to industry and commerce.

Lest it should be misunderstood, it is not that the Indian economy has not grown. In fact, the growth in certain core sectors has been phenomenal. The country is among the top producers, by virtue of sheer volume of output, of rice, wheat, cement, fertilizers, etc. However, despite being one of the largest producers of items such as fertilizer, the dependence on foreign technology has not diminished. On the contrary, whatever little gains the country has made in terms of developing indigenous technology have been lost in certain core industries, including fertilizers.

Population growth, moreover, has substantially nullified economic growth in several areas. Consequently, the per capita availability of many items in agriculture, industry and the services has declined over the years. Despite having a headstart in heavy industrialization in the Asia-Pacific region, India's rank among the major industrial countries dropped from 13th in 1965 to around 19th throughout the 1990s. Its major exports continue to be leather, gems and jewellery and woven cotton fabrics. In 2000, its share in world exports was around 0.6 per cent, less than half that in 1950.

Overregulation, protection and distortions in the emphasis of self-reliance and import-substitution has led to the neglect of quality, costs, delivery/supply schedules and customer orientation. As one industrialist puts it, 'In India anything and everything can be produced at any cost, quality, quantity and can still be sold for a profit.' Industrial sickness may be all-pervasive but the industrialists who contributed to such sickness, wilfully or otherwise, were permitted to set up new units with substantial support from public financial institutions. The result is that India has become a high-cost, low-performance economy, witnessing a tremendous lag in industry (peopled by the literate and the elite sections of India) despite significant achievements through the green (agriculture), white (dairy) and blue (fishery) revolutions (where the illiterate and indigent sections of society participate in overwhelmingly larger numbers) and in the frontier areas of technology such as nuclear, space and genetic engineering.

Labour may be cheap, but that does not necessarily hold true for the cost of labour. Again, capital may be scarce, but not its use. Since factor productivity is difficult to calculate because of gaps in the database, labour productivity is usually measured by dividing the output by the labour employed. When protective labour laws increased the rigidity in the labour market and made labour adjustment costlier and difficult, employers began to substitute labour with capital and through capital, with more advanced technology and equipment. This led to capital intensity and to a decline, both in absolute and relative terms, in the numbers employed in firms in the organized sector. This further led to the mistaken impression that labour productivity had started moving upwards (since increased output is divided by the numbers employed). Input shortages and infrastructure breakdowns (power and communications) led to the gross underutilization or non-utilization of many productive resources. Technology became not only capital intensive but also cost intensive. Capital productivity, despite capital being scarce, became a casualty (Table 1.2) By the end of the

TABLE 1.2 **Trends in Productivity and Growth: Manufacturing (Per Cent Per Annum), 1959–60 to 1988–89**

	1959–60 to 1979–80	1959–60 to 1965–66	1965–66 to 1979–80	1980–81 to 1988–89
Value added	5.5	9.1	5.0	7.0
Capital stock	8.6	13.4	7.0	7.5
Employment	3.3	4.0	3.5	−0.5
Capital–labour ratio	5.1	9.0	3.3	8.0
Total factor productivity	−0.5	0.2	−0.3	2.8
Labour productivity	2.1	4.9	1.4	7.5
Capital productivity	−2.8	−3.8	−1.9	−0.5

Source: I.J. Ahluwalia, op. cit.

1980s, despite the drive for self-sufficiency, the country had amassed a foreign debt of US$ 85,000 million (further increased to US$ 98,871 million by September 1999). It could no longer raise new funds externally and its internal capacity to generate capital surplus remained low. This made an overhaul of the economic policies an imperative and the stage was set for wholesome reform.

THE LABOUR MARKET CONTEXT OF ADJUSTMENT

Industrialization strategies affect society and labour and influence human resource and industrial relations policies at both the macro and micro levels. These strategies and policies should thus contend with the contextual elements of the labour market to ensure that economic and industrial development is in harmony with social and human progress. From this perspective it is necessary to take stock of some key factors of the labour market in India. Towards this end, the following is a brief review of the major concerns that underline the political economy of development in India.

Democracy and Development

India is industrialized in one sense and underdeveloped in another. There is a perception, which is not ill-founded, that most of the benefits of industrial and economic development have been aimed at or have concerned the top 20 per cent (in terms of economic status) of the population and have not reached the other 80 per cent. There is an argument that since the modest 'Hindu growth rate' (around 3.5 per cent) is only marginally higher than the rate of population growth, the benefits have not trickled down and that had the growth rate been higher (8.5 per cent or more), they would have trickled down in the long run. What will happen in the short run due to the changed policies cannot be predicted. Since structural changes are fraught with political risks in the short run, pendulum policies seem to result in one step forward, two steps back measures that only worsen the problem. In a democracy, decisions are often based on the lowest common denominator of consensus. Therefore, their effectiveness may be reduced considerably by delays and dilution. Yet these features do not and should not undermine the intrinsic merits of democracy.

India is the world's second-largest country in terms of population. It was a colony for centuries before it became independent but due to mass illiteracy the imperfections in its democracy were exacerbated in the first four decades following Independence. It is only in the 1990s that more than 50 per cent of its population has become literate and Kerala and one or two other north-eastern states, nearly 100 per cent literate. For nearly half a century, India's development strategy focused on a command economy in the state sector with the private sector playing an important but secondary role in the key areas of the economy. The transition to a globalized market economy was more out of disaffection with the performance of the state sector than a positive vote of confidence in the private sector. Public perception of the private sector is still fairly negative. Therefore, neither the autocratic policies of certain military regimes in developing countries nor the corporatist policies of various industrialized countries in South-East Asia and some western societies can be used as examples to suggest the harmonizing of the concerns of industrial relations and industrialization strategies. Hence, there is no right mix of industrial relations policies which are universally valid at a given stage of development. The balance between industrialization strategies and industrial relations policies has to be aligned to the stages of world development including the nature and degree of global interdependence, leverage of social and other clauses in trade agreements, etc.

Centre–State Relations and Unified Labour Policy

It appeared that the government was capable of articulating and implementing policies—whether right or wrong—in spheres including labour till the late 1960s when the same Congress Party was in power at the centre and in most states. But in 1969 and after, non-Congress parties and regional parties started coming to power in the states and twice at the centre. Over the years, the states have begun asking for greater provincial autonomy in matters including labour, which has been on the 'concurrent' list since British rule (that is, under the simultaneous jurisdiction of both the central and state governments). The problem is confounded by the definition of 'appropriate government', particularly in the case of central government undertakings. While the central government is responsible for the overall performance of such enterprises, labour management relations are, in several cases, under the jurisdiction of the government of the state in which the enterprise is located. Political differences among the parties in power not only cause problems for individual enterprises, but also result in government representatives basing their stands on the ideology of the ruling party at the centre and/or the states when policy issues are discussed at labour ministers' conferences. Given the diversity of the context, the seriousness of the political ferment and reversals of government policies over the years, one wonders whether India ever had or will ever have a unified labour policy.

Withdrawal of the State

In India, both labour and management have traditionally depended rather heavily on the state. Tripartite consultations and even bipartite relations are usually influenced by political considerations and state support. Budgetary deficits and structural changes tend to weaken and reduce the role of the state in social integration. This hampers political consensus. In periods of flux such as those that countries like India and several other developing countries are now facing, the need for state support for new initiative increases. Given the diminishing possibility of both state support and public resources, the main option is to focus on cooperative efforts at the firm/plant level in an adjust-or-perish spirit. The absence of mutual understanding about the commonality of interests between the other two social partners—labour and management—will lead to new social tensions. Therefore, while the state in India could do with fewer controls, it cannot afford more job losses in an already critical unemployment situation without creating mechanisms to mitigate the adverse effects. And, in the absence of social security of the type available in the Scandinavian and other industrialized countries, this problem assumes greater significance.

Employment Scenario

By mid-2000, India's population exceeded one billion. According to the 1991 census, the total workforce was 306.8 million (37.68 per cent of the total population of the country). Over 55 per cent of the workforce was illiterate and nearly 10 per cent, literate without any educational qualifications. Over 92 per cent of the workforce was employed in the unorganized sector and less than 8 per cent (26.75 million), in the organized sector. Formal HR/IR policies and practices are generally absent in the unorganized sector, which usually remains outside the purview of legislation, the trade union movement and professional management. Employers' organizations (EOs) have only a limited role to play in the sector and the Central Trade Union Organizations (CTUOs), which also claim to be concerned about the unorganized sector, often offer no more than empty words.

In India, the organized sector refers to the sector comprising public and private enterprises which are registered, come under the purview of any, some or several Act(s) and maintain annual accounts and balance sheets. Public enterprises include departmental and non-departmental enterprises in the public sector. In the private organized enterprises are included registered manufacturing, mining and quarrying, gas and water supply, private transport companies, registered schools, colleges and hospitals, and corporate trading activities and services.

In contrast, the unorganized sector comprises, exclusively, private sector units which are, if at all, only marginally affected or regulated by labour or industrial laws. Enterprises in this sector are usually very small (typically employing less than 10 persons) and are rarely unionized, provide low wages and harsh working conditions, are exploitative and are often largely unsafe.

The public sector accounts for over two-thirds (71 per cent) of the employment in the organized sector (19.2 million out of 27.06 million in 1992). Between 1970 and 1990, employment in the public sector grew at an annual rate of 2.9 per cent against 0.7 per cent in the private sector. Though top managerial remuneration is several times higher in multinational firms and the private sector than in the public sector, the average annual gross salary in public sector enterprises (non-departmental undertakings) in India, at Rs 49,197 in 1991, was one and a half times higher than in the private sector (CMIE, 1994).

Growing Unemployment

Although job creation has been a major concern and objective of successive five-year plans, fewer jobs have been created over the years, per Rs 10 million investment. In the 1950s, it was estimated that an investment of Rs 10 million in infrastructure would create 11,000 jobs.

Between 1980 and 1987, 70,000 jobs were added in the organized sector and capital formation in the public and private sectors exceeded Rs 700,000 million. Thus, a Rs 10 million investment generated just one job on an average in the organized sector through the greater part of the 1980s. Already, by the mid-1980s, parallel production, outsourcing, and sub-contracting became common practices to reduce the strength of full-time employments in the organized sector. The Nhava Seva port in the public sector employs 10 times less manpower and its wage cost as a proportion of the total operating expenditure is 12 times less than that of Mumbai. A public sector integrated steel mill set up at Visakhapatnam generated less than 14,000 jobs on an investment of over Rs 80,000 million.

The Amendments to the Industrial Disputes Act formulated during the Emergency in 1976 mandated prior permission from the government for lay-off, retrenchment and closure. Such legal provisions, court judgements and past collective agreements between employers and trade unions created rigidities in the labour market. However, higher adjustment costs seem to have reduced the demand for labour in firms in the organized sector, irrespective of whether they are owned by the government or by the private sector. A study of employment trends in 34 Indian industries, according to the Annual Survey of Industries Data for the period 1976–1982, pointed to a long-term decline in the demand for labour at around 17.5 per cent (Fallon and Lucas, 1991). The study noted significant inter-industry variations. Employment dropped by more than 5 per cent in 25 of the 35 industries, and by more than 15 per cent in seven of them. The rate of decline in employment was estimated to be over 33 per cent in textiles. Another study of 34 firms in Mumbai estimated an average reduction in employment of 20.5 per cent over the decade of the 1980s (Workers' Solidarity Centre Against Job Losses and Closures, 1989).

A Study of Six Industries

A study of plantations and textile (West Bengal), power (Andhra Pradesh), major ports, engineering (West Bengal and Andhra Pradesh) and the chemical and pharmaceutical industries (Maharashtra) points to a decline in full-time employment and unionization rates during the 1980s (Sarath, 1992) and to a rise in the incidence of casual and contract employment. The study of the chemical and pharmaceutical industry also points to the underreporting of employment by private sector firms (to the extent of 57 per cent). Data reveals that the actual number employed in the firms covered was, on an average, 57 per cent more than the number recorded by the Factories Inspector (presumably to overcome the burden of legal coverage since the coverage of several legislations progressively increases with the number employed).

Several studies (Goyal, 1984; Ramaswamy, 1988; Frensen, 1991) also point to a shift in employment from the organized to the unorganized sector through subcontracting and the emergence of atypical employment practices where employees work for an organization on a contractual basis (Mathur, 1989).

Against this background, the country was desperately searching for a middle way. As the then Prime Minister P.V. Narasimha Rao observed while addressing the World Economic Forum at Davos, Switzerland, in February 1994: Change has to be accepted as a result of deliberate and objective thinking. At the same time, those who wear the shoe and know where it pinches should be allowed full say in deciding how to mend it. In the new-found enthusiasm for change, governments should not go overboard and plunge large chunks of their people into mass misery; they have no right to do that . . . each society has to find its own 'middle way' suited to its genius and circumstances; and, this should be the approach that accepts change.

Clearly, the Indian case—in terms of both the magnitude and complexity of the challenges—calls for a different strategy than elsewhere. Given its strong democratic traditions and vibrant—even if weak and splintered—trade union movement, neither an autocratic nor a corporatist approach to industrial relations will work. Striking a balance between the requirements of economic development and social progress has not been an easy task. Therefore, the search for the 'middle way' has not yet produced a model that could be operationalized on a wider scale, though in certain specific local contexts at the firm/plant level both unions and managements have been able to work out an equilibrium.

Diversity in the Industrial Relations System

Given its diversity, it is difficult to generalize about the state of labour management relations in India even within the organized sector. Public sector industrial relations have its special problems due to Article 12 of the Constitution where the public sector is interpreted as the state, with the private sector multinational companies known to adopt different and unique approaches. Then there are significant differences based on sector (Venkata Ratnam and Verma, 1997) and/or location (Venkata Ratnam, 1997). There are companies where harmonious labour–management relations have prevailed for decades, but their numbers are relatively few. There are several types of employers, as Vaid's study (1974) points out: constitution-bound, paternalistic, exploitative. In exploitative companies, when gheraos and labour unrest took place after the Left-front government came to power in 1968, owners and managers were chased or done to death and company properties burnt. In constitution-bound companies, gheraos and unrest were symbolic gestures, not aimed at hurting anyone, physically or otherwise.

Tables 1.3 and 1.4 present data on industrial disputes—the causes, duration, and results of work stoppage respectively. The data is incomplete in the sense that it covers only reported disputes and the statistics of work stoppages and lockouts are contentious. The West Bengal government's annual reports on the labour situation indicate that in recent years 95 per cent of the work stoppages were caused by lockouts. Since the 1980s, unions have been increasingly resorting to tactics like work-to-rule (when work comes to a grinding halt with a strike) and go-slow so that workers do not lose wages. Thus covert methods are becoming more common than overt and direct industrial action.

Since industries are heterogeneous, the industrial relations scenario and the human resource practices vary. For instance, many high-tech information technology firms do not have unions at all.

The colonial heritage seems to have created a mindset problem in the principal actors which is yet to change. Labour–management relations are, by and large, rooted in adversarialism. Employers in general are still feudalistic, organizational structures are stratified, mirroring societal stratification, and the predominant belief and value system is unitarist, not pluralist. There are exceptions, though.

In a sheltered sellers market, employers benefit from perpetuating scarcities. Therefore, it is doubtful whether employers in India consider sound labour–management relations a prerequisite for corporate well-being.

TABLE 1.3 **Industrial Disputes by Public and Private Sectors, 1981–97**

	Disputes		Workers involved (in '000s)		Mandays lost (in '000s)		Wages lost (in Rs)		Value of production lost (Rs in crores)	
	Public	Private	Public	Private	Public	Private	Public	Private	Public	Private
1981	707	1,882	703	885	10,066	26,518	25.86	20.97	337.52	291.24
							(582)	(1,223)	(486)	(1,168)
1982	799	1,684	726	743	10,360	64,254	7.60	25.65	74.48	3,449.69
							(690)	(1,084)	(615)	(1,018)
1983	884	1,604	757	703	4,453	42,406	7.22	42.83	31.95	398.12
							(707)	(982)	(611)	(919)
1984	592	1,502	931	1,018	7,871	48,154	18.02	49.18	56.40	471.66
							(475)	(841)	(406)	(766)
1985	401	1,354	385	694	3,202	26,037	4.84	31.56	29.06	345.46
							(283)	(759)	(217)	(708)
1986	389	1,503	678	967	2,572	30,176	6.11	39.20	40.06	783.52
							(281)	(837)	(208)	(758)
1987	442	1,357	1,006	763	5,324	30,122	10.26	43.62	108.25	531.43
							(355)	(672)	(300)	(619)
1988	564	1,181	802	389	6,633	27,314	15.46	46.49	71.62	622.62
							(445)	(615)	(394)	(540)
1989	615	1,171	918	446	5,739	26,923	14.15	10.86	65.04	218.43
							(296)	(230)	(266)	(201)
1990	628	1,197	884	424	5,736	18,351	NA	NA	NA	NA
1991	653	1,157	788	554	4,145	22,284	NA	NA	NA	NA
1992	617	1,099	566	686	1,924	29,334	NA	NA	NA	NA
1993	359	1,034	565	389	2,292	18,009	12.15	25.17	115.99	544.67
							(318)	(431)	(267)	(403)
1994	316	885	523	323	1,316	19,667	11.08	18.16	46.77	435.22
							(288)	(364)	(249)	(331)
1995	343	723	725	723	4,794	11,496	38.92	15.38	146.3	308.45
							(310)	(303)	(254)	(265)
1996	381	785	267	381	1,156	10,343	8.77	8.11	39.64	84.76
							(209)	(106)	(171)	(98)
1997(P)	448	857	618	363	2,180	14,850	NA	NA	NA	NA
1998 (Jan Sep)(P)	482	136	303	129	1,760	6,100	NA	NA	NA	NA

Source: CMIE (1999).

Note: Figures in brackets indicate the number of cases to which the information regarding loss in Wages and Production relate to P = Provisional.

TABLE 1.4 Percentage Distribution of Disputes by (a) Causes (b) Duration and (c) Results, 1961–1990 (P)

	1971	1981	1985(P)	1990(P)	1995	1996
(A) Causes						
Wages & Allowances	34.3	29.7	22.5	25.2	30.9	25.0
Bonus	14.1	8.4	7.3	3.0	7.0	3.6
Personnel & Retrenchment	14.1	22.4	23.1	16.8	19.2	19.8
Leave & Hours of work	1.4	1.8	1.8	0.6	2.0	2.2
Indiscipline/Violence	3.6	9.9	16.1	17.0	15.3	21.6
Others	23.5	27.81	29.2	37.4	25.0	28.2
Total	100.0	100.0	100.0	100.0	100.0	100.0
Total No. of disputes to which % relates	2,723	2,453	1,700	NA	1,066	611
(B) Duration						
A day or less	25.4	22.9	15.6	27.6	27.4	34.7
Between 1 and 5 days	25.1	21.2	19.8	24.1	22.9	17.8
Between 5 and 10 days	14.8	12.2	14.6	9.8	9.3	6.5
Between 10 and 20 days	15.3	12.0	14.0	11.5	10.4	8.2
Between 20 and 30 days	5.8	8.7	8.1	5.2	8.1	5.0
More than 30 days	13.6	23.0	27.9	21.4	21.0	27.8
Total	100.0	100.0	100.0	100.0	100.0	100.0
Total No. of disputes to which % relates	2,670	2,281	1,542	NA	NA	NA
(C) Results*						
Successful	26.4	28.4	37.1	13.5	40.4	59.1
Partially Successful	23.4	26.8	28.4	26.7	11.2	19.9
Unsuccessful	34.4	40.5	31.8	58.0	45.7	17.2
Indefinite	15.8	4.3	2.7	1.6	2.7	3.8
Total	100.0	100.0	100.0	100.0	100.0	100.0
Total No. of disputes to which % relates	2,512	1,890	1,645	NA	NA	NA

Source: Ministry of Labour 1997. Pocket Book of Labour Statistics 1997, Simla.
Note: *Results are based on the extent to which workers'demands are met. Thus, 'unsuccessful' means that a worker's demands have not been accepted. 'Indefinite' means that no final decision was reached at the time of resumption of work. The information relates to those cases for which relevant information was available. NA = Not Available; P = Provisional.

There is excess capacity in several Indian industries due to the preemptive capacity creation strategies directed at eliminating competition. Some employers eventually got down to a situation whereby it was better that workers went on strike. For, if they reported for work when the order book position was poor, employers could not always provide enough productive work.

The key problem is the lack of trust. Workers consider employers 'Paisa chor' (money swindlers and surplus appropriators). Balance sheets are generally considered excellent pieces of fiction. Employers consider workers 'Kam chor' (lazy people who shun work). There is a need for communication and transparency in transactions.

HISTORICAL EVOLUTION

Colonial Period (Pre-1950)

During the colonial period the government's industrial relations policy was 'one of laissez-faire and selective intervention at the most' (NCL, 1969). The Trade Disputes Act, 1929 provided for state intervention in the settlement of disputes. The Act was subsequently amended in 1938, following the recommendations of the Whitley Commission (also referred to as the Royal Commission on Labour) (1931) and the experience of the only provincial legislation at that time in the industrially important Bombay province, called the Bombay Trade Disputes (Conciliation) Act, 1934. The Bombay Trade Disputes Act provided for (a) compulsory recognition of unions by employers; (b) right of workers to get their case represented by a union representative or a government officer; (c) certification of standing orders detailing terms and conditions of service; (d) setting up of an industrial court; and (e) prohibition of strike or lockout under certain conditions.

During this period, besides some departmental establishments like the railways and communications, much of the industrial activity was agro-based (jute and cotton textiles, tea, etc.). In the wake of the report of the Whitley Commission and special investigations by government-appointed committees into major industries like textiles, the government began to consider some special measures aimed at securing a modicum of welfare and security for employees.

Though the Whitley Commission recommended tripartite consultation, the colonial government did not accept this immediately. When the Government of India Act, 1935 placed labour in the 'concurrent' list, thereby empowering provincial governments to enact their own legislation, employer and worker representatives became concerned about the lack of uniformity in labour legislation and began to press for tripartite consultation. It was only during the Second World War that the tripartite consultation on labour was initiated, particularly to meet the exigencies of war and accelerate production.

In 1942, the government invited representatives of employer and worker organizations to participate in the tripartite Indian Labour Conference (ILC). Simultaneously, the Standing Labour Committee (SLC) was set up as a subcommittee of the tripartite conference. The basic objectives of the government in instituting the ILC and SLC were to (a) promote uniformity in labour legislation; (b) lay down a procedure for the settlement of industrial disputes; and (c) discuss matters of all-India importance to employers and employees.

Industrial disputes were settled on the basis of the examination of facts by a government-constituted authority or through public hearings based on independent investigations. The scope of legislation was limited and a formal machinery for handling grievances largely absent.

The exploitation of labour, declining real earnings and other adverse conditions during the Second World War; the political role of the trade union leadership in the freedom movement, which preferred a relationship of dependence on the government; and the perceived need to promote industrial harmony for ensuring economic development in consonance with central planning set the stage for extensive government involvement in regulation and dispute resolution and for a third-party role in determining wages and working conditions (wage boards earlier, and now government-mediated collective bargaining in the central public sector).

The Post-colonial Period (1947–1990)

Legal Framework: Labour is a concurrent subject. Both the central and state governments have the jurisdiction to legislate. Over 100 legislations govern the various aspects of human resources and industrial relations at the enterprise level. Several of these are amended. Additionally, there is a considerable amount of free interpretation of these laws, creating a body of what is known as 'judge-made law' While there is a plethora of legislation, the implementation is weak. The institutional framework for industrial relations includes consultative machinery and conciliation and arbitration machinery.

The consultative machinery is present at all three levels of the strategic choice framework indicated by Kochan et al. (1987). At the top tier, tripartite consultation is provided through ILC and SLC, as discussed earlier; at the enterprise level, there are joint management councils and work committees. Some committees like the canteen and safety committees are statutory. Although there is a lot of effort to promote worker participation, in more than half the government enterprises, where some machinery for worker participation was established in response to governmental directives, worker participation became nebulous due to a general lack of genuine commitment and involvement in the concept.

Several voluntary arrangements gained currency during the late 1950s in the wake of the Indo-China war due to the mesmeric influence of the union minister in charge of both Planning and Labour, G.L. Nanda: the Code of Discipline (1958), Model Grievance Procedure (1958), Code of Conduct (1958), Verification of Trade Union Membership (1958), Voluntary Arbitration (1959), Code of Efficiency and Welfare (1959) and Industrial Truce Resolution (1962). When these voluntary arrangements were discussed in tripartite fora the actors could not disagree openly with such lofty ideals. The moral appeal, though outstanding, soon waned. In retrospect, it appears the actors agreed to these because they were merely voluntary and non-adherence did not entail any sanctions (Mathur and Seth, 1969; Ratnam, 1992).

The dispute resolution machinery consisted of four levels: bipartite negotiations, conciliation, arbitration and adjudication. Soon after Independence, some trade unions favoured adjudication more than collective bargaining because they felt that they were relatively weak in relation to employers and adjudication would help restore the balance of power.

The conciliation machinery was generally found inadequate because the role of the conciliation officer was merely to arrange meetings between labour and management representatives and share/exchange information. The role, training, facilities, etc. of the machinery were not considered commensurate with the requirements.

Arbitration has not been popular in India at any time in the past. This is largely on account of a deep-seated adversarialism in labour–management relations and to some extent due to the absence of institutional arrangements. In the government sector, however, a board of arbitration was created in 1968 by setting up a joint consultative machinery to resolve differences between the government as employer and the general body of employees. In the cement industry, wages have been determined through arbitration on two occasions in the past, which is a rather unique experience in the Indian context. In the last two rounds of wage revision, however, this too ran into rough weather due to trade union dynamics.

Adjudication or compulsory arbitration is the last resort in redressing an industrial dispute. Labour courts, industrial tribunals and national tribunals with separate jurisdiction on the nature, scope and magnitude (local or regional or national import) of the dispute are set up for the purpose.

In addition, there are certain draconian legislations aimed at maintaining essential services (the Essential Services Maintenance Act, for instance). By invoking these, strikes/lockouts can be banned and industrial relations rights curbed for specified periods.

As already stated, the major problem in the legal framework lies in the plethora of legislation and the inadequate machinery for implementation. The Trade Unions Act which aimed at strengthening the union movement may have contributed to its weakening. The Central Act provided for registration, not recognition. *De facto*, if not *de jure*, all registered unions, irrespective of whether they are recognised or not and whether majority, minority, broad-based or craft or category unions, have come to enjoy industrial relations rights. Any seven members can register a union. Though some state laws, such as those in Maharashtra, provide for recognition, experience has indicated that it does not quite improve matters. The longest ever strike in India—the textile strike of 1982 which continued for over a year and has still (September 2000) not been officially called off—was the result of a fight between two rival leaders of trade unions, Datta Samant and R.J. Mehta, to gain control.

The Industrial Disputes Act, 1947 emphasized dispute resolution but there is little by way of creating an enabling environment. Other legislations like the Bonus Act, 1965, which intended to reduce strife on account of bonus disputes, actually led to increased strife.

The more people a firm employs the more the laws that apply to it. As shall be discussed later, to circumvent the limitations of such legislative 'harassment' employers often tend to substitute labour with capital, underreport numbers employed or resort to subcontracting, employment of casuals, etc.

Legal restrictions on introducing new work practices, the introduction of new technology and modernization, the adjustment of the workforce in line with changing business requirements through lay-offs, retrenchments or closure of business, etc. are some of the most current and contentious issues in the wake of the ongoing economic reforms. Managerial responsibility for decisions on these issues has been repeatedly questioned, before courts of law. Judicial interpretation on the matter of principles, rights and interests too has often been unpredictable and subject to judicial activism.

PRINCIPAL ACTORS IN THE INDUSTRIAL RELATIONS SYSTEM: THE WEAK TRIPOD

For a clearer perspective of the key players in industrialization strategies and industrial relations policies, it is useful to understand the actors who have played a major role. Dunlop's (1958) framework recognizes three principal actors in industrial relations: unions, employers and government. An earlier study of their roles in Indian industrial relations by Kennedy (1966) characterizes unions as militant, employers as legalistic and the government as tender-minded. In recent times even employers have been characterized as militant while the government continues to be unfocused in its goals.

The major problem in India today is that none of the three principal actors seem to be representative of the constituencies to which they belong.

Trade Unions

The trade union movement in India is over a century old. In the early 1990s, organized labour in India accounted for less than 8 per cent of the population. Membership of the unions submitting returns to the appropriate authority under the Trade Unions Act, 1926 was less than 2 per cent of the total labour force in the country as of 1994. As of September 2000, the latest information published by the Union Ministry of Labour, there were 56,872 registered unions, accounting for a membership of 4,094,000, of which 6,277 unions submit returns (Table 1.5). As seen from the table, though the number of registered unions has gone up by 33 per cent between 1980 and 1994, the average membership of unions submitting returns declined

TABLE 1.5 Verified Membership of Federation of Trade Unions between 1951–52 and 1994

	Registered Trade Unions*		Trade Unions Submitting Returns		Average Membership per Union	% of Women Members
	Number	Index (Base 1961–62 =100)	Number	Membership (in '000s)		
1951–52	4,623	39.81	2,556	1,996	781	6.6
1961–62	11,614	100.0	7,087	3,977	561	9.3
1971	22,298	194.0	9,029	5,470	606	7.1
1980	36,507	314.0	4,432	3,727	841	5.9
1985	45,067	388.0	7,851	6,433	823	9.4
1986	45,830	405.0	11,365	8,187	721	10.0
1987	49,329	424.7	11,063	7,959	719	9.4
1988	50,048	430.9	8,730	7,073	810	10.4
1989	52,210	449.54	9,758	9,295	953	11.7
1990	52,016	447.8	8,828	7,019	795	11.0
1991	53,535	476.6	8,418	6,100	725	9.7
1992	55,680	479.4	9,165	5,746	627	10.4
1993	55,784	480.3	6,806	3,134	460	15.9
1994	56,872	489.7	6,277	4,094	652	20.9

Note: P = Provisional and Incomplete
1. No. of Registered Trade Unions between 1977 to 1984 are provisional and estimated, and for other years they are incomplete.
2. Registered Trade Unions covers the Workers' Unions and Employees' Unions.

by about 25 per cent. It is doubtful, however, that these statistics give the true picture. It is amazing that in a country where mere registration by any seven employees of an enterprise carries *de facto* recognition, so few unions should be registered. By some estimates, the membership of the unions submitting returns under the Trade Unions Act constitutes only 30 per cent of the workforce in the organized sector. At 90 per cent, unionization is considered very high in the public sector, while in large-scale private sector establishments it could be well over 60 per cent. However, it is much less in small- and medium-scale units and virtually non-existent in the informal/unorganized sector, which employs over 90 per cent of the total labour force in the country.

Only one out of five registered unions is affiliated to one or the other of the 10 major national-level trade union federations. In 1990, it was agreed that unions with a verified membership of at least 500,000 across at least four states and four industries would be considered CTUOs for the purposes of representation on various national and international conferences, committees and councils. So far, no formal recognition has been accorded to any of the CTUOs on the basis of these norms. The 10 CTUOs that participated in the general verification on 31 December 1990 continue to enjoy representation on various committees. Some of them have a verified membership of less than 500,000 but over 100,000. Subsequently, the government chose to recognize only those unions with over 500,000 members in at least four industries and four states.

The number of employees covered by collective agreements on wages and working conditions works out to barely one per cent of the total labour force in the country. While these numbers by themselves are not large, the power of this vocal, predominantly urban minority can be gauged by their concentration in about 30 per cent of the parliamentary constituencies, which is disproportionate to their numbers. It must be noted that labour statistics in India are an eyewash. It is the footnotes, if any, that reveal more. The incidence of non-reporting of data or non-submission of returns is scandalously high even with respect to statutory returns.

The trade union 'movement' has developed in a hydra-headed fashion, with over a dozen national trade union federations split along ideological and other factional lines, each putting up exaggerated claims about its alleged membership strength. It is characterized by politicised polarization on many issues, including the one concerning the method of selecting the representative union. The World Employment Report (ILO, 1992) has tried its best to summarize the trade union situation in the country in the early 1990s: 'Indian unions are very fragmented. In many workplaces several trade unions compete for the loyalty of the same body of workers and their rivalry is usually bitter and sometimes violent. It is difficult even to say how many trade unions operate at the national level since many are not affiliated to any all-India federation. The early splits in Indian trade unionism tended to be on ideological grounds—each linked to a particular political party. Much of the recent fragmentation, however, has centred on personalities and occasionally on caste or regional considerations.'

Apart from the low membership coverage and the fragmentation of trade unions, several studies point to a decline in membership (Sheth, 1993; Sarath, 1992); the growing alienation between trade unions and their members (Sheth, 1993; Ramaswamy, 1988, particularly due to the changing characteristics of the new workforce (Sengupta, 1992); and the waning influence of national federations over the enterprise unions (Ramaswamy, 1988; Sarath, 1992). The new pattern of unionization points to a shift from organizing workers in a region or industry to independent unions at the enterprise level whose obsession is with enterprise-level concerns with no fora to link them with national federations that could secure for them a voice in policy making at the national level (Ramaswamy, 1988). Social movements like that of the Naxalites, struggles for regional autonomy in several states and emotion-charged protests over sensitive issues like Mandal and Mandir, particularly the former, have considerably weakened traditional trade union structures. The effect of the decline of communism in Europe on the Indian trade union movement, though significant, cannot be properly assessed at this stage.

> Trade unions are hard-pressed to live up to the rising expectations of the instrumental orientation of their members who consider membership in a union as a "meal ticket" (Sheth, 1991). It has resulted in a situation in Bombay, whereby, the arduous task of organizing a trade union from scratch has suddenly lost its relevance: the easier path to ascendance as a leader is to take over existing organizations. Raiding and poaching rather than laborious organizing are the norm. And yet, the fact is that, barring exceptions, the challenger enters not at his own initiative but at the behest of workers.
>
> (Ramaswamy, 1988)

The emerging dilemmas of trade unions in India have been appropriately captured by a veteran trade union leader of mill workers in Maharashtra who went on to become a general manager of a large public sector steel mill in West Bengal and a professor at the Tata Institute of Social Sciences:

> Technologies displace jobs and yet enable the workers affected to bargain for higher wages; unions resist closure of sick units but can hardly defend their being worked indefinitely as losing enterprises; unions do not generally like multinationals getting free access into the Indian industrial field but are attracted by the relatively higher emoluments and fringe benefits they offer; they

favour the growth of the small industry but do not like the work of large units being contracted out to ancillary small scale industries.

(Tulpule, 1993)

Employers' Associations

Employers' associations too have limited coverage and are riddled with problems of disunity. Over the years, the interests of foreign and native employers have given birth to two chambers and two employers' associations in the private sector.

There are three employers' associations in India: the All India Employers' Organization (AIEO) founded by the Federation of Indian Chambers of Commerce and Industry (FICCI) in Delhi; the Employers' Federation of India (EFI), founded by the Associated Chamber of Commerce and Industry (ASSOCHAM) in Mumbai, and the Standing Conference of Public Enterprises (SCOPE) in Delhi, which was set up by the central public sector undertakings. These three have formed a loosely federated umbrella organization called the Council of Indian Employers (CIE) for the purpose of relations with the government and international organizations like the International Labour Organization (ILO). Besides the above three employers' organizations, which are constituents of the CIE, there is a fourth organization—the All India Manufacturers' Organization (AIMO)—which primarily represents the interests of small- and medium-scale enterprises in the private sector. This organization too is accorded representation, separately, by the Ministry of Labour, in various tripartite fora, including the Indian Labour Conference (ILC) and the International Labour Conference.

The membership coverage of employers, particularly in the private sector is rather low. According to the 1980 economic census, India had 16.9 million non-agricultural enterprises. As of June 1990, there were over 1.96 million factories registered in India. But there are only 805 unions or associations of employers with 7000 members which are usually represented by the four major central organizations of employers (Nath, 1993). Of course, employers' organizations in India are registered not only under the Trade Unions Act, but also under the Societies Act. Nothing prevents them from being registered under the Companies Act either, though this is not a popular mode of organizing employers.

In 2000, the individual and association membership of the AIOE was less than 60 and 70 and that of the EFI, less than 200 and 40 respectively. Some members in both these categories are common. While the AIOE has a large following in northern India, the EFI has a greater following in western India. Both of them have some presence in the south and in the east. Employers' associations in the private sector do not have a substantial following. But SCOPE has a membership of nearly 95 per cent of the central public sector undertakings. Thus, SCOPE alone is considered representative among employers' associations. Despite that, SCOPE does not have much of a voice due to the delicate relations between its executive committee members and the government, the former being appointees of the latter.

Unions do not need to worry about solidarity among employers. But employers tend to feel threatened by solidarity among unions, notwithstanding the fragmentation within unions. Employers in India are hardly in a position to consider collective retaliation, as it was conceived of in the UK and elsewhere in the first half of the twentieth century. In fact, the problem that employers' associations find hard to grapple with is some of their members (or non-members) engineering trouble in competing firms in the hope of deriving undue advantage.

Government

State intervention in industrial relations in India is more direct and pervasive than in most industrialized countries, going well beyond the procedural and substantive laws regulating industrial relations. While during the colonial era the state may have been guided more by the 'need' to safeguard the commercial interests of the British, in the post-colonial era, state policy was 'necessitated by the larger need for regulation of the economy with focus on rapid overall growth' in the context of planned economic development and the concept of the welfare state as envisaged in the Constitution of India (NCL, 1969).

In India, the state is the largest employer besides being the regulator and enforcer of legislation. The government in India took on the role of regulator and enacted a series of protective, welfare-oriented legislations on the eve of and immediately following Independence. The resultant role conflict was obvious on several occasions. Several departmental and non-departmental enterprises it helped establish themselves violate the provisions of the Contract Labour (Abolition and Regulation) Act. The government agreed to the concept of a need-based minimum wage in a tripartite forum, but when it came to fixing the pay of civil servants, it said it could not pay because of resource constraints. It also can and did declare a variety of services as essential in order to prevent strikes and/or force striking workers to return to work.

The state has enormous discretion to intervene in industrial disputes not only when the dispute arises but also when an official or a minister apprehends a potential dispute. This has often led to the use of government machinery to influence trade union dynamics and industrial relations processes and outcomes.

It still sees its role as one of regulation. Its contribution in creating an enabling environment conducive for harmonizing industrial growth and social and employment relations has not yet been significant.

Its multifaceted role as employer, regulator, prosecutor and mediator in industrial relations puts it in a dichotomous position. Its legal and regulatory controls are often neutralized by informal arrangements among its own departments and enterprises, particularly with regard to contract labour, guidelines on pay, etc.

Government intervention in labour matters has increased the dependence of the private sector on it while in the public sector the government actually dominates industrial relations, granting little autonomy for enterprise management. Political interference has led to low accountability.

With labour in the concurrent jurisdiction of both the central and state governments, the emergence of regional parties and other newly formed political parties as the ruling elite at the state level and the mounting differences in centre–state relations have begun effecting industrial relations as well. The major problem in India today is that none of the three principal actors seems to be representative of the constituencies to which they belong.

Atrophied Tripartism

There are 44 tripartite committees at the national level. The apex tripartite mechanisms—the Indian Labour Conference and the Standing Labour Committee (SLC)—were set up in 1942 with the following objectives: (i) to promote uniformity in labour legislation; (ii) to lay down a procedure for the settlement of industrial disputes; and (iii) to discuss matters of all-India importance between employers and employees. These are non-statutory advisory bodies with flexible procedures whose deliberations are variously described as 'recommendations', 'decisions', 'conclusions', etc. A workshop on tripartism in India (ILO-APPOT 1993) observed that these objectives were still valid despite changes in the circumstances and the climate of industrial relations and notwithstanding their limited success, if any, in the last 50 years in realising avowed objectives.

Time and again, during the 1950s and early 1960s, the union labour minister, who also happens to be the ex-officio chairman of the ILC and SLC, had gone on record saying unanimous recommendations should be accepted by all parties. But, the government itself has, more than once, given evidence of its ambivalence and disregard for the unanimous recommendations of the tripartite body.

For instance, the 15th ILC (1957) resolved that the minimum wage should be need-based and defined the basis for calculation of need-based minimum wage (NBMW). But towards the end of April 1958, a secretary to the Government of India informed the chairman of the Second Pay Commission that, 'the Government desires me to make it clear that the recommendations of the Indian Labour Conference . . . should be regarded as what they are, namely, the recommendations of the Indian Labour Conference . . . Government at no time committed themselves to taking executive action to enforce the recommendations.' In 1964 the union labour minister tried to reverse the government stand when he stated that 'We have got to accept the unanimous recommendations of all tripartite bodies.' But subsequently, in 1968 and 1974, union ministers clarified the government policy: the tripartite committees' recommendations were not binding on the government, even if it was party to such deliberations and the recommendations were unanimous. The real problem lies in the fact that it is mainly the labour ministry which participates in tripartite discussions and there is no culture or practice of horizontal discussions with other ministries to include and bind the latter.

There are also glaring divisions and dissensions within the various interest groups, be it the government (centre–state relations), employers (diverse interests among them) or workers' trade unions (fragmentation). By the 1970s, tripartite meetings became rare and in the 1980s, several national trade union federations boycotted tripartite meetings. Between 1942 and December 2000, the ILC met on 37 occasions, though it was supposed to be an annual affair. The meetings were held more regularly up to 1972. Thereafter, for the next 15 years, the ILC met only once in three or four years on an average. In the 1990s, the economic crisis necessitated the revival of tripartite consultations (see Chapter 6). The meetings now began to be held regularly. For the first time in several years, the Prime Minister and several cabinet ministers attended the ILC held in the second half of the year 2000.

It is therefore not surprising that tripartism has atrophied over the years (Mathur and Sheth, 1969; Venkata Ratnam, 1989), with the principal actors losing their representative character. It is hard to sustain decisions taken without the mandate or support of the constituencies they are supposed to represent. Hence, indecision, politicised polarization and pendulum tactics often mark tripartite consultations. This was nowhere more apparent than during the deliberations on labour law reform in the early 1990s, in the committee headed by G. Ramanujam, President of INTUC. Initially, agreements were reached on many issues, though eventually the committee turned hydra-headed, with left unions and employer's representatives appending notes of dissent.

PARTICIPATION/CONSULTATION AT THE COMPANY AND SHOPFLOOR LEVELS

Since Independence, various schemes have been formulated to provide for employee participation/consultation at the company and shopfloor levels. Some of these are:

1947: Works Committees: The Industrial Disputes Act, 1947 provides for limited participation of elected representatives of workers in bipartite works committees with a view to promoting measures for securing and preserving amity and good relations between employers and workers. Some committees like the canteen and safety committees are statutory. The functioning of the committees are, however, not satisfactory due to the lack of clarity about their scope and functions and conflict between the elected representatives of the works committees and the trade unions operating in the enterprises.

1958: Joint Management Councils: The Industrial Policy Resolution, 1956 reiterated that, 'In a socialist democracy labour is a partner in the common task of development and should participate in it with enthusiasm. There should be joint consultation and workers and technicians should, wherever possible, be associated progressively in management.' Accordingly, in 1958, Joint Management Councils (JMCs) were introduced. They were supposed to be responsible for welfare, safety, vocational training, preparation of holiday schedules, etc. They were also to be consulted on matters relating to changes in work practices, amendment or formulation of standing orders, rationalization, productivity, etc. They did not receive much support from unions or management and the apparent similarity in the scope and functions of JMCs and works committees resulted in a multiplicity of bipartite consultative bodies.

1970: Employee Director in Nationalised Bank: Following the nationalization of banks in 1969, the government required all nationalized banks to appoint employee directors to their boards, one representing the workmen and the other representing the officers. The scheme entailed the verification of trade union membership, an identification of the representative union and an appointment of a worker director from a panel of three proposed to the government by the representative union. The tenure of an employee director was to be three years, though union membership verification need not occur even once in a decade.

In parallel, the government also began appointing labour representatives to the boards of several public enterprises; but these representatives had no direct link with the enterprise in organizing the union at the local level and were drawn from among the national leadership or on the basis of some other elusive criterion. There was no clarity about the role and function of worker directors.

1975: Amendment to the Constitution and the Workers' Participation: In 1975 the Constitution was amended and Section 43A inserted in the Directive Principles of the Constitution. The section provided that, 'The State shall take steps by suitable legislation or in any other way to secure the participation of workers in the management of undertakings, establishments or other organizations engaged in any industry.' Accordingly, the Scheme of Workers' Participation in Management at the shopfloor and plant levels in manufacturing and mining industries employing 500 or more workers was notified in 1975. Shopfloor and plant level councils were assigned specific functions relating to production and productivity, management of waste, reduction of absenteeism, safety, maximising machine and manpower utilization, etc.

1977: Scheme of Workers' Participation in Management: Another scheme, broadly similar to the 1975 scheme, was introduced in 1977 and extended to commercial and service organizations with 100 or more employees. Both schemes evoked some enthusiasm initially during the Emergency, but withered soon after the lifting of the Emergency and the change in government in 1977. In 1978, the new government constituted a special tripartite committee on workers' participation in management which recommended a three-tier participation at the levels of the board, plant and shopfloor. But the government did not last long enough to implement the recommendations.

The 1983 Scheme: In 1983, another new scheme was introduced and made applicable to all central public sector enterprises, except where specifically exempted, and a standing tripartite committee was set up by the Ministry of Labour to facilitate review and corrective measures. Implementation of the scheme was left to the administrative ministries concerned. Barely half of the central public sector enterprises introduced the scheme over the next decade, and several of these atrophied subsequently.

Workers' Share in Equity, 1985: The 1985–86 Union Budget made provisions for offering stock options to employees up to a total of at least 5 per cent of the total shares. This was intended to enhance workers' participation in management.

The 1990 Bill: The government's discontentment with the implementation of voluntary efforts resulted in the convening of a national seminar and the subsequent introduction of a bill in the Rajya Sabha in 1990 to introduce workers' participation at all three levels—board, plant and shopfloor—through legislation. The bill is still (September 2000) to be taken up for discussion.

Issues concerning the mode of representation, scope of the forums, levels of participation, coverage of the schemes, voluntary nature of the schemes, etc. still remain unresolved.

There has been much rhetoric about participation since Independence but in reality it remains elusive to this day. Walker (1975) observed, based on his global survey, that the world over it was confined largely to tea towels and toilets. One wonders whether in India it has extended even this far (Venkata Ratnam, 1992).

Unions and employers face major dilemmas with regard to participation. In India, as in several other erstwhile British colonies, there is no dearth of mechanisms for labour management consultation. But statutory arrangements have, by and large, remained dormant or unproductive. The few instances of apparently functional labour-management consultation processes often reflect the nature and style of management, partly motivated by industry characteristics and employee profile and partly by the management's desire to avoid unions or keep union influence under check. Similarly, unions are concerned about management strategies aimed at participatory mechanisms that seek to involve individual employees directly, undermining the union's role/influence.

Further, there is ambivalence about the true purpose and role of participation. Is it limited to giving workers and unions a say in management so that they, particularly, unions can pursue the sectarian interests of their members more vigorously? To what extent would unions accept the responsibility that goes with participation? Employers are sceptical about whether unions can and would like to accept responsibility. Unions too are generally wary of any scheme of participation that thrusts upon them more responsibility than effective power.

Unions generally want the participation process to start from the board level and percolate down to the shopfloor. Employers want to start it, gradually, and at the shopfloor. There are only arguments and hardly any agreement on this.

Consultative processes take time, and managers are wary of the costs and consequences of delays in decision making. It is apprehended that the greatest obstacle in the way of labour–management consultation is the rapidly changing environment (also see APO, 1991). This is compounded by the adversarial mode of labour–management relations, with a lack of mutual trust and, consequently, information sharing. Balance sheets of corporations in not only India, but the whole of South Asia are considered excellent works of fiction not only by trade unions, but also by government officials and perhaps, even by minority shareholders. This results in even Scanlon-type profit sharing incentive schemes turning non-starters.

TRADE UNIONS AND COLLECTIVE BARGAINING

India has ratified 38 International Labour Organization conventions but not those relating to the freedom of association and the right to collective bargaining. Although the Constitution of India guarantees the right of association, due to government apprehensions about granting this right to its employees, the ILO convention on the Freedom of Association has not been ratified. The preference for adjudicating disputes and in the absence of provisions for statutory recognition of unions (except in some states) and those requiring workers and employers to bargain in good faith, has resulted in collective bargaining making little headway. Despite adversarial relations, however, unions and managements have found it a better proposition to iron out differences across the table rather than take them to a third party. This is leading to a shift in the locus of power, causing inordinate delays and leading to frustration for both the affected parties.

Union Recognition

The central legislation on union recognition, the Trade Unions Act, 1926, provides for registration by any seven members, but does not mention recognition. Labour being a concurrent subject, some states, like Maharashtra, Gujarat, Uttar Pradesh and Madhya Pradesh, have separate laws providing for recognition. There have also been certain voluntary codes governing the criteria for union recognition, etc., but these codes are virtually buried for all practical purposes and have become part of industrial relations history.

There are two major problems with regard to union recognition:

1. All registered unions in India seem to enjoy industrial relations rights, *de facto*, if not *de jure*. This is so even if they happen to be based on unions craft, category or caste. Therefore, there is little incentive to aspire for recognition by the government or the employer particularly for representation at the enterprise level.

2. CTUOs are divided on the recognition criteria. The left-led union movement favours a secret ballot while the INTUC, affiliated to the Congress (I), is opposed to it. This has created a politicized polarization in resolving the recognition issue even though, under Congress rule in Andhra Pradesh, the secret ballot was introduced. Subsequently Orissa and West Bengal issued gazette notifications on rules pertaining to the secret ballot as a method of union recognition for collective bargaining. Kerala and Rajasthan too submitted proposals on the secret ballot for approval by the central government. Check-off is not favoured by most unions for fear that employers may exploit the system. Membership verification by the government machinery is time-consuming. Also, unions belonging to opposition parties are apprehensive about the ruling party favouring unions that are affiliated to it. Trade union amity is a far cry even in resolving matters relating to representation at the national and international levels in various tripartite fora.

A committee of labour ministers vetted the Ramanujam Committee findings on the subject and placed its conclusions before the apex tripartite forum, the Indian Labour Conference, in September 1992. Subsequently, officials of the ministry of labour presented their views based on which a draft bill was prepared suggesting amendments to the concerned legislation.

Reforms have been debated from the late 1960s, when the National Commission on Labour produced its monumental work. Since then the government of the day has, on at least three occasions, introduced industrial relations bills aimed at bringing 'comprehensive reforms'. On each of the three occasions, the government has fallen before the bills could be taken up for discussion.

Levels of Bargaining

Bargaining occurs at different levels in different industries.

Industry-level bargaining on a countrywide scale is common in core industries which are mainly concentrated in the public sector. These include coal, steel, banks, insurance and ports.

Industry-cum-regional-level bargaining is largely prevalent among common industries in the private sector. These include mainly textiles (cotton and jute), plantations and engineering.

In multiplant units, bargaining occurs in two stages. Company-wise agreements are usually supplemented with plant-level agreements. While the basic wage rates and some other benefits are decided at the company level, certain allowances, incentives, etc. are negotiated at the plant level, taking into account particular circumstances, needs, etc.

In collective bargaining in India, the role of the national federations of trade unions and of employers' organizations is limited to a small nucleus of industrial associations which have a long tradition of collective bargaining with their counterpart trade union federations of workers. Notable among such employers are the Ahmedabad Millowners' Association, Ahmedabad; the Bombay Millowners' Association, Bombay; the Indian Sugar Mills Association, New Delhi; the Tea Association of India, Calcutta; the Indian Jute Mills Association, Calcutta, the Cement Manufacturers Association, New Delhi; the United Planters Association of South India, Coonoor; the Southern India Millowners' Association, Coimbatore; the Indian Banks Association, Bombay; and the Indian Ports Association, New Delhi. The Confederation of Indian Industry, which till 1991 represented mainly the engineering industry, have traditionally negotiated region-cum-industry agreements for member firms who assigned to them in writing such responsibility. The role of industry associations in collective bargaining seems to vary depending upon the profile and background of industry and enterpreneurship. In a traditional industry like jute, with leadership largely in the hands of traders turned industrialists, entrepreneurs themselves conduct the negotiations. In the engineering industry, it is the professional managers who are in charge of negotiations. The variations in the collective bargaining processes and the distinct outcomes in each case merit detailed study and separate analysis.

In some industrial centres, both trade unions and employers, particularly in the public sector, have set up coordination committees to adopt a joint/collective strategy to deal with collective bargaining and related matters. This process started in Bangalore and Hyderabad and has spread to other places. Industry-wise coordination is also taking place with the commencement of industry-wise agreements in core sectors like coal, steel and oil which are presently dominated by the public sector. As we shall note, centralizing bargaining has already come under pressure and is likely to wither away at least for some time in the foreseeable future.

For government employees, a joint consultative machinery and a board of arbitration have been constituted. Pay scales for government employees are revised through pay commissions, which are usually adopted once every 12 years, or so. The significant gap between central government pay systems and industrial pay systems has created considerable discontent among public sector employees who feel they are adversely affected, particularly in the wake of some Supreme Court judgements pronouncing the public sector as the state.

Collective bargaining in India is different from that in many other countries. Some single plant firms may have unions numbering from zero to over 30. Some large, multi-plant engineering and steel companies in the public sector and departmental undertakings like the Railways have to cope with a few hundred unions each. While typically the tendency in negotiation has been to bar the gain to the other party and in the process make bargaining more coercive than collective, in the public sector, in the name of uniformity, the bargaining has become more competitive. In recent years, due to the economic crisis and the need to improve the levels of productivity there have, of course, been several innovative approaches in collective bargaining. In order to survive the ailing firms and save the threatened jobs, unions and managements, particularly the former, have been agreeing to a variety of concessions including wage and employment cuts, wage freezes, a moratorium on strikes and other trade union actions, changes in work practices, flexible deployment of the workforce, etc. In the process, of course, some unions have been able to commit employers in to regularizing the services of those who have remained casual labour for over several years (Venkata Ratnam, 1991). Productivity bargaining, though gaining currency, is yet to make much headway in view of the complexities in the measurement of factor productivity and sharing of gains particularly in the context of the glaring lack of mutual trust and acceptance. Several companies are planning to buy back the incentive schemes with a view to scrapping them because, over the years, they have resulted in reducing the norms and increasing the payments. In many firms, the agreed outputs can be achieved in half the time scheduled for the purpose. Despite unemployment, artificial labour shortages and restrictive work practices breed illegal practices with the connivance of the management and help workers increase unjustified earnings.

Economic difficulties and structural and other changes are resulting in a shift from national-industry-level to enterprise-plant-level bargaining and from national-level leadership to local leadership. This change in trend affects more the role and influence of CTUOs of employees than that of employers because it is mainly the former who wield greater influence in collective bargaining than the latter.

Subjects

Traditionally wages and working conditions have been the domain of collective bargaining. Over the years, however, anything and everything has become bargainable: staffing arrangements, crew sizes and composition, work norms, incentive and overtime payments, job and income security arrangements, technology and other changes, working tools, techniques and practices, staff mobility including transfers and promotions, rewards and punishments, individual grievances, discipline matters, etc. In fact everything—from recruitment to retirement and post-retirement benefits—has become a part and parcel of negotiation.

Duration of Agreements

Wage agreements used to be for a period of three years up to the mid-80s. In the mid-80s, several agreements were made, particularly in the public sector, which were for a duration of four years. As we shall see later, the government mandated these for a period of five years in the early 1990s and for 10 years towards the end of 2000, despite resistance from the unions.

PERIOD OF STRUCTURAL ADJUSTMENT (1991–2000)

Liberalization and Deregulation

In the wake of the New Industrial Policy (June 1991), industrial licensing was abolished in all but 18 industries related to the security and the social and environmental concerns of the country. Private sector competition was introduced, though selectively, in areas hitherto reserved for the public sector. The government has also declared that it has no plans of further nationalization. Majority foreign holding is now allowed in almost all industries except those which are of strategic importance. The system of capital issues control was abolished, the import-export regime drastically simplified and the rupee convertibility introduced on trade account. Budgetary support to public sector firms was withdrawn. Even reservations to the small scale sector were withdrawn in most cases.

IMPACT OF LIBERALIZATION ON INDUSTRIAL RELATIONS

There are doubts as to whether liberalization really leads to competition. The spate of mergers and acquisitions and the domination by a few brands or major players once again points out that in the era of globalization economies of scale matter. Though the number of players first increased due to the easing of entry barriers, eventually few have remained. Actually, in sectors like oil, air transport, telecom, banking, etc., there are doubts whether the number of players who will ultimately remain in the field will be fewer than the number before liberalization. Domestic enterprises find it hard to compete even in home territory because they are not used to competition and have, so far, mostly operated in a seller's market. Both captains of industry and academics are asking the government to liberalize the domestic economy first before exposing it to globalization. The private sector is asking for its privatization first. The Eleventh Finance Commission (2000) observed that economic liberalization has not resulted in the liberalization of PSEs from government controls. The dismantling of public monopolies has been accompanied by the creation of regulatory authorities which are subordinate to political and bureaucratic control. When ineffective regulatory authorities replace inefficient public utilities, the result is a transition from a bad to a worse situation. A chamber executive remarked, 'The evil of licensing is replaced by the devil of tendering.'

Technology is redefining competition. After nationalization, nationalized banks expanded their branch network into remote and rural areas and into virtually every street corner in urban areas. Eventually, many of them have remained unviable. The new, foreign banks with the latest technology are now open 24 hours a day, seven days a week through automatic teller machines. Not just that, E-banking has metamorphosed the banking industry. The CEO of a foreign bank said that, 'we cannot have a bank in every street corner, but we can place one in every home, every phone, every personal computer'.

The government has drafted the competition policy. What is important is that politicians, bureaucrats and captains of industry walk the talk and talk the walk. Thus far, they have only walked the walk and talked the talk. The basic ingredients of a competitive environment are still missing in India: it is marked by a demand-supply mismatch, information imperfections and a skewed distribution of resources, including purchasing power, etc. More importantly the much-needed reforms have eluded the public sector in the real sense. With most of the input and infrastructure—social and physical—still being in the hands of the government, the rest of the economy cannot gear up unless the public sector does. Still critical are reforms in the three pivotal areas of the legislature, judiciary and executive.

How different countries respond to the requirements of competitiveness may be a function of the particular stage of development it is in and the state of health of its economy. While different countries have different critical moments in history and pursue divergent industrialization strategies, it is usually observed that 'a less developed country begins the process of industrialization by creating some initial conditions conducive to investment. In industrial relations terms, it may translate to low wages and low unionization. This situation may attract initial investments by firms, which can take advantage of such labour market conditions. However, with increased investment, the initial labour market conditions inevitably change and there are pressures for higher wages and possibly unionization . . . . This reduces the initial advantage which attracted the new investment in the first place so other inducements are needed in order to retain attraction to external investors. This creates a critical juncture in the development process and places pressure on the existing industrial relations systems' (Sharma, 1995). The state at this stage may introduce measures such as wage controls and union repression or, alternatively, take recourse to upgrading skills and linking wages to productivity, and shift to a high wage, high value industrialization where workers get higher wages but wage costs become competitive. Wage controls cannot be prolonged and union suppression by itself cannot guarantee economic success. Therefore, these are not necessarily the answer. Yet it sometimes becomes necessary to create conditions necessary for inducing investment. Putting jobs before growth is like putting the cart before the horse. There can be growth without jobs, but there cannot be any new jobs without growth.

The policies of the international financial institutions (IFIs) have generally been criticized by most trade unions as being responsible for exacerbating the existing economic and social problems and worsening the industrial relations climate. Their policies would not have mattered much if the country had learnt to live within its means. IFI policies have affected urban India directly. Rural India has had an indirect and secondary impact. Some sectors have been affected badly and others not. Overall, India's performance in the post-reform period has been below its economic potential and negative on the social dimension.

However, India has not faced an economic crisis because: (a) it has retained control on capital outflows, (b) it has not supported full convertibility, (c) of the foreign exchange remittances by migrant workers of Indian origin and investments by NRIs, which has contributed to the accumulation of a sizeable exchange reserve base, and, (d) it has moved cautiously, and on a case by case basis, so far, in matters concerning disinvestment, etc.

Industrialization strategies affect society and labour and influence human resource and industrial relations policies at both the macro and micro levels. These strategies and policies should thus contend with the contextual elements of the labour market to ensure that economic and industrial development is in harmony with social and human progress. From this perspective it is necessary to take stock of some key factors of the labour market in India.

(a) The supply of labour is in excess of the demand for labour. The demand for capital is in excess of the supply of capital. Open unemployment may be less for reasons which will be explained later. But underemployment and disguised unemployment are high. So is the incidence of poverty and illiteracy. Taken together, these conditions make it difficult, regardless of the nature of laws, strength of trade unions and the political will of the government, to ensure job security and provide social protection to workers.

(b) Economic growth per se has not been low in India. But the modest 'Hindu' rate of growth has been nullified by the increase in the rate of growth of India's population. Hard economic conditions make even the government, with the best of intentions, less able, even if more willing, to safeguard the interests of workers and unions.

(c) Gupta's (1999) comparative study of the periods 1983–91 and 1991–98 points out that given the same rate of growth of GDP during both the periods, the incidence of poverty had increased and the rate of growth in employment had decelerated:

Changes in Poverty and Employment and GDP

Years	Changes in Poverty Ratio	Employment Growth Rate	GDP Growth Rate
1983–1991	−3.1	1.6	5.6
1991–1998	+2.7	1.1	5.7

(d) Alfred Marshal observed that if either or both the input and output of labour can be substituted, and if the proportionate costs of labour are high, the unions' capacity to achieve positive outcomes at the bargaining table would be low.

(e) Political instability may be perceived by some as good, at least in the short term, for workers and unions because in such circumstances governments are unwilling to take hard decisions and become increasingly sensitive to political risks.

(f) Pressure to restructure public finances is leading to government disinvestment in public enterprises mainly with a view to achieving the targets set for revenue realization in order to reduce revenue deficit. Selling capital assets to wipe out revenue deficits is not a wise proposition.

CHANGES IN LABOUR LAWS, LABOUR STANDARDS AND COLLECTIVE BARGAINING

Labour law reform has long been overdue. After the National Commission on Labour submitted its report in 1969, piecemeal efforts were made to amend the legislation. In the two decades that followed, comprehensive labour reform bills were introduced in Parliament on three occasions. But on each occasion before they could be discussed, the government changed. The bipartite committee headed by

G. Ramanujam, President of the Indian National Trade Union Congress, recommended some far-reaching changes in the Trade Unions Act and Industrial Disputes Act in 1990. The Labour Ministers' Conference and the 29th ILC meeting agreed to consider the implementation of at least the unanimous recommendations. The draft bill was ready but its timing considered inauspicious by a government with a fragile majority and faced with several other crises. In 1999, the government appointed a Second National Commission on Labour with former union labour minister Ravindra Verma as the Chairman to propose amendments to labour laws and suggest an umbrella legislation for the unorganized sector. While the administrative/employment ministries of the government and domestic and foreign investors have been bringing to bear pressure for the introduction of labour law reforms, trade unions have been insisting that until the Second National Commission on Labour submits its report no changes be proposed or brought about through an ordinance.

In India, the focus has generally been on subsidizing unprofitable enterprises rather than allowing for their liquidation. In 1987, the Board for Industrial and Financial Reconstruction (BIFR) was set up under the Sick Industrial Companies (Special Provisions) Act, 1985, to revive potentially viable sick industrial companies or recommend the closure of totally non-viable companies. Though the BIFR became operational in May 1987, it was only in December 1991 that the government chose to bring public enterprises within the purview of the BIFR through an amendment of the SICA. Yet, the past performance of the BIFR has revealed its inadequacies to meet the challenge. It cannot intervene until (a) seven years after a unit is established; and (b) the net worth of an enterprise is negative. Dilatory procedures and lack of authority, despite its quasi-judicial character, make it less potent to accomplish the task at hand.

The pressure is on the government to amend its attitude to the Intellectual Property Rights discussion, Super 301 clause, human rights issue, condition of employment in Export Promotion Zones and abolition of child labour. There is some action on these matters but they still lack momentum. The Bhopal gas tragedy has managed to put occupational safety and health issues on top of the agenda. Environmental issues seem to demand a trade off in as much as they create fresh hurdles even as old ones are removed and threaten jobs.

The prevailing mood seems to be that since we cannot do much about the factories already set up, let us take care of the new ones.

The barriers to entry have been eased. Exit restrictions, however, still apply. The problem lies not with prior notice for lay off, retrenchment, lockout or closure, but with prior permission from the government to implement any managerial decisions on the abovementioned aspects. Employers say that permission from the government is generally elusive and labour ministers agree that it is politically unwise for any minister to agree to closure or retrenchment. Somehow, though, closures and retrenchments do take place. Litigation in such cases, however, take decades. Employers, particularly multinational companies, want a clear-cut exit policy from the government rather than be forced to weather the current system by taking advantage of legal loopholes. The key point to be noted here is that while in a civilized society certain kinds of protection for labour are necessary, one must ensure that it does not become unduly restrictive giving rise to unintended dysfunctionalities and counter-productive consequences.

Employers in the small sector find it easy to keep units in limbo and not pay water, electricity and other dues in order to press their case for closure. In the large-scale sector, the experience is not as dismal. Where employers have done their homework and are clear about what they expect, they are able to have their way. Courts have given companies permission to close. When courts slap verdicts that entail financial commitments that employers 'really' consider render the unit unviable, employers are often able to impress upon the union to agree to terms which are much more unfavourable for the workers than those awarded by the court or simply start proceedings for sale or close. In some states, High Courts have agreed that prior permission for closure is not quite necessary.

On the collective bargaining front, there is an ascendancy in managerial rights (Venkata Ratnam, 1991 and 1992). New technologies and structural and other changes seem to have rendered union positions much more vulnerable today than at any time in the past 50 years. Labour–management cooperation pacts to save units on the brink of liquidation have entailed several sacrifices like cuts in salary, freezes in allowances and benefits, voluntary suspension of trade union rights and actions; commitments to agree to modernization and flexibility; and action points to increase production and profitability.

After nearly two decades of sustained but frustrated efforts to bring about uniformity in the pay structure of non-departmental central public sector undertakings, the Department of Public Enterprise announced a new policy that provides for decentralized bargaining of five year agreements (as against four year agreements in the mid- and late 1980s) based on enterprise viability, performance and profitability. The new policy clearly states that wage agreements should be for a period of 10 years, that any additional wage burden would not qualify for budgetary support and that companies should not be allowed to raise prices because of wage rises as they are now responsible for keeping unit labour costs in check. With over 40 per cent of the 232 operating central public sector units already being sick, the new circular has received a mixed response. Cash-rich profit-making companies like ONGC have given raises of almost 20 per cent over their previous wages while in the engineering sector (Bharat Heavy Electricals Limited, for instance), it was half of what the ONGC agreement provided for. In the ports it was about 56.5 per cent. Only banks have a five year agreement and a 12.5 per cent rise. Overall, profit earning public sector firms are giving much more than what workers would have got had the agreements been for a period of five years. Also, some allowances like conveyance are separately indexed in some firms where the agreements refer to x number of litres through a fixed amount. Though the government, particularly the Department of Public Enterprises (DPE), seemingly has pervasive influence and control over the way central public sector enterprises are run, in reality its guidelines are flouted with impunity and its authority, though not openly questioned, is frequently undermined. The DPE itself has shrunk since the mid-1980s and there was even a proposal to close it down.

Changes in Labour Welfare Laws, etc.

The 1990s have brought worker welfare back onto the centre stage. The preoccupation since the 1940s has been with welfare benefits while in service. Now the focus has shifted to post-retirement welfare benefits. The provident fund contribution of employers was raised in all but a few industries from 8.33 per cent to 10 per cent of wage/salary. The pension scheme has replaced the existing family welfare benefit scheme. The new pension fund scheme has been controversial for the following main reasons: In an earlier round of wage negotiations (late 1980s) a common plea was made in most agreements for the introduction of a third retirement benefit, i.e., for pension in addition to gratuity and provident fund. But the new pension scheme does not create a third benefit, merely replacing the existing benefit with a new one. The return on investment under the pension scheme is low and the government has withdrawn the financial contribution it was making to the Family Benefit Scheme while converting it and the Employee's Provident Fund contributions into a pension scheme. In the wake of pressure from trade union federations, the government has agreed to restore its earlier contribution.

REVIVAL OF TRIPARTISM

Structural adjustment reforms were announced in June 1991 without any consultation either with the state governments or with the organizations of employers and workers. The government approached the concerned parties after the decisions concerning the changes in macro-economic policies were made public. State governments, particularly those ruled by opposition parties, whose cooperation is inevitable for the success of reforms, considered this an affront. Organizations of employers and workers considered it a *fait accompli*. Neither had any information or data to evaluate the effects of the changes on them. Employers initially welcomed the proposals but later, on careful assessment, began to question the sequencing and place of these reforms which denied them (the employers) a level playing field on which to compete with multinationals.

The government formed a special tripartite conference and established Tripartite Industrial Committees in seven industries considered to be sick or prone to sickness (see Chapter 6). Social dialogue has been stymied due to political posturing and reluctance to take bold decisions. The conference, however, secured the limited purpose of releasing the pent-up aggression and deferring concrete actions to restructure enterprises, particularly in the central public sector.

There has been no change in the legal framework concerning employment security during the post-liberalization period. Both the executive and the judiciary have been showing greater responsiveness to market requirements. In the past, even if companies were sick, employee interests were secure. Now, even jobs in financially sound companies are not as secure. The dominant message is that enterprise success is a necessary, but not sufficient condition for job security. Employers argue about the need for proactive restructuring and justify downsizing as right sizing in order to prevent sickness and protect the interests of the remaining workforce in the organized sector.

Given the absence of a social safety net for the poor and the unemployed, the incidence of poverty is found to be higher among the employed rather than the unemployed. The really poor do not have the capacity to withhold their labour and settle for any job, even if at below minimum wage subsistence level.

Even though the rate of population growth has receded marginally, given its age distribution, the labour force in the country is projected to increase faster than the demand for labour over the next decade.

Trade unions have had a hard time in dealing with situations/arguments like the following:

- Restructuring leads to job loss. Non-restructuring does not avoid job loss. The job loss could be more with non-restructuring than with restructuring.
- New technologies shed few jobs and create many more jobs. For example, two successive revolutions in telecom—manual mechanical to electrical mechanical to digital cellular—have not only resulted in a loss of a few thousand Group C and Group D jobs in some public sector enterprises and erstwhile departmental undertakings but also created a few million jobs in STD/ISD booths in every nook and corner of the country's five lakh villages. Quality is an issue, but for many who do not have a source of livelihood some job is better than no job.
- In some units—for example, Sindri Fertilizers, some units of Indian Drugs and Pharmaceuticals Limited and Hindustan Engineering Corporation—there has been either no or low production for years together. In others—for instance Hyderabad Allwyn before privatization and the Kolar Gold Mines—the losses would have been less without production than with production. Expenses in the Kolar Gold Mines to produce 10 g of gold is nearly five times the market price of the same quantity of gold!
- Consumers and the community do not seem interested in how a company addresses itself to social issues like job creation. They are more interested in the cost and quality of products and services.

In the face of the private interests of the consumers and the public interests of the community the sectional interests of both employers/managements and workers/unions seem to have become secondary and/or relegated to the background. Consumer courts are awarding judgements undermining the rights of workers and public interest litigation on matters concerning environmental aspects, etc. This is resulting in court verdicts that subordinate the interests of workers and employers to those of the wider public and the community.

SOCIAL SAFETY NETS

Social safety nets are needed to provide assistance for maintenance (of self and family)/livelihood

(a) in the event of loss or reduction of income due to involuntary unemployment
(b) in the event of sickness, accident and invalidity, and for old age
(c) to the needier sections of the community in terms of redistribution of cash, goods and social services—education, health, subsidized housing, etc.

When we are discussing social safety nets in the context of increasing globalization, we are concerned mainly with social safety nets for the unemployed, particularly those rendered redundant due to restructuring to make the units that once employed them viable and competitive. Workforce reduction should be the last, not the first, option in restructuring. The provision of a social safety net is intended to take care of the vulnerable. Its purpose is to soften the adverse effects on the people displaced rather than make it easy for employers to get rid of people. It is underlined that not all sick units need to be closed or resort to workforce reductions. Similarly, profitable companies may not remain viable forever unless they adapt to changes. Productivity can be improved not only by denominator management (producing more with less people) but also through numerator management (producing more with the same number of people) where the demand for the product is not a problem. Experience reveals that the absence of a social safety net has resulted in delays or deferment of restructuring. Timely restructuring will avoid closure of units, which would otherwise become chronically sick. The longer the delay in restructuring the more chronic the problem becomes resulting in a harsher impact on labour.

In today's environment a large number of companies want to reduce the numbers they employ and cut the proportionate cost off the wage bill. Capital demands security for investment, and labour is concerned about the security of their jobs, careers and earnings. Income security is being considered an alternative to job security. The record of the National Renewal Fund created in 1991 is very disappointing, to say the least. It spent over 90 per cent of its money to 'voluntarily' retire over 200,000 employees in the PSEs. Its record in retraining and redeployment is very poor and it has not done anything regarding area regeneration and the setting up of an insurance fund (ILO, 1999).

Several countries have believed in the recent past that redundancy can be fought with retraining and redeployment, and that skills obsolescence can be prevented or minimized through retraining. But, when the new jobs created are less than the job losses plus the fresh additions to the labour force, redeployment will solve only the problem of redundant workers, not the unemployment of fresh entrants into the job market. Several companies have introduced schemes, which provide for higher compensation than that mandated by law to those who they want to retire 'voluntarily'. Profitable companies, proactively restructuring their enterprises through downsizing, may have the capacity and commitment to develop such schemes and make payments over and above legally mandated amounts. Sick and closed units, however, do not often have the capacity and commitment to pay even the legal dues. Social safety nets are needed to take care of the latter. In addition, social safety nets should also be considered in order to provide subsidies to industries which are economically depressed and facing financial difficulties with a view to arresting the retrenchment of workers (to keep employment within the enterprises during the crisis period) or to minimize the effect of lay-offs and retrenchments. The subsidies could cover in certain cases, up to 50 per cent of the total wage cost. Also, the relevant laws should be amended such that in the unfortunate event of the closure of enterprises and other liquidation procedures, workers' wages, severance pay, unpaid bonus, and other such outstanding payments should be the first charge on the liquidated assets of the concerned company or group of enterprises (ICFTU-APRO, 1998).

MNCs, PRIVATIZATION AND EPZs

Multinational Corporations (MNCs)

India needs foreign capital and technology resources to make optimal use of its vast natural and human resources and growing market for a variety of products and services. In the past, the policies of self-reliance and import-substitution restricted the scope for foreign capital and technology in India. The deregulation of foreign investment in India in 1991 can be considered a watershed. The extent of its liberalization and of the foreign investment climate is such that as a chief executive of one MNC put it, 'India has opened up its economy with far less discrimination than most other countries, including the Far East and South-East Asian economies at their commensurate state of development.'

The role of foreign direct investment (FDI) was recognized in India in its Industrial Policy Resolutions of 1948 and 1956 but not in the key industries, which were reserved for exclusive growth in the public sector till recently. The Foreign Exchange Regulation Act (FERA), 1973 put, barring certain exceptions, a ceiling of 40 per cent on foreign equity participation in India. Multinational Corporations (MNCs), which did not want to dilute their stake, were asked to leave the country. FERA has been a major deterrent to FDI in India till the New Industrial Policy (NIP).

The Monopolies and Restrictive Trade Practices Act was amended to remove the threshold limits with respect to assets in monopolies and dominant undertakings. In high priority industries, automatic permission is given for foreign equity of up to 51 per cent as against 40 per cent in the past. In several areas foreign equity of up to 100 per cent is permitted. The prior approval of the government is not required for investment in deregulated industries. This provides MNCs with greater flexibility in the planning and diversification of their operations. Specific high technology and priority industries are now given automatic approval to conclude foreign technology agreements within certain set guidelines. Permission is no longer necessary for the hiring of foreign technicians and the testing of locally developed technologies outside of India. The Foreign Investment Promotion Board (FIPB) negotiates with a number of large international firms to promote substantial investment and gain improved access to advanced technology and world markets. The bulk of investments in the post-1991 liberalization era has come through the FIPB route.

The main attraction for MNCs in India is the size of its market, which is not only large but also growing phenomenally. A vibrant democracy, a credible judicial system, a strong bureaucracy, competitive human and natural resources, and the continued popularity of English as a business language add to the attraction.

The Indian industry is concerned about the role of MNCs in India. In the early 1990s, many Indian companies engaged in foreign tie-ups and many foreign companies increased their stake in Indian operations. A spate of mergers and acquisitions, too, followed, with many alliances souring for one reason or the other. Established Indian brand names began to be replaced by foreign brand names and a new practice of charging royalty for the use of brand names, both by Indian and foreign companies, created a flutter.

Both Indian employers and Indian trade unions broadly share similar perceptions and concerns about MNCs which are along the following lines:

1. MNCs are interested in capturing the Indian market but not in building a manufacturing base in India. Continued import of components is cited as proof of this allegation. Very few Indian companies are being developed to source parts from India for the overseas operations of MNCs. Few exceptions include the case of Sundaram Fasteners which won a global tender to supply radiator caps for General Motors, worldwide. Recently, the Korean auto giant, Daewoo also acquired control over its Indian operations, increased its stake and set its eyes on developing the Indian unit to source auto components for its worldwide operations.
2. MNCs focus on the short-term rather than the long-term. MNCs are keen to generate and repatriate profits quickly.
3. MNCs are using India as a dumping ground to bring in technology and products which are being phased out in their home countries.
4. MNCs use Indian partners to establish a foothold in India on a 50/50 or 40/40 basis and to get speedy sanctions and approval. Once established, however, they seek to edge out, as in the story of the camel and the Arab the Indian partner.
5. MNCs set up joint ventures with Indian partners and simultaneously, also set up 100 per cent subsidiaries in competitive areas

without Indian partnership. They thus use the insights obtained through partnership with Indian companies in joint ventures to secure an unfair advantage, allowing the 100 per cent subsidiary to compete with the joint venture firm.

6. A significant proportion of MNC investment is geared towards either increasing their stake in existing businesses or, mainly, supplying second-hand machinery to relocate obsolete plants in their home/a third country to India. Such MNC investment does not generate many new jobs, and even if it does, obsolete plants become the breeding grounds for sickness and, therefore, job losses.
7. MNCs come to India like 'cowboys'. They choose a partner hastily, make mistakes and then want to break off the relationship. Alternatively, they get into alliances with different Indian companies for different product lines. In the telecom sector, all the joint venture partners who bid for cellular tenders have already parted company. Alliances in the deregulated airlines industry have also soured.
8. MNCs cause deindustrialization. The ghost of the East India Company still haunts the average Indian psyche. The East India Company came on business and colonized the country for over two centuries, contributing to the deindustrialization of the country. Now even established Indian brand names in several industries are not able to face or withhold foreign competition due to the financial muscle and brand image of foreign competitors in the auto (two, three and four wheeler), electronics (television sets), white goods (refrigerators, for instance) and soft drinks industries.
9. An impression is gaining ground, in the wake of the renegotiation of certain power projects, that MNCs have a tendency to pitch their investment costs and prices to a level which is higher than necessary, pushing up the prices that consumers have to pay. Confessions about huge development costs breed suspicion about corruption.
10. Since the mid-1990s, revelations about foreign exchange irregularities involving ITC-BAT and the controversy concerning the control of ITC by its UK partner, BAT has not augured well for the image of MNCs in India.
11. MNCs are capitalizing on the weaknesses of traditional and small-scale Indian businesses in rural areas by quickly patenting herbal

products and indigenous snacks (Bikaner bhujia, for instance). The entry of some multinationals into businesses like salt (the salt satyagraha launched by Mahatma Gandhi in Gujarat was an emotive movement during the freedom struggle) in the border areas of Gujarat, agriculture (Cargill) in Karnataka, ecologically unfriendly chemicals projects in Goa (Dupont's pact with the Thapars), and the use of India as a dumping ground for the disposal of dangerous chemicals wastes have rendered MNCs rather unwelcome in the minds of several Indians.

Kumar (1986) found that MNCs in Indian manufacturing pay higher than their local counterparts. In a subsequent study, Kumar (1990) explained this in terms of their tendency to employ qualitatively superior personnel than their local counterparts. Markensten's (1972) study of Swedish MNCs in India and Davala's (1996) case studies on six engineering and chemical firms in Mumbai and Bangalore confirm this. Davala (1996) characterizes the wage policies of MNCs as the following: 'The more you work, the more you get.'

Compared to their private sector counterparts, MNCs in India are generally known to adopt a policy of paying above average salaries to their workmen. During the 1990s, when General Motors decided to set up its manufacturing facility in Vadodara, the Vadodara Industrial Employers' Union reportedly met its chief executive and pleaded with him not to upset the local wage structure in the interest of maintaining employer unity in a region with predominantly medium- and small-sector units paying modest wages.

The working conditions in MNCs are usually better than that of their counterparts in the private sector. As observed earlier, '... trade unions hate multinationals, but like the pay and perks they offer ... (Tulpule, 1993).'

In many large MNCs in the chemical and pharmaceutical industry, union density rates are higher than the national average. But in the electronics industry, owned and controlled by MNCs, unionism is virtually absent even though a few private (ICIM, for instance) and several public sector electronics units are characterized by fairly high union density rates.

Unionism is very strong in both the public and the private sector banks in India, but not quite so in the foreign banks. Several foreign banks have registered unions, but most foreign bank managements do not recognize them. While some, like the Grindlays Bank, sign agreements with their unionized staff, and a few others choose to become members of Indian Banks Association and thereby become party to the industry level collective agreement, some foreign banks refuse to sign agreements directly with their unions. A proper measure of industrial relations in such organizations is not the number of mandays lost, but the number of court cases concerning unfair dismissals and other forms of discrimination and exploitation of labour in which they are embroiled.

Collective bargaining in India is size specific. Large companies employing more than 300 persons typically have collective bargaining, excepting in the insurance business. Till date, MNCs have not been allowed to operate in the insurance sector, though in the future they may. Most MNCs, other than in electronics and a few in banking, have collective bargaining.

Japanese investors are apprehensive about the ad hoc management of unions and industrial relations in the context of multiplicity, plurality, ambiguity and uncertainty. The Japanese MNC representatives of the Kansai Productivity Centre, who visited India in the late 1990s, told the author that they would like to identify and deal with a collective bargaining agent directly. But unfortunately, union structures and recognition policies do not provide such clear-cut arrangements for determining collective bargaining agents.

In India, generally, high wages and high exploitation go together. In many cases, workers can secure high wages, relative to other firms in the region, through hard bargaining and militant unionism. The same can generally be considered true of MNCs, particularly the chemical and pharmaceutical industries, but not so much the engineering industry and certainly not MNCs in the electronics industry.

One MNC located on the outskirts of Delhi signed an agreement in 1995 with its individual employees to the effect that it would increase emoluments by a few hundred rupees if they agreed not to join/form a trade union.

Typical Indian private sector industrialists are comfortable with the enormous diversity in the legal framework of India and many of them manage the complexity and uncertainty if they are clear about their purpose. MNCs, in contrast, generally expect clear-cut legal measures because they want to be seen as good corporate citizens, at least with regard to legal compliance.

MNCs provide the social security measures mandated by law. These include provident fund and gratuity, but not pension as of date. Several MNCs, however, have pension funds for their senior executives, not for their workers.

The aim of the Tripartite Declaration of Principles on Social Policy and the Code for Multinational enterprises 'is to encourage positive contribution which MNCs can make to economic and social progress and to minimize and resolve the difficulties to which their various operations may give rise, taking into account the United Nations Resolutions advocating the Establishment of a New International Economic Order'.

Workers' organizations are generally not consulted on investment matters, particularly with regard to policy changes on investment and assets, and other operations of MNCs. The INTUC acknowledges that MNCs are expected to play an important role in promoting economic and social welfare by providing more employment opportunities and raising the living standards of workers.

The INTUC states that the establishment of MNCs is regulated in accordance with the national development priorities of the government. Some of the leftist trade unions do not subscribe to this view. The fact is that the Companies Act, the Monopolies and Restrictive Trade Practices Act and the Foreign Exchange Regulation Act regulate the entry and operation of MNCs. The same set of labour laws that are applicable to domestic firms apply to MNCs as well. Although there is no separate permanent machinery for consultation with workers' and employers' organizations concerning the operation of MNCs, the existing tripartite machinery and parliamentary fora are used for holding discussions on MNCs. The employers and workers in MNCs are represented by their respective central organizations. There are no exclusive organizations of workers and employers for MNCs.

Privatization

The economic liberalization in India since 1991 has resulted in a major policy shift, permitting the entry of the private sector in areas hitherto reserved exclusively for the public sector. This has ensured a measure of competition for public sector monopolies in sectors like transportation, electricity, oil, telecom, banking and insurance, to mention a few. Along with this covert route, the government has also resorted to the disinvestment of less than 20 per cent of the shares in about 50 central public sector enterprises. Throughout the 1990s, employees have also been offered shares in central public sector undertakings as a sop to ease workers' opposition to privatization. Though some national federations of trade unions opposed the move initially, workers and several unions in some profit-earning sectors demanded the earmarking of a higher proportion (up to 26 per cent) of shares for them. When the shares of several of these enterprises began declining, the initial euphoria among workers subsided.

The government appointed a Disinvestment Commission in 1996–97 and referred about a quarter of the companies under its control to it for advise on their privatization. The Disinvestment Commission has made recommendations, from time to time, individually on about 50 central public sector undertakings. Successive governments have not, however, followed up on any of the major recommendations. Scooters India, the first PSE at the national level to have been considered for privatization in the early 1990s because of its persistent losses, did not find a suitor because the government was not willing to allow for any reduction in the workforce. It has since diversified its product portfolio and begun to earn profits. In 1999, the government replaced the Disinvestment Commission with the Disinvestment Department and a Cabinet Committee on Disinvestment.

The main elements of the central government's policy on PSEs, announced in the Union Budget for 2000–01, include the following: (a) restructuring and reviving potentially viable PSEs, (b) closing down the PSEs which cannot be revived, (c) bringing down government equity in all non-strategic PSEs to 26 per cent or lower, if necessary, and (d) fully protecting the interests of workers. There are dissensions within the ruling alliance and among the opposition parties on this, with the left parties vehemently opposing disinvestments. In regard to protecting the interests of workers, even if retrenchment is ruled out, downsizing cannot be, particularly because PSEs themselves have started downsizing. The Steel Authority of India, which proposes to reduce its workforce by at least one-third, has even created a board-level position—Director, Restructuring—and engaged international consulting firms to consider shedding non-core activities and divest non-performing assets. The only major means of dealing with labour redundancy seems to be through voluntary retirements that give four times the normal retrenchment compensation and a promise of employee stock options in disinvested firms. Recent trends in the stock market have dampened the euphoria about employee stock options even in the ICE—information, communication and entertainment—industries.

In January 2000, Modern Bakeries became the first central public sector undertaking to have been sold to Hindustan Lever, the Indian subsidiary of the Anglo-Dutch multinational, Unilever. Another 17 units were listed for privatization. These include Maruti Udyog, where Suzuki is the majority partner, Air India and some companies in the petroleum sector. Besides several trade unions there is, however, considerable resistance from the alliance partners in the government as well as from several opposition parties. Among the trade unions, it is only the Indian National Trade Union Congress which does not have any ideological opposition to privatization as such even though the Congress Party, with which it has strong links and which initiated the economic liberalization process, has begun to question the stripping of national assets. It is seen from Table 1.6 that disinvestments have picked up in 1998–2000.

TABLE 1.6 **Disinvestment in Public Sector Undertakings**

Year	Target (Rs crore)	Achievement (Rs crore)
1991–92	2500	3038
1992–93	2500	1913
1993–94	3500	Nil
1994–95	4000	4843
1995–96	7000	362
1996–97	5000	380
1997–98	4800	902
1998–99	5000	5371
1999–2000	10000	1479*

*(till 31.12.99).
Source: Economic Survey 1999–2000, pp. 119.

The finances of some state governments are in a much worse condition than others including that of the central government. These governments privatized some units owned and controlled by them before the central government could do so. States like West Bengal, which continue to be under left-front rule, have found it more difficult to mobilize public opinion to sell state-level public enterprises like the Great Eastern Hotel in Calcutta. In the largest state of Uttar Pradesh the privatization of a cement factory, accomplished with considerable bloodshed and the killing of several people in police firing, had to be reversed in the wake of political instability that resulted in a change in government. The same state took a tough stand with striking power men in early January 2000 over the privatization of electricity distribution because of its dependence on international borrowings to carry on reforms for its sustenance.

The experience with several private airlines and passenger road transport services in some states has not been positive. Privatization of electricity transmission and distribution in Orissa was initially deemed a success and held as a model. But when a massive cyclone uprooted the electricity transportation system in most parts of the state, private sector operators were unable to fully restore the infrastructure. In the neighbouring state of Andhra Pradesh, privatized distribution was followed by a phenomenal rise in electricity tariffs, incurring the wrath of the public. Voltas Limited, an otherwise profitable private sector unit, took over the refrigeration units from Hyderabad Allwyn, the state-owned public sector giant in Andhra Pradesh. This adversely affected the company's bottom line and the Chief Executive, who favoured the acquisition, had to quit. Subsequently, however, the Hyderabad unit started earning a surplus, encouraging Voltas to commit more in terms of investment. All things considered, there are doubts in certain quarters about the nature of the private enterprise in India and its capacity to mobilize the needed resources and manage its businesses effectively.

Social dialogue on privatization—particularly deliberations on the future of the Indian Iron and Steel Company, nationalized textiles mills and Indian Drugs and Pharmaceuticals Limited—in the special tripartite committee meeting and tripartite industrial committee meetings has only helped to delay hard decisions, in the process rendering the sickness of these units more chronic. It is not only trade unions but also the political and bureaucratic leadership which is against privatization. The absence of civil service reforms and political reforms has ensured that neither has there been any real privatization nor any true liberalization of public sector managements from political and bureaucratic controls.

The government had offered for takeover a few sick units to trade unions but the unions were not quite willing to go for the bait. There is a growing realization in the government that a mere ownership change will not help companies improve their performance. Therefore, the government is now proposing to disinvest more than 50 per cent of the shares and bring these units under the effective control of private management. A section of the civil service and politicians themselves continue to resist this move because ownership and control over public sector enterprises has provided political sustenance for them. In contrast, the management in some PSEs is said to be hand in glove with private sector lobbyists in anticipation of an extended (beyond normal superannuation) and lucrative career. There is a move to introduce the concept of golden share.

There has been a shift in the government's approach to privatization. Yet, there is no clear-cut policy. Ad hocism continues, with a concern for achieving revenue targets from disinvestment. Perceived political risks and social tensions are prevailing upon the government to go slow on reforms.

Export Processing Zones

The government is impressed with the success of the Chinese Special Economic Zones (SEZs) and the union minister for commerce is keen to replicate these in India. A section of Indian employers welcomed the idea in the hope that it would give them the right to hire and fire employees. In the wake of vociferous protests from trade unions, the minister was forced to assure them that such zones would not be exempt from the labour laws of the country. However, going by past experience, even if the labour laws in such zones were not discriminatory, it would be difficult to unionize and secure protection of the kind that organized labour in the rest of the country enjoys.

In India, the organized sector refers to the sector comprising public and private enterprises which are registered and come under the purview of any/some or several Acts and which maintain annual accounts and balance sheets. Public enterprises include departmental and non-departmental enterprises in the public sector. In the private organized enterprises are included registered manufacturing, mining and quarrying, gas and water supply, private transport companies, registered schools, colleges and hospitals, and corporate trading activities and services.

In contrast, the unorganized sector comprises, exclusively, private sector units which are, if at all, only marginally affected or regulated by labour or industrial laws. Enterprises in this sector are usually very small (typically employing less than 10 persons) and are rarely unionized, with low wages, and harsh, exploitative and often largely unsafe working conditions.

NEW TRENDS IN INDUSTRIAL RELATIONS

The response of employers and trade unions to industrial relations is often driven by the context in which the interface between the two social partners occurs. It is possible to discern at least five distinct scenarios where the balance of power seems to swing in either's favour, influencing possible outcomes. Based on this typology it should be possible to read the signals early enough and predict the degree of choice and discretion that parties may have in influencing industrial relations outcomes.

Scenario 1

This is a situation of rising input costs and declining output prices. Cash flow problems limit opportunities for further investment, modernization and growth. Productivity improvement becomes imperative to maintain existing levels of profitability. Major constraints persist in continuing to do more with limited resources over a longer period. The resultant squeeze in employment, wages, benefits, etc. creates a sense of helplessness and causes tensions/conflict in human resource/industrial relations. Such companies are numerous.

Scenario 2

Several companies have, over a period of time, multiplied their business turnover and profitability through: (a) the setting up of parallel production facilities; (b) loan/lease licence arrangements; (c) subcontracting; (d) franchising, etc. This has rendered production/services more lucrative for employers. As output/services in a unit become less critical employers seem to develop a sense of independence, forcing unions to come to terms with management proposals. Several multinationals (Bata, Hindustan Lever and a host of pharmaceutical companies, for instance), which had earlier conceded to union demands in a cost plus situation, are now beginning to take (undue?) advantage of the increased vulnerability of unions in the liberalized environment since the late 1980s.

Scenario 3

When companies become bankrupt due to mismanagement etc., employers have to yield to union pressure to give up control and may be forced to accept employee buy-outs by worker cooperatives, for example. In quite a few cases (Kamani Tubes and Central Jute Mills, for instance), workers are able to revive sick units and sustain their profitability with support from the professional management.

Scenario 4

When economic, structural, technological and other changes make enterprises bankrupt, trade unions often agree to several concessions of the following type to revive the unit and save threatened jobs: (a) downsizing, including retrenchment of a section of the workforce; (b) wage and benefit cuts and freezes; (c) cost of living and other allowance freezes; (d) suspension of trade union rights for collective bargaining and industrial action for a certain period; and (e) agreeing to changes in work norms and work practices and greater managerial discretion in maintaining discipline, production and productivity, etc. In almost all companies—both public and private sector—whose cases are referred to the Board of Industrial and Financial Reconstruction (BIFR) for revival, these concessions have become the norm rather than the exception. The latest in the series is the multi-unit public sector firm, Indian Drugs and Pharmaceuticals Limited.

Scenario 5

When neither the trade union nor the employer seems to show adequate concern and sensitivity to workers' interests, workers are seen to ignore both employers and union and take charge of the situation. They are seen not to prefer a strike nor are they prepared to face a lockout. They simply occupy the plant and run it to keep their jobs and earn their livelihood. The most recent such case is that of the Kanoria Jute Mills in Calcutta.

Scenario 6

The new, high-tech, service and information, communication and entertainment industries with non-traditional work places, work patterns and employment contracts (individual, not collective) have a young, diversified, ambitious and non-union workforce with a different set of aspirations. Here the focus is not on the usual aspects of industrial relations. Even the traditional notions of employment relations are increasingly being questioned. The evolving pattern of the future course of employment in this as yet small, but growing sector which has caught the imagination of the urban, educated present and future generations is, as yet, difficult to figure out.

CONCLUSIONS AND IMPLICATIONS FOR POLICY

At the time India became an independent nation in 1947, it was one of the few major industrial powers in the whole of Asia. But in the 1990s, it is at the bottom of the newly industrializing countries.

India has allowed itself to get marginalized in a world that has become increasingly interdependent. India's share in world exports declined from 1.4 per cent in 1955 to 0.5 per cent in 1990; its share in world imports also declined from 1.3 per cent to 0.7 per cent during the corresponding period. Significantly, however, in the wake of the first phase of reforms during 1984–85, India's exports and imports picked up substantially. Certain international developments like the Gulf War, however, precipitated the balance of payments crisis.

India's competitiveness in terms of its human resources is considered to be the least. The World Competitiveness Report (IMD and WEF, 1990) puts India at the bottom of the 10 newly industrializing countries in terms of the competitiveness of its human resources. The World Competitiveness Report examines the competitive advantage of human resources on the basis of skills, motivation, flexibility, age structure and health of the people. The criteria included in this factor are: population, employment, unemployment, educational attainment, vocational training, public expenditure on education, management quality, income levels and health factors.

During the 1990s, the UNDP Report on Human Development ranked India in the bottom 35 of 160 countries in terms of the Human Development Index that takes into account three parameters, i.e., longevity (life expectancy), knowledge (adult literacy) and decent standard of living (per capita income). In terms of the Human Freedoms Index, covering 40 indicators of freedoms to exercise choices in cultural, social, economic and political affairs, India scored 14 points to obtain a medium freedom ranking (11–30 points) (UNDP, 1999).

One lesson that India has learnt is that 'inward looking country strategies (have) failed, outward looking country strategies (have) succeeded'. Hence, the shift from import-substitution to export-orientation and the concomitant thrust on productivity and quality.

The following observations can be made concerning the existing institutional framework of industrial relations in India in the light of Kochan et al.'s (1987) three tier strategic choice model.

For the top tier of strategic decision making, a superstructure of tripartite concertation was built and in the quarter century (1947–72) since Independence, such tripartite institutions as the ILC and SLC served a useful role and provided a major thrust towards voluntarism in the face of the preference to adjudication over collective bargaining. However, since the early 1970s, tripartite consultations and voluntarism have suffered a setback.

Political developments since the late 1960s and the subsequent fissures in centre–state relations, the rigid polarization of views on major aspects of industrial relations within and among the actors, particularly unions, and a host of other factors not all of which are clear as yet for want of a system analysis, have rendered macro-level efforts somewhat unproductive. Major reforms in industrial relations either did not enjoy popular support or have suffered from the absence of the much-needed political will or both.

The middle tier suggested by Kochan et al. refers to such factors as the employment relationship and personnel policy formulation, collective bargaining, labour legislation and labour administration at enterprise level. Here, too, the scenario is equally infirm.

There is a surfeit of legislation along with collective bargaining in a less than congenial environment. Some critics discern a certain sense of free-for-all—a laissez-faire situation—with many undercurrents and new equations in industrial relations (Ramaswamy, 1988). Some point to the growing size of the 'working non-employees' which, unchecked, may reduce the sphere of the labour force with regard to 'employment relationship' to cause significant shifts in personnel policy (Mathur, 1989).

At the third tier, i.e. the shopfloor level, the strategic choices relate to the organization of work and the workplace environment. The last two decades have shown considerable innovation and experimentation at this level (also see De, 1984); yet, much of it has not been sustained in organizations where they have been tried or tested. The principal thrust of management here is to gain greater flexibility in organizational work and the allocation and utilization of human resources. Here, too, employees and trade unions seem to question the motives and bona fides of moves made:'flexibility for whom and for what ends?'

A charitable interpretation of the current industrial relations scene in India would be to call it very complex. A critical view could be that it is chaotic. Whatever it is, the changes in the international economic order and the geopolitical environment in the wake of the breaking down of the Berlin wall, the transition in Central and East European countries, and the end of Cold War; the changes in the macro economic and social environments, technological and structural changes; and the changing worker profile (Sengupta, 1992), work organization, work environment, etc. call for fresh perspectives on our thinking, our beliefs, our philosophy and our value system concerning the management of people at the workplace and elsewhere. The dynamic change process warrants a fresh look at the institutional and legal framework as also the roles of the principal actors. Changes in industrialization strategies call for changes in labour management policies, too, to obtain the requisite balance between the social system and the technical systems in our organizations in order that organizations fulfill the purposes for which they are created.

Workplace changes point to a reduction in manufacturing employment, downsizing as right sizing, the ascendancy of employer rights and the increasing vulnerability of unions due to technological, economic, structural and other changes. In employment relations the following shifts are discernible. The shift to a market economy being decisive and irreversible, at least in the foreseeable future, organizations will need to do more with limited resources to be viable, competitive, productive and profitable. The focus will be on productivity, profitability and quality improvement.

The agenda for reform should concern itself with the following:

1. Develop a vision for A.D. 2000 and draw up an action plan that focuses more on changing mind-sets rather than argue about the content of legal reform.
2. Strike a balance between western (North America and West Europe) and eastern (China, Japan, South-East and Far East) models of industrial relations with a view to developing the so-called 'middle path' that marries the imperatives of globalization, tending towards a market economy, with considerations of equity and social justice in the context of widespread underemployment, unemployment and poverty.
3. Consider where protection of the kind a civilized society ought to afford becomes restrictive and counterproductive, and develop a dual consideration for economic viability, competitiveness of enterprise and the quality of work-life as well as a reasonable measure of social protection for workers.
4. Strengthen the representative character of each of the three social partners and forge strategic alliances among them and also with the community, national and international.
5. Review the institutional framework for industrial relations in the context of the new paradigms and changing dynamics of centre-state relations and the need for less developed states to evolve an investor-friendly climate.
6. Recognize and value the guiding principles of the freedom of association, right to collective bargaining, access to information, and consultation and communication at all levels.
7. Document experiences of building trust, rapport, two-way communication and information at all levels.
8. Create better jobs, a better environment and a growing and competitive economy.
9. Develop skills and mechanisms for continuous training and retraining to develop a creative, adaptive and willing workforce.
10. Build the voice of and the stake for people around and meet their expectations within the context of the need for creating high-performance work systems.

REFERENCES

All India Trade Union Congress (AITUC) (1990). *34th Session of AITUC: Report, Resolutions and All Documents,* Madras: AITUC.
Ahluwalia, I.J. (1992). *Redefining the Role of the State: India At Crossroads.* Paper presented at the Korea Development Institute, Senior Policy Forum on Private Sector-led Development Strategy and the Role of Government in Developing Countries at Seoul, Korea, October 15–17. New Delhi: Centre for Policy Research. Mimeo.
Asian Productivity Organisation (APO) (1991). *Labour-Management Consultation in Asia.* Tokyo: Asian Productivity Organization.
CMIE (Center for Monitoring Indian Economy) (1994). *Basic Statistics Relating to the Indian Economy.* Bombay: CMIE. August.
Davala (ed) (1992). *Employment and Unionism in Indian Industry.* New Delhi: Frederick Ebert Foundation.
Davala, S. (1996). *Multinationals and Labour Policies.* New Delhi: Frederick Ebert Foundation.
De, N.R. (1984). *Alternative Approaches to Work Design.* Geneva: ILO.
Dunlop, J.T. (1958). *Industrial Relations System.* New York: Holt.
Fallon, Peter R. and Robert E.B. Lucas (1991). *The Impact of Changes in Job Security Regulations in India and Zimbabwe,* The World Bank Economic Review, Vol. 5(3), pp. 395–413.
Frensen, J. (1991). *Subcontracting and Inequality: The Case of Hindustan Lever in India.* Nijmegen: Third World Centre, Catholic University of Nijmegen.
Goyal, S.K. (1984). *Small Scale Sector and Big Business.* New Delhi: The Corporate Study Group of the Indian Institute of Public Administration.
Gupta, S.P. (1989). *Planning and Development in India: A Critique.* New Delhi: Allied.
Gupta, S.P. (1999). 'Trickle down Theory Revisited: The Role of Employment and Poverty,' V.B. Singh Memorial Lecture, 41st Annual Conference of the Indian Society of Labour Economics, IGIDR, Mumbai, November 18–20.
ICFTU–APRO (1998). *Building Trade Unions into the 21st Century.* Singapore: International Confederation of Free Trade Unions—Asia Pacific Regional Office.
International Institute for Management Development (IMD) and World Economic Forum (WEF). *The World Competitiveness Report, 1990.* Geneva: IMD and WEF.
International Labour Organization (1992). *World Employment Report.* Delhi: ILO.
International Labour Organization (1999). *National Renewal Fund.* Delhi: ILO.
International Labour Organization–Asian Pacific Project on Tripartism (1993). *Tripartism in India.* Bangkok. Mimeo.
Indian National Trade Union Congress (INTUC) (1993). *25th INTUC Session Report: May 1988 to April 1993.* Cuttack: INTUC.
Johri, C.K. (1992). *Industrialism and Industrial Relations in India.* New Delhi: Oxford University Press.
Kannappan, S. (1993). *Industrial Relations and Employment Policy in India.* The Indian Journal of Labour Economics, April-June 1993, pp. 133–142.
Kennedy, V.D. (1966). *Unions, Employers and Government: Essays on Indian Labour Questions.* Bombay: Manaktalas.
Kochan, T.A., H. Katz and R.B. McKersie (1987). *Transformation of American Industrial Relations.* New York: Basic Books.
Kumar, N. (1986). 'Foreign Participation, Market Structure and Employee Compensation in Indian Manufacturing'. *India Journal of Industrial Relations,* 31(3): 297–309.

Kumar, N. (1990). *Multinational Enterprises in India: Industrial Distribution, Characteristics and Performance.* London and New York: Routledge.

Markensten, K. (1972). *Foreign Investment and Development: Swedish Companies in India.* Lund: Student Literature.

Mathur, A. (1989). *Industrial Restructuring and Union Power: Micro-Economic Dimensions of Economic Restructuring and Industrial Relations in India.* New Delhi: ILO-ARTEP.

Mathur, K. and N.R. Sheth (1969). *Tripartism in Labour Policy: The Indian Experience.* New Delhi: Shri Ram Centre for Industrial Relations.

National Commission on Labour (Government of India) (1969). *Report of the National Commission on Labour.* New Delhi: Government of India.

Ramaswamy, E.A. (1988). *Worker Consciousness and Trade Union Response.* New Delhi: Oxford University Press.

Reserve Bank of India (1979). *Reserve Bank of India Bulletin.* July, p. 449.

Sengupta, A.K. (1992). *New Generation of Organised Workforce in India: Implications for Managements and Trade Unions,* in J.S. Sodhi and S.P.S. Ahluwalia (Eds.) *Industrial Relations in India: The Coming Decades.* New Delhi: Shri Ram Centre for Industrial Relations and Human Resources.

Sharma, B. (1995). *Aspects of Industrial Relations in ASEAN.* Singapore: Institute of Southeast Asian Studies.

Sharma, B.R. (1992). *Managerial Unionism: Issues in Perspective.* New Delhi: Shri Ram Centre for Industrial Relations and Human Resources.

Sheth, N.R. (1991) *Some Thoughts on our Trade Unions.* Ahmedabad: Indian Institute of Management.

Sheth, N.R. (1993). *Labour Relations in the New Economic Environment.* Vikalpa.

Singh, N.K. (1987). *Human Resource Development in Indian Public Sector.* New Delhi: Standing Conference of Public Enterprises.

Tulpule, B. (1993). *New Industrial Policy, Employment and Structural Adjustment in India.* Indian Worker, August.

United Nations Development Programme (UNDP) (1999). *Human Development Report.* New York: Oxford University Press.

Vaid, K.N. (1974). *Gheraos, Lock-outs and Labour Unrest in West Bengal.* New Delhi: Shri Ram Centre for Industrial Relations.

Venkata Ratnam, C.S. (1989). *Employers' Dilemma.* Bombay: Employers Federation of India and SOLAR Foundation.

Venkata Ratnam, C.S. (1991). *Unusual Collective Agreements.* New Delhi: Global Business Press.

Venkata Ratnam, C.S. (1992). *Managing People.* New Delhi: Global Business Press.

Venkata Ratnam, C.S. (1993). *Adjustment Through Privatization: A Case Study of India.* Geneva: ILO Interdepartmental Project on Structural Adjustment. Mimeo.

Venkata Ratnam, C.S. (ed) (1997). *Industrial Relations in Indian States.* New Delhi: Global Business Press.

Venkata Ratnam, C.S. and Anil Verma (1997). *Challenge of Change: Industrial Relations in Indian Industry.* New Delhi: Global Business Press.

Walker, K.F. (1975). *Workers Participation in Management: An International Perspective.* Geneva: IILS Bulletin.

The Workers Solidarity Centre Against Job Losses and Closures (1989). *Report of the Workshop on Job Losses and Industrial Closures.* Seminar on Social Movements, Human Rights and the Law. Bombay: 27–30 Dec.

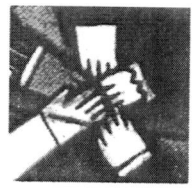

Two

Labour–Management Relations and the World in Transition

This chapter is presented in four parts. Part I reflects on the changing geopolitical situation and related developments and their implications for industrial relations. Part II discusses emerging trends and Part III raises some key issues both at the macro and micro levels. Part IV offers broad conclusions.

THE WORLD IN TRANSITION

Changing Geopolitical Map

The geopolitical map of the world has been changing rapidly since the late 1980s. Very little is left of communism after the fall of the Berlin wall and the convulsions in Central and Eastern Europe and that too, only in Cuba and northern China. Perhaps the same may happen to capitalism. In any case, neither communism nor capitalism today exists the way Adam Smith, Schumpeter and Karl Marx envisioned it should while writing their treatises.

The transformation in the geopolitical set-up has had its ramifications on industrial relations as well. In some countries, like in the USA (Kaufman, 1992) and the UK (Blyton and Turnbull, 1994), industrial relations are in a decline as a result of changes in trade unions, collective bargaining and modern human resource policies and practices. In contrast, in some other countries, particularly in Eastern and Central Europe which did not have a tradition of industrial relations—the way it is understood in democratic societies—industrial relations systems are emerging and taking root.

A basic concern in many countries is that public policies and labour institutions have not adjusted adequately to the fundamental shifts that have been occurring in the structure and nature of employment (ILO, 1994). This is not a recent phenomenon, though. As Schregle (1981) has observed, the legal system of industrial relations in India has remained, due to several difficulties, the same as it was at the time of Independence in 1947 even though significant reforms have been called for in several areas. More recently, a correlation has been found between industrialization strategies and industrial relations policies (Kuruvilla and Ratnam, 1996). Kuruvilla and Ratnam have contrasted the export-oriented industrialization strategies of South-East Asia with the import-substitution policies of South Asia. The government's protectionist strategy coexists with industrial relations pluralism, relative inefficiency and high labour costs. In the first stage of export-oriented industrialization strategies, the emphasis shifts to achieving competitiveness in export markets through measures that ensure a compliant labour movement and favourable labour cost structures for inward investors. However, in the second stage, downward pressure on labour cost and repression of trade unions gives way to: a reduced role for the state through decentralization; education and training policies to raise the skill levels of the workforce; and the search for flexible, productive, high-performance workplaces. Usually, the erosion of labour standards has been seen to be a transitory phenomenon in South-East Asia and East Asia during the early stage of industrial development. This has normally been followed by improvements in labour rights.

Convergence to Mixed Economies

Economic systems have been converging and today all countries, without exception, are mixed economies. This movement towards a market economy is pervasive. In 1978, two-thirds of the world's labour force lived in countries largely insulated from international markets by prohibitive trade barriers and capital controls, or by planned trade. By the year 2000, less than 10 per cent of workers were living in countries that are disconnected from world markets (World Bank, 1995). Whether such a convergence will weaken the role of ideological barriers in industrial relations and pave the way for transforming political unions into business unions and conflictual relations into cooperative relations remains to be seen.

Given the limited time-frame and pendulum-like shifts in the fortunes of parties with diametrically opposite ideological backgrounds, the evidence available is inadequate to permit any broad conclusions.

Democratization

The surge of democracy, rise in literacy levels, revolutionary developments in microelectronics, satellite and telecommunications technologies, the integration of financial and product markets and the emergence of workers with expectations of working in high-performance organizations in an increasingly competitive global economy are some of the characteristics which are fast becoming universal.

Economic development cannot be explained as a uniform phenomenon (Kerr, et al. 1961; Kerr, 1971). The Asian experience indicates that economic development in the newly industrialized countries was subject to different strategies at different stages and with different outcomes. Globalization and the resultant changes in macro-and micro-level institutions and organizations should not undermine human rights at work and in the wider society. Newly industrializing countries should view functional democracy as an important ingredient of the industrial relations system. These concerns were articulated at the 10th World Congress of the International Industrial Relations Association (Towers, 1996; see also Zapata, 1996) and the Third Asian Industrial Relations Congress at Taipei in 1995. Today, more than ever before, there is growing recognition of basic human rights and freedoms including freedom of association and collective bargaining. Concern for international labour standards is manifest in the form of social charters and social clauses, the latter seeking compliance for international trade with international labour standards (see Chapter 10 for a detailed discussion).

Ownership Changes

In the 1970s, the political structure of industrial relations changed with widespread nationalizations, particularly in the developing countries. In the 1980s and 1990s, the pendulum swung backwards with denationalization. Along with denationalization, deregulation, decentralization and devolution became recurrent themes in most parts of the world. Now, the arguments for limiting and redefining the role of the state have also been gaining currency. Widespread changes in ownership such as in Eastern and Central Europe have important implications for trade unions and collective bargaining. Several studies point to industrial relations institutions taking contrasting forms (Egorov, 1996; Bamber and Peschanski, 1996; Venkata Ratnam, 1991; Edgren, 1990). Some of these studies point to the ascendancy in the role of employers and workers' organizations as the state gradually curtails its own role. The need for establishing an effective labour relations machinery at the preliminary stage of economic transformation along with a psychological transformation in the parties' attitude to collective bargaining has been highlighted by Egorov.

Structural Adjustment Pressures

In the 1970s, the oil price shocks forced industrialized market economies to restructure themselves and their enterprises. In the 1980s and 1990s, exchange, debt and deficit crises and widespread inflation and unemployment compelled most developing countries and economies in transition to transform their economies and enterprises. In several countries, structural changes led to downsizing, decentralizing of firm-level collective bargaining, trade-offs between wages and jobs and the sacrifice of the accumulated rights of workers and unions and new human resource policies whereby industrial relations have a non-union focus (ILO, 1984; Venkata Ratnam, 1996; Ozaki, 1999).

Externally driven transformation is leading towards new and convergent patterns of industrial relations (Aglietta, 1979; Piore and Sabel, 1984; Kochan et al., 1986). The Taylorist and Fordist systems of work organization are giving way to neo-Taylorist, post-Fordist work systems and Tayotoism. Piore and Sable (1984) point to a radical disjuncture between a 'mass-production economy' and one based on the principle of flexible specialization, the former signifying the era of Taylor and Ford and the latter heralding the era of Tayotoism. Tayotoism emphasizes lean production and flexible specialization. Changes in the workplace are brought out largely through new responses in collective bargaining that marked assertive, if not aggressive, employers seeking to restore some of the 'lost' managerial prerogatives (ILO, 1984; Venkata Ratnam, 1996). It is not surprising though, that already there is disenchantment with Tayotoism and analysts concerned about its weaknesses are exploring 'Beyond lean production' (IILS, 1993). Unless otherwise stated, most studies being country-specific, the conclusions are based on ethnocentric preoccupations and predilections.

Bronstein (1995) reviews the changes in the industrial relations system in Latin America since the 1980s. He notes that Latin America underwent far-reaching changes during the 1980s and early 1990s. However, not all these changes were along the same lines. On the one hand, Bronstein finds that there was greater respect for human rights and, as a result, new and wider avenues for freedom of association and autonomous collective bargaining. On the other, significant changes in the economic policies affected the regulatory framework of individual labour relations, which led to other forms of tension. He also points to the decline in industrial conflict, blurring of the ideological divide, lowering of the level of 'guaranteeism' of legislation and the advances in social dialogue and tripartite consultation. But, some of these, in Bronstein's view, were the product of isolation from the current economic environment and an interlude that may end any time. Thus a return to the past is not ruled out.

New Human Resource Policies

There is global concern about the new human resource policies and practices and their impact on industrial relations.

The broad trend towards decline in employment in the manufacturing sector, low union density in 'sunrise' sectors, decentralized collective bargaining, and direct communications with and involvement of workers can be seen as efforts at political restructuring of industrial relations. Kochan, et al. (1986) identify a trend towards industrial relations without collective bargaining. This is not limited to North America. In Australia and New Zealand, there is individualization of contracts, which is nullifying the legislative measures regarding, among others, pay equity. In the UK too as Blyton and Turnbull (1994) demonstrate, 'the determination of pay and conditions . . . is not solely achieved through collective bargaining'.

The 12th World Congress of International Industrial Relations Association (IIRA), organized at Tokyo in 2000 discussed atypical employment practices which are becoming typical. The next World Congress of IIRA scheduled to be held at Berlin in 2003 has, as its theme, 'Beyond the traditional employment contract . . .'. It is being recognized that the new human resource policies impinge heavily on not only industrial relations but also on the family and home.

Diverse Trends in Labour–Management Relations

It is difficult to visualize a single model of industrial relations which is apt for Asian countries like Burma, Nepal, India, China, Japan and Singapore in the foreseeable future. Generalizations are misleading, and classifications problematic, but, as Schregle (1981) reassures, they can be 'useful for anyone who wants to come to grips with comparative industrial relations'.

Schregle (1981) argues:

> Without going into details, there can be no disagreement that industrial relations in the United States and in Canada (more precisely in its English-speaking provinces) are very different indeed from those of Western Europe, in their historical development and concepts, in their basic characteristics, and in their value systems. Even within Europe, the divergence between different countries is enormous. There are worlds between, for instance, the industrial relations system of Italy and that of Norway, or between that of the Federal Republic of Germany and that of the United Kingdom, or between those of France and Austria . . . . Suffice it to remind ourselves that even the . . . member countries of the European Community have up to now been unable to develop even in a very limited or general way something that could be called an EEC approach to labour relations, in spite of the 'harmonization' efforts of the Commission of the EEC in the labour field.

Schregle's observations are as relevant today as at the time he first made them. Subsequently, Hyman (1994) has observed that stereotypes of industrial relations in Western Europe are open to challenge: 'Danes and Norwegians commonly object to being treated as mere variants of the Swedes. Austrians emphasize the contrasts between their system and the German one; the French and Italians may be more conscious of their mutual differences than their similarities. Inherent in such controversies are crucial questions of the value and limitations of cross-national generalization in industrial relations.'

In the Asian context, it is, likewise difficult to think of one model of industrial relations. Kuruvilla and Ratnam (1996) identify two primary strategies which were adopted by the state in South Asia and South-East Asia as circumstances changed: the import substitution industrialization strategy which focused on low-technology consumer and industrial goods for local consumption and subsequently focused on heavy industries; and the export-oriented industrialization strategy which focused on attracting foreign investment into light industry for export and subsequently on upgrading technology to achieve higher value-added production. The latter required skills development. Another plausible broad categorization can be three-fold: the South Asian contentious (adversarial), the East Asian consensual (particularly Japan, not Korea or Taiwan) and the South-East Asian compliance models. Yet, if an in-depth analysis were to be made, one would find not only similarities but also glaring contrasts between models as obtaining in Singapore and Hong Kong, or Singapore and Malaysia, even as Indonesia and the Philippines provide conspicuous contrasts on either ends of the continuum of unilateralism and pluralism respectively. In 1999, after the East Asian economic crisis, the new regime in Indonesia ratified a host of ILO conventions all at once. What it actually means to Indonesia's industrial relations systems remains to be seen.

Within India itself, if one looks at Bihar, unions have a strong presence in the public sector but not in the private sector, except in Jamshedpur. The approach of trade unions to productivity improvement in the private sector in West Bengal, also differs from its approach towards the public sector undertakings owned or controlled by the central government. Moreover, the differences among the parties in power at the state and central level contribute significantly to such diverse approaches. Here, it is important to consider whether whenever there is a pressure for change there is a general tendency to try out approaches (concerning trade unions, collective bargaining, tripartism/bipartism, etc.) different from the ones currently in vogue in a particular context, irrespective of whether they are still being adopted in settings where they once worked.

National Systems of Industrial Relations

National systems of industrial relations influence and are influenced by the way in which employers (whether the predominant form of capital is state, proprietary, managerial or collective) and workers are organized (craft, industry or enterprise), as also by labour institutions, the legal framework, stage of development, culture, history, etc. Within a nation, there is diversity across provinces or states based on the relative need for investment and job creation, and across industries or sectors depending on whether they are labour intensive or capital intensive and whether they operate in protected or competitive markets. Within an industry, at the enterprise, firm or plant level, there can be diversity depending upon the influence of cyclical forces (birth, growth, maturity and decline). Locke (1992) argues that the strategic choices of labour and management lead to outcomes that challenge the concept of national industrial relations. His explanation is that in certain industries or sectors, the diversity within industrial relations systems will be greater than the diversity across systems. Smith (1994), quoting Tolliday and Zeitlin (1991), asserts that national models of labour regulation 'should be understood not as homeostatic and self-producing systems of action but as complex and contingent historical constructions whose unity and coherence always remains open to empirical question'.

Thus it can be said that the wider the unit of analysis of industrial relations systems and practices, the greater the degree of abstraction. At each level of analysis—international, national, regional, sectoral, enterprise—the subunit differences become pronounced. Industrial relations are not only culture specific, but vary widely on account of historical, institutional, technological and other differences.

EMERGING TRENDS

Myriad Paradoxes and Tensions

Globalization coexists with growing regionalization. The European Union, the North American Free Trade Agreement, the ASEAN Free Trade Association, and the more recent South Asian Free Trade Association coexist with the signing of the agreement on the World Trade Organization (WTO) at Markash. Doubts persist regarding the tensions between free trade and fair trade and the paradox of how different nations can cope with managed trade. Nations must come to terms with their own sovereignty vis-à-vis the autonomy of the actors of an economic system, and address themselves to the twin goals of standardization and flexibility and the pursuit of efficiency and equity. Communism has failed and capitalism as it existed in the earlier centuries has disappeared. We have become used to both state and market failures. Therefore, we continue to search for alternative models and ultimately settle for a middle path that everyone seems to be advocating for in countries like India and even the UK. Against such a background, one key question, as Drekker (1995) puts it, is: Can industrial relations practitioners ensure that the human resource function is not subordinate to uncontrolled capitalism by developing a standard relating that function to a bilateral or tripartite code of conduct and behaviour?

The Influence of Contextual Factors and Critical Historical Events

As stated earlier, industrial relations are influenced by history, culture and other contextual factors which include not only the stage (predominantly agricultural, industrial, services/high-tech economies), nature (inward- or outward-looking strategies) and phase (in business cycle) of development, but also values, philosophy, institutions and leadership. As Fong (1990) argues, the 'distinctive economic features did not develop (in East Asia, for instance) in a vacuum, but are linked to a set of equally distinctive social and cultural features including a this worldly, culturally homogenous population imbued with an achievement-oriented work ethic, a high degree of respect for education and material success; a strong sense of group and family solidarity; a long period of political stability and social harmony; and effective institutions run on meritocratic principles'. Fong, however, hastens to add, 'The causal nature of the link between economic success and socio-economic features is far from clear.'

Critical historical events also influence subsequent developments (Collier and Collier, 1991). The developments in most dynamic Asian countries bear this out. The same can be said about the Eastern and Central European countries in transition. While in some dynamic Asian countries it resulted in pre-emptive state subordination of trade unions (Deyo, 1989), in the latter it is resulting in the liberation of trade unions from state subordination. Kochan (1994) observes an increased importance of the role of enterprise-specific strategies and decisions, thereby requiring decentralization of industrial relations activity in countries with a tradition of national or industry-wide collective bargaining. All this points to the need for a better understanding of the complexity of the environment (social/economic; micro/inter-organizational; national/international; formal/informal) in which industrial relations are practised (Thomson and Warner, 1981).

Several general patterns and conclusions have emerged from studies of changing employment relations in various countries by teams of national scholars in Asia (Verma, Kochan and Lansbury, 1995; Bamber, 1995) and OECD countries (Locke, Kochan and Piore, 1995). Most countries are under intense pressure to adapt their traditional practices in response to increased global competition and rapid changes in technology. The process is not, however, without intra- and inter-country variations in the pace of change and the degree to which different industrial relations systems have been able to adapt through incremental adjustments rather than fundamental transformations. There is a growing thrust on industrial relations activities at the enterprise level and decentralized systems and structures in industrial relations. Workplace changes reflect a growing concern for flexibility and competitiveness. As a result, skills development and contingent compensation are gaining importance with the attendant effect of increasing wage inequities. Trade unions in all countries also face major challenges as the pace of restructuring is intensifying, the workforce becoming more diverse, and the average size of enterprises declining. They are experiencing difficulties in maintaining membership in traditional industries and organizing themselves in new industries. Trade union difficulties are not restricted only to sharing a decline in membership, but also to resisting employer initiatives to wrest job control. Worker representation and worker participation in decision making is under stress, with the focus shifting in several cases from union representation to direct participation and worker empowerment.

CHANGING ROLES OF THE PRINCIPAL ACTORS

Government

In some countries like Japan and Germany, the government's attitude to business and industry is one of partnership to promote the growth of the national economy. In others, for political reasons, the government views private business with suspicion. Unless the government's attitude towards private business is positive, little can be accomplished through changes in other spheres—which will then be no more than cosmetic.

The government's role is changing. Strengthening of the forces of deregulation, denationalization and disinvestment is causing the state to gradually withdraw from some social and economic sectors. Governments are increasingly under pressure to become facilitators rather than regulators and controllers. Legal reform is under way in many countries and overdue in several others. Madrid's (1994) analysis of the situation in Argentina provides the much-needed caution for the state everywhere: The increase in the powers of employers is 'giving a market authoritarian character to the employment relationship. As a result, the principles of labour law have faced a crisis with declining protection afforded to workers and the disregard, in fact or in law, of the guiding principles of the ILO'.

Rising unemployment, underemployment and inflation, fall in living standards, increasing disparity in incomes and growing imbalances in the development of different regions within a state are influencing some governments to adopt policies aimed at wooing domestic and foreign investment but wily-nilly nullifying the accumulated social benefits and rights. Export-oriented production activities and zones where such firms are located are exempt by governments in several developing countries, such as Bangladesh, from the purview of certain labour laws and trade union and workers' rights. This is a matter of great concern. In Sri Lanka, the change in government escalated expectations about the reversal of such regressive policies which led to about 80 strikes in the last quarter of 1994 in the export-processing zone near Colombo airport alone. Liberalization and globalization presuppose that the differences in competition within and across national borders will vanish. In that case, the relevance of separate export-processing zones and 100 per cent export-oriented units and special conditions for labour standards in such zones/enterprises will and should disappear. In India, labour is on the concurrent list of the Constitution. In some states where investment is inadequate and job losses are mounting, public policy concerning labour market reforms have been particularly harsh on workers and unions. The industrial and labour policy changes in Kerala, the easing of requirements for labour inspection in Rajasthan, the relatively higher incidence of approvals for closure, retrenchments, etc., in Tamil Nadu (Government of India, 1996a), and the cancellation of the registration of a few thousand unions in West Bengal for non-submission of statutory returns to the Registrar of Trade Unions (Sen, 1996) in good time illustrate the changes at the state level (see also, Chapter 5). The central government has also tried to usurp more power from the states through exclusive control over industrial relations issues in regard to multinational corporations, contract labour in central public sector undertakings and introducing a proposal for a national minimum wage (Government of India, 1996b).

The 1998 ILO Declaration on Fundamental Principles defines and sets in motion the mutual steps for ensuring universal compliance with minimal, core labour standards covering the abolition of child and forced labour, elimination of discrimination and promotion of equality. International pressure through WTO, Non-Governmental Organisation (NGO) campaigns, social labelling and consumer labelling will aid the ILO initiative (see also, Chapter 10).

Employers

Drawing on the works of Lazonick (1991) and Chandler (1962), Taira (1994) explains,

> The comparative history of business organization and human resource utilization suggests a linear and upward evolution of

capitalism: from England's proprietary capitalism in which an individual capitalist owned a firm, to America's and Germany's managerial capitalism in which numerous individuals subscribed to the capital of a firm managed by professional managers, to Japan's collective capitalism in which control of the firm is democratized and in which workers also take on some managerial functions and assume risks, augmenting the managerial resources of the firm . . . . Organizational and human resource efficiencies as well as scale of organization increase along this evolutionary path. Firms under managerial capitalism are larger and more efficient than those under proprietary capitalism. Likewise, firms under collective capitalism are larger and more efficient than those under managerial capitalism. The scope of inter-firm coordination of economic activities under collective capitalism is larger than under any other type of capitalism, because of alliances among firms . . . . To sum up, managerial capitalism overtakes proprietary capitalism, and collective capitalism overtakes managerial capitalism.

Though in several countries significant sections of employers in the organized private sector have welcomed structural changes, they argue that these changes should be achieved through policies that give an impetus to local industry to expand and grow. Encouragement to multinationals, easing of restrictions on expatriate employment and ownership of the means of production and other resources are reminiscent of colonialism. Also, employers' interests vary depending on whether they represent foreign or domestic interests—large or small—export- or import-oriented businesses, etc. (Venkata Ratnam, 1994). Market reform policies lead to improved business climate and performance. However, the opposite is equally true. In Nigeria, one cement plant incurred substantial foreign debt in the late 1970s in order to finance expansion, but after devaluation the local cost of this debt rose five-fold.

In India, when liberalization and globalization measures were initiated in parallel, some domestic companies found that their foreign debt on capital investment multiplied overnight due to devaluation. Fresh capital for long-term capital and working capital needs could only be borrowed in India at much higher interest rates than their competitors from overseas, and imported materials and components too became costlier. As a result, some domestic entrepreneurs had a 30 to 50 per cent strategic cost disadvantage. Also, countries in dire need of foreign investment offer incentives that are attractive to foreign investors but considered detrimental to the interests of domestic investors (Venkata Ratnam, 1994).

Privatization of Central and East European economies resulted in the emergence of employers as an interest group, distinct from the state (Egorov, 1996; Thirkell, 1994). In Central and East European countries no separate employer function was officially recognized till 1989 'since everybody was supposedly united in the construction of socialism. Industrial relations, taken for granted in pluralistic societies, did not exist. The prevailing ideology made no allowance for any possible conflicts of interests. Trade unions were anything but independent and were as a rule used to organise and administer social services and run personnel departments in the state enterprises. Now employers' organizations are emerging in these countries as elsewhere' (ILO, 1994). The challenges before employers organizations throughout the world are many. 'The changes in the system of government and economic management, with emphasis on pluralism and economic liberalization, have thrust employers and their organizations into the centre stage of economic development debate and action. The role of the private sector as an engine of development has gained credibility. Recognition of this is one thing, but for the government to divest themselves of some of the tools of power will take time. The struggle for true partnership in development will not be easy (ILO, 1994).'

Trade Unions

Over time the labour movement has changed from craft unionism to industrial unionism to enterprise unionism. Taira (1994) argues, 'One may graft stages of production technology and the labour movement on the Lazonick model of capitalist evolution.' Production technology has changed from craft production, to mass production, to lean production, roughly co-varying with proprietary, managerial, and collective capitalism. As he argues further, 'For lean production, workplace innovations are largely firm-specific and often carefully guarded as intellectual property. Productivity and gain sharing are maximised when employees put in long years of service and get involved in continuous Kaizen. To ensure employment security and improve terms of employment, the union is just as much concerned about the conditions of the firm as management. The union then becomes increasingly localised and autonomous.' The ultimate localization of a union is an autonomous enterprise union. Enterprise unionism is one of the four pillars of the industrial relations system in Japan. The trend towards enterprise unionism is growing in the US too (Weiler, 1990).

At one time, bringing together workers across an entire industrial sector was considered essential to take wages out of competition and ensure the equitable distribution of wealth. Now, in several countries enterprise-based unionism is becoming the predominant form of union organization. Of course, enterprise-based unions do not exist in isolation and still are, in many cases, federated across sectors or industries and further, at a different level, into national centres.

Union membership is declining in traditional industries in several countries. Union organization is becoming difficult in new industries. 'In the countries that have changed to democracy and are moving towards the market economy, the newly constituted trade unions are coming up against all manner of constraints, their difficulties aggravated by an excessive fragmentation which is scarcely conducive to that unity of expression and participation so indispensable to these organizations if they aspire to play an effective part in the consolidation of trade union structures and policies and in the genuine participation in their economic and social life' (ILO, 1992).

Since the 1980s, as in the US (Strauss et al., 1991), in Western Europe (Hyman, 1994) too, unions have been on the defensive. In Japan as well, union density declined from 45.3 per cent in 1947 to 24.2 per cent in 1993 (Tsuru, 1994). Tsuru suggests that the shifts in employment patterns and the disinterest of non-union workers in unionization are the major determinants of decline in union density. The explanations for low or declining union density vary across countries even within Asia (Frenkel, 1993; Verma et al., 1995; Venkata Ratnam et al., 1995; ICFTU–APRO, 1995). Revolutionary changes in technology are shifting the locus of control away from blue-collar to white-collar workers and managers and the dramatic decline in employment intensity in many sectors of manufacturing is not only eroding the traditional base of the unions but also destabilizing the traditional trade union structures. Standing and Sziraczi (1992) are certain that the overall rate of unionization will decline, particularly as unions find it hard to become established in the type of small-scale firms that are emerging. Organizing the unorganized in the small and tiny sectors will indeed be a major challenge for trade unions in the years ahead. The ongoing Internet debate on trade unions in 2000 and some of the recent successes unions have had in countering employer militancy through cyber unionism and Internet campaigns provide useful pointers to the new challenges and opportunities before trade unions.

Frenkel's (1993) analysis of the factors affecting trade union characteristics in nine countries in the Asia Pacific region tests several hypotheses and theoretical approaches. It portends little change in countries that follow state corporatist policies (e.g. China and Singapore), moderate change in countries which follow state exclusionary policies (Thailand, Malaysia and Hong Kong) and major changes in countries where state collaborativism is nurtured with autonomous market-bargained corporatism (New Zealand). The exceptions to his categorization, he notes, are Japan and Australia which, though they both follow state corporatist and state collaborative policies, may see only moderate change.

In India, trade unions may be on the decline in old industries, and difficult to organize in new high-tech industries. But the vast untapped informal sector that accounts for 90 per cent of the main workers as per the 1991 census holds much promise for the resurgence of the trade union movement, should it take up more seriously the organizing of the labour force in the informal sector.

New Actors on the Horizon

Traditionally, all aspects relating to industrial relations were considered matters for discussion between organizations of employers and workers with (tripartism) or without (bipartism) the involvement of the government. But, gradually the consumer and the public have begun to play an increasingly decisive role. Also, where the principal social partners are not addressing the real issues concerning, for instance, child labour, gender inequities, unorganized labour, environment and occupational safety, NGOs and other public interest groups are seeking to step in and fill the vacuum effectively. Where trade union leaders are reluctant or indifferent, social groups and public interest groups are taking up these causes. Pressure is building up from all sides for public policy to pay attention to the neglected sectors of society. Information technology and the media are also playing a much greater role in bringing into sharp focus what otherwise may have been suppressed or marginalized.

Tripartism

In many countries with dual economies, tripartism has become the exclusive club of a vocal minority in the formal sector, excluding over 60 to 90 per cent of the workforce in the informal sector. In periods of major economic pressures, countries that do not have a tradition of tripartism are taking recourse to it, while those with traditions of tripartism are increasingly taking recourse to bipartism. Seemingly, we are passing through a phase 'where several environmental pressures increase the probability that the pattern of relationship among the actors will be re-assessed and modified in fundamental ways' (Kochan, 1983).

Tripartism is under strain, often even where it has once thrived on the initiative and patronage of the state and where the state is now slowly withdrawing from certain sectors of the economy (ILO, 1994). Freeman (1992) has argued that there is not enough evidence about tripartite social pacts having contributed substantially to social and economic development. There has been a trend two of the three major social partners aligning themselves to achieve something they both feel is collectively desirable. For instance, since 1983, eight versions of the Social Accord have been reached in Australia without involving employers. Recently, some Swedish employers withdrew from tripartite fora. In several economies in transition both workers' and employers' organizations have found themselves in a fait accompli situation as the governments first took decisions and later sought to involve them in implementation. Widening of the social dialogue and the experimentation with non-traditional forms to fight social exclusion are still in their infancy.

The World Bank (1995), while addressing workers' concerns, makes the case for company unionism but rules out any role for them in national economic policy formulation. This is in contrast to the role currently played by unions in countries such as Singapore, for instance.

Cooperative Collective Bargaining

Collective bargaining occurs at various levels: plant/firm, industry, industry-cum-region or at the national level. In several countries the shift from centralized bargaining to decentralized enterprise-level bargaining is pervasive and is affected by and, in turn, affecting some of the changes in union organization as described earlier. In low-income industrializing countries, less than 15 per cent of the workforce is engaged in the formal sector and collective bargaining covers barely two to three per cent of the workforce. In industrialized countries, the weakening of unions, new technologies and new human resource policies, are leading to a further shift from enterprise-based collective bargaining to individualized bargaining.

At another level, as Galbraith (1995) argues:

> At one time there was the all-embracing and continuing struggle between capital and labour, employers and the working masses. Democracy was a thin disguise for this conflict; political voice was on one side or the other, and most frequently, one cannot doubt, on the side of the capitalists. Unacknowledged but ever present and accepted by all were the bearded face and long arm of Karl Marx. Capital and labour, capital versus labour; what else is there? . . . Now no longer. The capitalist has been swept into the great corporate bureaucracy. International competition has weakened what once were the evident powers of monopoly and oligopoly. Where once in the United States, Canada, Britain and other of the older industrial countries there was fear of corporate power, there is now deep concern for corporate incompetence and weakness. This has greatly changed the terms of what was once the class struggle.

Indeed, there is anxiety and apprehension about employer survival and, often, a financial commitment by labour thereto. The class struggle may soon become a pale ghost of its past, with workers and unions agreeing to a variety of trade-offs between wages and jobs, and cuts or freezes in their wages, benefits and even basic worker/trade union rights to save companies from liquidation and preserve threatened jobs (ILO, 1984; Venkata Ratnam, 1991 and 1995; Ozaki, 1999).

The trade-offs may be perceived as suicide pacts and hence trade unions may find them unacceptable. However, there is ample evidence to suggest that if there is an option, with or without opposition from trade unions, every opportunity is to be availed to avert or minimize job losses and other trade-offs that could adversely affect the interests of the employed. But when it is imperative, particularly in companies in crisis than in growing and profitable companies, adjustment pressures for survival at the enterprise level are leading to greater involvement of local unions and, consequently, to local union leaders acquiring power at the expense of national union leadership. What Fashoyin (1990) says about the developments in Nigeria is applicable to India as well:

> There is a discernible trend towards greater cooperation and collaboration between unions and managements in their efforts to deal decisively and realistically with the employment consequences of the recession. Management involves opinions and suggestions from unions and workers, and their leaders are allowed access to company data which traditionally were exclusive to the management. Also, unions have gone out of their way to solve problems traditionally regarded as the responsibility of management.
>
> The current level of cooperation between unions and management (cooperation which has developed for the most part outside the established consultative machinery) is no doubt a transient phase, not destined to lead to an end to adversarial relations. On the other hand, the introduction of fundamental economic restructuring will emphasise the competitiveness of industry through deregulation and privatization and thus increase the need for labour management cooperation to improve the efficiency of enterprises. In the final analysis, the question then seems to revolve around the pace of economic recovery and growth and the genuineness of both parties' commitment to security of employment as a joint union management objective.

A New Generation of Workforce

Workforce diversity is increasing. In industrialized countries of West Europe and North America, an industrial worker typically used to be a white male. This is not true any longer. In North America, the proportion of white males in the workforce will soon be less than 20 per cent while the share of women is likely to reach 50 per cent. Globalization is easing the earlier restrictions of expatriate employment.

With the advent of microchip-based technologies there has been a progressive decline in employment intensity in manufacturing, resulting in a greater emphasis on skills development. Cheap labour no longer provides a competitive edge.

Sharing information, shedding power at the shopfloor level upwards, and distributing profits and gains are becoming a necessity, not a choice. The new generation knowledge workers can show commitment and exercise initiative only when management is through consensus rather than through direction and control. Direct two-way communication, proper grievance redressal mechanisms, systems for sharing and empowerment are becoming the rule, particularly in organizations which have been able to adjust to the changing scenario and cope with the rapid pace of myriad changes and the resultant challenges.

MACRO ISSUES IN INDUSTRIAL RELATIONS

From the foregoing analysis the following are identified as the macro issues in industrial relations: labour law/labour market reform, unemployment and poverty, egalitarianism, and development objects, basic human rights and international labour standards. The macro issues in Indian context—work organization, skills formation, compensation and work organization—are discussed separately in Chapter 11.

Labour Law/Labour Market Reform

At the heart of the current industrial relations debates is the concern over the imposition of macroeconomic policies that have a bearing on social and labour issues as well.

As a result of structural changes, labour reforms have led to a reduction in guarantees, including job security, minimum wages, working conditions and social security provisions. In India, legal reform has been stymied for the last half century due to tender-minded governments, politicized polarization among social partners and atrophied tripartism. Despite numerous committees and commissions that have debated on the subject of legal reform in India, legislative initiatives have been woefully inadequate to promote harmonious labour–management relations. Instead of acting on at least the Ramanujam Committee recommendations, and the work of the National Labour Law Association (NLLA) in drafting a labour code (NLLA, 1994), another bipartite committee was constituted afresh to consider comprehensive labour law reforms. That committee could not build on the existing consensus. Instead, its working led to the exacerbation of existing differences. In October 1999, the Second National Commission on Labour was appointed to recommend, among others, measures to revamp the labour laws. It cannot be expected that legal reforms on social and labour matters will address squarely the issues of globalization and competitiveness in countries like India because of the huge and complex problems of poverty, unemployment and the government's inaction in the area of social security. Therefore, it would be prudent for employers and unions to collectively promote sound human resource policies where employees have a say and a stake and both labour and management cooperate even as they compete to maintain a delicate balance of mutual interest.

The macroeconomic policies and regulations regarding minimum wages, job security and social security have been the subject of heated debate, with the World Bank coming down heavily against them till recently and the ILO taking the opposite view. The World Bank is of the view that minimum wage regulations tend to raise not only the cost of welfare but also that of labour in the formal sector and leads to a reduction in the demand for labour (World Bank, 1990). The ILO, on the other hand, considers that, 'Minimum wages have an important role to play in protecting low income groups—structural adjustment also calls for a sound industrial relations system and a commitment to tripartite dialogue. Over the long run suppression of free industrial relations jeopardizes prospects for economic development (ILO, 1991b). The 1980s highlighted—the need to regulate the labour market' (ILO, 1991a).

Freeman (1992) presented an exhaustive assessment of the contrasting views of the World Bank and the ILO on the value of institutional interventions in developing country labour markets insofar as they relate to government regulation of wages, mandated contributions to social funds, job security and collective bargaining. The World Bank, he argued, treats them as causing distortions while the ILO stresses the potential benefits of such interventions. Freeman further argued that there is little support for the notion that interventions are major impediments in the way of resource allocation, structural adjustment, or stabilization programmes, although in some cases they have sizable costs. Interestingly, however, he noted that there is little evidence on the value of social pacts and related consultative modes of adjustment favoured by the ILO.

Based on the calculation of standard deviations of log earnings among manufacturing industries using data from the ILO Yearbook of Labour Statistics (ILO, 1991c), Freeman examined the trends in interventionist and non-interventionist economies and observes that interventions reduce rather than increase wage differentials in the industrial sector. Many countries set minimum wages too low or are too lax in enforcing the law for the regulation to have much effect. Freeman also cites the experience of continental European countries where job guarantees resulted in smaller job losses in the declining steel industry than in the laissez-faire UK.

Unemployment and Poverty

In modern welfare states, job creation is seen as a responsibility of the state. In several countries, job creation is also seen as a responsibility of employers. Employers, however, seem to differ in their perception on whether job creation is incidental to or the raison d'etre for all economic activities.

In some countries, unemployment is viewed more as a political rather than a socio-economic problem. With the result, in such countries job creation—indeed the right (right, not duty) to work—becomes a major element of the election manifesto, which, when unfulfilled, causes frustration and loss of credibility of the government.

The World Bank (1995) argues that it is the demand for labour, not the supply of it, which makes the difference to job and wage growth. Improving real wages of employees, profits of enterprises, real worth for consumers' money and sustainable growth should be the guiding principles of public policies.

In matters such as job search, job skills training, placement and outplacement, tripartite initiatives, including neighbourhood communities at the local enterprise level, are more likely to produce substantial and substantive results. Active labour market policies including vocational and skills training are better planned and implemented at the local level. This appears to be the experience of Japan and Norway. In the wake of the California riots in the early 1990s, the Clinton administration promoted the idea of an inner-city job campaign to minimize social unrest. This does not mean that social dialogue at the national level is futile. The success of the Social Accord in Australia in creating more jobs than were targeted during the period of Mark VII of the Accord is well acknowledged and demonstrates the value of such cooperation even if it was only between two of the three social partners, in this case, between the union and the government.

Egalitarianism

In present-day modern welfare states, social justice must be an integral part of all developmental planning. Approaches such as, growth first and justice later are as contentious as, 'chicken or egg, which came first?' Exhortations by political leaders to 'sacrifice today for a better tomorrow' fall on deaf ears in societies where the rich continue to get richer and the poor poorer. The Philadelphia declaration, 'Poverty anywhere is a danger to prosperity everywhere' has, in most countries, remained empty rhetoric.

The stark reality is that labour policy often fails to protect the vulnerable. Although 90 per cent of the developing countries have some form of social security system, at best it covers only workers in the formal sector: just 15 per cent of the labour force in low-income countries and 30 per cent in middle-income ones (World Bank, 1995).

All societies are striving to enable their population to share the gains of continuous and rapid economic change. As Reich (1995) cautioned, 'Persistent unemployment/underemployment, declining wages and living standards undermine the moral core of capitalism and democracy . . . . In a democracy people will vote for economic dynamism only if they have a fair chance of benefitting from it.'

Economic growth cannot be an excuse for inhuman exploitation. Falling growth rates in the economy, and rising inflation and unemployment, constrain governments to woo foreign investment and create additional jobs. This leads them to adopt competitive labour policies, which wipe out a substantial part of the accumulated social gains. 'When some countries employ forced labour or child labour in export production, or when they repress trade union rights in export processing zones or special economic zones, the effect is to place their neighbours under pressure to implement similar policies in order to compete in the world market. This is particularly evident when governments are striving to attract investment from MNCs (ICFTU, 1995).'

Development Objects, Basic Human Rights and International Labour Standards

Schregle (1981) argues: 'The national development . . . has its price, it requires sacrifices. The workers' effective right to have their interests represented by strong and efficient trade unions provides the only sure guarantee that the bill of development will not be footed exclusively or primarily by the workers but that the burden will be more or less equitably shared by all.'

The rapid development of certain dynamic Asian economies may make some wonder about the nexus between democracy and development. Sengenberger and Campbell (1994) challenge the widespread belief that labour standards impede the functioning of free markets and the consequent assumption of a trade-off between economic growth and labour standards or, in labour market terms, between job creation and high labour standards. They argue that standards are essential supports and enabling devices for superior economic—not just social—outcomes. They hold the view that this is especially the case in situations of industrial decline and harsh competition, because standards prevent a relapse into parochial and short-term oriented behaviour.

CONCLUSION

The major transition and transformation in industrial relations can be summed up as follows: democratization offers many opportunities for turning industrial relations systems away from unitarism to pluralism. This means that economic development cannot be at the cost of human rights at work and in the wider society. The linkage between labour standards and international trade attempts to achieve this. Even though there is some polarization of views in this regard between the developed and the developing countries, workers' organizations in the developing countries have opposed such linkage in international fora even as they pressurize their respective national governments for improvements in labour standards.

Diversity in industrial relations systems is increasing at the national, sectoral and enterprise levels. The context of development and the strategy for industrialization at the national level, the stage of industry at the sectoral level and the position of the firm in the business cycle at the firm level accounts substantially for such diversity.

While industrial relations systems are on the decline (in the US and UK for instance) in some countries which have had a long tradition, they are emerging in some and growing in others. Democratic and social pressures cause the scope of industrial relations to extend beyond trade unions and collective bargaining to incorporate all aspects concerning people at work (Kochan, 1986). In several countries, hitherto-formal industrial relations systems and government policies have focused on 10 to 15 per cent of the workforce in the formal sector. But now, new actors on the horizon such as customer groups, citizen groups and NGOs are pressing for industrial relations to include such concerns as social clause, social vulnerability, social exclusion, social protection and social security and social action to deal with all forms of discrimination based on gender, for instance and abuse as in the case of child labour. For long, ILO and other institutions have envisaged and encouraged a role for organizations of both workers and employers even at the firm level in such macro concerns as population planning.

Adjustment pressures will continue because it is an ongoing phenomenon. Since enterprise survival is imperative for individual well being, whatever be the approaches and outcomes, ultimately they should reflect fairness and equity, faith in the power balance among social partners, concern for the individual without neglecting the collective interests of the community and, above all, integrity and trust.

Employment-related aspects have always dominated concerns related to industrial relations and continue to do so. In the context of globalization and liberalization, there has been a shift in focus. Earlier, under export-oriented industrialization policies, labour rights were compromised in export-processing zones. Now, the whole market, domestic and international, has become an export-processing zone. Therefore, a segmented approach in public policy will not work. Gradually, new systems of social security nets which provide income security without job security are evolving. Trade unions resist this, but are not always able to avoid it.

The output of industrial relations has so far been measured in terms of the network of rules and regulations, strikes and lock-outs, grievances and indiscipline, etc. But with the traditional measures having proven inadequate, the search for identifying positive parameters has begun. New technologies and changing workplace and worker demographics are bringing about a transformation in workplace governance which will result in a greater say and stake for employees, customers, as well as the country.

REFERENCES

Adams, R.J. (1993). 'All Aspects of People at Work: Unity and Division in the Study of Labour and Labour Management' in Roy J. Adams and Noah M. Meltz (eds). *Industrial Relations Theory: Its Nature, Scope and Pedagogy*. London: IMLR Press/Rutgers University and The Scarecrow Press, Inc.

Aglietta, M. (1979). *A Theory of Capitalist Regulation: The U.S. Experience*. London: New Lexicon Books.

Baldry, C. (1994). 'Convergence in Europe: A Matter of Perspective?' *Industrial Relations Journal*. 25(2). pp. 96-109.

Bamber, G.J. (1987). *International and Comparative Industrial Relations: A Study of Industrialised Market Economies*. St. Leonards: Allen and Unwin.

Bamber, G.J. (1995). Rapporteur's Report. 3rd Asian Industrial Relations Association. Taipei (Mimeo).

Bamber, G. and V. Peschanski (1996). *Industrial Relations Journal* (UK). 27(1) March. pp. 74-88.

Blyton, P. and P. Turnbull (1994). *The Dynamics of Employee Relations*. Basingstoke: Macmillan.

Bronstein, A.S. (1995). 'Societal Change and Industrial Relations in Latin America: Trends and Prospects'. *International Labour Review*. 134(2). 163-185.

Chandler, A.E. (1962). *Strategy and Structure,* Mass: MIT Press.

Collier, R.B. and D. Collier (1991). *Shaping the Political Area*. Princeton, N.J.: Princeton University Press.

Deyo, F.C. (1989). *Beneath the Miracle: Labour Standards in the New Asian Industrialism*. Berkeley: University of California Press.

Dore, R. (1973). *British Factory–Japanese Factory: The Origins of National Diversity in Industrial Relations*. Berkeley and Los Angeles: University of California Press.

Drekker. (1995). Rapporteur's Report on Track 5 of the IIRA World Congress Washington, DC, U.S.A.

Dunlop, J.T. (1958). *Industrial Relations Systems*. Cambridge Mass: Harvard University Press.

Edgren, G. (1990). 'Employment Adjustment and the Unions: Case Studies of Enterprises in Asia'. *International Labour Review*. 129(5) pp. 629–648.

Egorov, V. (1996). 'Privatization and Labour Relations in the Countries of Central and Eastern Europe'. *Industrial Relations Journal* (UK). 27(1) March. pp. 89–100.

Fashoyin, T. and S. Matanmi (1996). *Industrial Relations Journal* (UK). March 27(1). pp. 38–49.

Fashoyin, T. (1990). 'Economic Recession and Employment Security in Nigeria'. *International Labour Review*. 129(5). pp. 649–664.

Fong, P.E. (1990). 'Industrial Restructuring, The State and Employers in Asia-Pacific Countries'. Paper presented at the ILO/APINDO South East Asia and Pacific Employers' Symposium on the Role of Employers' Organisations in the Informal Sector and the Industrial Restructuring at Bali, Indonesia, 13–16 March. Bangkok: ILO (Mimeo).

Frenkel, S. (ed) (1993). *Organized Labour in the Asia-Pacific Region: A Comparative Study of Trade Unionism in Nine Countries*. Ithaca, New York: ILR Press.

Freeman, R.B. (1992). 'Labour Market Institutions and Policies: Help or Hindrance'. Proceedings of the World Bank Annual Conference on Development Economics. Supplement to the World Bank Economic Review and the World Bank Research Observer. Washington DC: World Bank. pp. 117–156.

Galbraith, J.K. (1995). *The World Economy Since the Wars: A Personal View*. London: Mandarin Paperbacks.

Gladstone, A. et al. (eds) (1992). *Labour Relations in a Changing Economy*. New York: Walter de Gruyter.

Government of India (1996a). 'Annual Report, 1995-96—Ministry of Labour'. New Delhi.

Government of India (1996b). 'Agenda: 33rd Session of the Standing Labour Committee'. New Delhi: Ministry of Labour. 13 September.

Hyman, R. (1994). 'Industrial Relations in Western Europe: An Era of Ambiguity'. *Industrial Relations*. 33(1) January. pp. 1–22.

ICFTU (International Confederation of Free Trade Unions) (1995). 'Conclusions of the ICFTU-Asian Pacific Regional Organization and Japan Institute of Labour Regional Symposium on International Competitiveness, Trade and Investment—Challenges for Trade Unions'. Singapore: ICFTU-APRO. 1–5 August 1995.

IILS (International Institute for Labour Studies) (1993). ' Lean Production and Beyond: Labour Aspects of a New Production Concept'. Geneva: IILS.

International Labour Conference, 81st Session (1994).'Report III Part 4B: Freedom of Association and Collective Bargaining'. Geneva: ILO.

ILO (International Labour Organisation) (1984). 'Collective Bargaining: A Response to Recession'. Geneva: ILO.

ILO (1991a). 'World Labour Report'. Geneva: ILO.

ILO (1991b). 'Report of the Director General to the 78th Session'. Geneva: ILO.

ILO (1991c). 'ILO Year Book of Labour Statistics'. Geneva: ILO.

ILO (1992). 'Democratisation and the ILO: Report of the Director-General'. International Labour Conference. 79 Session 1992. Geneva: ILO.

ILO (1994). 'Visions of the Future of Social Justice: Essays on the Occasion of the ILO's 75th Anniversary'. Geneva: ILO.

ILO (1994a). 'Collective Bargaining: A Response to Recursion'. Geneva: ILO.

ILO (1995). 'World Labour Report'. Geneva: ILO. Also the reports for the previous years.

Kaufman, B.E. (1992). 'The Origins and the Evolution of the field (India 1996b) of Industrial Relations in the US'. Ithaca, New York: ILR Press.

Kerr, C., Charles A. Myer and F. Harbison (1971). 'Postscript to Industrialism and Industrial Man'. *International Labour Review*. 103. pp. 519-540.

Kerr, C., et al. (1961). *Industrialism and Industrial Man*. Cambridge Mass: Harvard University Press.

Kochan, T.A. (1983). Report for the International Industrial Relations Association, Sixth World Congress, Kyoto, Japan, 28-31 March. Vol. IIA, pp. I-XII.

Kochan, T.A. (1994). 'Shaping Employment Relations for the 21st Century: Challenges Facing Business, Labor, and Government Leaders'. Key note address at the Conference on Changing Employment Relations and Human Resource Management in Asia held at Chung-Hua Institution for Economic Research, Taipei on 28 June.

Kochan, T.A., H. Katz and R. Mckersie (1986). *The Transformation of American Industrial Relations*. New York: Basic Books.

Kochan, T.A. and M. Weinstein (1994). 'Recent Development in US Industrial Relations'. *British Journal of Industrial Relations*. 32:4. December. pp. 484-504.

Kuruvilla, S. and C.S. Venkata Ratnam (1996). 'Economic Development and Industrial Relations in South and Southeast Asia: Past Trends and Future Developments'. Paper presented at the IIRA 10th World Congress at Washington DC. 31 May-4 June 1995. *Industrial Relations Journal* (UK). 27(1). March. pp. 9-23.

Lazonick, W. (1991). 'What happened to the Theory of Economic Development?' in P. Higgonnet, D.S. Landesand Henry Rosovsky (eds). *Favorites of Fortune*. Cambridge, MA: Harvard University Press.

Locke, R.M. (1992). 'The Demise of the National Union in Italy'. *Industrial and Labour Relations Review*. 45: 229-249.

Locke, R.M., T.A. Kochan and M. Piore (eds) (1995). *Employment Relations in a Changing World Economy*. Cambridge, MA: MIT Press.

Locke, R.M., T.A. Kochan and M. Piore (1995). 'Reconceptualizing Comparative Industrial Relations: Lessons from International Research'. *International Labour Review*. 134(2). pp. 139-161.

Madrid. J.C.K. (1994). 'The ILO and Current Trends in Principles of Labour Law in Argentina' in W. Sengenberger and D. Campbell. 1994. *International Labour Standards and Economic Interdependence*. Geneva: International Institute for Labour Studies.

National Labour Law Association (1994). *Draft Labour Code*. Delhi: NLLA

Ozaki, M. (1999). 'Negotiating Flexibility'. Geneva: ILO.

Piore, M. and C. Sable (1984). *The Second Industrial Divide*. New York: Basic Books.

Reich, R. (1995). 'Address to the delegates of the 10th World Congress of International Industrial Relations Association'. Washington DC. IRRA. May 31-June 4.

Schregle, J. (1981). 'Negotiating Development: Labour Relations in Southern Asia'. Geneva: International Labour Organisation.

Sen, R. (1996). 'Industrial Relations in West Bengal'. IIRA Newsletter, June.

Sengenberger, W. and D. Campbell (1994). 'Creating Economic Opportunities: The Role of Labour Standards in Industrial Restructuring'. Geneva: International Institute for Labour Standards.

Smith, A.E. (1994). 'New Technology and the Process of Labor Regulation: An International Perspective' in J. Belanger et al. (eds). 'Workplace Industrial Relations and the Global Challenge'. Cornell International Industrial and Labour Relations Report No. 25. Ithaca, New York: ILR Press.

Standing, G. and G. Sziraczi (1992). 'Labour Market Issues in Eastern Europe's Transition' in *International Labour Review.* p. 142.
Strauss, G. Daniel, G. Gallagher and Jack Fiorito (eds) (1991). 'The State of the Unions.' Madison, WI: Industrial Relations Research Association. Madison: IRRA.
Taira, K. (1994). 'Workplace Productivity, Macroeconomic Performance and World History' in Japan Institute of Labour. 1994. *Human Resources Management and Economic Development in Asia.* Proceedings of the 1994 Asian Regional Conference on Industrial Relations. Tokyo: JIL.
Thirkell, J. et al. (1994). 'Labour Relations in Transition in Eastern Europe'. *Industrial Relations Journal.* 25(2). pp. 84-95.
Thomson, A. and M. Warner (1981). *The Behavioural Sciences and Industrial Relations: Some Problems of Integration.* London: Grower.
Tolliday, S. and J. Zeitlin. (1991). 'Conclusion: National Models and International Variations in Labour Management and Employer Organization' in S. Tolliday and J. Zeitlin (eds). 'The Power to Manage?' London: Routledge. pp. 273-343.
Towers, B. (1996). 'Report and Commentary to the Special Issue from Track 5 of the IIRA 10th World Congress'. *Industrial Relations Journal* (UK). 27(1). March. pp. 4-8.
Tsuru, T. (1994. 'Why Has Union Density Declined in Japan?' *Japan Labour Bulletin.* 1 November. pp. 5-8.
Venkata Ratnam, C.S. (1991). *Unusual Collective Agreements.* New Delhi: Global Business Press.
Venkata Ratnam, C.S. (1994). 'Appropriate Structural Adjustment Policies: The Perspective of Employers' Organisations in Selected Countries'. Working Paper of the Interdepartmental Project on Structural Adjustment. Geneva: ILO.
Venkata Ratnam, C.S. (1995). 'International Trade, Investment and Competitiveness— Trade Union Strategies in a Globalizing Economy: A Case Study of India.' Singapore: ICFTU/APRO.
Venkata Ratnam, C.S., G. Botterweck and P. Sinha (eds) (1995). *Labour and Unions in a Period of Transition.* New Delhi: Friedrich Ebert Foundation.
Venkata Ratnam, C.S. (1996). 'Future of Work: New Paradigm in Labour Management Relations'. *Indian Journal of Industrial Relations,* October.
Verma, A.T. Kochan and R.D. Lansbury (eds) (1995). *Growing Asia: Changing Trends in Employment and Industrial Relations.* London: Routledge.
Weiler, P.C. (1990). *Governing the Workplace: The Future of Labor and Employment Law.* Cambridge, MA: Harvard University Press.
World Bank (1990). *World Development Report 1990.* New York: Oxford University Press.
World Bank (1995). *World Development Report 1995: Workers in an Integrated World.* New York: Oxford University Press.
Zatapa, F. (1996). 'Labour Relations, Economic Development and Democracy and the 21st Century'. *Industrial Relations Journal.* 27(1) March. pp. 65-73.

THREE

Economic Development and Industrial Relations: The Case of South and South-East Asia*

INTRODUCTION

The South and South-East Asian region is distinctive in economic terms for several reasons. These regions account for roughly one half of the world's population. Parts of South-East Asia were the fastest growing areas in the world till 1997. Between 1965 and 1990, the average rate of economic growth has exceeded 5 per cent per annum in South-East Asia, compared to only 1.8 per cent in South Asia, 2.2 per cent in the OECD countries, 1.7 per cent Latin America, and 0.2 per cent in subSaharan Africa. South-East Asia has a high export growth; in some countries it exceeded 12 per cent per annum, whereas world exports grew at only 5.5 per cent during 1970–1992. The average savings rates in several South-East and South Asian countries are high, in some cases as high as 30 per cent of GDP. In recent years, the

---

* Jointly written with Dr Sarosh Kuruvilla of Cornell University the main author of this chapter. Presented at the Xth World Congress of Industrial Relations at Washington DC and reproduced with some revisions and with permission from Industrial Relations (UK), 1996.

South and South-East Asian region has accounted for about 50 per cent of the inflow of foreign direct investment to developing countries.

A World Bank report which tries to explain the dramatic growth of South-East Asia is largely inconclusive since it finds support for two competing explanations, namely the neo-classical and the revisionist (World Bank Research Report 1993). The neo-classical explanation stresses the importance of such factors as low inflation, a stable legal and political framework, open economic systems and undistorted prices; the revisionist highlights deliberate state intervention via protection and price distortions. However, there is consensus in the World Bank report, as well as in the writings of various experts, that industrial relations and human resource policies of governments have been critical to the success of these economies.

Although the foregoing overview suggests certain uniformity in Asian development, it is important to note here that the Asian region is also very diverse economically. Whatever the criteria chosen, the region is representative, be it in terms of area, population, gross national product (GNP), political ideology, unemployment levels, poverty, literacy and so on. Table 3.1 provides some sense of the diversity in Asian economies.

TABLE 3.1 Economy and Social Indicators: Selected Countries 1993

Country	Population (Million)	GNP/Capita 1992 (US$)	Labour Force (%)			Literacy (%)
			Agri.	Ind.	Services	
Hong Kong	5.80	15,360	0.2	23.5	76.3	90.0
Singapore	2.80	15,360	0.3	37.5	62.2	92.0
South Korea	22.60	6,790	7.0	46.2	46.8	96.8
Taiwan	22.44	10,196	3.7	42.6	53.7	
Malaysia	18.80	2,790	16.1	43.9	40.0	80.0
Thailand	56.10	1,840	13.1	37.4	49.5	93.8
Philippines	65.20	770	22.6	35.0	42.5	90.4
Indonesia	191.20	670	17.9	42.9	39.3	84.4
Vietnam	69.50		38.2	24.6	37.2	88.6
Cambodia	8.80	240	49.4	16.3	34.4	37.8
China	1,187.40	470	16.7	58.4	24.9	80.0
India	880.10	350	32.5	27.3	40.2	49.8
Pakistan	124.90	400	25.7	26.0	48.3	36.4
Sri Lanka	17.70	500	21.8	28.6	49.6	89.0

Source: 1994; Human Development Report 1994, UNDP. Washington DC.

Industrial relations systems in the region exhibit diversity as well. This chapter examines the inter-relationship between economic development and industrial relations in Asia, and in particular, the trends in industrial relations over the last decade. This is followed by a detailed review of the implications of the current international context for industrial relations in the future.

ECONOMIC DEVELOPMENT

Economic development of the South-East Asian region has occurred in different time periods. In contrast to Japan whose economic development received a spurt after postwar reconstruction (the Japanese economy took off from a diversified industrial base), there was rapid growth among the Asian tigers (NICs, Singapore, Korea, Hong Kong, and Taiwan) during the 1960s and early 1970s. The 'emerging 'tigers namely, Malaysia, the Philippines, Thailand, and Indonesia, grew fastest in the 1980s, while Asian Countries, notably China, Vietnam, Cambodia, Laos and India, were the fastest growing economies in the 1990s.

In order to set the stage for discussing industrial relations and labour policy, two aspects of Asian economic development merit particular attention. The first aspect has been the strong role played by the state in economic development. Contrary to Western Europe and the US where economic development has been led by private enterprise, in South and South-East Asia, it has been managed by the state. However, there are variations in the role of the state across countries. For instance, in Japan and Korea, the state influenced the nature of investment, the choice of industries and the number of firms that could enter the economic sector, and often, as in the case of Korea, actively financed private sector investment. In the case of South-East Asia, the state's role has been more facilitative, creating the conditions necessary for attracting foreign investment. In South Asia, particularly India and Pakistan, the state has reserved for itself the responsibility of economic development through large public sector industries. As will be argued later, the role of the state has implications for labour and industrial relations as well.

The second significant feature of economic development in the region has been the existence of a clearly conceptualized industrialization strategy. In East and South-East Asia, the successful economies have followed an outward looking, export-oriented industrialization (EOI) strategy. By contrast, in China and South Asia, the industrialization strategy has been inward looking and focused on import-substitution. Kuruvilla (1995) suggests the existence of two primary industrialization strategies; the import-substitution industrialization (ISI) strategy and EOI although within each strategy there are variations.

In the case of ISI, there is a first stage of 'simple' ISI based on the development of low technology consumer and industrial goods for local consumption. The focus of this strategy is to promote the growth of locally owned industries catering to the relatively large domestic market in order to conserve foreign exchange and to promote industrialization and local entrepreneurship The second stage of ISI is characterized by the development of heavy industries, such as the railways, atomic energy, steel, heavy chemicals, defence and space industries, where the focus has been on creating a diversified industrial base that will fuel future growth. For example, the ISI adopted by Singapore, Malaysia, the Philippines, South Korea, and Taiwan during the early stages of their development can be classified as 'simple' while 'advanced' ISI was characteristic of India's and China's industrialization strategy until the 1990s.

Similarly, the EOI strategy exhibits variation. Typically, the first stage EOI in South-East Asia was characterized by its focus on the low-cost production of light manufacturing goods for exports, largely financed by foreign investment, multinational companies in the electronics, electrical, textile, and footwear industries being the main investors. This strategy has aimed to create employment and enhance foreign exchange earnings to repay foreign debts in the case of both Malaysia and the Philippines; in Singapore and Taiwan, this strategy was the only growth avenue given that their relatively smaller markets and lack of local capital could not sustain an ISI strategy (Huff, 1987). Second stage EOI is characterized by its stress on the technological upgradation of first stage EOI industries, a move to higher value added products, and innovations in the manufacturing process (Rasiah forthcoming) The second stage EOI in Singapore and Malaysia has been accompanied by efforts to diversify the industrial base of the economy, and is seen in the investment in large industrial projects in iron and steel, chemicals, and automobiles in several Asian countries such as Singapore, Malaysia, Korea and Taiwan.

What is also important is that the fast growing Asian countries continue to be at different levels of industrialization. For example, Singapore, Taiwan and South Korea are all at the second stage EOI with more high value added manufacturing and higher cost and skilled labour requirements. Singapore is at a critical juncture in its industrialization where it is shifting to a service dominated economy. Malaysia and Thailand are rapidly entering the second stage, while the Philippines and Indonesia are currently low-cost first-stage EOI countries. Cambodia, Vietnam and Laos are emerging out of their ISI phases and aggressively becoming export-oriented economies. India and China, both of which have for years followed a heavy and capital-intensive inward looking ISI strategy, are now gradually shifting to become EOI economies.

The link between industrialization strategies and industrial relations policies at the national level as well as at the level of the workplace is best illustrated by Kuruvilla (1995) in Table 3.2. He examines four countries, Singapore, Malaysia, Philippines and India, although the argument is true for several countries in the Asian region.

Such an association is prevalent in South-East Asia as well. Apparently, certain kinds of industrialization strategies and certain kinds of national labour policies go hand in hand.

In ISI, labour policy is largely pluralistic. Given that the strategy is inward looking and therefore protected against external competition, most Asian governments have not attempted to significantly regulate industrial relations. In fact, labour policies of most South Asian countries, for example, of India and many other South-East Asian ones, during their brief ISI periods emphasized pluralism in industrial relations. In a discussion on India it is noted that the ISI strategy and existing industrial relations policies are mutually sustaining. The protection afforded to the Indian manufacturer from foreign competition, and a guaranteed internal market, has in the view of several observers created huge inefficiencies in several fields, including labour costs. In other words, a protectionist ISI strategy was congruent with a highly protectionist IR system that impinged negatively on the development of collaborative and flexible industrial relations.

In the first stage of EOI, the primary focus of industrial relations policy at the national level was on cost containment. Except in Korea

TABLE 3.2 **Economic Development Strategies, Industrial Relations Policies and Workplace IR/HR Practices**

	ISI	EOI
1st Stage	• National IR policy focus: Pluralism and stability • Political choices resulting in country specific institutional arrangement to meet IR policy goals • Predominant pattern of workplace industrial relations practices 　▪ Passive human resource practices 　▪ Paternalistic IR practices 　▪ Pluralistic system 　▪ Relatively Tayloristic work organization	• National IR policy focus: Cost containment • Political choice resulting in country specific institutional arrangement to meet IR policy goals • Predominant pattern of workplace industrial relations practices 　▪ Cost containment oriented HR practices 　▪ Union avoidance and suppressive IR practices
2nd Stage	• National IR policy: Pluralism, stability and productivity • Political choices resulting in country specific institutional arrangements to meet IR policy goals • Predominant pattern of workplace industrial relations practices: 　▪ Active HR practices to increase productivity 　▪ Collaborative industrial relations practices 　▪ Pluralistic system	• National IR policy focus: Workplace flexibility and skills enhancement • Political choices resulting in country specific institutional arrangements to meet IR policy goals • Predominant pattern of workplace industrial relations practices: 　▪ Aggressive HR practices promoting skills development and flexible pay 　▪ Dynamic work organization 　▪ Positive non-union HR practices 　▪ Highly flexible HR systems

Source: Kuruvilla (1995).

and Japan where investment was from within, in all the other countries of Asia, export orientation has been based on the competitive advantage of low-cost labour financed by foreign investment. It was the need to attract and retain foreign investment that drove economies to enact industrial relations policies geared towards cost containment. For example, both Malaysia and the Philippines enacted rules that restricted the amount of overtime, refused to legislate equal pay for equal work in export-oriented industries where most of the labour was female, and did not bring foreign investors within the purview of most of the labour and employment legislation.

The first stage EOI strategy was also predicated on providing investors with cheap, flexible and highly compliant labour. Here again, the approach of most countries has been to suppress the growth of trade unionism. Deyo (1989) has made a strong case that Asian industrialization has been based on some degree of labour subordination. Several countries have banned unionization (for example, unionization in the export-oriented electronics industry in Malaysia was banned until 1988), or otherwise restricted the ability of workers to form unions. In other cases, authoritarian regimes have suppressed union activity. South Korea, Taiwan, Malaysia, the Philippines and Indonesia have all at one time or another severely restricted the ability of workers to form unions. There is evidence that the goals of an EOI and a restrictive and exclusive labour policy are highly congruent (Kuruvilla, 1995).

However, in more advanced export orientation based on higher technology, the focus of labour policies has shifted from cost containment and union repression to the development of highly skilled and flexible, yet productive, labour. Again, in all countries that have embarked on second stage EOI, there have been efforts to reform the education system to provide better qualified workers to the growing export industry, and to develop skills through incentives offered by the government. In Malaysia and Singapore for example, the government has introduced the concept of Skills Development Fund (Chew and Chew, 1995), whereby employers must pay a certain percentage of payroll costs into the fund. They can reclaim a part of their contributions only if they invest in training. Both Korea and Taiwan have a history of skills development through vocational training centres. In addition, almost all countries have decentralized bargaining structures to enable bargaining to reflect the unique conditions of individual industries and firms (Kuruvilla and Erickson, 1994). These are all indications of a qualitative shift in the focus of labour and industrial relations and human resource policies at the national level following change in the industrialization strategy.

The most interesting case, and one that further supports the above industrialization and industrial relations framework, is that of India. After 40 years of ISI, the shift of the Indian economy in 1991 to an export-oriented one is bringing to bear tremendous pressure on the industrial relations system to change (Venkata Ratnam, 1993). Clearly it is moving towards increased workplace flexibility. This illustrates the argument that the Asian industrial relations policy is closely and intimately connected with the industrialization strategies of their countries, as outlined in Table 3.2.

INDUSTRIALIZATION: INDUSTRIAL RELATIONS AND HUMAN RESOURCE PRACTICES

Apart from its effect on macro-level industrial relations and human resource (IR/HR) policy, the industrialization strategy also affects the nature of IR/HR practices in firms. In studying the effects of industrialization on IR/HR practices in several firms in the ISI and EOI sectors in Malaysia and the Philippines, Kuruvilla finds the following. First, there are differences in IR/HR practices as between the ISI and EOI sectors in each country. In the ISI sector, firms appear to be following more 'passive' human resource practices. While in the EOI sector, the human resource practices show more diversity, but suggest a pattern of more 'aggressive' and flexible IR/HR practices, that appear to fit the pattern of 'new human resource systems'. Second these differences between the industrialization regimes are present in both countries. Third, IR/HR practices under the more advanced EOI strategy in Malaysia differ from those in the first stage EOI in the Philippines. This is best illustrated by the electronics industry, which constitutes the bulk of the EOI sector in both countries.

Industrialization's effects on IR/HR practices work indirectly through the various mechanisms used by countries to attract a certain type of foreign investment, and in creating two distinct sectors within the economy. The ISI sector, which is protected from external competition, has relatively less need to adopt competitive human resource practices than do export-oriented sectors which have to compete internationally. In addition, given that export-oriented sectors are typically dominated by foreign investment, it is only natural that the diffusion of human resource innovations from investor countries will reach these sectors quicker. The difference in workplace-level IR/HR practices across the two sectors is found in other Asian countries as well (Kuruvilla, 1995 and Bhatt and Miller 1984).

INSTITUTIONAL VARIATIONS IN SOUTH AND SOUTH-EAST ASIAN INDUSTRIAL RELATIONS SYSTEMS

Despite the close connection between industrialization and macro-level industrial relations and micro-level industrial relations practices, there are considerable variations in the specific institutions that countries have adopted to attain national-level policy goals. In other words, although there is a commonality in terms of macro-level goals, there is considerable divergence in the rules, legislation and institutions in different countries for attaining these goals.

The variations in institutional arrangements are largely a product of political choices made by the state, as well as the institutional IR/HR history of the parties (Kuruvilla,(1996). This section aims to give a sense of the differences in terms of approach to labour legislation and institutions in South and South-East Asia.

Labour Protection

Typically, the first plank in Asian labour policy is on labour protection, that is labour standards, laws and welfare policies. There is a remarkable similarity in labour protection legislation across all Asian economies. All these economies are characterized by advanced legislation mandating annual leave, casual leave, maternity leave and child care and legislation regarding overtime, working hours, safety and health, restrictions on terminations, severance pay, annual bonus and retirement benefits. Protective labour legislation is advanced, certainly more so than in the US, and the commonalties are explained more by the willingness of these economies to follow established ILO conventions with regard to these issues.

However, despite similar legislation, there is wide variation in the enforcement of these laws. So far, Singapore is perhaps the only country where all labour standards laws are enforced in full. Several countries have revised labour standards laws downward (for example, the Philippines), arguing that they are too advanced for developing economies. There is some truth in this argument, given that the models of legislation in Scandinavia have been the basis for many of these laws. In other cases (for example Taiwan), enactment of the labour standards legislation has been the basis for increased union activity and the cause of increased labour management conflicts (Lee, 1995). In general terms however, the labour standards laws 'on the books' in Asian countries are relatively advanced (Kuruvilla and Pagnucco, 1994).

Labour Relations

It is in the area of labour relations that one sees vastly different institutional regulations in Asia. Here we discuss several issues such as bargaining structure, union structure, the subjects of bargaining, and the right to strike.

Bargaining Structure

Fundamentally, there have been two approaches to bargaining in Asia. The first, characterized by Singapore, was a highly centralized bargaining system with wage increases suggested by the tripartite national wages council economy wide. In Korea and Taiwan, centralization has been the norm during authoritarian regimes. However, in most other Asian countries, bargaining has been decentralized to the industry and firm level.

In terms of the bargaining structure at the workplace, most countries allow only one union per workplace. However India and recently Korea have adopted multiple union systems. The absence of a sole bargaining agent has led to a large number of industrial disputes and an escalation in inter-union conflict and rivalry, inhibiting the development of stable and cooperative industrial relations (Venkata Ratnam, 1993).

During the last decade, the bargaining structure in Asia has moved towards increased decentralization. For example, Singapore has completely abandoned its centralized wage determination principle, in favour of more flexible wages that reflect the differential competitive position of each industry and firm. To further facilitate decentralization, in the early 1980s. Singapore also mandated the formation of 'house' or enterprise unions, based on the argument that a change in union structure would enhance workplace flexibility. There is a trend as well towards increased decentralization in the union structure in

Malaysia which also has enterprise union legislation, as does Taiwan. In other countries such as Thailand, India and the Philippines, bargaining and union structures are highly decentralized for the most part, and in Korea, the situation is in flux as labour policy has not yet been determined.

Union Federations

There are a few countries where there is only one trade union federation. These federations are normally closely linked and identified with the political party in power. However, only one country allows union involvement in national level decisions. Singapore, for example, has created a tripartite framework in which the National Trade Union Congress (NTUC) and the Singapore National Employers Federation (SNEF) has representation on all important national bodies, including the National Wages Council, the Economic Development Board, the Housing Board and in boards and enterprises in every sphere of government (Chiang, 1988). This form of European style social partnership is not found anywhere else in Asia. This tripartism has been achieved also because of the creation of an enterprise union structure in which all enterprise unions are affiliated to one major federation, the NTUC.

The more common model in this region is the multiple trade union federations. Japan, Malaysia, the Philippines, India, Thailand, all follow this model, although none of the federations have any significant influence on national policy making. More recently, Korea recognized one single union federation while other federations (illegal) continue to exist. The variation in the number of federations is large. While most countries have two or three major federations (mostly one for the private sector and one for the public sector), India has over 10 major federations, Pakistan seven, and Thailand eight. The Philippines, which has a highly fragmented labour movement, reports over 155 federations (Offreneo, 1993).

With the exception of Singapore, formal tripartism in other countries is either non-existent or weak. Most Asian countries have attempted to institutionalize tripartism through formal bodies or meetings with varying degrees of success. Efforts are mostly in the form of codes of conduct that are voluntarily agreed to by significant employer and union federations. For example, in India, the Code of

Conduct on Industrial Discipline outlines the principles to be applied in dismissal and in union recognition; in Indonesia, there is a 1982 joint statement on labour relations to maintain industrial peace; Malaysia has a code of conduct for 'Industrial Harmony and Areas for Cooperation'; the Philippines has a joint communiqué of the 'National Tripartite Conference on Wages, Employment, and Industrial Relations; while Thailand has the 'Code of Practice for the Promotion of Labour Relations'.

However, these codes have had limited success, largely due to the unwillingness of trade unions or employer organizations to follow them completely, as well as on account of the problems concerning inter-union or inter-federation rivalry and problems with the concept of consultation as compared with that of negotiation, resulting in the difficulty of drawing clear distinctions between tripartite consultation and tripartite negotiations. As Venkata Ratnam (1993) suggests, these codes have to be seen in the 'political contexts in which they are agreed upon and the quality of the environment and the nature of implementation, both of which leave much to be desired'. Our general finding here is that with the exception of Singapore, the single or multiple federation models does not seem to have yielded any significant influence for trade unions in national decision making.

The Subjects of Bargaining

There are variations in the subjects of bargaining. At one extreme is the model in India where unions and employers are allowed to bargain over any issue. At the other extreme are countries that restrict the subjects of bargaining. Singapore and Malaysia, for example, do not allow bargaining regarding transfers, promotions, work assignments, redundancies, layoffs and retrenchment. In its EOI phase, Korea did not permit bargaining over wages, although this changed after 1987. Taiwan's labour law does not permit bargaining over issues connected with the introduction of new technology. Another restriction often found in several countries is the requirement that collective bargaining agreements be certified by the industrial court (Singapore and Malaysia), which empowered the industrial court to refuse certification, if collective bargaining agreements contain provisions considered detrimental to the national interest.

The Right to Strike

One distinctive feature of Asian economies is that there are several administrative restrictions on the right to strike. The primary motivation to restrict this right has been the argument that industrial conflict should not hamper economic development. The administrative restriction found in all Asian countries is the prohibition of the right to strike in essential industries. There is considerable variation in what constitutes 'essential', with some countries like Singapore having more industries under this classification than other countries. In addition, the right to strike in the public sector is also restricted in most countries.

The right to strike is circumscribed in other ways too. For example, in India, Singapore and Malaysia, a strike or a lockout must be called off once an industrial dispute is under third party mediation, conciliation or arbitration. Some countries like Singapore and the Philippines mandate taking a strike vote by secret ballot, while other countries like Korea enforce a two week cooling off period before strikes can occur. According to the ILO yearbook of labour statistics, the number of strikes declined in every Asian country during the decade of the 1980s, with the exception of Korea and Taiwan, where the number of strikes rose sharply after democratization in 1987 (Park and Lee, 1995).

STYLIZED MODELS IN SOUTH AND SOUTH-EAST ASIA

The above discussion suggests the existence of several different models in South and South-East Asia. It may be noted that most Asian countries in the region have adopted models that have features of these stylized models. Further, there have been shifts within these models as industrialization strategies have shifted.

The Tripartite and Flexible Singapore

The essential feature of this model includes equal partnership between trade unions, employers and government in all aspects of macro economic and macro-social policy. Wage bargaining is thus de facto centralized given the tripartite representation on the National Wages

Council. However, the level of trade union influence at the national level is not proportionate to the influence at the workplace level. At the workplace, the accent of the model is on providing employers with considerable flexibility to react to changing economic conditions.

The key outcomes of this model have been largely positive. In Singapore, while social partnership at the national level has ensured that workers have a steady improvement in living standards through the country's economic development policies, the model has shown that it is possible to use labour policy to make the transition from the first stage EOI to the second stage EOI (Katz, Kuruvilla and Turner, 1994). The changes and enhancements made to the model such as the change in union structure to enterprise unions in 1981 further enhanced flexibility. However, workplace democracy and participation does not guarantee the model, unless it happens due to the changing nature of the workforce and skills. In the mid 1980s, the National Wages Council decentralized its wage recommendations, consistent with the needs of flexibility.

State–Employer-Dominated Exclusionary and Flexible Model

This model primarily suggests a strong role for the state with employers having greater bargaining power than trade unions. Here, trade unions have very little influence over national issues. In Malaysia, trade union federations are registered as societies, not unions. In this model, there is relatively little centralization. Workplace industrial relations are largely similar to those in the Singapore model, emphasizing flexibility. In the export-oriented sectors, there is a very low incidence of unionism.

In terms of outcomes, this model has performed very well in those countries that have successfully adopted EOI, ensuring increases in real wages and employment. However, these increases have often come at the expense of union representation, given that the current system permits employer tactics and strategies to effectively oppose union formation. Stability in industrial relations has been achieved by some degree of coercion, while flexibility has been promoted through institutional features.

The Pluralistic, Decentralized and Fragmented Model

This model is prevalent in the Philippines, which has a pluralistic industrial relations system wherein it is easy for trade unions to form but where they have little influence at the national level. Another feature of this model is the extensive fragmentation of trade unions (there are about 160 federations). The lack of unity of the labour movement and the intense inter-union rivalry has resulted in very weak trade unions.

Further the model has had little success in increasing real wages or workplace democracy. As Pagnucco (1994) suggests, employers are free to pursue anti-union strategies with remarkable success. In the interest of economic development, government legislation, which has changed between periods of dictatorship and democracy, is focused at limiting the ability of unions to strike freely.

The Politicized Multi-Union Model

Mostly characteristic of India and other South Asian countries, in this model, trade unions are highly politicized and their affiliation with political parties not only helps them influence national-level policy making but has also been instrumental in getting favourable protective legislation for organized workers (Kuruvilla, 1995). Union formation, recognition and functioning are well protected by law, and bargaining is highly decentralized.

While providing organized workers with considerable protection, this model proved detrimental to the development of efficiency and workplace flexibility. For example, the principle of allowing multiple unions in each workplace has resulted in intense inter-union rivalry which impinges on the development of long-term collaborative relationships between workers and management (Reddy, 1978). In addition, the inability of the employer to lay off or retrench workers of closed industries without government permission (which has been useful in protecting employment) has created inefficiencies (Kuruvilla, 1995). Most significantly, politicization of unions and the concept of outside political leaders functioning as enterprise union leaders has led to political interference in the workplace (Ramaswamy, 1993). Therefore, this model leans towards equity and protection at the expense of efficiency and flexibility. It may however, be noted that with economic liberalization in India, since 1991, there has been considerable pressure for reform in workplace industrial relations.

The Newly Democratic Transitory Model

This model is characteristic of industrial relations in Korea and Taiwan. In both countries, the shift from authoritarian to democratic forms of government has completely destabilized established patterns of industrial relations. In both countries there has been an increase in strikes and union militancy after democratization. Earlier entirely under state control, industrial relations is now allowed to float freely. Employers, who have never had to deal with unions, thus have very little experience in negotiations. In this situation, new industrial relations policies are required. But in both countries, the democratic state has been slow to put in place a new set of industrial relations policies. Although a transition phase in Asian industrial relations, it has relevance for other emerging economies in Asia, particularly Myanmar, Cambodia, Vietnam, all of which are also moving from authoritarian systems to more democratic ones.

The foregoing five stylized models capture the variation in approaches to industrial relations in South-East Asia. Note that most countries adopt variations on one or two of these models. Most importantly, these models are also undergoing change with rapid economic development. The next section outlines the emerging trends in South and South-East Asian economies over the last decade.

IMPORTANT INDUSTRIAL RELATIONS OUTCOMES AND TRENDS

Having described the variation in approaches to industrial relations, this section discusses some significant trends in South and South-East Asian industrial relations over the last decade.

Weak and Declining Unions

There has not been a tradition of strong unions in Asia. In the most obvious indication of trade union strength, namely, density of unionization, Asian trade unions lag far behind their western counterparts. In 1993, South Korea had the highest unionization rate, with a union density of nearly 30 per cent of the non-agricultural workforce. Apart from Taiwan and South Korea, which reported an increase in trade union density following their 1987 democratization, almost all other countries in Asia have experienced a decline in trade union density. In Japan, union density declined from a high of 30 per cent in 1985 to 22.7 per cent in 1992, while Singapore's declined from 25.5 per cent of the labour force in 1976 to 14.4 per cent in 1992 (Begin, 1995). Every other industrialized Asian nation has also seen declines in union density during the 1980s and 1990s, though not of the same order or magnitude.

The density of unionization however is not always related to the power that trade unions have in the region. For example, India's trade union density (expressed, as a percentage of the total workforce) is only 2.6 percent. However, the political orientation of trade unions and their close ties with the country's political parties has ensured that the labour movement has a political influence greater than the number of trade unions suggest. Labour is the swing vote in at least 30 per cent of all parliamentary constituencies (Venkata Ratnam, 1993). In other words, trade union influence and power are not determined by sheer numbers, but by the institutional network in which unions operate and the specific exclusionary and inclusionary policies of the state.

The shifts in industrialization strategy from ISI to EOI have negatively impacted the ability of unions to form and to bargain collectively. In the South-East Asian nations in particular, restrictions on union formation in certain sectors and export processing zones, on the subjects of bargaining and on real wages have dampened the ability of unions to grow and the enthusiasm of people to join them. Apart form Singapore where unions have considerable influence at the strategic level of the economy, union influence has declined with the decline in union density. In countries such as the Philippines, the intense fragmentation of the labour movement (155 federations and 5,600 independent unions) as noted earlier (Offreneo, 1993) has weakened unions. Even in India where ties between unions and political parties have been historically strong, economic liberalization has polarized relations, given that the political party in power has often been pro-liberalization, while its trade union arm has been less supportive of liberalization.

The fastest growing sector in most Asian economies is the export-oriented sector, consisting of firms in the textile, electronics and garments industries. This is also a sector that is almost completely union free. An ILO report criticizing governments for banning unions in export sectors raised protests by governments. When criticized for being authoritarian regarding unions, governments point out that real wages, even those for low skilled workers, have risen quite steadily in the post colonial period, and that this has been achieved with declining income inequality (ILO, 1994). With the increasing adoption of the export-oriented model of development, one significant trend in Asian industrial relations was the rise of the non-union model during the 1990s.

Decentralization in Bargaining and Workplace Flexibility

As mentioned earlier, another significant trend is the shift towards decentralization in bargaining. This movement is quite consistent with developments in the advanced European and North American nations (Katz, 1993). Decentralization in bargaining in several Asian countries appears to be part of a larger movement towards increased workplace flexibility. In every Asian country there is a clear movement towards highly flexible wages, the breakdown of industry-wide bargaining structures, and the spread of enterprise unions. The increasing need for workplace flexibility can be traced to several factors, notably the shift to more high-tech EOI, the adoption of increasingly complex micro-electronic technologies, particularly in the export sectors, and increased competition and globalization on an international scale. India is a good example of this trend, with the movement among employers for workplace flexibility following India's strategy towards being a more liberalized economy. Decentralization and workplace flexibility are highly correlated with the level of development and integration internationally.

Worker Participation

Although worker participation in decision making was institutionalized in several countries in the form of joint labour management committees (most countries have one such institution), these institutions have not been noteworthy for their success, as already stated.

In the fast growing South-East Asian nations, there is now a resurgence in worker participation, fuelled by different reasons. This trend is noticeable particularly in the high technology export-oriented electronics sector. For example, Rasiah suggests that higher end processes such as chip design, wirebonding and research and development operations are increasingly being located in Malaysia (Rasiah, 1988). Work organization in the electronics industry mirrors practices followed in the advanced countries, while human resource management techniques are based on the development of skills with high pay and employee involvement in an increasingly non-union environment (Rasiah, 1988).

Increased Emphasis on Training, Productivity and New Payment Forms

The shift to higher technology intensive industries for export, and the diffusion of new technologies that call for more skilled and participative workers also brought with it changes in the methods of wage payment. For example, in Malaysia, under the low cost EOI phase compensation policies in the electronics industry were geared towards keeping costs low (Grace, 1990). Wages were kept to minimum levels, and the government's persistent refusal to enact the equal pay for equal work legislation, allowed the industry to employ young women at wages less than 60 per cent the average wage for males (Grace, 1990). Workers were paid by a variety of piece rates and production incentives above the daily base rate (Rasiah, 1988).

In the high tech EOI phase, pay systems began to look like the pay systems in more advanced economies. New forms of work organization brought with them new methods of training and wage payment systems. Wages were tied to learning new skills, and Rasiah notes that in many semiconductor companies, a production worker needed to know at least three processes to become a super operator with salaries reaching almost 750 M$ a month (US$301 Rasiah, 1988). The average wage in the electronics industry was about 350 M$ (US$ 167) per month.

In addition to pay systems, increased attention is being paid to training in order to upskill the workforce to sustain the high-tech EOI strategy. Governments as well as firms have demonstrated an increase in training efforts. For example, in Penang (Malaysia), electronics companies that are fierce competitors in the global market have begun collaborative efforts for skills development. They have formed a skills development centre, where each company contributes equipment and training professionals to train skilled workers for the entire industry (Sharma, Verma and Kuruvilla, 1994). Such firm-level efforts are of course, buttressed by national level efforts to increase workforce skills, via the introduction of skills development funds (in Malaysia and Singapore), or by extensive restructuring of the education sector.

Increased Focus on Job Security

One consequence of the rapid development of the Asian region has been the shortage of labour in several countries (although this is less true of South Asia, China, the Philippines and Indonesia). Labour shortage has, in turn, brought about increased job security in the South-East Asian economies. For example, in Singapore and Malaysia, the use of temporary or casual workers declined considerably in the 1980s, while international subcontracting increased. In addition, Singapore, Malaysia, South Korea, Taiwan, have all introduced guest worker programmes, absorbing the surplus skilled and unskilled labour from the Philippines, India, Indonesia and Pakistan.

Decline in Industrial Conflict

One very clear trend has been the decline in the number of strikes in South and South-East Asia. At the low end, Singapore reported zero strikes during period (Table 3.3). At the highest end, the number of strikes in India also declined substantially over time. A decline in strikes however does not mean that labour–management cooperation increased or is increasing. For example, in Malaysia and the Philippines, the decline in strikes was accompanied by an increase in industrial disputes. In other cases, the decline is highly correlated with the decline in unions. In Korea and Taiwan, the increase in strikes was a direct outcome of democratization. But even in these countries, there has been a decline since 1990 (in Korea, however the economic crisis and resultant workforce reductions resulted in a nationwide strike in 1997).

TABLE 3.3 Union Density and Incidences of Strikes in Selected Asian Countries, 1980 and 1992

Country	Union Membership Density		Number of Strikes	
	1980	1992	1980	1992
Hong Kong	16.1	21.2	37	15
Singapore	24.5	14.5	0	0
South Korea	20.1	30.0*	407	322
Taiwan	20.4	34.9	626**	1,860**
Malaysia	16.0	10.1	39	17
Thailand	11.3	7.0	18	9
Indonesia	3.0		198	61
India	1.1	2.6	2,797	1,825

* Estimated.
** Figures include all disputes, not just strikes.
Source: Foreign Labor Trends, US Department of Labor.
Note: Union density is not calculated in the same way in all countries. In some countries union members are calculated as a percentage of the civilian workforce, while in others it is calculated on the basis of the non-agricultural workforce.

Integration of Industrial Relations Policies with Other Macro-level Policies

The single most important trend in successful South-East Asian economies is the increased integration across macro-level policies in the interest of economic development. For example, industrialization policies are linked to industrial relations. The experience of Singapore and Malaysia has demonstrated that for successful upskilling and moving to higher technology EOI, industrial relations policies need to be integrated with education policies (to provide skilled workers), human resource policies (for increased training), immigration policies, active labour market policies (to meet labour shortages) and financial and tax policies (to continue to attract the right kind of foreign investment.)

LESSONS TO BE LEARNT FROM THE FAST DEVELOPING ASIAN ECONOMIES

It may be emphasized here that trends are more apparent in the South-East Asian countries. South Asia however demonstrates a much more traditional picture of industrial relations, although conditions are changing rapidly in India. The industrial relations systems of Pakistan, Bangladesh, Nepal and Sri Lanka continue to be largely static.

Future Challenges

The twenty-first century presents a vastly different economic and social environment for South and South-East Asia, with attendant implications for industrial relations policy and practice. We briefly describe the major developments, then examine the lessons from past experience and suggest a principle that could guide the development of industrial relations in the twenty-first century.

There are both global and regional economic imperatives to consider. The deepening of globalization is paradoxically coexistent with a resurgence of regionalism. At the global level is the growing integration of product markets and even labour markets. The position of Asian countries in the international division of labour is rendered increasingly precarious with these changes, as capital moves more freely. In addition, efforts to link industrial relations issues such as labour rights to trade liberalization through the WTO following GATT will force countries to re-examine labour policy. All these factors exert a push to be more competitive. Clearly then, industrial relations systems must also change to ensure economic competitiveness and equity, as well as provide the stability and flexibility to adapt quickly to changing international market conditions.

At the same time, internal factors peculiar to each economy are bringing pressure to bear for a change in industrial relations as well. In the successful countries of South-East Asia, there is a growing shortage of labour and an increasingly well educated and wealthy workforce demanding more say in industrial and economic decision making and showing signs of greater and greater dissatisfaction with existing authoritarian regimes. In addition, in the emerging countries, such as Laos, Cambodia and Vietnam, democratization and economic liberalization are exerting pressure to enact new industrial relations policies for economic growth. The experience of Indonesia in the mid 1990s is particularly instructive in this regard, given its rapid economic development and its poor labour rights record. In the South Asian countries, where organized workers have had a highly protective set of labour regulations, the pressure to open up their markets and drop protectionist barriers has resulted in demands for more efficient industrial relations practices.

Further, the movements towards the creation of regional economic blocs such as AFTA (ASEAN Free Trade Area) and APEC (Asia-Pacific Economic Zone) also imply the necessity of harmonization of industrial relations policies for the success of these efforts. Informal arrangements such as the plethora of regional growth triangles that are being formed require the setting up of new and common standards of industrial relations across these countries (Sharma, Verma and Kuruvilla, 1994). Clearly, this presents several opportunities for industrial relations reform in this region in the new country.

What have we learnt from the South-East and South Asian experience so far? We have learnt that in the successful countries of South-East Asia, industrial relations policies and practices are closely tied to economic development strategies. As economic development strategies change so do these policies and practices. We have learnt that the focus on efficiency with the erosion of labour rights is largely a transitory phase for successful economies. While economic success has not resulted in an increase in labour rights, democratization forces of successful economies have resulted in an increase in labour rights. We have also learnt that in the long run, suppression of labour movements results in destabilization in industrial relations. We have also witnessed the rise of progressive human resource practices in non-union environments, particularly in the competitive export sectors of several economies. In addition, new micro-electronic technologies bring with them new forms of worker participation in firm-level decision making, new wage and benefit policies and increased job security. Finally, we have learnt that industrial relations must be congruent with macro policies such as education, training and immigration to facilitate economic development.

Most significantly, the growing and widespread adoption of the Asian model of development (from first stage EOI to service-oriented economies) and the differential positions of Asian countries in the ladder of Asian development have provided newly developing Asian countries with a model of development and industrial relations. For instance, the emerging economies of Laos, Cambodia, and Vietnam are adopting the development strategies of Singapore and Malaysia.

The Asian industrial relations experience shows trends of both convergence and divergence. Convergence lies in the congruence between industrial relations policies and industrialization for economic development while divergence lies in the diverse industrial relations institutions and regulations adopted by different countries that are consistent with their unique political and cultural circumstances.

Wide variation in the countries in Asia prevent us from making a uniform prediction or prescription regarding the future of industrial relations. Nor is it possible to identify an optimal industrial relations system. Industrial relations choice must be locally determined, and rooted in the national, cultural and institutional contexts. The Asian experience shows us that even when there is similarity in thinking at the conceptual level, there is significant divergence at the practical level based on the contexts in which the concepts are implemented. At this point, all we can offer are the past lessons of successful countries (described earlier) and the desired goals for an ideal industrial relations system.

We posit that for industrial relations systems to help in both economic development and democracy, the challenge lies in promoting their stability and flexibility so that the twin goals of both 'efficiency' and 'equity' are met. The pure efficiency model can be faulted for its long-term suppression of labour rights which leads to conflict and to the destabilization of industrial relations, as was the case in Korea and Taiwan, as well as to weak unions unable to participate in workplace decision making. The pure equity models can be faulted for the ability of their workplaces to react flexibly to a changing environment.

In adopting the principles of stability and flexibility in industrial relations such that the goals of both efficiency and equity are met, several fundamental changes in the roles of industrial relations actors are necessary. In particular, decentralization of industrial relations implies that states must devolve more power and control over industrial relations issues upon employers and labour to develop solutions that reflect their unique interests and concerns. Structural and legislative changes may be necessary to ensure that labour and management have the ability to mutually resolve their disagreements. The role and willingness of the state in interpreting and acting in the public interest are all being questioned (Adams, 1992). Clearly, with increased decentralization in industrial relations, the traditionally strong role of the state in Asia will come into question. Stephen Frenkel (1993) makes several critical arguments regarding the future scenario that are worth noting. Yet, in countries like India, the state will continue to play a major role in the informal sector which currently accounts for over 92 per cent of the labour force.

To meet the goals of efficiency and equity in industrial relations, not only the roles of parties, but also those of their underlying values will come under scrutiny. There must be a redefinition of the commitment of the actors to the principles of pluralism, freedom of association and worker rights. Clearly economic forces will push for greater flexibility and efficiency. However, the issues of equity and stability can be addressed only by the parties themselves, in particular, in the South-East Asian context. The role and legitimacy of trade unions or other representative bodies of workers needs to be understood and enhanced.

In addition, if actors at the national level cannot develop institutions and solutions meet the requirements of efficiency and equity, there will be pressure from actors at the local level or the regional level for such efforts, given the drift toward globalization and regionalization as well as decentralization of industrial relations systems.

It is also important for countries to rethink the purpose of industrial relations rules and regulations. According to Kuruvilla and Erickson (1994), the purpose underlying the introduction of industrial relations legislation in the 1940s in most countries of the world was to minimize industrial conflict. In the 1990s, they argue, the purpose is to promote productivity, flexibility, and in some cases, increased workplace democracy. The industrial relations system of the twenty-first century must come to grips with these issues.

Finally, for industrial relations to effectively promote democracy there must be a change in the definition of workers and the ambit of existing labour legislation. In most Asian countries, only industrial workers appear to have coverage, leaving agricultural workers, rural farm workers, contingent workers, casual and contract labour, and workers and employees in shops and establishments and small businesses outside the purview of industrial regulation.

The goals of stability and flexibility and equity and efficiency presuppose many changes in the established ways of conceptualizing industrial relations. It is our view that to achieve these goals individual countries must devise their own systems and institutions that are congruent with their national culture, institutional history, and other macro policies. Widespread acceptance of these goals is the only concrete principle that we can suggest for the industrial relations actors of the twenty-first century.

REFERENCES

Adams, R.J. (1992). 'The role of the State in Industrial Relations'. D. Lewin, O. Mitchell and P. Sherer (eds). *Research Frontiers in Industrial Relations and Human Resources.* Madison: Industrial Relations Research Association.

Arudsothy P. and C. Littler (1993). 'State Regulation and Fragmentation in Malaysia'. Stephen Frenkel (ed). *Organized Labour in the Asia-Pacific Region: A Comparative Study of Trade Unions in Nine Countries.* Ithaca: H.R. Press.

Begin, J. (1995). 'Industrial Relations in Singapore'. S. Frenkel and J. Harrod (eds). *Industrial Action and Labour Relations: Contemporary Research in Seven Countries.* Ithaca: H.R. Press.

Bhatt, B.J. and E.L. Miller (1984). *Industrial Relations in Foreign and Local Firms in Asia.* Management International Review, pp. 62-75.

Chew S.B. and R. Chew (1995). 'Impact of Development Strategy on Industrial Relations in Singapore'. A. Verma, T. Kochan and R. Lansbury (eds). *Employment Relations in the Growing Asian Economies.* London: Routledge. pp. 62-88.

Chiang, T.B. (1988). *The Administration and Enforcement of Collective Agreements in Singapore.* Bangkok: International Labour Organization. pp. 239-246.

Deyo, F. Beneath (1989). *The Miracle: Labour Subordination in East Asian Development.* Berkeley: University of California Press.

Frenkel, S. (1993). *Organized Labor in the Asia-Pacific Region: A Comparative Study of Trade Unions in Nine Countries.* Ithaca: ILRR. Press.

Grace, E. (1990). *Short Circuiting Labour: Unionizing Electronic Workers in Malaysia.* Kuala Lumpur: Insan.

Huff, W.G. (1987). 'Patterns in the Economic Development of Singapore'. *Journal of Developing Areas.* pp. 305-325.

International Labour Organisation (1994). *World Labour Report.* Geneva: ILO. (Also see volumes for the years 1990 to 1993.)

Lee, J.S. (1995). 'Economic Development and the Evolution of Industrial Relations in Taiwan 1950-1993'. A. Verma, T. Kochan and R. Lansbury (eds). *Employment Relations in the Growing Asian Economies.* London: Routledge. pp. 88-119.

Katz, H.C. (1993). 'The Decentralization of Industrial Relations: A Literature Review and Comparative Analysis'. *Industrial and Labor Relations Review.* 47, pp. 3-22.

Katz, H.C., S. Kuruvilla and L. Turner (1994). 'Trade Unions and Collective Bargaining'. *Impediments to Competitive Labour Markets: An overview of Policy and Research issues.* Washington DC: The World Bank.

Kuruvilla, S. (1994). 'The Influence of Development Strategy on Workplace Human Resource Practices: Case Studies in Malaysia and the Philippines'. *Human Resource Management Journal.*

Kuruvilla, S. (1995). 'Industrialization Strategy and Industrial Relations Policy in Southeast Asia', *Industrial and Labor Relations Review.*

Kuruvilla S. and C. Erickson (1994). 'Critical Junctures in Industrial Relations Transformation'. Paper presented at the Fourth Bargaining Group Conference, Toronto.

Kuruvilla S. and A. Pagnucco (1994). 'NAFTA, AFTA, and Industrial Relations in Asia'. Harry C. Katz and Maria Cook (eds). *North American Industrial Relations.* Ithaca: Institute for Collective Bargaining.

Offreneo, R. (1993). *Changes in the Workplace.* Manila: University of Philippines. Mimeo.

Pagnucco, A. (1994). 'The Problem Solving Industrial Relations System in Singapore and Philippines'. Master's thesis, Cornell University.

Park Y.B. and M.L. Lee (1995). 'Economic Development, Globalization, and Practices in Industrial Relations and Human Resource Management in Korea'. A. Verma, T. Kochan and R. Lansbury (eds). *Employment Relations in the Growing Asian Economies*. London: Routledge. pp. 27–62.

Penang Skills Development Center. *Training for Change: The Way to a Better Future*. Penang: PSDC.

Rasiah, R. (1988). 'Production in Transition Within the Semi-conductor Industry and its Impact on Penang'. *Journal of Malaysian Studies*. pp. 85–111.

Rasiah, R. 'Changing Organization of Work in Malaysia's Electronics Industry'. *International Labour Review*, Forthcoming.

Ramaswamy, E.A. (1993). 'Indian Management Dilemma: Economic Versus Political Unions'. Asian Survey. pp. 976–990.

Reddy, Y.R.K. (1978). 'Determination of Collective Bargaining Agency: Search for a Procedure'. *Indian Journal of Industrial Relations*. pp. 73–86.

Sharma, B., A. Verma and S. Kuruvilla (1994). 'Strategic Economic Cooperation and Growth Triangles in Southeast Asia'. Paper presented at the Changing Employment Relations and Human Resource Management Conference in Asia, Taipei, Chung Hua Institute for Economic Research.

Venkata Ratnam, C.S. (1993). 'Impact of New Economic Policies on the Role of Trade Union'. *Indian Journal of Industrial Relations*. pp. 56–77.

Venkata Ratnam (1994). op. cit. See also Schregle, J. *Labor Law in South East Asia, First Andres Bonifacio Annual Lecture Series*. Manila: University of Philippines. Mimeo.

World Bank Research Report (1993). *The East Asian Miracle: Economic Growth and Public Policy*. New York: Oxford.

FOUR

The Economic and Social Dimensions of Structural Adjustment Reforms

The debt and foreign exchange crisis precipitated by the disintegration of the erstwhile Soviet Union—then a major trading partner and the Gulf War, dried up foreign exchange remittances by migrant Indian workers in West Asia.

When the government approached the IFIs for stabilization and adjustment loans, the IMF wanted India to be fiscally more prudent and reduce its monetized deficit. The Washington Consensus' package included:

- Reduction in fiscal deficit through cutting down of government expenditure
- Drastic reduction in subsidies
- Lowering of tariff and non-tariff barriers on foreign trade
- Removal of public policy preferences in the form of reservations for the public sector, small-scale sector, etc.
- Reform/Removal of industrial licensing
- Withdrawal of restrictions on entry of foreign capital and regulations on foreign exchange
- Dismantling anti-monopoly legislation, etc.

Prior to that, as Dreze and Sen (1995) have argued, 'Indian economic planning offered good illustration of horrendous overactivity in controlling industries, restraining gains from trade, and blighting competitiveness; and, soporific underactivity in expanding school education, public health care, social security, gender equity, and land reform'.

As Debroy (1998) observes:

> If competitiveness can be measured as a share of world exports, there has been a steady erosion in India's international competitiveness since independence. India's share in world exports declined from 2.5 per cent at the time of independence to 0.5 per cent in 1997. The protected and profitable domestic market offered little incentive to turn towards an extremely competitive export market. Industrial licensing regime in the period up to 1991 proved arbitrary and non-transparent, encouraging lobbying and rent seeking behaviour. Discouraging imports through tariffs is difficult in the post-WTO regime. Slashing imports to maintain balance in balance of payments position is not an easy option for India in view of its dependence on oil imports, etc.

Exports increase only during periods when exchange rates depreciate. The poor quality of inputs, the uncertain and inadequate infrastructure, the low quality and the high cost of output, and the non-adherence to delivery schedules are among the problems that persist on the export front. These continue to have an adverse impact on the external sector.

India has pursued the policies of the IFIs selectively in foreign investment, industry and trade. While to an extent the same holds true for physical infrastructure and the financial sector, the opposite is true of the insurance and labour market reforms. There is a semblance of political consensus on economic reforms, but not on labour market reforms. According to Bhagwati (1993), the initial speed and scope of the Indian reforms was adequate, but not so the speed of the residual reforms in the public sector and labour market reforms which are the focal points of resistance in terms of the organized labour in India. Sen (1996) considers that India was too conservative in keeping government underactivity in social infrastructure intact, while trying to cure governmental overactivity in trade and manufacturing. Bhattacharya (1998) agrees that financial repression in India has decreased: reserve requirements have come down; interest rates have been deregulated, and real interest rates have risen to very high levels; and that direct credit to the government too has decreased. However, their full impact on savings, growth, investment, employment and poverty alleviation is still to be felt (Babu 1992, Sengupta 1994, Rao 1994, Wadhwa 1994, Kapila 1995, Joshi and Little 1996, Kelkar and Bhanoji Rao 1996, Guha 1997a, Chelliah 1998). Overall, the performance of the economy in the post-reform period has been below its potential. On the social front the record is even more bleak.

THE ECONOMIC SITUATION

The World Employment Report 1998–99 (ILO 1998) observes that, 'India's economic performance has fluctuated in the 1990s due to both economic liberalization and weather'. One might add political instability too. One can assess the economic situation only from official data, with their manifold limitations. During the 1990s, there was no dearth of controversy over the estimates of various wings of the government and semi- and fully-autonomous academic/research bodies and interest groups like the chambers of commerce. There was a major difference of opinion between the conclusions of the Planning Commission and the finance ministry over the mid-term assessment of the Eighth Five-Year Plan and considerable delay in the finalization of the Ninth Five-Year Plan. In popular academic writing, titles such as 'poverty of poverty estimates' and 'unemployability of employment data' are not uncommon.

The data presented here and elsewhere on the Indian economic and social situation needs, therefore, to be taken with a sack of salt. It must be added that this problem is not unique to India alone, but common across most developing countries. Although the growth rate has been higher than earlier, it has not been sustained or sufficient to significantly reduce the current levels of underemployment and to absorb new job seekers productively in quality jobs.

GDP Growth

Stabilization measures resulted in the significant contraction of the growth rate in 1991–92. GDP growth in the agriculture sector suffered the most and was erratic in alternate years. The same was true, to an extent, of mining and quarrying, manufacturing and construction. Overall, industry performed well and the services sector fared even better. Table 4.1 presents the GDP growth in India during 1981–98.

TABLE 4.1 **GDP Growth, 1981–1998**

(% Per Year)

	1981–90 Avg.	1990–91	1991–92	1992–93	1993–94	1994–95	1995–96	1996–97	1997–98*
GDP at factor cost	5.7	5.4	0.8	5.3	6.2	7.8	7.2	7.5	5.0
Agriculture and allied	3.6	3.8	–2.3	6.1	3.7	5.1	–3.0	7.9	–2.0
Industry	7.2	7.2	–1.3	4.2	6.6	10.4	12.5	6.4	5.7
Mining and quarrying	8.5	10.7	3.7	1.1	1.78	5.9	8.4	–0.3	6.3
Manufacturing	7.6	6.1	–3.7	4.2	8.4	11.9	14.0	7.4	6.1
Electricity, gas and water	8.8	6.5	9.6	8.4	6.3	9.4	7.3	5.0	6.4
Construction	4.9	11.6	2.2	3.4	0.9	6.2	9.7	5.2	3.2
Services	6.5	5.2	4.9	5.4	7.7	7.7	10.4	8.1	8.9

*Provisional.
Source: Economic Survey, 1999–2000; CSO, National Accounts Statistics, 1997–98 Advance Estimates.

Debt, Balance of Payments and Exchange Reserves

India's major problems have been high debt and a negative balance of payments position. Its external debt has increased in the post-reform period (Table 4.2). The IMF and rupee debts have decreased, but all other sources of debt increased during 1991–98. With a view to suppressing the real magnitude of the debt burden, the government, while calculating the debt ratios, sometimes does not take into account the NRI and foreign currency deposits which have matured. The balance of payments position (Table 4.3) and foreign exchange reserves (Table 4.4) have improved. Despite the devaluation of the rupee immediately after liberalization, the continuing erosion of the value of the rupee vis-à-vis the dollar in the post-reform period (Table 4.5) and a steep reduction in tariffs (Table 4.6), exports have not grown as fast as imports. Indian exports have still to become competitive. Though the World Bank (1998) argues, based on data shown in Table 4.7, that India's share increased from 0.53 per cent to 0.62 per cent between 1990 and 1997, during the corresponding period tariffs fell from 127.7

per cent to 34.2 per cent. The share of Indian merchandise exports in world merchandise exports increased by a mere 0.09 per cent against a nearly 400 per cent reduction in tariffs. Trade liberalization, devaluation and tariff reduction have had a mixed impact on different industries.

TABLE 4.2 **India's External Debt, 1991–98**

(Million)

	1991	1994	1995	1996	1997	1998
1. Multilateral	403,860	821,990	898,190	981,730	1,050,660	1,170,520
2. Bi-lateral	273,780	545,800	637,610	657,400	628,910	674,600
3. IMF	51,320	158,120	135,450	81,520	47,140	26,220
4. Export credit	83,740	163,070	208,760	184,320	210,440	266,500
5. Commercial borrowings	197,270	387,820	409,150	476,420	514,540	670,680
6. NRI & foreign currency deposits	200,300	397,290	390,060	378,020	395,270	471,890
7. Rupee debt	251,990	316,340	303,150	281,500	269,780	232,040
8. Total long-term debt (1 to 7)	1,462,260	2,790,430	2,982,370	3,040,910	3,116,740	3,512,450
9. Short-term debt	167,750	113,750	134,480	166,370	241,530	203,200
Total debt (8&9)	1,630,010	2,904,180	3,116,850	3,207,280	3,358,270	3,715,650
External debt as % of GDP	28.0	33.1	30.0	26.3	23.8	23.8

Source: Government of India (1999). Economic Survey, 1998–99. Delhi. p. 94.

TABLE 4.3 **Balance of Payments 1991–2000**

(US$ Billion)

	Actuals				Estimates		Projections
	1990–91	1994–95	1995–96	1996–97	1997–98	1998–99	1999–00	2000–01
Total exports of GNFS	23.0	33.0	39.7	42.4	43.6	45.7	49.4	55.3
Merchandise (FOB)	18.5	26.9	32.3	33.8	34.7	35.6	38.2	42.3
Non-factor services	4.6	6.1	7.4	8.6	8.9	10.0	11.2	13.0
Total imports of GNFS	31.5	41.4	51.2	54.3	58.0	62.2	68.7	75.5
Merchandise (CIF)	27.9	35.9	43.7	48.1	50.3	54.4	59.8	66.5
Non-factor services	3.6	5.5	7.5	6.2	7.7	8.2	8.9	8.9

(Contd.)

Dimensions of Structural Adjustment Reforms 137

	1990-91	1994-95	1995-96	1996-97	1997-98	1998-99	1999-00	2000-01
Resource balance	-8.5	-8.4	-11.5	-11.9	-14.4	-16.6	-19.3	-20.2
Net factor income	-4.0	-3.7	-3.5	-3.6	-3.5	-3.3	-3.1	-3.5
Factor receipts	1.1	0.9	1.4	1.1	1.1	1.2	1.7	1.9
Factor payments	5.1	4.6	4.9	4.7	4.2	4.6	4.8	5.4
Interest (scheduled)[a]	5.0	4.4	4.6	4.5	3.8	4.2	4.4	4.7
Other factor payments[b]	0.1	0.2	0.3	0.2	0.4	0.4	0.4	0.6
Net private current transfers	2.1	8.1	8.5	11.1	11.3	11.5	12.9	13.2
Current receipts	2.1	8.1	8.5	11.1	11.4	11.6	13.0	13.3
Current payments	0.0	0.0	0.0	0.1	0.1	0.1	0.1	0.1
Current account balance[c]	-10.3	-4.1	-6.5	-4.4	-6.2	-8.5	-9.5	-10.5
Official capital grants	0.5	0.4	0.3	0.4	0.3	0.2	0.3	0.3
Foreign investments	0.1	4.9	4.8	5.8	4.7	2.0	6.5	8.5
Direct foreign investments	0.1	1.3	2.1	2.5	3.1	3.0	3.5	4.5
Portfolio investments	0.0	3.6	3.7	3.3	1.6	-1.0	3.0	4.0
Net long-term borrowing	5.9	3.2	1.5	2.8	5.3	3.6	6.6	5.9
Disbursements	7.1	7.5	7.6	6.5	9.6	9.0	11.6	11.9
Repayments (scheduled)[a]	2.7	5.2	7.0	7.2	4.2	5.4	5.0	6.0
Other capital flows	1.0	2.4	-2.1	1.6	0.9	-0.7	-0.7	-0.6
Net short-term capital	1.0	0.6	0.8	1.7	n.a.	n.a.	n.a.	n.a.
Bilateral balanced with Russia	-1.2	-1.0	-1.0	-0.7	-0.8	-0.7	-0.7	-0.6
Errors and omissions	1.1	2.8	-1.9	0.6	1.7	0.0	0.0	0.0
Changes in net international reserves	2.9	-6.9	2.0	-6.2	-4.2	3.2	-2.2	-3.7
IMF (Net)	1.1	-1.2	-1.7	-1.0	-0.6	-0.4	-0.3	0.0
Changes in gross reserves	1.8	-5.7	3.7	-5.2	-3.6	3.6	-2.0	-3.7
Memorandum items: Current Account Balance/GDP	-3.5	-1.3	-2.0	-1.2	-1.6	-2.3	-2.5	-2.5
Gross foreign reserves	2.3	21.2	17.4	22.7	26.3	22.6	24.6	28.3
In months of imports (Goods)	1.0	7.1	4.8	5.7	6.3	5.0	4.9	5.1
External debt (% of GDP)	30.5	33.4	28.4	25.0	24.7	26.5	26.6	26.2
Debt service (% of total current receipts)	32.4	25.6	21.6	23.2	18.6	17.8	16.9	15.2
NRI inflows (net)	1.5	0.8	0.9	3.5	3.1	0.0	1.0	1.0
Interest payments on NRI deposits	1.3	1.0	1.2	1.6	1.2	1.3	1.1	1.2

(a) World Bank Debt Reporting System (DRS), these numbers differ from RBI.
(b) Returns on foreign investments.
(c) Current account balance differ from GOI, on account of interest payments (DRS) and official capital grants (treated as a financing term).

Source: Government of India, RBI, Ministry of Commerce, IMF: World Bank Debt Reporting System; World Bank Staff estimates.

TABLE 4.4 External Reserves

(US$ Billion)

	Foreign Exchange	SDRs	Reserve Position in the Fund	Reserves Excluding Gold	Gold*	Reserves Including Gold	Use of IMF Credit	Net Reserves
1980–81	5,850	603	405	6,858	370	7,228	327	6,901
1981–82	3,582	473	405	4,460	335	4,795	964	3,831
1982–83	4,281	291	393	4,965	324	5,289	2,876	2,419
1983–84	5,099	230	518	5,847	320	6,167	4,150	2,017
1984–85	5,482	145	483	6,110	325	6,435	3,932	2,503
1985–86	5,972	131	554	6,657	416	7,073	4,290	2,783
1986–87	5,924	179	626	6,729	470	7,199	4,291	2,908
1987–88	5,618	97	376	6,391	507	6,898	363	3,246
1988–89	4,226	103	630	4,959	473	5,432	2,364	3,067
1989–90	3,368	107	634	4,109	487	4,596	1,493	3,102
1990–91	2,236	102	—	2,338	504	2,842	2,623	219
1991–92	5,631	90	1	5,722	542	6,264	3,451	2,812
1992–93	6,434	18	297	6,749	557	5,306	4,798	2,508
1993–94	15,068	108	300	15,476	583	16,059	5,040	11,019
1994–95	20,809	19	332	21,160	695	21,855	4,312	15,743
1995–96	17,044	82	311	17,436	645	18,090	2,374	15,715
1996–97	22,367	2	295	22,664	620	23,284	1,313	21,971
1997–98	25,975	1	284	26,260	596	26,856	664	26,192

— Not available.

Source: IMF, International Financial Statistics' various issues.

Note: IMF Credit refers to use of IMF Credit within the General Resources Account (GRA) excluding Trust Fund Structural Adjustment Facility (SAF) and Enhanced Structural Adjustment Facility (ESAF) loans.
(a) Valued at 35 SDRs per fine troy ounce.

TABLE 4.5 Exchange Rate Movement

(Indian Rupees to One US$ 1966–98)

Currency	Currency		
	Official	Unified	Market@
Prior to June 1966	4.76		
June 6, 1966 to mid-December 1971	7.50		
Mid-December 1971 to end-June 1972	7.28		
1971–72	7.44		
1980–81	7.89		
1990–91	17.95		
1991–92	24.52		
1992–93	26.41		30.65
1993–94		31.36	

(Contd.)

Currency	Currency		
	Official	Unified	Market@
1994-95		31.40	
1995-96		33.46	
1996-97		35.50	
1997-98		37.16	
1998-99		42.30	
8 June 1999		43.03	

Source: IMF International Finance Statistics (IFS) and Reserve Bank of India.
Note: The fiscal year runs from April 1 through March 31.
@ A dual exchange rate system was created in March 1992, with a free market for about 60% of foreign exchange transactions. The exchange rate was reunified at the beginning of March 1993 at the free market rate.

TABLE 4.6 **India: Tariff Structure, 1990–98**

(In Per Cent)

	Sector					
	Whole Economy	Agricultural Products	Mining	Consumer Goods	Intermediate Goods	Capital Goods
1990-91	128	106	n.a	142	133	109
	(41)	(48)		(33)	(42)	(32)
1995-96	40.8	25.1	30	54.4	43.7	33.1
	(19)	(24.9)	(15.6)	(26)	(13.5)	(12.4)
1996-97	38.6	25.6	24.8	45.4	38.8	33.6
	(19)	(21.1)	(11.9)	(27.1)	(13.2)	(12.2)
1997-98	34.4	24.6	24.4	39.8	34.7	29.7
	(14.8)	(17.7)	(11.9)	(20.5)	(10.3)	(9.4)
1998-99	40.2	29.6	29.4	45.9	40.7	35.3
	(15.3)	(18.8)	(12.3)	(20.7)	(11.1)	(10.2)
1990-91	87	70	n.a.	164	117	97
1994-95	33	17	31	48	31	38
1995-96	27.2	14.9	27.6	43.1	25	28.7
1996-97	24.6	14.7	22	39	21.9	28.8
1997-98	25.4	14	21.9	33.8	26.1	24.7
1998-99	29.7	16.1	19.5	39.3	31.5	30.1

Source: World Bank Staff Estimates, the rates are based on the 1997-98 and 1998-99 editions of the Easy Reference Customs Tariff, Academy of Business Studies.
Note: Standards deviations are in parenthesis in 1990-91, mining is included in intermediates.
Total customs duty is calculated as a sum of the basic customs duty, the special duty of customs and the special additional duty. Special additional levy is levied on the value of the imports as well as the basic duty value, the special duty value, and the additional countervailing duty value.
Figures for 1997-98 include the 35 special duties imposed in September 1997.

TABLE 4.7 India's Share in World Trade Rose when Tariffs Fell

Year	World Merchandize Exports FOB (US$ bn)	India's Merchandize Exports FOB (US$ bn)	Share (%)	Tariff (%)
1980	1,921.8	8.6	0.45	
1981	1,900.8	8.3	0.44	
1982	1,753.8	9.3	0.53	
1983	1,712.9	9.1	0.53	
1984	1,818.7	9.4	0.52	
1985	1,849.4	9.1	0.49	
1986	2,035.3	9.4	0.46	
1987	2,392.7	11.33	0.47	
1988	2,730.5	13.2	0.48	
1989	2,966.7	15.9	0.54	
1990	3,377.6	17.9	0.53	127.7
1991	3,477.5	17.6	0.51	127.6
1992	3,731.4	19.6	0.53	94.0
1993	3,724.9	21.5	0.58	71.0
1994	4,238.3	25.0	0.59	55.0
1995	5,079.1	30.7	0.60	41.0
1996	5,249.6	333.0	0.63	38.6
1997	5,455.0	33.9	0.62	34.2

Source: International Financial Statistics, IMF; Annual Report, WTO, various years.
Note: Tariffs before 1990 were in excess of 130%.

Foreign Investment

There is much ado about foreign investment. Despite far-reaching changes in policies to attract foreign investment, India has not become a favourite destination for foreign capital. The actual flow during 1991–98 was 21.7 per cent of the $54,268 committed, approved flow (Table 4.8). Despite the size of its economy, India's share in the developing countries was between one per cent and 2.2 per cent during 1994–97. Mauritius, the US and South Korea were major sources of foreign

TABLE 4.8 Foreign Direct Investment

(US$ Million)

	1991	1994	1995	1996	1997	1998
Approved	325	4,332	11,245	11,142	15,752	6,132
Actual Flows	155	958	2,100	2,383	3,330	2,073
Actual Flow as % of Approval	47.7	22.1	28.7	21.4	21.1	33.8
India's share in developing countries	N.A	1.0	2.29	2.8	2.2	N.A.

Source: Government of India. (1999). Economic Survey, 1998–99. Delhi. p. 87.

direct investment flows into India in the 1990s. A large part of the foreign direct investment in the post-reform period has gone into increasing the stake in existing businesses (and industries). In some cases, investment has gone into adding new manufacturing capacities or modernizing the existing ones. The latter type of investment has often reduced the current level of labour intensity and/or affected existing domestic businesses (for example, the white goods industry). What little foreign investment has flowed into the country has resulted in a decline of, not an addition to, direct employment in the concerned areas. Telecom might be regarded as a possible exception. Neither the Planning Commission nor any of the ministries have worked out the employment elasticities based on new technologies to be able to study the impact of investment growth and employment in different sectors. There are no such studies even by academic or other research institutes in the country.

The Asian crisis has highlighted the perils of uncontrolled mobility of capital. Fortunately, India has decided that capital account liberalization should be carefully calibrated to minimize the risks of disruption.

It is wrong to consider that foreign investment is bad. Majumdar and Chibber (1998), in their study (for the years 1988 to 1994) of over 1,000 firms with varying degrees of foreign ownership in India, found that firms with over 51 per cent of foreign ownership had fared much better in exports. Ghemawat and Patibandla (1998) have also shown how the skill-intensive industry reduced the dependence of competitive industries on inefficient domestic suppliers and infrastructure and enhanced domestic competitive conditions. Of course, not all industries were similarly placed so as to have a similar beneficial impact.

Tables 4.9 and 4.10 present the position of finances of the central government and state governments respectively as a per cent of GDP for the period 1990–91 to 1997–98. The total revenue of the central government as a per cent of GDP has declined marginally over the years, largely due to the reduction in trade tariffs. The share of income tax, however, has improved despite a steep cut in tax rates. This is due to better tax compliance following the cuts and the introduction of special schemes like the voluntary disclosure of income (VDIS). Revenue expenditure has been higher than the revenue income in all the years despite reduction in subsidies and grants to states. Interest payments went up following the increase in debt. Salaries of government employees also went up due to the 40 per cent increase

TABLE 4.9 Central Government Finances, 1990–98

(% of GDP)

	90–91	91–92	92–93	93–94	94–95	95–96	96–97	97–98**	98–99*
A. Revenue	10.3	10.7	10.5	9.3	9.5	9.8	9.9	9.8	10.0
Tax revenue	8.0	8.1	7.7	6.6	7.0	7.3	7.3	7.0	7.2
Corporation tax	1.0	1.3	1.3	1.2	1.4	1.5	1.5	1.5	1.6
Income tax–VDIS	1.0	1.1	1.1	1.1	1.2	1.4	1.4	2.0	1.3
Excise duties	4.6	4.6	4.4	3.9	3.9	3.6	3.5	3.4	3.5
Customs	3.9	3.6	3.4	2.7	2.8	3.2	3.4	2.9	3.0
Other	0.3	0.4	0.5	0.3	0.2	0.3	0.3	0.3	0.3
Less: state's share	2.7	2.8	2.9	2.7	2.6	2.6	2.7	3.1	2.5
Non-tax revenue	2.2	2.6	2.8	2.7	2.5	2.5	2.6	2.8	2.8
Interest receipts	1.6	1.8	1.8	1.9	1.6	1.6	1.7	1.8	1.7
B. Revenue Expenditure	13.7	13.3	13.1	13.3	12.7	12.5	12.4	12.9	12.9
Interest payments	4.0	4.3	4.4	4.5	4.6	4.5	4.7	4.6	4.6
Subsidies	2.3	2.0	1.7	1.6	1.3	1.2	1.3	1.4	1.4
Food	0.5	0.5	0.4	0.7	0.5	0.5	0.5	0.5	0.6
Fertilizer	0.8	0.8	0.9	0.6	0.6	0.6	0.5	0.5	0.5
Others	1.0	0.7	0.4	0.3	0.2	0.1	0.3	0.3	0.4
Defence	2.0	1.9	1.7	1.8	1.7	1.7	1.6	1.9	1.9
Grants to states	2.5	2.5	2.5	2.6	2.1	1.9	1.8	1.7	1.7
Other	2.9	2.7	2.8	2.7	3.0	3.3	3.1	3.3	3.4
C. Capital Expenditures	2.3	1.9	1.9	1.6	1.5	1.2	1.0	1.2	1.3
Defence	0.9	0.8	0.8	0.8	0.7	0.7	0.7	0.7	0.6
Economic services	1.2	0.9	1.0	0.7	0.7	0.4	0.4	0.7	0.9
Other	2.3	1.9	1.9	1.6	1.5	1.2	1.0	1.2	1.3
D. Gross Loans	3.9	3.0	2.5	2.7	2.5	2.2	2.3	2.5	2.2
To states and UTs	2.7	2.1	1.9	1.9	1.9	2.2	2.3	2.1	1.8
To PEs	0.7	0.6	0.4	0.6	0.5	0.4	0.5	0.5	0.5
Other	0.5	0.3	0.2	0.2	0.1	0.1	0.1	0.1	0.1
E. Recovery of Loans	1.1	1.0	0.9	0.8	0.7	0.6	0.6	0.7	0.6
F. Net Lending	2.6	1.9	1.4	1.8	1.8	1.6	1.7	1.9	1.6
G. Disinvestment in PEs	0.0	0.5	0.3	0.0	0.5	0.0	0.0	0.1	0.3
Fiscal deficit (GoI definition)	8.3	5.9	5.7	7.4	6.1	5.5	5.2	6.1	5.6
Primary deficit	4.3	1.6	1.3	2.9	1.5	1.0	0.6	1.5	1.0
OCC deficit	0.2	0.5	0.1	0.0	0.1	0.2	0.8	0.1	0.3
Fiscal deficit	8.6	6.4	5.8	7.5	5.9	5.7	6.0	6.0	5.3
Fiscal deficit	8.6	6.9	6.0	7.4	6.5	5.7	6.0	6.0	5.6
Financed by: Reserve Bank of India (net)	3.1	1.0	0.5	0.2	0.1	1.9	0.1	0.3	n.a.
Marketable securities (net)	0.9	1.9	2.6	4.8	1.9	3.1	2.1	1.8	2.1
Other domestic borrowing (net)	3.8	2.2	1.9	1.9	3.5	0.4	2.7	3.9	3.3
External borrowing (net)	0.6	0.9	0.8	0.6	0.5	0.0	0.2	0.1	0.1

Source: World Bank (1998).
Note: * = budget estimates; ** = estimates.

TABLE 4.10 **State Government Finances**

(% of GDP)

	80–81	90–91	91–92	92–93	93–94	94–95	95–96	96–97RE
Revenue receipts	12.0	12.6	13.2	12.9	13.0	12.7	12.3	12.1
Tax revenue	7.7	8.4	8.6	8.6	8.5	8.4	8.3	8.4
States own taxes	4.9	5.7	5.8	5.6	5.7	5.8	5.7	5.7
State share in central taxes	2.8	2.7	2.8	2.9	2.7	2.6	2.6	2.7
Non-tax revenue	4.4	4.2	4.6	4.4	4.5	4.3	3.9	3.7
Of which: Grants from centre	2.0	2.5	2.5	2.5	2.6	2.1	1.9	1.8
Revenue expenditure (A + B + C)	11.0	13.4	14.0	13.6	13.5	13.3	13.0	13.6
A. Developmental (1 + 2)	7.7	9.1	9.5	9.0	8.7	8.2	8.0	8.5
1. Social services	4.4	5.2	5.0	4.9	4.8	4.7	4.8	4.9
2. Economic services	3.4	3.9	4.4	4.1	3.9	3.5	3.2	3.6
B. Non-developmental	3.1	4.1	4.3	4.5	4.6	5.0	4.8	4.9
Of which: Interest payments	1.1	1.6	1.8	1.9	1.9	2.0	2.0	2.1
To centre	0.7	1.0	1.1	1.1	1.2	1.2	1.2	1.0
To others	0.4	0.6	0.7	0.8	0.8	0.8	0.8	0.9
C. Transfer to local bodies	0.2	0.1	0.2	0.2	0.1	0.1	0.1	0.2
Net current balance	1.1	–0.8	–0.8	–0.7	–0.5	–0.6	–0.7	–1.5
Capital expenditure (A + B + C)	3.8	2.5	2.1	2.2	2.1	2.1	2.1	2.0
A. Development (1 + 2)	2.3	1.7	1.6	1.5	1.5	1.8	1.6	1.4
1. Social services	0.3	0.2	0.3	0.2	0.2	0.2	0.2	0.3
2. Economic services	2.0	1.4	1.3	1.2	1.3	1.5	1.4	1.2
B. Non-developmental	0.1	0.0	0.0	0.0	0.0	0.0	0.1	0.1
C. Loans and advances (net)	1.5	0.8	0.5	0.7	0.5	0.3	0.4	0.5
Gross fiscal deficit	2.8	3.3	2.9	3.0	2.6	2.8	2.8	3.5
Finance by instrument: Market loans	0.2	0.5	0.5	0.5	0.5	0.4	0.6	0.5
Loans from centre (net)	0.9	1.8	1.5	1.2	1.2	1.4	1.3	1.3
Small savings and provident funds	0.3	0.6	0.5	0.5	0.5	0.5	0.4	0.5
Other	1.4	0.5	0.4	0.7	0.3	0.4	0.5	1.2
Memo items: Primary deficit	1.7	1.7	1.2	1.1	0.7	0.8	0.8	1.4
Total debt outstanding	17.6	20.6	20.5	20.2	19.8	19.2	19.0	19.2

Source: World Bank (1998).

after the award of the Fifth Central Pay Commission. The fiscal deficit declined by over 3 percentage points between 1990–91 and 1997–98. Part of this reduction could be attributed to proceeds of disinvestment of capital assets in the public sector while a significant portion of the fiscal deficit was earlier met through the Reserve Bank of India. In the post-reform period this reliance was offset by market borrowings.

In the states too, revenue receipts decreased and revenue expenditure increased in all the years of reference. As Table 4.11 shows, most states showed a negative change in social and economic expenditure and in interest payments between 1990–91 and 1996–97.

TABLE 4.11 Change in Social and Economic Infrastructure and Interest Spending (1990–91 and 1996–97)

(Change in Percentage Points of GSDP)

State	Social[1]	Economic[2]	Interest Payment
Andhra Pradesh	−0.8	0.7	0.6
Bihar	0.1	−2.2	1.3
Gujarat	−0.3	−1.2	0.5
Haryana	−0.3	−0.6	0.4
Karnataka	0.0	−1.4	0.3
Kerala	−0.1	−0.2	1.0
Maharashtra	−0.2	−0.5	0.1
Madhya Pradesh	−0.1	−0.1	0.6
Orissa	0.1	−1.7	0.8
Punjab	−0.4	−0.9	2.0
Rajasthan	0.7	0.0	1.0
Tamil Nadu	−0.7	0.1	0.6
Uttar Pradesh	−0.4	−0.5	1.2
West Bengal	−0.6	0.8	1.1
14 states average	−0.2	−0.6	0.8
All states[3]	−0.4	−0.4	0.5

Source: *RBI Bulletin* various issues as compiled by World Bank (1998).
Note: 1996–97 is revised estimate.
[1] Refers to total expenditure on health and education.
[2] Refers to power, irrigation and transport—capital outlay and loans.
[3] All states as a proportion of GDP at factor cost.

Privatization

Privatization in India has so far been more covert than overt, particularly in the central sphere. Here, too, the evil of licensing has been replaced by the devil of tendering, such as in the telecom sector.

The government, following the IFIs' advice, set up a disinvestment commission and sold shares in 40 of about 240 central public sector enterprises. In all central public sector enterprises where disinvestment took place, the government retained its controlling interest (see Table 4.12 for year-wise details of shares disinvested between 1991 and 1997). Thus, disinvestment enabled the government to reduce fiscal deficit by treating capital receipts to reduce revenue deficits but it did not help improve the performance of the enterprises concerned. The government implemented only a few of the recommendations of the

Dimensions of Structural Adjustment Reforms 145

TABLE 4.12   Year-wise/PSU-wise Details of Shares Disinvested Since 1991–92

S No.	Name of the PSE	Percent of Central Government Holding						
		1991	1992	1993	1994	1995	1996	1997
1.	Andrew Yule	71.3	62.8	62.8	62.8	62.8	62.8	62.8
2.	Bharat Earthmovers Ltd	100	80	80	80	60.1	60.1*	60.1*
3.	Bharat Electronics Ltd	100	80	80	80	75.9	75.9	75.9
4.	Bharat Heavy Electricals Ltd	100	80	79.5	79.5	67.7	67.7	66.2
5.	Bharat Petroleum Corpn Ltd	100	80	69.6	69.6	66.2	66.2	66.2
6.	Bongaigaon Refineries & Pet Td	100	80	74.6	74.6	74.5	74.5	74.5
7.	CMC Ltd	100	83.3	83.3	83.3	83.3	83.3	83.3
8.	Cochin Refineries Ltd	61.2	55	55	55	55.1	55	55
9.	Dredging Corpn Ltd	100	98.6	98.6	98.6	98.6	98.6	98.6
10.	Fertilisers & Chem. (Travancore) Ltd	100	97.5	97.4	97.4	97.4	97.4	97.4
11.	HMT Ltd	100	95.1	90.3	90.3	90.3	90.3	90.3
12.	Hindustan Cables Ltd	100	96.4	98	98	98	96	96
13.	Hindustan Copper Ltd	100	100	98.9	98.9	98.9	98.9	98.9
14.	Hindustan Organic Chem. Ltd	100	80	80	80	56.9	56.9	56.9*
15.	Hindustan Petroleum Corp Ltd	100	80	70	69.7	60.3	51.0*	51.0*
16.	Hindustan Photofilms Mfg Co. Ltd	100	87.5	87.5	87.5	87.5	87.5	87.5
17.	Hindustan Zinc Ltd	100	80	75.9	75.9	75.9	75.1	75.1
18.	Indian Petrochemicals Corp. Ltd	100	80	81	62.4	62.4	61.4	61.4
19.	Indian Railway Const. Co. Ltd	100	99.7	99.7	99.7	99.7	99.7	99.7
20.	Indian Telephone Inds Ltd	99.7	79.7	77.8	77.7	77	77	77
21.	Madras Refineries Ltd	84.6	67.7	67.7	51.8	51.8	51.8	51.8
22.	Mahanagar Telephone Nigam Ltd	100	80	80	80	67.2	65.7#	56.0#
23.	Minerals & Metals Trading Corpn	100	99.3	99.3	99.3	99.3	99.3	99.3
24.	National Aluminium Co Ltd	100	97.3	87.2	87.2	87.2	87.2	87.2
25.	National Fertilizers Ltd	100	97.7	97.7	97.7	97.7	97.7	97.7
26.	National Mineral Dev Corp Ltd	100	100	98.9	98.4	98.4	98.4	98.4
27.	Neyveli Lignite Corpn	100	93.9	93.9	94.2	94.2	93.3	93.3
28.	Rashtriya Chemicals & Fertilizers	100	94.4	92.5	92.5	92.5	92.5	92.5
29.	Shipping Corpn of India	100	81.5	81.5	81.5	80.1	80.1	80.1
30.	State Trading Corpn	100	92	91	91	91	91	91
31.	Steel Authority of India Ltd	100	95	89.5	89.5	89	88.9#	88.9#
32.	Videsh Sanchar Nigam Ltd	100	85	85	85	85	82	64
33.	Container Corpn of India	100	100	100	100	80	76.9#	76.9#
34.	Indian Oil Corpn	99.9	99.9	99.9	99.9	96.1	91	91
35.	Oil & Natural Gas Corpn Ltd	100	100	100	100	98	96.1	96.1
36.	Engineers India Ltd	100	100	100	100	94	94	94
37.	Gas Authority of India Ltd	100	100	100	100	96.6	96.6	96.6
38.	Indian Tourism & Dev Corp	100	100	100	100	90	90	90
39.	Kudremukh Iron & Ore Co Ltd	100	100	100	100	99	99	99
40.	Industrial Devt Bank of India	100	100	100	100	100	72.1	72.1

* These companies had floated public issues. Percentage of Government holding after proposed public issue is not known.
\# Figures are provisional as the shares sold in October 1995 are yet to be transferred in favour of successful bidders.
Source: Economic Survey, 1997.

Disinvestment Commission. Ultimately, it curtailed the Commission's powers and status and replaced it by the Department of Disinvestment. For the first time since 1991, a central public sector company, Modern Bakeries, was sold to the Indian subsidiary of the Anglo-Dutch multinational Hindustan Lever Limited.

The experience of increased private sector competition in domestic airlines and passenger road transport in Delhi has not proved positive. The performance of the non-banking private sector financial institutions and scams in the stock markets have eroded the confidence of middle-class investors.

In the absence of civil service reforms, public sector reforms have remained mostly on paper. Economic reforms have thus not been an unmixed blessing. Still, the need and rationale for economic reforms cannot be questioned, even though their content remains controversial.

THE SOCIAL DIMENSIONS

Table 4.13 presents data on select characteristics like population, income, consumption/distribution patterns and other social indicators like health, education and nutrition. Table 4.14 presents data for the period 1991 to 1998 on economic reforms based on economic and social parameters. Despite impressive industrial recovery (Gupta 1998), employment grew by hardly 0.6 per cent in 1995–96 and 0.2 per cent in 1996–97, suggesting a fast (and continuing) decline in employment intensity in the organized sector. Employment in the civil service reduced marginally in the first four years of the post-reform period, but grew subsequently. Overall, unemployment is rising and will rise over the next few years, even if economic growth is twice as high as it was in 1997–98. Estimates are confusing and conflicting, whether it is poverty or productivity. Inflation has been tamed on paper, but the price rise of daily wage goods continues to be stiff. Minimum wages are a mockery. The organized sector usually pays much more than the minimum wage. In the unorganized sector, compliance is weak and enforcement feeble. Workforce reductions loom larger as economic decision making dithers due to political compulsions.

TABLE 4.13   India—Social Indicators

	Latest Single Year			Same Region/Income Group	
	1970-75	1980-85	1990-95	South Asia	Low Income
Population					
Total Population, mid-year (mill)	613.3	765.1	945.1	1,265.8	3,236.2
Growth rate (% annual average)	2.3	2.1	1.8	1.9	1.8
Urban Population (% of population)	21.3	24.3	27.1	26.6	29.1
Total fertility rate (births/women)	5.6	4.4	3.1	3.4	3.2
Poverty					
(% of population)					
National Headcount Index	—	—	35.0	—	—
Urban Headcount Index	—	—	30.5	—	—
Rural Headcount Index	—	—	36.7	—	—
Income					
GNP Per Capita (US$)	180	280	380	380	490
Consumer Price Index (1987=100)	—	83	238	—	—
Food Price Index (1987 =100)	—	83	238	—	—
Income Consumption Distribution					
(% of Income or Consumption)					
Lowest Quintile	5.9	—	9.2	—	—
Highest Quintile	49.4	—	39.3	—	—
Social Indicators					
Public Expenditure					
Health (% of GDP)	—	—	0.7	0.8	1.5
Education (% of GNP)	—	3.4	3.8	3.0	3.6
Social Security & Welfare (% of GDP)	—	—	—	—	—
Net Primary School Enrolment Rate					
(% of age group)					
Total	—	—	—	—	—
Male	—	—	—	—	—
Female	—	—	—	—	—
Access to Safe Water					
(% of population)					
Total	31	54	81	78	76
Urban	80	80	85	83	80
Rural	18	47	79	74	72
Child Malnutrition (% under 5 yrs)	—	—	66	—	—
Life Expectancy at Birth (years)					
Total	50	52	63	62	63
Male	51	52	62	61	62
Female	49	51	63	63	64
Mortality					
Infant (per thousand live births)	132	101	65	73	68
Under 5 (per thousand live births)	202	173	85	93	94
Adult (15-59)					
Male (per thousand population)	324	261	229	239	231
Female (per thousand population)	353	279	219	230	206
Maternal (per one lakh live births)	—	460	437	—	—

Source: World Development Indicators 1998 CD-ROM, World Bank (1998).

TABLE 4.14 Economic Reforms and Labour—Select Parameters

Aspect	Change during Post-reform Era (1990s)
Estimated employment in organized public and private sectors	Increased from 267.33 lakh in 1991 to 279.41 in 1996.
Employment in civil service	Increased from 190.57 lakhs in 1991 to 194.29 in 1996. There was a marginal decline in central government employees strength which was offset by the increase in employee strength in state government, quasi government and local bodies.
Employment in central public sector	Reduced by 200,000 from 21.79 lakhs in 1991-92 to 19.78 lakhs in 1996-97.
Employment in organized private sector	Increased from 76.77 lakhs in 1991 to 85.12 lakhs in 1996.
Unemployment	The number of persons in the live registers of employment exchanges rose from 36.3 million in 1991 to 38.1 million in 1997.
Workforce reductions	30% redundancy estimated in organized sector employing about 28 million. The 243 central public sector alone shed 200,000 jobs during 1991-97 through means other than retrenchment.
Poverty	The government claims that the incidence of poverty is declining. The critics argue about the poverty of poverty estimates.
Inflation	All India Consumer Price Index nearly doubled in 7 years: It rose from 951 in 1990-91 to 1803 in 1997-98. The rate of inflation is claimed to be low during the 1990s.
Minimum wages	The range of minimum wages at minimum level ranged from Rs 9.25 to Rs 114.16 as on 31.3.98. In Delhi it was Rs 68.60. Minimum wage enforcement continues to lax.
Social sectors and human development index	The Economic Survey, 1997-98 (p. 16) acknowledges that "the shortcomings in our social sectors—such as education, health, water supply and sanitation and housing—in relation to both our own aspirations as well as performance levels achieved by other Asian countries becomes increasingly stark and unacceptable. India's rank in UNDP's Human Development Index is 138 out of 175 in the year 1998.
Industrial unrest: No. of strikes and lockouts	58,62,000 workers were involved in strikes and lockouts (3921,000 in strikes and 19,41,000 in lockouts) during 1992-97.
No. of workers laid off	410,428 workers were affected by lay-offs during 1992-97
No. of workers retrenched	15,534 workers were retrenched during 1992-97
No. of closures and workers affected by closures	94,429 workers were affected due to closure of units during 1992-97

Source: Annual Report of Ministry of Labour, Government of India for the year 1997-98 (various pages) and Economic Survey submitted to the Parliament by the Finance Minister in the relevant years.

In the social sector, India's track record is poor. It has the dubious distinction of being the home of a record number of illiterates worldwide. Where industrial unrest is concerned, when strikes are under control, lockouts are on the rise—worker violence replaced by employer militancy. The number of workers affected by layoffs, closures and 'voluntary' reductions may be small in relative terms but in absolute terms it is a worrisome figure. Overall there is little room for comfort or complacency. However, since India did not go all out for quicker and rapid economic changes, unlike many other countries in Asia, it could keep social costs in check.

Statistics show that the rate of labour productivity has been consistently rising since the mid-1980s. In the two years (1992–93 and 1993–94) following the stepping up of economic reforms (for which Annual Survey of Industries Data is available), the overall gains in total factor productivity have been impressive at 8.9 and 10.2 per cent respectively (Gangopadhyay and Wadhwa 1998). Gains in productivity have been associated with falling unit labour costs since the mid-1980s, particularly in industries such as textiles, leather, metal products and other manufacturing industries which are spearheading India's export growth. In these industries, rising labour productivity, deepening capital and falling labour costs were accompanied by a rise in the growth rate of employment and wages.

The rise in labour productivity should be seen in the context of productivity improvement through capital investment and resultant mechanization; increased use of casual and contract labour; and, a steady reduction in workforce in the organized sector mainly through natural attrition and voluntary separations. Johri (1995) questions whether labour has become a redundant resource in India's post-reform quest for productivity and quality to gain competitiveness. Indeed, in more cases than not, companies are becoming productive and profitable at the cost of unskilled/redundant labour. While the Bengal Chambers of Commerce (1997) study of 26 firms, including nine multinational corporations, confirms this, Kuruvilla's (1997) analysis of postglobalization trends in human resources/industrial relations reinforces it.

To sustain productivity improvement it is necessary to ensure that the rate of expansion of industrial and economic activity is high enough to generate more jobs than are lost in the short-term/transition stage itself. The Asian economic crisis and political instability have, however, resulted in a slowdown. If this slowdown continues, labour productivity improvement will be at the cost of labour. Existing jobs will have to be sacrificed to make enterprises viable. New jobs will be fewer than those displaced. With slow growth, the trickle down of benefits will not take place. The result will be that while the rich may become richer, the converse will also be true: the poor will become poorer.

With its population crossing the billion mark, India has only 28 million workers with a semblance of job security. Public provision of education, health, housing and social security being virtually negligible, even this relatively pampered sector is in the throes of a crisis with job loss sans social safety nets.

The discussions on alternative safety nets remain on paper and the National Renewal Fund (NRF) initiative has become a national redundancy fund (Table 4.15). Established in February 1992, the NRF was supposed to (a) provide compensation to employees affected by restructuring/closure of industrial units; (b) provide assistance to retrain and redeploy employees affected by modernization/restructuring; and, (c) contribute to area regeneration. However, over 90 per cent of the funds were used only to 'voluntarily retire' 109,000 redundant public sector employees. Of these about two-thirds were surveyed, one-third counselled, one-fifth retrained and about one in 18 redeployed. Not all the training was relevant or appropriate and even those who were redeployed were not redeployed to use the skills for which they were trained. Studies on how those voluntarily retired fared subsequently confirm mixed results (Guha 1997, Gupte 1986).

TABLE 4.15 Performance of National Renewal Fund 1992–98

Aspect	Total from 3.2.1992 to 31.3.98
Financial allocation	Rs 22,227 million
Expenditure incurred	Rs 20,830 million
Expenditure on voluntary separations	Over Rs 18,000 million (90% of total expenditure of NRF)
No. of workers who took voluntary retirement with NRF funds	109,000 workers. The number of people who took voluntary retirement with company's own funds would be at least twice this number.
No. of Employee Assistance centres (EAC)/Employee resource centres (ERC)	557 EACs in 16 states and 47 ERCs in 47 central public sector undertakings
No. of workers surveyed by EACs	66,662
No. of workers counselled	33,791
No. of workers retrained	26,304
No. of workers redeployed	6,712

Source: Ministry of Industry, Government of India.

The Indian experience with social safety nets in the wake of structural adjustment reforms confirmed the concerns expressed by the ILO (1999):

- They cover very few people and offer low levels of protection (p. 38)
- They apply to less than 10 to 20 per cent of the labour force (p. 39)
- Their administration (of social protection measures) is often poor, with inadequate record keeping and high costs (p. 41)

Poor design and administration and excessive emphasis on workforce reduction rather than dealing with the problems of redundancy through retraining are the primary causes for the dismal record of the NRF. Due to apprehensions about the low quality and high cost of administration, employers' organizations in India have spurned the government's proposal to introduce a skills development fund of the kind that exists in Singapore and Malaysia. Trade unions contend that this is an employers' ruse to avoid a levy on turnover/profits. Yet, trade unions too are as unhappy as are employers' organizations about the record of the government in managing other social security measures like the Employees' State Insurance Scheme and the Provident Fund Scheme. While there is a recognition of the problem, there is not enough resoluteness among the social partners about solving it. This is largely because the state behaves both like an elephant and an ostrich.

Table 4.16 presents the sorry situation with regard to human resources as a source of competitive advantage. India is second to none in terms of its skilled workforce. The problem, however, is that it is woefully inadequate to meet the country's needs. Technology increases the demand for skilled labour. ILO (1998) asserts, based on an UNIDO industrial statistics database for 1997, that in India the share of employment in the high-skilled manufacturing industry as a percentage of total manufacturing employment increased from 30 per cent in 1980 to 34.6 per cent in 1993. In the future, the study notes, it is not always that 'higher' skills will be required, but 'different' skills definitely will be. Job losses may be more due to skill gaps than due to competitive pressure on costs.

TABLE 4.16 Global Competitiveness of Indian Labour

Item	Scale*	Rank**
Country has abundant labour force	6.77	1
Average workers are unproductive	2.94	51
Hiring and firing practices are severely restricted	2.16	53
Labour regulations impede adjustment of working hours to meet changes in demand	2.16	49
Labour regulations impede adjustment of working hours to meet changes in demand	5.05	8

* All questions are scaled from 1 (lowest) to 7 (highest)
** India's rank amongst 53 countries ranked in the 1998 Global Competitiveness Report.
Source: 1998 Global Competitiveness Report.

The preferred alternative, therefore, is to raise labour productivity through investment in developing a skilled, flexible and adaptive workforce—in infrastructure and in research and development. Table 4.17 presents a comparison between the organized and unorganized sectors in terms of compensation and contribution. Compensation is the total remuneration paid to employees. Contribution is measured in terms of the operating surplus income generated.

TABLE 4.17 Compensation and Contribution in the Organized and Unorganised Sectors

Aspect	Organized Sector		Unorganized Sector	
	1990–91	1994–95	1990–91	1994–95
Compensation to employees (Rs million)	1,051,980	1,776,260	582,530	994,000
Operating surplus and mixed income (Rs million)	487,490	1,112,500	2,134,190	3,754,220
Ratio of operating surplus and mixed income to compensation to employees	46.3%	62.3%	366.36%	377.69%

Source: CMIE (1998). National Income Statistics, February 1998 (Chapter 14: Factor Incomes).

Between 1990–91 and 1994–95, the percentage change in compensation to workers in both the organized (168.5 per cent) and the unorganized (170 per cent) sector remained more or less similar. The unorganized sector fared marginally better. Contribution, however, increased by 228 per cent in the organized sector and 176 per cent in the unorganized sector. Employee compensation in the organized sector was 2.16 times and 1.5 times the operating surplus income generated in the sector during 1990–91 and 1994–95 respectively. The corresponding figures for the unorganized sector were 0.27 and 0.26.

On an average, 28 million employees in the organized sector received Rs 20,805 and Rs 35,500 annually between 1990–91 and 1994–95 respectively. Their counterparts in the unorganized sector, who number approximately 282 million, received Rs 9,297 and Rs 17,257 respectively during the corresponding years. The compensation gap between the organized and unorganized sectors came down during the five-year period between 1990–91 and 1994–95. In 1990–91, employees in the unorganized sector received 44.59 per cent of the compensation received by the employees in the organized sector. By 1994–95, the percentage rose to 48.6 per cent.

The wage gap between the public and private sectors is wide and has increased in the post-reform period. The gap works in favour of workers in the public sector who get about 1.5 times more than their counterparts in the private sector. It works negatively at and above the manager level in favour of private sector managers. This is considered to have created a flight of talent from the public to the private sector. Based on a study of about 20 per cent of the central public sector undertakings, Hakeem and Ratnam (1997) point out, that this has not happened and that there has been no brain drain in the public sector. Some argue that the brain drain is preferable to having brains in the drain. In recent years, non-residents Indian have helped brain drain by contributing to a brain trust and brain gain in the burgeoning knowledge sector.

Strikes and Lockouts

Economic reforms have made workers and unions vulnerable, because the focus has shifted from labour to the market. This is evident from a comparison of the terms of reference of the first National Commission on Labour appointed in 1966 with the proposed terms of reference of the second National Commission appointed in October 1999. While the first commission was asked to examine the working conditions of workers and their social welfare, the second commission is being asked to examine the need for labour law and labour policy changes in the context of liberalization, globalization and privatization. Trade unions have naturally protested against such formulation of the terms of reference and suggested that the terms of reference and the composition of the commission should be finalized in consultation with them. During the 1990s, despite several strike notices by trade unions belonging to different political parties to demonstrate their dislike of the economic reforms, the incidence of mandays lost due to strikes and lockouts declined. A few industries (mining, engineering and jute/cotton textiles) and a few states (Andhra Pradesh, Tamil Nadu, Maharashtra and West Bengal) account for a large proportion of mandays lost. More mandays were lost due to lockouts than due to strikes. The proportion of mandays lost due to lockouts was 95 per cent in most years against 5 per cent mandays lost on account of strikes. Strike as a weapon of last resort for trade unions seems to have been blunted with workers in most situations not being very keen to go on strike. This is partly due to the fact that a variety of allowances are linked to attendance and participation in a strike could mean tremendous loss of income for workers. Therefore, in the 1980s and 1990s, workers and unions have explored covert rather than overt forms of conflict wherever possible. But outsourcing, parallel production, contractualization and casualization, recessionary conditions, loss of control over jobs due to technological change are among the other factors that have blunted the strike weapon in the past 15 years.

Employment

The concern over jobless growth is mounting. There is stagnation or reduction in employment in several industries in the organized sector. In 1990–91 India had a backlog of 17 million unemployed. With the rate of growth of the workforce (3.2 per cent to 3.5 per cent) being more than twice the rate of growth of employment (1.5 per cent), the number of unemployed nearly doubled during 1991–97. The number of unemployed in 1999 was more than the number employed in the organized sector, which has a semblance of protection and unionization. In 1998, there were 38 million job seekers registered in the employment exchanges as against 31 million employed in the organized sector.

The employment intensity in the organized Indian industry has been declining. While some studies (Fallon and Lucas 1991) attribute it to the rigidity in labour laws and labour market institutions, others (ILO 1996) consider labour market rigidity as 'a' reason, not 'the' reason for the decline in employment intensity. Labour market rigidity seems to have had a diverse impact on different sectors. While it has not seemed to deter the large private sector firms from rationalizing their workforce and closing down unviable units, the public sector has not been able to exercise similar options due to the lack of operations freedom for managements at the enterprise level and the threat perception of political risks by the ruling party/coalition.

In any case, only about eight per cent of the workforce is protected, while over 92 per cent is unorganized, unprotected and vulnerable. Technological changes, competitive pressures and opportunities to outsource, casualize and contractualize labour, and parallel production have accelerated the pace of decline in labour intensity.

Though employment opportunities have expanded in the unorganized sector, there is concern about the poor quality of jobs and the decline in safety, security, wages and welfare. Decasualization, feminization and possible decline in unionization are the issues. The incidence of unemployment is higher among the educated, reflecting a mismatch between acquired and required skills.

There was a silver lining in the 1998–99 budget. Section 80 JJAA was inserted which provides tax incentive to employers with over 100 employees who engage new regular labour. It provides for 30 per cent aggregate wages of new workers to be deducted from the profits of the company. Its real impact on job creation remains to be seen.

Poverty

Poverty is on the rise. Its incidence is higher in rural areas than in urban areas, and more among the employed than the unemployed. In the absence of credible systems of social security, the poor in India cannot afford to remain unemployed and hence seek employment even if it is at below-subsistence or below-poverty level (Hashim 1998).

Venkata Ratnam (1999) quotes Tendulkar who provides a word of caution on five counts: (i) a casual connection is not necessarily warranted without closer examination just because a priori possibilities of an adverse impact of reforms on poverty and the observed worsening of the poverty situation during the reform process happen to coincide; (ii) public outlays impacting on poverty are a function of political economy and need not be related to the underlying rationale of reform-related policies; (iii) improving the quality and cost effectiveness of public outlays is an integral part of the reform process, so same reduced outlays can be more effective; (iv) due consideration be given to regional variations in administrative and organizational capabilities and corresponding variations in the effectiveness of utilization of the same amount of public outlays; and (v) the focal point of reforms being the urban organized industrial sector, and given the close financial, administrative and organizational links of the government machinery with the urban than the rural sector, reform-related policies can have immediate and greater impact on the urban organized sector with a second-order impact on the urban informal sector, and a lagged direct impact on the rural sector. The immediate impact on the rural sector is more likely to be indirect via its effects on the structural factors.

Physical and Social Infrastructure

Physical and social infrastructure is poor, inadequate and becoming unaffordable (ADB 1998). Public provision of public goods/services is declining.

Rising Inequality

Income distribution is becoming more skewed at both the individual and the regional levels. If unattended this can affect social harmony and political stability. As a well-known author has remarked, further neglect of this aspect may give birth to a violent Gandhi in the new millennium. Growing social tensions are already creating unstructured situations in some parts of India that undermine civil, police, legislative and judicial administration. East-west polarization and increasing inequalities are leading to a resurgence of diversionary tendencies among local groups fighting for a separate identity and statehood.

PUBLIC POLICY AND ITS EFFECTS ON LABOUR

Labour policy so far has focused mainly on the organized sector. The Working Group Report on Labour for the Ninth Five-Year Plan (1997–2002) promises to focus on the unorganized sector, as well.

There ought to be a link between the economic system, the industrialization strategy and industrial relations policies. Comprehensive labour law reforms seem to be considered inauspicious because thrice in the past has the government of the day fallen soon after the introduction of a bill attempting comprehensive reforms. Labour laws are archaic. Thick laws and thin implementation often makes laws a mockery and provides incentives for lawlessness. The coverage/applicability of most laws is linked to a certain threshold number. When it is linked to a threshold salary limit, the majority of workers in the organized sector are not covered as they draw more salary than that stipulated. When linked to the number employed, employers have started reducing the workforce in existing as well as greenfield sites. In several cases, rosters do not reflect the total number employed, with many being employed under fictitious names that change every few months or informally engaged without a proper record of employment. If there is no proof of hiring, there can be no proof of firing. Since labour is in the concurrent list of the Constitution, as will be discussed in the next chapter, some state governments are taking new initiatives to woo investment (Venkata Ratnam 1997).

THE SCENARIO OF POLITICS AND GOVERNANCE

The Congress government approached the IMF and the World Bank for financial assistance soon after it was voted to power in June 1991. The foreign exchange crisis was such that the government had to pledge its gold. Between 1995 and 1999, political instability deepened. Parliament had to be dissolved thrice and the country had five prime ministers in as many years.

Despite political slogans opposing economic reforms, there is near-unanimity among political parties in their approach to foreign direct investment. If at all, it is the chambers of commerce and industry and captains of industry who have voiced strong reservations about the possible negative fallout of post-reform policies on foreign direct investment to the domestic industry in terms of both control and competition. The concerns of the Bombay Club and Confederation of Indian Industry (CII) about foreign investment and multinationals respectively substantiate this argument.

In India the language of the ruling party and the language of the opposition party are the same regardless of the party in power or in the opposition. For instance, the same party opposes privatization if it is in the opposition and pursues it when it becomes the ruling party. It could be that a particular party may be in power in a state that has adopted privatization but since it is not part of the ruling coalition at the centre, it vigorously opposes privatization at the national level. As Sanjay Baru (1999) observes,

> The absence of a system of 'shadow' governments has meant that political parties freely adopt populist and irresponsible postures when in the opposition and do precisely the opposite thing when in government. In opposition, the Congress Party opposes what it wanted to do in office. In office, the BJP seeks opposition support for what it opposed before joining government. Those who campaigned against India joining the WTO, sought legislative support for the Patents Bill, those who proposed negotiations for a CTBT, now refuse to allow the government to sign the treaty! Such are the ironies of an anarchic democracy.

There is little transparency in the reform process. The government agreed to certain terms and conditions with the IMF and the World Bank without discussion in Parliament at the national level or with state governments or with the other social partners (representatives of workers' and employers' organizations, etc.) A special tripartite committee was set up subsequently to seek the cooperation of employers' organizations and workers' organizations in the implementation phase. Social partners participate not in policy formulation, but at the implementation stage. Even at this stage, not enough attention is paid on inventing, creatively, multiple solutions to each problem. Naturally the other social partners consider it *fait accompli* (see chapter 6).

The documents and correspondence of and between the government and IFIs is usually not made public and is considered 'top secret'. Hence, in the absence of a convincing and detailed explanation about the rationale of the change, the social partners and the general public find it difficult to understand or appreciate the policies. Since the reform process has not been participatory, the opportunity to create common/public ownership of the proposed structural changes in the economy too has been undermined. The differences between the central and the state governments, between and among different departments/ministries within the central government, between politicians within the party pushing the changes and the bureaucracy which is supposed to assist it has resulted in a situation where even those who are in charge often lack consistency, credibility, conviction, and accountability.

The quality of politics and political leadership though important, has not received much attention. As Baru (1999) observes,

> [in India] From the point of view of an ordinary citizen, the real opportunity and challenge for economic reforms is at the state level. Normal and daily interaction between citizens and government is mostly at the local (city, town or village) and provincial (state) level. Rarely do they (the ordinary citizen) interact with the national government . . . except when they use railway and telecommunication services.

Big business persons deal mainly with the central government in matters concerning licensing (now become mostly redundant), finances and other regulations. But they need to interact with the state governments in matters ranging from inspection under various legislations to infrastructure (water, electricity, etc.) environment and a variety of taxes and duties (other than those levied by the central government).

In India since 1969, the parties in power in several states happened to come under the control of those opposed to the party in power at the centre. The influence of the regional parties began to grow. Most chief ministers and regional leaders have been pressing for greater decentralization and the devolution of power. Also, as Baru (1999) asserts,

> There is no evidence to suggest a strong positive correlation between the level of development of a state and the commitment of local political leadership to economic reforms . . . In a rapidly developing state like Andhra Pradesh, where a newly emergent business class has secured increased leverage within a largely farmer-dominated legislature of the past, the Telugu Desam, which was liberally supported by the local business elite, has been more committed to liberalization, reform and decentralization than the Congress Party . . . Yet individual leadership matters . . . Within the Telugu Desam, N.T. Rama Rao was more in favour of populist policies while his successor Chandrababu Naidu was a pro-reform leader.

Those who have made politics their business can also be expected to be pro-reform. Competitive pressures to attract investment and create jobs in backward states also partly explains the interstate variations. A backward state like Orissa, for example, has taken the lead in the privatization of electricity boards.

Also, as Baru (1999) argues,

> Political leadership in this context means different things at the national and state levels. State-level political leaders will remain committed to greater growth and development at their state level, widening regional disparities are not their concern. On the other hand, the national leadership must ensure regional differences are not accentuated and uneven economic growth does not end up creating new political threats and challenges to a federal polity.

The position of ministries responsible for labour has also been a major area of concern (ILO 1999): 'Over the years, the position of ministries responsible for labour has been changing. Many ministries of labour now have relatively narrow areas of responsibility and when it comes to broader issues of economic and social policy, their voices are often not heard.' Government policies have impact not only on competitiveness and enterprise viability, but also on workers and employers through many other ministries, particularly those of finance, industry and planning.

One of the major criticisms about government policies at the behest of IFIs concerns the Enron project in India in the power sector. US-based multinational Enron has been given 16 per cent sovereign guaranteed return, but the people who work for Enron or even for the state-owned companies do not have sovereign guarantee for their jobs and earnings. It is dubbed as a partisan approach to give guarantee to capital, but not to labour.

Sanjay Baru (1999) quotes Panandikar who adds a new dimension to the analysis of politics and governance in India. He observes that the urban, educated forward caste leaders' vision of India is of building a strong, industrial and modern technological state. The new power elite in India, who mainly come from rural, agricultural, backward communities do not share this vision. Their focus is on rural and agricultural issues and the welfare of the people belonging to their castes/communities who feel that they did not have a fair share of the fruits of development in the first few decades following Independence.

In the short run of up to about fifteen years, Indian political economy will perhaps be greatly influenced by the increasingly vocal and politically powerful backward and scheduled castes. In the long run, say by the year 2015, the Indian middle class, growing at the rate it is, will be the most formidable influence on Indian political economy for the rest of the twenty-first century making India a major political and economical global player.

In some states in India like Andhra Pradesh, as Sanjay Baru observes elsewhere, the legislature was dominated by the farmer class for a long time, but now the business class wields greater leverage. The new paradigm in the politics and policies of the state can be attributed partly to the leadership and partly to the increased role of the business class.

THE EMERGENCE OF CRISIS/STRUCTURAL WEAKNESSES

The external debt crisis of India precipitated in early 1991 due mainly to: (a) the drying up of foreign exchange remittances by Indian workers in West Asia following the Gulf War; and (b) the collapse of the Soviet Union, then India's largest trading partner. The structural weaknesses and the impending crisis was signalled earlier by the Economic Advisory Committee, Ministry of Finance, Government of India (1989): despite a better growth rate in the 1980s, 'The pattern of growth, (and) methods of financing employed . . . have been such that, at the end of the decade, it would appear that the strategy of growth pursued, especially over the last five years, needs some critical modifications'.

In the mid-1980s, India's current account deficit nearly doubled, to 2.3 per cent of GDP; external debt multiplied two-and-a-half times; and, debt servicing burden as a per cent of export earnings also doubled, to 30 per cent. As the balance of payments position worsened, there were difficulties in rolling over short-term debts and the outflow of non-resident Indian deposits began at an alarming note. Inflation began to soar and the fiscal crisis deepened.

In early 1991, India went to the polls, after a period of political instability during 1989–91. By mid-1991, the new government took on the reigns of a sick economy and had little choice but to pledge its gold reserves and negotiate a stand-by arrangement with the IMF, followed shortly by negotiations for the structural adjustment loan (AIMA, 1998).

The performance of the Indian economy in the post-reform period has been below par due partly to the country's poor physical and social infrastructure. To overcome the structural weaknesses, the government has to refocus its role and public investment (ADB 1998) even as it concentrates on wooing foreign investors.

THE IMPACT OF THE PROGRAMME

IFI policies have affected urban India directly. Rural India has felt an indirect and secondary impact. The impact was more on some sectors and less or insignificant in others. At the national level, the most profound impact was on the delicensing of trade liberalization and on reduction in financial repression. Some states have pursued the policies of the IFIs more vigorously than have others.

Overall, India's performance in the post-reform period has been below its potential economically and below acceptable levels in the social dimension. The results have thus been a cause for concern. Notwithstanding the current slow down, the rate of growth in GDP during the 1990s has been higher than in previous decades. India continues to be dependent on agriculture which, in turn, is dependent on the vagaries of the weather. Manufacturing has shown near stagnation. The tertiary sector has shown the fastest growth.

The WTO agreement makes capital mobile, not labour; it provides free access for the products of the developed countries to markets of the developing countries, but developing countries would still find it difficult to freely access the technologies of the developed countries. Against this background, trade and industry liberalization is viewed with apprehension that this could lead to de-industrialization.

The current account deficit has declined. The trade balance and reserves position has shown significant improvement, due largely to the remittances of Indian workers in West Asia/Middle East. Investment in physical infrastructure has improved. Foreign Direct Investment flows touched the magic US$ 10 billion mark. Over half (7 per cent during 1991-97) the FDI flows are in the infrastructure sector as against only 14 per cent for consumer goods.

The telecommunications network has expanded rapidly. The power sector has not grown. Financial and trade sector reforms have made some headway. The insurance sector reforms have received the assent of the Parliament. There are problems with the regulatory authorities in the infrastructure industries: one might prefer an inefficient public monopoly to an ineffective regulator. Foreign direct investment flows have occurred more to acquire controlling interest in existing enterprises, edge out domestic joint venture partners or expand businesses in non-core, fast food areas, etc. The promised investment flows into core sectors like energy and infrastructure have slowed down due to a maze of legal and political complexities. Some of the manufacturing companies are becoming traders and franchisees.

The social sector continues to suffer. The prices of basic goods and services like food, electricity, water transport and education have increased. The choice and quality of consumer durable goods have increased. The prices of consumer durable goods have also decreased. The IFIs have recently started paying attention to social and labour issues. Otherwise, their policies for most part of the reform process since the early 1970s have been aimed at growth, not equity; enterprises, not employment (despite evidence about jobless growth in recent decades); economic gains, not social pains. Typically, in tune with the approach of many industrialized countries, the IFIs have shown greater concern for combating inflation, not unemployment. The solutions for the developing countries cannot be based on the problems of the developed countries.

Competition has increased in certain areas and decreased in others. Mergers and acquisitions at the national and global level have decreased competition in certain areas and created oligopolistic situations in segments such as soft drinks, detergents, etc. The number of jobs created is more than the number of jobs displaced. The quality of jobs, however, is a major concern because while jobs were lost in the organized sector, most of the new jobs are in the unorganized sector with low job security, low wages, poor working conditions and greater exposure to risks of safety and occupational health. While skilled workers are able to retain their jobs and improve earnings, unskilled workers are the worst affected. Before liberalization, government jobs were considered secure and well paying, but not any longer. Some state governments have resorted to privatization and closure of units without paying the promised separation money or paying off past dues completely.

In India, due to the absence of adequate social security provisions, the really poor cannot remain unemployed and hence seek employment even at sub-subsistence level. As a result, the incidence of poverty among the employed (18 per cent) is twice that of the unemployed. Little wonder then that the structural adjustment programmes dictated by the IFIs have generally come in for severe indictment. Bimal Jalan (1976) lists the following charges: (a) The policies are imposed without recognizing the diversity of country circumstances; (b) The one-size-fits-all approach could cause more harm than good; (c) The social costs of adjustment and reform could cross the limits of tolerance; and, (d) The 'success stories' are few as evident from the need for repetitive IMF assistance.

The ILO (1999; 13) avers,

> Globalization and economic restructuring favour flexible modes of employment, many of which lie beyond the reach of labour legislation and social protection and are characterized by low incomes and high levels of insecurity.

The problem is not just one of growth, but also of equity. Increase in poverty, unemployment and skills mismatch/obsolescence cannot be attributed to the IFIs' policies alone because these problems persisted even before. Yet, the fact that these trends became more persistent and intense, become a focal point of concern in reviewing these developments in the context of the ongoing economic 'reforms'.

The impact of the IFI policies in India is less severe/drastic than in many other countries undergoing structural changes largely because of the cautious approach of the Government of India. India did not face the problems of the flight of foreign capital due to three main reasons: (a) India retained its controls on capital outflows; (b) India did not go in for full convertibility; and (c) Foreign exchange remittances by migrant workers of Indian origin and investments by NRIs has contributed to the accumulation of a sizeable exchange reserve base.

India has dilly-dallied on privatization of the public enterprises at the national level. It has followed a policy of covert rather than overt privatization. Its disinvestments policies have lacked coherence and consistency. The government has stripped off its assets without losing controlling stake. The reform of public enterprises is suffering largely because it cannot fructify fully until the civil service, which controls the public sector, is reformed.

ALTERNATIVE STRATEGY AND POLICY OPTIONS

Nations lose their stature if they become defaulters. They lose their sovereignty when they are unable to balance their budgets and have to borrow from transnational sources. In a country like India, these sources become unpopular if they seek to confiscate the gold from the women in order to overcome the debt/exchange crisis. The last but the best option for the nation is to take concrete steps to reduce debt and seek a better balance between imports and exports through appropriate mechanisms. Simultaneously measures must be taken to boost domestic savings to the level of the investment needs commensurate with developmental objectives and goals. Given the average low level of per capita income and the skewed distribution of incomes, private savings can be considered fairly high in India. The need is to increase government savings. This is possible by cutting down unproductive expenditure but without undermining the need for additional investments in augmenting the physical (water, energy, transport and communications in particular) and social (health and education in particular) infrastructure.

It is advisable to reduce the dependence on international financial institutions. If a country borrows from the IMF and the World Bank it has to listen to their dictates. There is need for a national consensus on national finances—sources and uses—such that the social partners can chalk out the priorities in a manner whereby the country can conduct its affairs having regard for its means and potential.

As the UNDP (1987) declared, 'Economic development should be the means and social development should be the goal.' ILO (1999; 12) stresses that 'Principles and rights at work provide the ground rules and the framework for development; employment and incomes are the way in which production and output are translated into effective demand and decent standards of living. Social protection ensures human security and civil inclusion, and enabled economic reform.'

While evolving policies for economic development their impact on social development should be assessed. In India, academic groups, specially those with a shared ideological perspective, have initiated a public debate through the annual publication of an alternative survey of the Indian Economy. They vigorously put forth their candid views on the policies that ought to be pursued and others that should not. The following illustrative listing of some such arguments brings out the substance in the criticism of the relevant policy prescriptions of the IFIs (Delhi Science Forum, 1998):

- **Treatment of the Public Sector Disinvestments Proceeds** The Economic Survey, 1996–97 provides a new definition for the concept of the 'fiscal deficit'. 'The fiscal deficit is defined as the difference between the revenue receipts (net) plus non-debt capital receipts and the total expenditure including loans net of repayments.' Non-debt capital receipts arise from the sale of assets. In the present instance, such receipts arise from the sale of government equity in public sector enterprises. This is not only odd, it is an accounting fudge; and by taking a capital receipt into the revenue account as a normal receipt, we are violating all canons of accounting honesty. True, this has been happening all these years. Indeed, if authorities like the IMF have cheerfully accepted this fudging of accounts, it is only because the sale of government enterprises to private parties is wholly consistent with their ideology and economic principles.
- **Competitiveness of the Domestic Industry** If Indian industry is to be placed on the path to recovery a combination of some degree of protection against displacement by imports and a faster pace of expansion of the home market is an absolute necessity . . . (p. 40).
- **Health Sector** The World Bank's strategy to encourage the private sector to play a role in provision and financing of primary health care was despite the observation that public hospitals provided cheaper and equitable services, particularly to the poor, that the burden of out-of-pocket expenditure for health fell disproportionately on the poor, that the overall share of public sector in health was very inadequate, and that there was a decline in funds for operationalization and maintenance of programme activities.
- **Pharma Industry** Contrary to the reforms ideology the market does not regulate prices of drugs—as demand primarily depends

on prescription habits of doctors, disease profiles, drug resistance, etc.. The oligopolistic nature of the industry, where few companies have monopoly within various therapeutic groups, makes the operation of the market even more infructuous (p. 94).

The growing concern about the adverse effects of the policies of the IFIs has opened the way for fruitful interaction between the ILO, the World Bank, the IMF and the UNCTAD. As ILO (1999) observes,

> The financial crisis in Asia, in Russia and in Brazil have significantly altered the public perception of what constitutes sustainable economic and social policies. There is an increasing realization that adjustment and structural reforms need policies and institutions for social consensus, employment and social protection. There is a moment of opportunity to integrate these social perspectives into the policy framework of the Bretton Woods institutions . . . (It is important to) link macroeconomic policy to labour markets and poverty eradication policies, and to articulate the role of social institutions and fundamental rights at work in development policy.

The IFIs' policies as articulated by the World Bank (1995) in its World Development Report assume a homogenous labour market with an elastic supply of labour, the conditions for an improvement of wages are seen to be increasing the demand for labour in the formal sector. Hence the World Bank emphasizes export growth, particularly of manufactured goods.

With a vast reservoir of surplus labour in agriculture and the informal sector in the developing world, the key to raising workers' earnings in these economies is to increase the supply prices of such labour—and this can only be done with policies that augment labour productivity in agriculture. In many cases overemphasis on export growth might detract from this objective.

The list of elements that an alternative strategy should exhibit is illustrative:

- The creation of better and productive jobs should be a key developmental objective.
- An increase in the level of domestic savings to meet investment needs commensurate with developmental objectives/goals.

Government savings are currently much lower than private sector savings.
- Deficit financing becomes tolerable up to a point if it leads to increased availability of productive goods/assets and boosts effective demand. At the same time there is every need to reduce fiscal deficit through cutting down unproductive expenditures on administration through restructuring/reengineering government administration.
- Strengthening financial market supervision and regulation, improving infrastructure reforms and emphasizing transparency and market discipline, introducing uniform, international accounting standards and promoting good practices in the area of governance.
- Stepping up investment in physical and social infrastructure. Such investment may come from public, private and foreign sources.
- Privatization is not a panacea for public sector ills. Provision of public goods and services continues to be a government responsibility. Without effective regulatory mechanisms, blind reliance on the market mechanism for the provision of public goods and services can be disastrous. Based on social dialogue, there could be a reprioritization of and a refocusing on areas where the public sector needs to play a different/enhanced role. Performance improvement should be the key motive. The proceeds of disinvestments of public sector shares/assets should not be used to set off fiscal deficit. A separate fund should be created from the disinvestments proceeds to help turnaround sick public sector units and to strengthen the public sector.
- Reforms in parliamentary democracy and civil service are critical to the success of economic reforms and public sector reforms. Structural changes in the economy can be impeded by the deficiencies in the political and administrative decision-making processes.
- Labour market deregulation alone cannot provide a lasting solution. Putting in place proactive labour market policies and delivery mechanisms can be. It is, however, important to have a (a) clear enunciation of the rights and responsibilities of employers and workers/unions; (b) unambiguous and easily understandable legal and institutional framework; (c) predictable arrangements concerning union recognition, collective bargaining, skills development, flexibility and workforce adjustment; (d) well defined, clear-cut and time-bound procedures for grievance

redressal; and (e) administrative and judicial system that can be trusted for its transparency, expediency, efficiency, and accountability.
- Improving productivity in every sphere—particularly in the agriculture and informal sectors—and enhancing competitiveness of Indian enterprises is critical. The government should promote competition through anti-trust laws because the shift to a market economy has not necessarily resulted in increased competition in many sectors.
- Corruption at all levels, particularly at higher ones, is jeopardizing the country's economic progress. Transparency International lists India among the top ten corrupt nations in the world. The evil needs to be eradicated.
- India is home to one out of every three illiterate persons in the world. In the 21st century, the future is going to be bleak for those who do not have the knowledge, skill and attitude. We must declare a war against illiteracy, want and deprivation. The first step in this journey is educating and empowering people with the necessary skills for employability. Currently even the few who are educated are without a job. The existing mismatch between acquired and required skills and proactive labour market policies and effective labour market institutions must be bridged.

THE TRADE UNION PERSPECTIVE

The ILO (1999; 51) observation that 'in developing countries, where the formal sector is typically small, trade unions may have political influence that exceeds their membership base' holds true for trade unions in India. It is equally true that, as elsewhere, trade unions in India too 'are having to come to terms with the effects of globalisation and international competition. Thus, trade unions are increasingly entering into bargains that cover not just wages and protection but also competitiveness and productivity. They have to reinforce the necessary knowledge and analytical skills for this purpose. In addition, workers' organizations need to develop a capacity for macroeconomic analysis so that they can more effectively defend their members' interests. Since many corporate decisions are being taken at a global level, unions are also networking across sectors and over national borders.'

Trade unions in India would also do well to pay heed to what the ILO (1999; 51) is saying:

> Trade unions will need to continue to diversify their activities, both internally and externally. Internally they are increasing their appeal to workers by offering a new range of services, such as legal and financial advice or help with upgrading skills. Externally they are strengthening their position by seeking new alliance through civil society—with environmental groups, for example, or women's associations, or community associations. In making common cause with such groups, many trade unions have been able to secure broad public support for important employment issues such as the plight of lower paid workers.

Indeed, at a seminar organized by the Indian Industrial Relations Association and Friedrich Ebert Foundation, telecom trade unions have stressed the need to align their interests with those of customers. Telecom employees have also contributed immensely to the improvement of the performance of the public sector telecom units. Another impressive development is related to the significant turnaround of the Delhi Transport Corporation that has earned goodwill for the Corporation and helped reverse the decision to privatize city transport services in the national capital.

Such positive examples, however, remain rare and have not yet become the trend or the pattern. Some national centres of trade unions in India became myopic due to political polarization, prolonged political instability in the country and confusion over ideological interests vis-à-vis local/enterprise-level interests.

Trade unions are not united at the national level in their response to the challenges posed by the IFI's policies regarding initiatives taken in social development. The Indian National Trade Unions Congress (INTUC) welcomed the new economic policies in 1991. The Hind Mazdoor Sabha (HMS) did so, initially, with some caution. Over the years, both have generally acknowledged the need for reforms and supported some aspects of economic reform based on the policies of the IFI. They have not got bogged down by sheer ideological opposition, but have weighed the pros and cons and considered whether and what alternatives exist. Both the INTUC and the HMS are deeply concerned about the adverse effects of unemployment and poverty and the negative fallout of the dismantling of the public sector. In contrast, the other three major national centers of trade unions—the Bharatiya Mazdoor Sangh (BMS), the All India Trade Union Congress (AITUC) and the Centre of Indian Trade Unions (CITU) have totally condemned and rejected the Washington-consensus-based policies even though the parties to which they are affiliated or to whom they are close have been supportive of some of the economic reforms as partners in ruling coalitions either at the centre or in the states (Masilamani 1995).

On issues relating to privatization, labour policy/law reform and wages and working conditions, including social security, all the national centres of trade unions have carved out issue-based unity and organized collective campaigns, joint action programmes and even strikes. Even those unions who had earlier shunned technological changes are now beginning to welcome them provided it does not lead to job loss and provided the labour rendered surplus through such changes is retrained and redeployed. In this, the trade unions are concerned about protecting the interests of their members. They have, however, lost sight of the fact that in a growing unemployment situation this will not provide a lasting and satisfactory solution. For, the interests of the existing workers are protected against the claims of new entrants into the labour market. Trade unions have also not availed of the opportunity to play a proactive and positive role in the retraining and redeployment efforts with the result that the retraining and redeployment efforts under the National Renewal Fund have gone awry.

Issue-based unity among the trade unions has been witnessed in several cases at the sectoral or industry level. Trade unions are united in their opposition to reforms in the insurance sector. In the telecom sector, however, there is no unity between the employee unions in the Department of Telecom and the equipment manufacturers in the public sector like Indian Telephone Industries Limited.

Trade unions have been successful in avoiding the overt privatization of public enterprises at the central level, delaying reforms in the insurance sector and preventing labour law reforms. The year 2000 began with a series of aborted strikes in key sectors like banks, ports and electricity. The insurance reforms bill has been passed and Modern Bakeries has been privatized by outright sale. When the Government resisted, unions seemed unable to effectively stall the move. Corporate restructuring through downsizing has been taking place in a fairly big way in the private sector where the unions have been able to do little by way of resistance. In the public sector, however, they have been far more successful in averting restructuring that could hurt the interests of labour. The exceptions have been in the core and competitive industries—steel for instance—where the competitive pressures seem to impact and soften the perspective of the trade unions concerned. Trade unions have generally disliked voluntary separations. But, downsizing has become imminent and they have not been able to prevent their members from availing the so-called golden handshakes under which separation compensations have been far higher than what the law has provided for. Some trade unions have initially been reluctant to the idea of workers owning shares in the firms they are employed particularly in the context of disinvestments due to ideological annoyance with the concept of 'worker capitalism'. Still, they have not been able to prevent their members rush for shares in companies whose book values and share prices have been grossly undervalued.

On occasions where the viewpoints have differed, some of the federations have not joined. INTUC has not supported some strikes and, in some occasions, either BMS has chosen to opt out or has been kept out by the other federations. For instance, when the proposal for constituting the second national labour commission was mooted, the other four federations separately issued a memorandum to the government and did not take BMS into confidence. Political differences have been instrumental for the divisions in the ranks of the workers' organizations.

Eventually, the trade unions have realized that all parties do more or less the same thing when in power. The distrust among the trade unions towards political parties has begun to grow. Whether this will eventually free such of those trade unions which have become pawns in the hands of the political parties remains to be seen.

Trade unions in India have not yet come up with alternative strategies and policies. They have undersood the weaknesses of the past, protectionist regime but have failed to understand the processes of liberalization, privatization and globalization because they have felt that the dice has been loaded against them.

G. Sanjiva Reddy, President, Indian National Trade Union Congress (INTUC) observed recently that:

The protectionist policy followed by the government in the post-independence period only resulted in making the industries weak. Products of such industries therefore became uncompetitive because of their inferior quality. In the open competition the companies would not be able to compromise on the quality of the product. Liberalization has benefited the country to some extent, but the country's industrialists are yet to get ready to face the tough competition from abroad. Management is mainly responsible for the large number of sick industries. Management has made more than 600,000 small industries sick while more than 125,000 large-scale industries too face the same problem. This has resulted in the retrenchment of a large number of workers many of whom are facing a very tough time. Workers are never given their due credit. When the company profits the management is praised. The moment the company's performance suffers, the workers are blamed. This situation must change and the workers' contribution must be given full credit.

The biggest challenge for trade unions is that the IFI policies have unleashed a market economy where a large proportion of the labour force is made a redundant resource. They find it difficult to accept large-scale workforce reductions and/or job displacements from the organized to the unorganized sector without a credible system of compensation or social safety net.

Market economy policies are resulting in situations where the organized labour's interests seem to come into conflict with those of organized consumers. The trade unions know, for instance, that they cannot defend public ownership merely for the well being of their members that they should refocus their strategies aligning the interests of their members with those of consumers. After all, their members are also consumers of public goods/services.

The big question is, will the government continue to 'make haste slow'? The Union Budget 1998–99 and the subsequent announcements of the Union Ministers for Finance and Industry seem to point out, as Hind Mazdoor Sabha (HMS Bulletin, June–July 1998) commented editorially, 'Hard times are ahead for workers' in view of, among others, the following:

- Decline in budgetary support to public sector enterprises

- No provision for modernization/revival of national textile and jute mills
- Proposed closure of nine non-viable, loss-making units through the voluntary retirement scheme
- Up to 75 per cent reduction of government equity in profitable, non-strategic public sector enterprises
- 10 per cent new accretion of provident funds to be invested in select private sector securities

CONCLUSIONS

The economic challenges and the social development issues that are currently being debated in the wake of the policies of IFIs are not new to India. The country has been facing them even before the structural adjustment reform process started. During the post-reform period they have come to the centre-stage and became even more critical than ever before. National states lose their sovereignty when they live beyond their resources and begin to borrow from other countries/international financial institutions. When change is the only constant, status quoism has no place in any society. Pattern maintenance and adaptation to change are the two conflicting pursuits that are key and critical to survival and progress in any civilization.

Social and economic change becomes smooth when there is a wider social dialogue in the design and implementation of relevant policies. If social dialogue is atrophied or becomes a ritual or a *fait accompli*, it does not produce the necessary political and social consensus. The resultant tension among the actors and the institutions in the system would result in below par or counterproductive outcomes.

Increasing employment opportunities, reduction of poverty and inequalities and augmenting skills development are the four key tasks. The perception and priorities of the political leadership has been and continues to be different at the national and state level in a federal policy. Also it has been and will continue to be different whether the party concerned is part of the ruling coalition or in the opposition. When petty party/sectional interests override national concerns, political polarization vitiates the environment and affects the quality of the decision-making and implementation process.

The rights of workers and trade unions can be made more secure when the economy and the enterprises become strong. The workers' jobs and income become more secure and protected when there is a shortage of labour, both in terms of numbers and skills. Enterprise promotion and employment generation together with skills formation and upgradation should be pursued in a manner where the socio-economic development becomes more balanced and equitable. Improving investments in physical and social infrastructure holds the key to the productive utilization of available resources. The government should refocus its role in these areas.

Organized labour is beginning to distrust political parties. For, they seem to oppose 'new economic policies' while in opposition and follow them when they are in power. Governments seem to have unlimited capacity to do what they do not say and say what they do not do. Often desperate times need desperate solutions. Governments acting under the pressure of debt and exchange crises are unable to sustain the avowed promises they make due to political compulsions. They can deny their adherence to unpopular policies until the time they approach the World Bank and the IMF. Once they approach the Bretton Wood twins, it is no longer a secret.

Organized labour is not able to impede economic changes, particularly when dissatisfaction with public provision of public services/utilities is higher than the distrust of market forces. Economic reforms are carried out on a negative vote despite the lack of consensus and despite the concern for social and economic consequences.

The government are damned if they do not undertake the 'reforms', and damned if they do. When one is unsure, it is wise to tread cautiously—slowly, but steadily. Consistency and predictability in policies and actions is essential. Political instability and the lack of a popular mandate may weaken the resolve—whatever direction it is heading towards—of the government. The resultant vacillation is reflected, often, in pendulum politics, in policies and programmes that keep swinging from right to left, left to right and so on without resting at some point.

Economic reforms based on the Washington consensus—the prescriptions of the IMF and the World Bank—are increasingly being questioned. We need to explore more fully the Third Way, which not only India but others also (Tony Blair of the UK, for instance) have been advocating. As regards labour, legislation needs to be aligned with the emerging policy shift in economic and industrialization policies. Otherwise, the mismatch between the two can hurt both the economy and labour. Workforce reduction in the organized sector continues unabated. Any further delay in putting in place a credible system of compensation and social security for the affected workforce can cause untold misery and result in social crisis and political unrest. The key issue is to deal with the huge problem of redundant/obsolete workforce with minimal social cost.

Economic development should be the means and human development, the goal. Further neglect of the growing problem of unemployment, poverty and inflation and the alarming situation in respect of public provision of basic education (including employable skills training) and health for all will have counterproductive outcomes socially, politically and economically. The Asian Development Bank (ADB, 1998, pp. 187–219) asserts that without an initial skills base, no amount of new/high technology imports will lead to sustained development. Along with investment in human resources, which provides the social infrastructure, the role of investment in physical infrastructure to provide energy, roads, transportation and modern telecommunication system should not be ignored.

The conflicting demands on public policy towards social and labour issues, requires a delicate balancing act. Flexible conditions in the labour market can be created only when the transitional problems of change are taken care of. Public policy should aim at creating more jobs than are displaced within the short term. Mere emphasis on retraining and redeployment will not solve the problem. Skills retraining and social safety net efforts need to be reviewed. Simultaneously, local level initiatives for job creation should explore the linkages between hinterland resources and opportunities.

The database on labour in India is time-barred, inadequate and unreliable. Empirical studies are rare in India. As a result assessments are impressionistic, anecdotal or based on experiences and limited to case studies which are not necessarily representative. This raises questions about objectivity and, occasionally, even doubts about the paralysis of analysis due to the poverty of poverty data, unemployability of unemployment data and counterproductive information base on productivity, etc. Much of the labour on labour statistics just does not deliver. For a systematic and objective assessment of the link between the intent, content and outcome of public policy changes we need to pay urgent attention to the creation of a timely, adequate and reliable database. In the absence of such a database, debates on policy outcomes would be dysfunctional and obstruct political consensus and labour and social issues.

REFERENCES

Ahluwalia, I.S. and I.M.D Little (1998). *India's Economic Reforms and Development: Essays for Manmohan Singh*. New Delhi: Oxford University Press.

All India Management Association (AIMA) (1998). *Towards India Inc. Strategies for Competitiveness*. Background papers for the 25th National Management Convention at Calcutta. New Delhi: AIMA.

Alternative Survey Group (1999). *Alternative Economic Survey 1 of Structural Adjustment*. New Delhi: Rainbow Publishers Limited. Lokayan and Azadi Bachao Andolan. p. 88.

Asian Development Bank (1998). *Asian Development Outlook*. Manila: ADB.

Babu, V.V. (1992). *India's Economic Reforms and Security Perceptions*. New Delhi: Economy and Trade.

Baru, S. (1999). 'Managing the Politics of the Economy'. Paper presented at the National Management Forum, 1999 on Managing the Indian State organized by the All India Management Association at Delhi on 28 May 1999. New Delhi: AIMA. Mimeo.

Bengal Chamber of Commerce (1997). *Productivity on the Rise in West Bengal*. Calcutta.

Bhagwati, J. (1993). *India in Transition*. Delhi: Oxford University Press.

Bhattacharya, B.B. (1998). *Financial Reforms and Financial Development in India*. New Delhi: Excel Books.

Chandrasekhar, C.P. and Jayati Ghosh (1999). 'The Indian Economic Reform Process and the Implications of the Southeast Asian Crisis'. Paper presented at the National Workshop on Economic Reforms and Labour: Lessons for India from the East Asian Experience organized by the International Labour Organization at Delhi, 25-26 May 1999. New Delhi: International Labour Organization. Mimeo.

Chelliah, R.J. (1998). *Towards Sustainable Growth: Essays in Fiscal and Financial Sector Reforms*. New Delhi: Oxford University Press.

CMIE (1998). *National Income Statistics*. Mumbai. February 1998, Chapter 14.

Debroy, B. (1998). 'Reforms and the External Sector'. *Productivity*. 39(3). October-December. pp. 361-372.

Delhi Science Forum (1998). *Alternative Economic Survey*. New Delhi.

Desai, A. (ed) (1998). *Economic Reforms—The Next Step*. Vols. 1&2. *The Golden Jubilee Celebration of India's Independence August 1997-August 1998 Symposium Papers*. New Delhi: Rajiv Gandhi Institute for Contemporary Studies and Frank Bros & Co. (Publishers) Ltd.

Dreze, J. and Sen, A. (1995). *India—Economic Development and Social Opportunity*. Delhi: Oxford University Press.

Fallon, Peter R. and Robert E.B. Lucas (1991). 'The Impact of Changes in Job Security Regulations in India and Zimbabwe'. *The World Bank Economic Review*. 5(3), pp. 395-413.
Gangopadhyay, S. and W. Wadhwa (1998). 'Economic Reforms and Labour'. *Economic and Political Weekly*. 30 May, pp. L40-47.
Ghemawat, P. and M. Patibandla (1998). 'India's Exports since the Reforms'. *Economic and Political Weekly*. 16 May, pp. 1196-1198.
Government of India—Economic Development Council. (1989). 'Report on the Current Economic Situation and Priority Areas for Action'. Ministry of Finance. December.
Guha, B.P. (1997a). *Challenges of Economic Reforms: Impact on Labour and Industrial Relations*. New Delhi: BR Publications.
Guha, B.P. (1997b). *Voluntary Retirement Schemes*. New Delhi: Shri Ram Centre for Industrial Relations and Human Resources.
Gupta, S.P. (1998). *Social Security: Burden of the Backlog*. The Observer Group of Publications: Agenda 2000. pp. 1329-1330.
Gupte, V. (1986). *Voluntary Retirement Schemes*. Mumbai: Maniben Kara Institute and New Delhi: Friedrich Ebert Foundation.
Hakeem, M.A. and C.S. Venkata Ratnam (1997). 'Is There a Brain Drain in the Public Sector?' New Delhi: Standing Conference on Public Enterprises. Mimeo.
Hashim, S.R. (1998). 'Employment and Poverty—Aspects Requiring Policy Focus'. Valedictory address at the Conference of the Indian Society for Labour Economics at Hyderabad. 31 December.
Hind Mazdoor Sabha (1998). *Impact of New Economic Policies on Industrial Relations at Company Level*. Report of HMS-ICFTU-RDTP National Training Workshop. 25-26 April. New Delhi: HMS.
ILO-SAAT (1996). *Economic Reforms and Labour*. New Delhi.
ILO (1998). *World Employment Report, 1997-98*. Geneva.
ILO (1999). *Decent Work*. 87th International Labour Conference—Report of the Director-General. Geneva.
IMD (1997). *World Competitiveness Report*. Lausanne.
Jalan, B. (1996). *India's Economic Policy: Preparing for the 21st Century*. New Delhi. Viking.
Johri, C.K. (1995). 'Work Ethos and Globalisation of Indian Economy'. *Indian Journal of Industrial Relations*. 30(3), January, pp. 297-307.
Joshi, V. and I.M.D. Little (1996). *India's Economic Reforms 1991-2000*. Delhi: Oxford University Press.
Kapila, U. (1995). *Recent Developments in Indian Economy. Part IV—After 4 Years of Economic Reforms*. New Delhi: Academic Foundation.
Kelkar, V.L. and V.V. Bhanoji Rao (1996). *India: Development Policy Imperatives*. New Delhi: Tata McGraw-Hill.
Kotler, P. (1994). *Marketing Management: Analysis, Planning, Implementation and Control*. Englewood Cliffs: Prentice-Hall.
Kuruvilla, S. (1997). 'Globalisation and Industrial Relations'. Paper prepared for the ILO. New York: Cornell University. Mimeo.
Kuruvilla, S. (1999). 'Impact of Globalisation on Economies and IR/HR Systems—Theory and Evidence'. A. Sivananthiran and C.S. Venkata Ratnam (eds). *Globalisation and Industrial Relations in South Asia*. New Delhi: Indian Industrial Relations Association and ILO-South Asia Multidisciplinary Team.

Mazumdar, D. (1997). 'Labour Markets, Trade Patterns and Workers' Living Standards'. *Economic and Political Weekly.* 1-8 March, pp. 463-474.
Majumdar, S.K. and P. Chibber (1998). 'Are Liberal Foreign Investment Policies Good for India?' *Economic and Political Weekly.* 7 February, pp. 267-270.
Marshal, A. (1930). *Principles of Economics.* London: Macmillan. pp. 385-386.
Masilamani, S. (1995). *Economic Reforms and Trade Unions in India.* New Delhi: Friedrich Ebert Foundation and Shri Ram Centre for Industrial Relations and Human Resources.
Porter, M. (1980). *Competitive Strategy.* New York: Free Press.
Rao, S.L. (1994). *Economic Reforms and Indian Markets.* New Delhi: Wheeler.
Sen, A. (1997). 'Development Thinking at the Beginning of the 21st Century'. London School of Economics Suntory and Toyota International Centres for Economics and Related Disciplines. The Development Economics Research Programme Working Paper 2. March.
Sen, R. (1996). 'The Future of Trade Unionism and Trade Unions in the Future'. *IIRA Newsletter.* March. pp. 15-20.
Sengupta, N.K. (1994). *Unshaking Indian Economy.* New Delhi: Vikas.
Shyamsunder (1998). 'Economic Reforms and Industrial Relations System in India. Some Issues for Discussion'. *Economic and Political Weekly.* 6 June, pp. 1379-1384.
The Statesman (1998). 'Proposal to Retire 11,000 Workers from Nine PSUs'. 9 September.
UNDP (1994). *Human Development Report.* Washington DC: UNDP.
UNDP (1997). *Human Development Report.* New York: Oxford University Press.
UNDP (1998). *Human Development Report.* New York: Oxford University Press.
Venkata Ratnam, C.S. (1997). *Competitive Labour Policies and Labour Laws in Indian States.* LARGE (Legal Adjustments and Reforms for Globalising the Economy) Policy Paper 24. New Delhi: Allied Publishers.
Venkata Ratnam, C.S. (1998). 'Multinational Companies in India'. *The International Journal of Human Resource Management.* 9(4) August, pp. 567-589.
Venkata Ratnam, C.S. (1999). 'The Reform Process and Social Dialogue'. Paper presented at the National Workshop on Economic Reforms and Labour: Lessons for India from the East Asian Experience organized by the International Labour Organization at Delhi. 25-26 May 1999. New Delhi: International Labour Organization. Mimeo.
Wadhwa, C.D. (1994). *Economic Reforms in India and the Market Economy.* New Delhi: Allied Publishers.
World Bank (1995). *World Development Report: Workers in an Integrating World.* New York: Oxford University Press.
World Bank (1995). *Achievements and Challenges.* Washington DC: World Bank.
World Bank (1998). *India: 1998 Macroeconomic Update.* Washington DC: World Bank.

FIVE

Competitive Labour Policies and Labour Laws in Indian States

In the wake of the so-called 'New Economic Policy' (NEP), there was widespread expectation in certain quarters that the time had come for labour policies to be dovetailed with industrial policies so that both moved in a unified direction. There was much talk about the so-called 'Exit Policy'. Till 6 December 1992, the Congress Party had the tacit support of the Bharatiya Janata Party (BJP) whereby the former could show a decisive shift towards the right. But the Ayodhya crisis snapped the Congress's support base in the Vishwa Hindu Parishad (VHP) and the BJP. The Congress Party had to anchor itself to the left for support. Then came the 'prestigious' speech of the prime minister at the Davos conference where he said something to the effect that 'People did not elect me to deprive them of their livelihood'. The pendulum stopped swinging thereafter due to the compulsions of successive coalition governments which increased the political uncertainty following three general elections during 1996 and 1999. In October 1999, the government constituted the Second National Commission on Labour at the recommendation of the Indian Labour Conference.

The impact of the new policies on labour and other social issues has been a major source of concern. New investments are taking place not where job losses are the most but where job losses are relatively less. As a result, job creation, if at all, is not occurring where it is needed most. Productive employment creation and the maintaining of the social order being the responsibility of the state, state governments will have to strive hard to preserve employment and create a conducive environment for further job creation. It then becomes imperative for them to review their industrial and labour policies to woo investment and facilitate the growth of industry and business for further job creation. Whether and how state governments can make a difference in adopting and practising competitive labour policies is, then, a moot question.

Labour is in the concurrent list of the Constitution. According to Article 246 of the Constitution of India, both Parliament and state legislatures can enact laws on aspects relating to employment, trade unions, industrial disputes, social security, etc. Generally speaking, the state government is the appropriate authority for administering central laws, too, in most cases.

The Government of India articulated and implemented policies on social and labour issues till the late 1960s when the same party used to rule at the centre and in most states. Post 1969, however, non-Congress and regional parties began coming into power in the states and four times at the centre. State governments then began to ask for greater provincial autonomy including in matters relating to labour, which has been on the 'concurrent list' since British days. Both trade unions and employers' organizations submitted memoranda reflecting their views on labour issues to the Sarkaria Commission set up in the 1980s to review centre–state relations. The problem has been compounded by the definition of 'appropriate government' particularly in the case of central government undertakings with plants or operations extending to more than one state. While the administrative ministry in the central government is responsible for the overall performance of the enterprise, labour–management relations in plants comes, in several cases, under the jurisdiction of the government of the state where the enterprise is located. Political differences among the parties in power cause, not infrequently, problems for individual enterprises. Also, when major policy issues are discussed at labour ministers' conferences, government representatives take a stand on the lines of the ideology/position of the ruling party at the centre and/or the states. Given the diversity of the context, the seriousness of the political ferment and pendulum-like swinging of government policies over the years, one wonders whether India has ever had or will ever have a unified labour policy.

PLURALISM AND DIVERSITY AT THE STATE LEVEL

Section 2 (a) (i) of the Industrial Disputes Act lists the establishments/industries carried on by or under the authority of the central government or by a railway company or concerning any such controlled industry as may be specified in this behalf by the central government or in relation to industrial disputes concerning a list of specific establishments/industries in the central sphere for which the central government is the appropriate government while the remaining industries/establishments are in the state sphere even for the implementation of central laws. The issue becomes complex in a steel plant with captive mines. If the plant is in Bihar, the state government will have jurisdiction on labour matters in the steel plant but the central government will be the appropriate authority on issues relating to labour employed in the mines of the same company in the same state. Over the years, the interpretation of the term 'appropriate government' has, nevertheless, been subject to several judicial pronouncements, some of which have given rise to divergence from the scope of the definition originally envisaged by the government under the act.

India is known for its regional imbalances, which have become further skewed over time. According to the 1991 census, 50 per cent of the 285 million main workers were in seven states while India comprised twenty-five states and seven union territories. Three states, namely, Maharashtra, Gujarat and Tamil Nadu, accounted for over 43 per cent of the disbursements by all India financial institutions up to March 1994. These three states also accounted for 40 per cent of the total foreign investment approvals for the period 1991–1994. If the size of a state and its population are reckoned, the per capita disbursement by all-India financial institutions at Rs 3,598 was 13.5 times higher than that for Bihar (Rs 265). Even during the plan period, the four richest states, which have 40 per cent of the population, attracted almost 48 to 49 per cent of investment and the five poorer states, with about 50 per cent of population, had only 42 per cent of the public sector investments (Observer Research Foundation 1996). Even in terms of sheer size, Uttar Pradesh has a population of 139 million while Sikkim has a population of only 0.4 million. In between there are eight maritime states—which include Maharashtra with a population of 79 million and Kerala with a population of 29 million—which account for 80 per cent of the revenue of the central government.

State governments are in business too. According to a report of the Comptroller and Auditor General of India, the number of state government companies increased significantly from 168 in 1969–70 to 840 in 1986–87 and to over 1,000 in the 1990s. In every state, the state electricity boards and state road transport corporations were the biggest, with a total investment of over Rs 137 crore in 1986–87, spread unevenly across states. The electricity boards had a negative return of 13 per cent on average. The cumulative losses of 514 state government enterprises were over Rs 20 billion.

Some state governments are endeavouring to make adjustments and improve their image so that they can attract investment and save/create jobs. While the central government did not resort to even a single overt privatization till the end of 1999, many states have gone ahead with open privatization. Raipuria (Observer Research Foundation, 1996) refers to the privatization and restructuring of electricity boards (Meghalaya, Orissa, Andhra Pradesh, Haryana, and more recently Uttar Pradesh), profit-sharing with employees (Rajasthan Roadways), renewal fund on the lines of the National Renewal Fund (Rajasthan) for employees of sick units which were closed, issue of project-specific bonds (Gujarat and Rajasthan) and promotion of tourism through the private sector (Sikkim). Andhra Pradesh, Orissa, Karnataka and many other states also resorted to open privatization. Several state governments have a variety of welfare programmes as well. Some political parties continue to oppose privatization of central public sector undertakings in their own states, regardless of whether they are in opposition or a part of the ruling coalition at the Centre even though in their own states as a ruling party they pursue privatization, often vigorously. Among these, the employment guarantee schemes in Maharashtra and West Bengal and the welfare funds/schemes in Kerala and Tamil Nadu merit mention.

The industrial relations scenario in different states in India presents glaring contradictions. In West Bengal, politically affiliated trade unions, particularly those subscribing to the leftist ideology, are widespread. In Maharashtra—which is the hub of economic activity and widely acclaimed as the commercial capital of the country—enterprise-level unions, which are independent and unaffiliated to any central federation or political party, have a major presence. In Karnataka, particularly, Bangalore, which has been christened the Silicon Valley of India, many firms in the new, non-traditional, high-tech industries are 'union-free'.

In some parts of Gujarat, 'footpath unionism' is growing. Briefless lawyers, among others, can mobilize signatures of seven disgruntled employees, register a union and pursue their individual grievances on the lines of contingent litigation. The leaders of such unions will have a sizeable share in the compensation that such workers might get. In Maharashtra, the growing sickness in textile mills and opportunities to reap a bonanza through the real estate business in sick and closed mills opened new vistas for a formidable link between real estate underworld mafia and trade unions. In some of the industrially and socially backward areas of Andhra Pradesh and Bihar, for instance, radical social movements in some cases assumed the role of trade unions also and began to pursue the cause of workers through militant means, undermining the role of traditional trade unions and making a mockery of the authority of the employer, the district administration and the local police.

Unions may be declining in some parts of the country, but not in Orissa, where union leadership is focused on organizing small- and medium-scale industries. Interestingly, 50 per cent of the labour courts and industrial tribunals in the country are located in three states, viz., Maharashtra, Madhya Pradesh and Gujarat (Table 5.1)

CHANGES IN LABOUR LAW/POLICY AT THE STATE LEVEL

During the post-liberalization period, the central government has dilly-dallied on labour reform due to the fear of political risks. Given the pressure for wooing investment and generating new jobs, some state governments have announced far-reaching changes.

TABLE 5.1 State-Wise Details of Labour Courts and Industrial Disputes

The Number of Labour Courts (LCs), Industrial Tribunals (ITs) and Labour Court-cum-Industrial Tribunals (LC & IT) set up by State Governments and Union Territory Administrations as on 31.10.1998.

Sl.	Name of the State/ Union Territory	No. of Labour Courts (LCs)	No of Industrial Tribunals (ITs)	No. of Labour Courts-cum-Industrial Tribunals (LC & IT)	Total
1.	Andaman & Nicobar	1	1	0	2
2.	Andhra Pradesh	6	2	3	11
3.	Arunachal Pradesh	0	0	0	0
4.	Assam	2	3	0	5
5.	Bihar	14	3	0	17
6.	Chandigarh	6	0	1	7
7.	Dadra & Nagar Haveli	1	0	0	1
8.	Daman & Diu	1	0	0	1
9.	Delhi	10	3	0	13
10.	Goa	1	0	1	2
11.	Gujarat	41	17	0	58
12.	Himachal Pradesh	0	0	1	1
13.	Haryana	0	0	7	7
14.	Jammu & Kashmir	0	0	1	1
15.	Kerala	4	5	0	9
16.	Karnataka	12	4	0	16
17.	Lakshadweep	0	0	0	0
18.	Meghalaya	1	0	1	2
19.	Maharashtra	40	28	0	68
20.	Manipur	0	1	0	1
21.	Madhya Pradesh	26	5	0	31
22.	Mizoram	0	1	0	1
23.	Nagaland	1	1	0	2
24.	Orissa	3	1	0	4
25.	Punjab	6	1	0	7
26.	Pondicherry	3	1	0	4
27.	Rajasthan	1	1	7	9
28.	Sikkim	0	0	0	0
29.	Tripura	3	3	0	6
30.	Tamil Nadu	10	1	0	11
31.	Uttar Pradesh	19	6	0	25
32.	West Bengal	2	9	0	11
	Total	214	97	22	333

Recognition of Bargaining Agent

In India, the Trade Unions Act, 1926, which is a central legislation, provides for registration, not recognition. Unions generally press for collective bargaining rights, and shun any legislation on recognition. Some state governments (for instance, Maharashtra, Gujarat and Rajasthan) have provided for certain criteria through state-level labour laws. For years Andhra Pradesh has been following secret ballot as a method of trade union recognition. Between 1991 and 1996, two state governments—Orissa and West Bengal—introduced, for the first time in the country, secret ballot through tripartite social dialogue at the state level for the purpose of trade union recognition. The Kerala legislature also passed a similar legislation which is awaiting the assent of the President of India, before the new law on secret ballot in that state comes into operation.

The problem with secret ballots, however, is that it does not resolve all the contentious issues. For example,

- The complexities associated with the campaigning for and conduct of elections.
- Would the tenure of recognition be coterminus with the currency of a subsisting collective agreement?
- What would be the role and rights of unrecognized union(s)?
- What happens in states that choose to give individuals the right to raise industrial disputes on any aspect, including those aspects which were a part of the union–management agreement?
- Inability or indifference to deal with situations that produce different results in membership verification even as secret ballot results in the concerned enterprises continue to be valid.

While secret ballots in Orissa have thrown up quite a few surprises due to anti-incumbency negative vote, West Bengal is yet to make the secret ballot a preferred way of choosing a collective bargaining agent. Orissa has been holding secret ballots, but West Bengal chooses to defer secret ballots except when demanded by parties at the enterprise level.

Simplified Labour Inspection

From June 1991 to September 2000, some state governments simplified the process of labour inspection. In Uttar Pradesh, a labour inspector can carry out inspection only after prior consent of an officer of the rank of Labour Commissioner or District Magistrate.

Box 1

TRADE UNION RECOGNITION RULES IN SELECT INDIAN STATES

ORISSA: In pursuance of the Industrial Policy Resolution of Orissa, 1992, and as per the unanimous resolution of the State Implementation and Evaluation Committee, the Verification of Membership and Recognition of Trade Union Rules, 1994 was brought into force with effect from 1 November 1994. The special features of these rules include:

- Where only one union is functioning at least for a period of one year after registration, it will be recognized as the sole bargaining agent.
- The union which secures the maximum number of votes, but not less than 30 per cent of the total number of votes polled, shall be entitled to be recognized. In the event of two or more unions getting an equal number of votes, the union having the longer period of existence after registration shall be declared duly voted by the employees.
- In the event of none of them securing 30 per cent votes, the labour commissioner shall constitute a 'Negotiating Committee' for the industry based on the number of votes polled by each union in the verification process subject to the condition that each union shall have at least one member on the negotiation committee. The total membership of the committee shall not exceed nine.
- In order to qualify to be represented in the negotiation committee, a union must have secured a minimum of 10 per cent of the total number of votes polled.

MAHARASHTRA: Under the BIR Act, 1946, registered unions are classified as follows:

- Representative union with at least 25 per cent membership in an industry in a local area.

(Contd.)

- Qualified union with at least 5 per cent membership in an industry in a local area.
- Primary union in an undertaking with at least 15 per cent membership and complying with the conditions laid down in respect of the approved union.

To mitigate interunion rivalry, a code of discipline was adopted at the 16th Indian Labour conference and a procedure for verification of strength was laid down, which must be followed by unions for getting recognition. Where there are several unions in an industry, the one with the largest membership will be recognized as the representative union.

The BIR Act, 1946 was initially made applicable to the textile, sugar and transport industries and cooperative banks. It was extended to some other industries such as engineering throughout the state via the Bombay Industrial Relations (Extension and Amendment) Act, 1964.

RAJASTHAN (Proposed rules): To be eligible for registration, a union should have at least 15 per cent of its workforce employed in the unit of an industry. When two or more unions fulfil the above condition, the union having the largest membership of workers employed in the unit of the industry shall be registered.

Rajasthan has reduced the scope of labour inspection, simplified forms and exempted several establishments from the purview of labour inspection. The system of separate inspection under industrial labour laws has been done away with. Instead, there is going to be only a common inspection of industry in accordance with a checklist prepared for the purpose. The number of inspections under labour laws have been reduced to 5 per cent of the establishments in the small-scale and tiny sectors and 10 per cent in other sectors selected on a random basis. Small-scale industrial units are now required to send only one return and display one common notice covering all labour laws. The state government has special powers to prohibit strikes or lockouts in general or in connection with any industrial dispute, if, in the opinion of the state government, it is necessary for securing public safety or convenience or maintenance of public order of supplies and services essential to the life of the community or for maintaining industrial peace.

Andhra Pradesh too has simplified the number and the contents of the forms under the AP Factories Rules and has issued the revised formats on CD-ROM.

New Thrust in Labour Policy

The Kerala government announced a labour policy, as part of its new industrial policy in 1994, which contained, among others, the following provisions:

- The entrepreneur will have the full right over hiring of labour and shall not be inhibited by any claims from the sons of the soil displaced persons from acquired land, construction/contract labour and dependants of employees.
- All restrictive labour practices, including intimidation, *gherao* and *dharna* inside the factory, harassment of managers and their families and extortion of any kind including 'attimari' will be treated as criminal offences and dealt with accordingly.
- The management will have the prerogative to deploy workers in any section of the unit as part of a multicraft approach.
- Disciplinary action against individual workmen will be taken in accordance with the procedure provided in the Industrial Disputes Act.
- Unions will be recognized for participation in labour–management negotiations only if they have a minimum membership of 15 per cent of the total number of employees. The government will bring about a comprehensive legislation for this purpose.
- The government will encourage long-term agreements. Long-term enhancement in wages will be linked to productivity. The possibility of long-term bonus settlement will also be explored.
- The government will do all that is in its power to avoid work stoppages during the first five years of a project. Even after the first five years, any dispute that might arise, involving stoppage of work and lowering of production, will be discouraged.
- In all new enterprises with an investment of Rs 300 million or more, an officer of the labour department of appropriate status

and with adequate power will be exclusively appointed at the cost of the government for the first five years to ensure that labour disputes do not lead to any stoppage of work.
- The viability of an industrial unit depends to a considerable extent on whether construction activity can be completed within the scheduled time and at the estimated cost. Work stoppages, whether due to labour dispute or non-fulfilment of obligations by contractors will not be tolerated.
- Industrial relations committees will be constituted in all existing and potential industries. These committees, it is hoped will ultimately create an atmosphere of complete understanding between labour and management in all industrial areas.
- Existing institutional machinery will be strengthened and innovations introduced to ensure that disputes are resolved quickly and without any disruption of productive activity. A joint cell of the labour department will be constituted to study what changes need to be made in laws, rules and regulations and in the administrative and institutional arrangement to achieve these objectives.

Many of these policy procurements have remained on paper, and more so when the left front alliance replaced the Congress as the ruling party in the state.

Permissions for Closure, Retrenchment or Lay-off

Under Chapter V-B of the Industrial Disputes Act, 1947, prior permission of the appropriate government is required for closure, retrenchment and lay-off. The general feeling in India is that the government usually refuses permission for closures, retrenchment and lay-offs. But it is not quite so. As seen from Table 5.2 the central government has been more liberal in granting permission than any state government. Information on the subject is not available from all states, including some industrially important states such as Maharashtra and West Bengal. The situation varies from state to state. In Tamil Nadu, during 1991–95, 38 per cent of the applications for closure/retrenchment/lay-off were considered in favour of employers, 53 per cent in favour of workers and in the remaining 11 per cent a decision was kept in abeyance. Evidently, of course, there were more permissions for lay-offs, than for retrenchment. West Bengal, a state ruled by the

TABLE 5.2 Applications Received Under Chapter V-B of the ID Act, 1947 for Permission for Closures, Retrenchment and Lay-off in Industries During 1991–95

State/U.T.	Closures				Retrenchment				Lay-off			
	A	B	C	D	A	B	C	D	A	B	C	D
Andhra Pradesh	17	1	8	8	3	–	3	–	22	5	15	2
Assam	–	–	–	–	4	–	4	–	2	–	2	–
Goa	–	–	–	–	1	–	1	–	2	–	2	–
Gujarat	6	6	–	–	21	5	12	4	23	2	14	7
Manipur	–	–	–	–	1	1	–	–	3	1	1	1
Nagaland	–	–	–	–	1	–	–	1	–	–	–	–
Orissa	–	–	–	–	–	–	–	–	1	1	–	–
Punjab	–	–	–	–	4	–	2	2	4	–	2	2
Tamil Nadu	22	6	11	5	2	1	1	–	2	–	2	–
A and N Islands	1	–	–	1	21	7	14	–	56	25	28	3
Daman and Diu	–	–	–	–	–	–	–	–	–	–	–	–
Delhi	2	–	2	–	–	–	–	–	–	–	–	–
Pondicherry	1	–	1	–	–	–	–	–	–	–	–	–
Rajasthan	1	–	1	–	3	1	2	–	–	–	–	–
State Sphere	50	13	23	14	61	15	39	7	115	34	66	15
Central Sphere	21	16	5	–	39	18	21	–	4	–	4	–
Grand Total	71	29	28	14	100	33	60	7	119	34	70	15

– = Nil.
A = No. of applications received.
B = No. of cases in which permission was granted.
C = No. of cases in which permission was not granted.
D = Under process/withdrawn/court case.

Source: Government of India (1996). Annual Report, 1995–96, Ministry of Labour, New Delhi, p. 28.

Note: Information in respect of remaining states/union territories is awaited.

Marxist party for over two decades, was among states more cautious in granting permission for lay off or retrenchment or closure. But this is the state where, for several years, 95 per cent of the mandays lost due to industrial strife were on account of lock-outs, and only 5 per cent due to strikes.

Wages

The role of the state in fixing minimum wages is a hotly debated issue in the context of global competition. There is no uniform wage policy for all sectors of the economy. Wage costs as a percentage of turnovers vary from less than 2 per cent in certain petrochemical firms to over 100 per cent in sick units. In many firms in different sectors they are usually well below 20 per cent. In fact, they vary widely even in a single company. For instance in Coal India, wage costs are less than 15 per cent in new, open-cast mines in Mahanadi Coalfields and 60 per cent in old, sick, underground mines in Eastern Coalfields and Bharat Coking Coal Limited. The average labour cost for Coal India as a whole is less than 30 per cent.

Although the Minimum Wages Act, 1948 is a central legislation, state governments (and the central government where it is the 'appropriate government') are responsible for the constitution of tripartite minimum wages advisory bodies to recommend minimum wages. Often state governments tend to be populist, and unilaterally declare hikes in minimum wages because they are sure that unions will back them in ratification and hence opposition if any from employers can be easily overcome. Minimum wages in India vary widely across states (Table 5.3) and within a state across sectors. For instance, as of 1 October 1998, in Maharashtra alone, minimum wages for unskilled workers vary from Rs 42.46 to over Rs 85.92. In Kerala range between Rs 30 to Rs 157.81. In Delhi, the range of minimum and maximum wages at minimum wages level is nil (Rs 90.30).

Adherence to wage board recommendations is also not uniform throughout the country. Wage boards have become unpopular for a variety of reasons. Currently, there is only one wage board working as against nearly 20 in the 1970s. The recommendations of the Bachawat Wage Board in the mid-1980s were not implemented by 910 out of 1563 newspaper establishments even till a decade later. Meanwhile, another wage board was set up in 1995 which submitted its report in 1999. Over two-fifths of the newspaper establishments which did not implement the recommendations were located in West Bengal and Bihar. In West Bengal, 15 of 420 establishments implemented the Bachawat award, fully or partially, while in Bihar, 112 of 245 establishments implemented it (fully or partially). Although over one-third of the newspaper establishments in the country are located in these two states, the percentage of establishments complying with the wage board recommendations is abysmally poor in these states.

TABLE 5.3　State-wise Details of Minimum Wages (As in 1999)

Central/State Government/ Union Territory	No. of Employments for which Minimum Wages have been Fixed/Revised	@ Range of Minimum Wages Per Day (in Rs)	
		Minimum	Maximum as on 1.10.98
(1)	(2)	(3)	(4)
(i) **Central Government**	44	46.22	84.12
(ii) **State**			
1. Andhra Pradesh	60	27.00	63.19
2. Arunachal Pradesh	25	35.60	37.60
3. Assam	62	32.80	55.80
4. Bihar	74	38.61	51.00
5. Goa	23	21.00	125.00
6. Gujarat	49	58.80	79.20
7. Haryana	56	70.12	73.12
8. Himachal Pradesh	24	26.00	45.75
9. Jammu & Kashmir	18	30.00	30.00
10. Karnataka	59	26.00	74.00
11. Kerala	40	30.00	157.81
12. Madhya Pradesh	36	49.46	56.46
13. Maharashtra	62	42.46	85.92
14. Manipur	5	44.65	49.50
15. Meghalaya	22	35.00	35.00
16. Mizoram	3	45.00	45.00
17. Nagaland	36	25.00	25.00
18. Orissa	83	42.50	42.50
19. Punjab	60	54.07	60.96
20. Rajasthan	38	32.00	44.00
21. Sikkim*	–	–	–
22. Tamil Nadu	60	22.40	82.72
23. Tripura	11	17.70	36.00
24. Uttar Pradesh	65	42.02	64.21
25. West Bengal	45	36.55	79.99
(iii) **Union Territories**			
26. Andaman & Nicobar Islands	5	50.00	86.77
27. Chandigarh	44	52.09	71.93
28. Dadra & Nagar Haveli	43	38.00	44.00
29. Daman and Diu	72	50.00	60.00
30. Delhi	29	90.30	90.30
31. Lakshadweep	9	41.46	41.46
32. Pondicherry	4	19.25	65.00

@ Excludes employments where wages were fixed on piece-rate basis.
* Minimum Wages Act, 1948 is yet to be extended and enforced.
Source: Government of India (Ministry of Labour) Annual Report, 1999–2000 p. 55.

The central government monitors about 18 of 68 central legislations on the various aspects of labour. More than half the states do not submit even statutory returns to the Labour Bureau, like the number of unions registered in their respective states and the number of workers enrolled in these unions. The data on mandays lost and accidents and the impact of both is also only cursory. Hence, the facts contained in the usually dated annual publication of the Labour Bureau invariably fail to present a true and fair picture of the labour scene in the states.

LIMITS TO THE POWERS OF THE STATES

There is a limit to the role and powers of the state governments, though. They are duty-bound to refer their enactments and amendments to the centre for the assent of the President of India. The central government may on its own, or upon being referred to by the President, tender advice to form the basis for the President's decision. The usual practice of the President's office is not to act rather than turn down the proposals for changes *per se*. Some years ago, the Tamil Nadu government raised the limit of the number of employees required in an establishment for application of certain central legislations (like the Factories Act and the Industrial Disputes Act) as well as for prior approvals for lay-offs, lock-outs and closures. Similarly, it took many years for Andhra Pradesh to get Presidential approval for its legislations concerning workers' participation in management and insurance for workers' affected by structural changes. Finally, of course, Andhra Pradesh did not go ahead with its proposals.

Thus it is seen that in the absence of the centre's concurrence, state-level initiatives on labour and social matters can make a mockery of labour being a concurrent subject in our Constitution. This, in short, is the snakes and ladders story of competitive labour policies in the country's political set-up. The potential for states to adopt competitive labour policies to woo investors appears enormous, but this entails political and social risks. Therefore, there is need for caution and restraint. Also, in the wake of the pressure to link international trade with social clause and the 1998 ILO Declaration on Fundamental Principles, it might become necessary for maintaining uniformity and consistency in aligning core labour standards—freedom of association, right of collective bargaining, non-discrimination, equal remuneration, child labour and forced labour—as envisaged in the relevant conventions of the ILO.

MARGINALIZING STATE GOVERNMENTS?

The agenda for the 33rd session of the Standing Labour Committee (September 1996) proposed that the central government may be the appropriate government with respect to: All central public sector undertakings/companies where the central government holds the majority of the paid-up capital; an establishment or undertaking having branches in more than one state; multinational companies; and disputes of national importance as may be specified by the central government through notification.

Further, under the present law, state governments are the appropriate government for contract labour even in respect of most of the industries under the central sphere. It is proposed to also bring contract labour within the central sphere in respect of all industries for which the central government is the appropriate government. Hitherto, even though minimum wage legislation is a central law, the fixation of minimum wages is the responsibility of state governments. Minimum wages vary widely across different states as several of them follow different criteria. The resultant disparities have largely been responsible for the flight of capital and labour. From time to time trade unions have demanded a national minimum wage. The National Commission on Labour (1969) considered that a uniform minimum monetary wage was neither feasible nor desirable. The 28th Indian Labour Conference (1985) discussed the subject and recommended that till such time as a national minimum wage is feasible, it would be desirable to have a regional minimum wage. A fresh proposal before the Standing Labour Committee seeks to introduce a national minimum wage.

Thus, effectively, the proposed changes seek to bring multinational companies, contract labour and minimum wage fixation, which are currently under the purview of state governments, under the jurisdiction of the central government.

Discussions with some of the representatives of employers and workers reveal that neither favours further devolution of labour matters from the concurrent to the state list. The employers, particularly, feel that the state governments tend to be more populist. Several even favour a transfer from the state to the central list. Most recognize the need for uniformity.

ISSUES FOR CONSIDERATION

Based on the foregoing analysis, the following issues emerge:

1. There is a need for a thorough review of the centre–state relations in the sphere of labour with respect to legislation, labour administration and labour judiciary. In a federal set-up, states shall have the power to legislate, and will be accountable for enforcing the provisions of law. The key issue, however, is how much uniformity and how much diversity can states have in labour matters.
2. In the context of a globalized market—an international trade regime (World Trade Organization) seeking to enforce international labour standards and eliminate the unfair competitive advantage based on exploitative wages, denial of the basic rights of freedom of association and collective bargaining, neglect of safety, health and environment and the non-provision of basic social and social security services—should wages and other aspects of compensating and caring for labour be taken out of competition? Is there not a need for a unified labour policy and labour laws on aspects concerning the core labour standards? (See also Chapter 10.)
3. Some states in India have been lagging behind, industrially and economically. Some have acquired a reputation for being hard to deal with. How can this perception be changed? Would legal changes influence the environment and the habits of people such that the 'desired' changes are conducive to further investment and job creation?
4. If harmonizing labour policies is a goal, changes in labour laws alone may not be sufficient and adequate. There is need for harmonizing the attitude/approach of the labour bureaucracy and labour judiciary through specialist cadres and continuing educational inputs that engender sensitivity towards both the socio-cultural and business imperatives in a rapidly changing world.

5. The focus should be people and harmonious relations among them, not laws and regulations. There is a need to evolve a culture of coexistence and codetermination in a spirit of mutuality and reciprocity, objectivity and fair play, trust and transparency. Citizens' attitudes to laws are contingent not merely on the quality of laws and law enforcement but a variety of other aspects that are woven into the fabric of society. In other words, laws alone cannot provide the ideal solution.

REFERENCES

Freeman, R.B. (1992). *Labour Market Institutions and Policies: Help or Hindrance.* Proceedings of the World Bank Annual Conference on Development Economics. Supplement to the World Bank Economic Review and World Bank Research Observer. Washington DC: World Bank. pp. 117-156.
Government of India (1996a). *Agenda: 33rd Session of the Standing Labour Committee, New Delhi, 13 September.* New Delhi: Ministry of Labour.
Government of India (1996b). *Agenda: 33rd Session of the Indian Labour Conference, New Delhi 23-25 October.* New Delhi: Ministry of Labour.
Government of India (1996c). *Annual Report, 1995-96.* New Delhi: *Ministry of Labour* (also 1998-99 report).
Government of India (1996d). *Report of the Working Group on Labour Policy: Ninth Five Year Plan (1997-2002).* New Delhi: Ministry of Labour.
International Labour Organisation (1991). *Report of the Director General to the 78th Session.* Geneva: ILO.
Nair, K.R. (1996). 'Kerala'. Venkata Ratnam, C.S. (ed.). *Economic Changes and Industrial Relations in Indian States.* New Delhi: Global Business Press.
Observer Research Foundation (1996). *Economic Reforms: The Role of the States and the Future of Centre State Relations.* New Delhi.
Papola, T.S. and G. Rodgers (eds) (1992). *Labour Institutions and Economic Development in India.* Geneva: International Institute for Labour Studies.
Venkata Ratnam, C.S. (1996). *Welfare to Moneyfare: A Study of Social Security Clauses in Collective Bargaining.* A study sponsored by UNDP and the Centre for Development Studies. New Delhi: International Management Institute.
World Bank (1995). *World Development Report—Workers in an Integrated World.* Washington DC: World Bank and Oxford University Press.

Appendix I
List of Important Labour Acts (as on 31-12-1991)

FACTORIES

Central

1. The Indian Boilers Act, 1923. Amended in 1929, 1937, 1939, 1942, 1947, 1949, 1952 and 1960.
2. The Cotton Ginning and Pressing Factories Act, 1925. Amended in 1939, 1942, 1950 and 1951.
3. The Factories Act, 1948. Amended in 1949, 1954, 1976 and 1987.

States

1. The Cotton Ginning and Pressing Factories (Bombay) (Amendment) Act, 1936. Amended in 1957.
2. C.P. and Berar Cotton Ginning and Pressing Factories (Amendment) Act, 1936 and 1947*.
3. The C.P. and Berar Cotton Ginning and Pressing Factories (Second Amendment) Act, 1947*.
4. The Cotton Ginning and Pressing Factories (Madras) (Amendment) Act, 1953.
5. The Cotton Ginning and Pressing Factories (Saurashtra) (Amendment) Act, 1956.

MINES

Central

1. The Mines Act, 1952. Amended in 1959 and 1983.
2. The Coal Mines (Conservation and Development) Act, 1974. Amended in 1985.

---

* Not in force in Maharashtra.

3. The Mines and Minerals (Regulation and Development) Act, 1957.
4. The Coking Coal Mines (Nationalisation) Act, 1972.
5. The Coal Mines (Nationalisation) Act, 1973.
6. The Coal Mines Nationalisation Laws (Amendment) Act, 1986.

State

1. The Bengal Mining Settlement Act, 1912.

PLANTATIONS

Central

1. The Tea Districts Emigrant Labour (Repeal) Act, 1970.
2. The Plantations Labour Act, 1951. Amended in 1953, 1960 and 1981.

State

1. The Jalpaiguri Labour Act, 1951.

TRANSPORT

Central

1. The Indian Railways Act, 1980. Amended in 1948, 1950, 1951, 1954, 1955, 1956 and 1957.
2. The Dock Workers (Regulation of Employment) Act, 1948. Amended in 1951, 1962, 1970 and 1988.
3. The Merchant Shipping Act, 1958. Amended in 1966, 1976 and 1977.
4. The Motor Transport Workers Act, 1961.

State

1. The Motor Transport Workers (West Bengal) (Amendment) Act, 1979.

SHOPS AND COMMERCIAL ESTABLISHMENTS

Central

1. The Weekly Holidays Act, 1942. Amended in 1951.

States

1. The Andhra Pradesh Shops and Establishments Act, 1966. Amended in 1969.
2. The Assam Shops and Establishments Act, 1948.
3. The West Bengal Shops and Establishments Act, 1963. Amended in 1965 and 1981.

4. The Bihar Shops and Establishments Act, 1953. Amended in 1959.
5. The Bombay Shops and Establishments Act, 1948. Amended in 1949 and 1960.
6. The Delhi Shops and Establishments Act, 1954. Amended in 1960 and 1970.
7. The Jammu & Kashmir Shops and Establishments Act, 1966.
8. The Kerala Shops and Commercial Establishments Act, 1960.
9. The Madhya Pradesh Shops and Commercial Establishments Act, 1958. Amended in 1967.
10. The Madras Shops and Establishments Act, 1947 (Also applied to Andhra Pradesh with certain modifications).
11. The Madras Catering Establishments Act, 1958. Amended in 1961.
12. The Mysore Shops and Establishments Act, 1961.
13. The Orissa Shops and Establishments Act, 1956. Amended in 1958.
14. The Punjab Shops and Commercial Establishments Act, 1958.
15. The Rajasthan Shops and Commercial Establishments Act, 1958.
16. The Saurashtra Shops and Establishments Act, 1955.
17. The Uttar Pradesh Dookan Aur Vanijya Adhisthan Adhiniyam, 1962.
18. The Pondicherry Shops and Establishments Act, 1964.
19. The Himachal Pradesh Shops and Commercial Establishments Act, 1969.
20. The Goa, Daman and Diu Shops and Establishments Act, 1973. Amended in 1984.
21. The Punjab Shops and Commercial Establishments (Haryana) (Amendment) Act, 1976.
22. The Gujarat Shops and Establishments (National Festivals and Other Holidays) Amendment Act, 1980.
23. The Gujarat Shops and Establishments (Employees' Life Insurance) Act, 1980.
24. The Bombay Shops and Establishments (Gujarat) (Amendment) Act, 1980.

WAGES AND BONUS

Central

1. The Payment of Wages Act, 1936. Amended in 1937, 1940, 1948, 1957, 1964, 1976, 1977 and 1982.
2. The Minimum Wages Act, 1948. Amended in 1954, 1957, 1961 and 1984.
3. The Payment of Bonus Act, 1965. Amended in 1959, 1972, 1973, 1974, 1975, 1976, 1978, 1980 and 1985.
4. The Equal Remuneration Act, 1976. Amended in 1987.

States

1. The Payment of Wages (Bombay) (Amendment) Act, 1953.
2. The Payment of Wages (Bombay) (Amendment and Validation) Act, 1959.

3. The Payment fo Wages (Madras) (Amendment and Validation) Act, 1959.
4. The Payment of Wages (Mysore) (Amendment) Act, 1952.
5. The Payment of Wages (Saurashtra) (Amendment) Act, 1955.
6. The Minimum Wages (Rajasthan) (Amendment and Validation) Act, 1969.
7. The Payment of Wages (Madhya Pradesh) (Amendment) Act, 1964.
8. The Tamil Nadu Payment of Subsistence Allowance Act, 1981.
9. The Payment of Wages (West Bengal) (Amendment) Act, 1981.
10. The Minimum Wages (Bihar) (Amendment) Act, 1988.
11. The Kerala Motor Transport Workers' Payment of Fair Wages Act, 1971. Amended in 1988.
12. The Andhra Pradesh Payment of Salaries and Pension and Removal of Disqualifications Act, 1953. Amended in 1989.

INDUSTRIAL HOUSING

Central

1. The Indian Dock Labourers Act, 1934. Amended in 1949, 1950, 1951, 1963 and 1964.

States

1. The Madhya Pradesh Housing Board Act, 1950.
2. The Uttar Pradesh Industrial Housing Act, 1955.
3. The Andhra Pradesh Housing Board Act, 1956.
4. The Punjab Industrial Housing Act, 1956.
5. The Mysore Housing Board Act, 1962.
6. The Assam State Housing Board Act, 1972.
7. The Jammu and Kashmir Housing Board Act, 1976.
8. The Tamil Nadu State Housing Board (Amendment) Act, 1977.

SAFETY AND WELFARE

Central

1. The Indian Dock Labourers Act, 1934. Amended in 1950 and 1951.
2. The Mica Mines Labour Welfare Fund Act, 1946. Amended in 1950, 1951 and 1980.
3. The Coal Mines Labour Welfare Fund Act, 1947. Amended in 1951, 1972 and 1981.
4. The Coal Mines (Conservation and Safety) Act, 1952. Amended in 1961.
5. The Iron Ore Mines Labour Welfare Cess Act, 1961. Amended in 1970.
6. The Limestone and Dolomite Mines Labour Welfare Fund Act, 1972.
7. The Beedi Workers Welfare Fund Act, 1976.
8. The Beedi Workers Welfare Cess Act, 1976. Amended in 1981.

9. The Iron Ore Mines and Manganese Ore Mines Labour Welfare Fund Act, 1976.
10. The Iron Ore Mines and Manganese Ore Mines Labour Welfare Cess Act, 1976. Amended in 1982 and 1983.
11. The Cine Workers' Welfare Fund Act, 1981. Amended in 1987.
12. The Dock Workers' (Safety, Health and Welfare) Act, 1986.
13. The Dangerous Machines (Regulation) Act, 1983.

States

1. The Bombay Smoke Nuisance Act, 1912. Amended in 1953.
2. The Bombay Labour Welfare Fund Act, 1953. Amended in 1956, 1961, 1966, 1970 and 1987.
3. The Uttar Pradesh Sugar and Power Alcohol Industries Labour Welfare and Development Fund Act, 1950.
4. The Uttar Pradesh Labour Welfare Fund Act, 1965.
5. The Mysore Labour Welfare Fund Act, 1965.
6. The Punjab Labour Welfare Fund Act, 1965.
7. The Maharashtra Mathadi, Hamal and other Manual Workers (Regulation of Employment and Welfare) Act, 1969. Amended in 1973.
8. The Tamil Nadu Labour Welfare Fund Act, 1972. Amended in 1982.
9. The Assam Tea Plantations Employees' Welfare Act, 1959.
10. The West Bengal Labour Welfare Fund Act, 1974. Amended in 1980.
11. The Kerala Toddy Workers' Welfare Fund (Amendment) Act, 1978.
12. The Punjab Labour Welfare Fund (Haryana) Act, 1965. Amended in 1978 and 1988.
13. The Gujarat Cashew Workers' Relief and Welfare Fund Act, 1979.
14. The Kerala Labour Welfare Fund Act, 1975.
15. The Kerala Coir Workers' Welfare Fund Act, 1987.
16. The Kerala Cashew Workers' Relief and Welfare Fund Act, 1979. Amended in 1987.
17. The Kerala Handloom Workers' Welfare Fund Act, 1989.
18. The Maharashtra Private Security Guards' (Regulation and Employment and Welfare) Act, 1981.

SOCIAL SECURITY

Central

1. The Fatal Accidents Act, 1855.
2. The Workmen's Compensation Act, 1923. Amended in 1924, 1925, 1929, 1933, 1937 (twice), 1938, 1939, 1942, 1946, 1948, 1959, 1962, 1976, 1977 and 1984.
3. The Employers' Liability Act, 1938. Amended in 1951 and 1952.
4. The War Injuries (Compensation Insurance) Act, 1943. Amended in 1950.

5. The Employees' State Insurance Act. 1948. Amended in 1951, 1966, 1975, 1984 and 1989.
6. The Coal Mines Provident Fund, Family Pensions and Bonus Schemes Act, 1948. Amended in 1950, 1951, 1965, 1971, 1972 and 1975.
7. The Employees' Provident Funds and Miscellaneous Provisions Act, 1952. Amended in 1953, 1956, 1958, 1960, 1962, 1963, 1965, 1971, 1973, 1976 and 1988.
8. The Maternity Benefit Act, 1961. Amended in 1972, 1973, 1976 and 1988.
9. Personal Injuries (Emergency Provision) Act, 1962. Amended in 1971.
10. The Personal Injuries (Compensation Insurance) Act, 1963. Amended in 1971.
11. The Seamen's Provident Fund Act, 1966.
12. The Payment of Gratuity Act, 1972. Amended in 1984 and 1987.

States

1. The Assam Tea Plantation Provident Fund Scheme Act, 1955.
2. The Bengal Rural and Unemployment Relief Act, 1939. Amended in 1941.

INDUSTRIAL RELATIONS

Central

1. The Trade Unions Act, 1926. Amended in 1928, 1942, 1947, 1960 and 1964.
2. The Industrial Employment (Standing Orders) Act, 1946. Amended in 1950, 1961, 1963, 1982 and 1983.
3. The Industrial Disputes (Bihar) Act. Amended in 1948, 1949, 1950, 1951 (thrice), 1952, 1953, 1954, 1955, 1956, 1957, 1964, 1965, 1971, 1972, 1976, 1982 and 1984.
4. The Industrial Disputes (Banking Companies) Decision Act, 1955. Amended in 1957 and 1972.
5. The Industrial Disputes (Banking and Insurance Companies) Act, 1949. Amended in 1952.
6. The Industrial Disputes (Appellate Tribunal) Act, 1950. Amended in 1956.
7. The Industrial Disputes (Amendment and Miscellaneous Provisions) Act, 1956.
8. The Working Journalists and Other Newspaper Employees' (Conditions of Service) and Miscellaneous Provisions Act, 1955. Amended in 1962, 1978, 1979 (Ordinance) and 1991.
9. The Working Journalists (Fixation of Rates of Wages) Act, 1958. Amended in 1962.
10. The Trade Unions (Recognition) Act, 1977.
11. The Industrial Reconstruction Bank of India Act, 1984.
12. The Administrative Tribunals Act, 1985. Amended in 1987.

States

1. The Bengal (West) Industrial Disputes Amendment Act, 1958. Amendment Act, 1958. Amended in 1971, 1973 and 1974.
2. The Bihar Essential Services (Maintenance) Act, 1947.
3. The Industrial Disputes (Bihar) (Amendment) Act, 1959.
4. The Bombay Adjudication Proceedings (Transfer and Continuance) Act, 1947.
5. The Bombay Industrial Relations Act, 1946. Amended in 1948 (thrice), 1949, 1953, 1955 and 1966.
6. The Bombay Industrial Relations (Gujarat Extension and Amendment) Act, 1961. Amended in 1962 and 1964.
7. The Industrial Employment (Standing Orders) (Bombay Saurashtra Amendment) Act, 1953.
8. The Industrial Employment (Standing Orders) (Bombay Amendment) Act, 1955 and 1957.
9. The C.P. and Berar Validation of Awards and Continuance of Proceedings (Industrial Disputes) Act, 1947.
10. The C.P. and Berar Industrial Disputes Settlement Act, 1947. Amended in 1947, 1951 and 1955.
11. The Indian Trade Unions (Madhya Pradesh Amendment) Act, 1963.
12. The Trade Unions (Madhya Pradesh Amendment) Act, 1968.
13. The Madhya Pradesh Industrial Relations Act, 1960. Amended in 1965.
14. The Madhya Pradesh Industrial Employment (Standing Orders) Act, 1961. Amended in 1965.
15. The Industrial Disputes (Madras Amendment) Act, 1959.
16. The Industrial Employment (Standing Orders) (Madras Amendment) Act, 1960.
17. The Mysore Essential Services (Maintenance) Act, 1943.
18. The Industrial Disputes (Mysore Amendment) Act, 1953.
19. The Maharashtra Recognition of Trade Unions and Prevention of Unfair Labour Practices Act, 1971.
20. The Mysore Industrial Disputes (Amendment and Repeal) Act, 1959.
21. The Mysore Labour (Administration) Act, 1952.
22. The Industrial Disputes (Orissa Amendment) Act, 1953.
23. The Industrial Disputes (Orissa Amendment) Act, 1958. Amended in 1987.
24. The Industrial Disputes (Rajasthan Amendment) Act, 1970.
25. The Industrial Disputes (Saurashtra Amendment) Act, 1963.
26. The Uttar Pradesh Industrial Disputes Act, 1947. Amended in 1950, 1951, 1953 and 1983.
27. The Uttar Pradesh Industrial Disputes (Amendment and Miscellaneous Provisions) Act, 1956. Amended in 1957.
28. The Maharashtra Industrial Relations (Validation of Certain Proceedings) Act, 1972.
29. The Bomaby Industrial Relations (Gujarat Amendment) Act, 1972.

30. The Bombay Industrial Relations and Industrial Disputes (Gujarat Amendment) Act, 1972.
31. The Industrial Disputes (Maharashtra) Act, 1947. Amended in 1973 and 1974.
32. The Industrial Disputes (West Bengal Amendment) Act, 1980.
33. The Industrial Disputes and Maharashtra Unemployment Allowances Payment to Workers in Factories (For Temporary Period), (Amendment) Act, 1981.
34. The Industrial Establishments (Conferment of Permanent Status to Workmen) Act, 1981.
35. The Industrial Disputes (Tamil Nadu Amendment) Act, 1982.
36. The Industrial Disputes (Madhya Pradesh) Act, 1947. Amended in 1983 and 1988.
37. The Tamil Nadu Industrial Establishments (Conferment of Permanent Status to Workmen) Act, 1981. Amended in 1985.

PROTECTION OF CHILDREN

Central

1. The Children (Pledging of Labour) Act, 1933.
2. The Employment of Children Act, 1938. Amended in 1939, 1948, 1949, 1951 and 1978.
3. The Child Labour (Prohibition and Regulation) Act, 1986*.

INDEBTEDNESS

States

1. The Assam Money Lenders' Act, 1934. Amended in 1954.
2. The Bengal Workmen's Protection Act, 1934. Amended in 1940.
3. The Bihar Workmen's Protection Act, 1948.
4. The Bombay Agricultural Debtors' Relief Act, 1947.
5. The Bombay Money Lenders' Act, 1946. Amended in 1948.
6. The C.P. and Berar Adjustment and Liquidation of Industrial Workers' Debt Act, 1936.
7. The C.P. and Berar Protection of Debtors' Act 1937.
8. The Agriculturists Loan (Coorg Amendment) Act, 1936.
9. The Coorg Debt Conciliation Act, 1940.
10. The Coorg Money Lenders' Act, 1939. Amended in 1946.
11. The Madras Debtors' Protection Act, 1934.
12. The Madras Workmen's Protection Act, 1941.

---

* The Employment of Children Act, 1938 has since been repealed by the Child Labour (Prohibition and Regulation) Act, 1986.

13. The Punjab Registration of Accounts Act, 1930.
14. The Punjab Relief Indebtedness Act, 1934.
15. The Punjab Debtors' Protection Act, 1936.
16. The Punjab Regulation of Money Lenders' Relief Act, 1954.
17. The Saurashtra Agricultural Debtors' Relief Act, 1954.
18. The Kerala Agricultural Workers' Act, 1974.
19. The West Bengal Relief of Rural Indebtedness Act, 1975.
20. The Tamil Nadu Debt Relief Act, 1976.
21. The Rajasthan Scheduled Debtors (Liquidation of Indebtedness) Act, 1976.
22. The Gujarat Rural Debtors Relief Act, 1976.

MISCELLANEOUS

Central

1. The Cotton Industry (Statistics) Act, 1926. Amended in 1950.
2. The Employment Exchanges (Compulsory Notification of Vacancies) Act, 1959.
3. The Collection of Statistics Act, 1953.
4. The Apprentices Act, 1961. Amended in 1972 and 1986.
5. The Beedi and Cigar Workers' (Conditions of Employment) Act, 1966.
6. The Contract Labour (Regulation and Abolition) Act, 1970.
7. The Central Labour Laws (Extension to Jammu and Kashmir) Act, 1970.
8. The Bonded Labour System (Abolition) Act, 1976.
9. The Sale Promotion Employees (Conditions of Service) Act, 1976. Amended in 1986.
10. The Coconut Act, 1977.
11. The Domestic Workers (Conditions of Service) Act, 1977.
12. The Essential Services Maintenance Act, 1981.
13. The Cine Workers and Cinema Theatre Workers (Regulation of Employment) Act, 1981. Amended in 1988.
14. The Inter-State Migrant Workmen (Regulation of Employment and Conditions of Service) Act, 1979.
15. The Repealing and Amending Act, 1988.
16. The Bharat Petroleum Corporation Limited (Determination of Conditions of Service of Employees) Act, 1988.
17. The Labour Laws (Exemption from Furnishing Returns and Maintaining Registers by Certain Establishments) Act, 1988.
18. The Life Insurance Corporation (Amendment) Act, 1981.

States

1. The Bombay Tenancy and Agricultural Lands Act, 1948.
2. The C.P. and Berar Regulation of Manufacture of Beedis (Agricultural Purpose) Act, 1948.

3. The Hyderabad Public Contractors' Labour Regulations and Fair Wage Clauses, 1951.
4. The Jammu and Kashmir Collection of Statistics Act, 1960.
5. The Kerala Industrial Establishments (National and Festival Holidays) Act, 1958.
6. The Madras Compulsory Labour Act, 1958.
7. The Madras Industrial Establishments (National and Festival Holidays) Act, 1958. Amended in 1964.
8. The Madras Beedi Industrial Premises (Regulations and Conditions of Work) Act, 1958.
9. The Orissa Compulsory Labour Act, 1948.
10. The Kerala Cigar and Beedi Industrial Premises (Regulation and Conditions of Work) Act, 1961.
11. The Pondicherry Industrial Establishments (National and Festival Holidays) Act, 1964. Amended in 1971.
12. The Punjab Industrial Establishments (National and Festival Holidays and Casual and Sick Leave) Act, 1965.
13. The U.P. Industrial Establishment (National Holidays) Act, 1961.
14. The Uttar Pradesh Industrial Undertakings (Special Provisions for Prevention of Unemployment) Act, 1966.
15. The Bombay Lifts Act, 1939 as extended to the province of Delhi.
16. The West Bengal Payment of Subsistence Allowance Act, 1969.
17. The Himachal Pradesh Industrial Establishments (National and Festival Holidays and Casual and Sick Leave) Act, 1969.
18. The Uttar Pradesh Prohibition of Bonded Labour Act, 1975.
19. The West Bengal Rural Employment and Production Act, 1976.
20. The Himachal Pradesh Essential Services (Maintenance) (Amendment) Act, 1979.
21. The Madhya Pradesh Labour Laws (Amendment) and Miscellaneous Provisions Act, 1981.
22. The Tamil Nadu Manual Workers (Regulation of Employment and Conditions of Work) Act, 1982.
23. The Karnataka Khadi and Village Industries Act, 1956. Amended in 1983.
24. The Maharashtra Tax Laws (Levy, Amendment and Repeal) Act, 1989.
25. The Andhra Pradesh Factories and Establishments (National Festivals and Other Holidays) Act, 1974 and Rules, 1974.
26. The Punjab Industrial Establishments (National Festival Holidays and Casual and Sick Leave) Haryana Amendment Act, 1976.
27. The Karnataka Industrial Establishments (National and Festival Holidays) Act, 1963. Amended in 1975 and 1985.

Six

Social Dialogue and the Reform Process

For the purpose of this Chapter, reforms mean structural adjustment reforms and social dialogue means dialogue between and among the social partners. Social and political consensus is necessary to make reforms/changes in any area at any level. Consensus is possible when all stakeholders are included in the consensus-building process so that they are representative enough and are able to arrive at decisions for collective benefit and well-being. As the renowned social scientist, Alwin Gouldner observed, 'Respect for norms depends on the manner of their formulation.'

Social dialogue has hitherto been limited to discussions between the government and representatives of organized labour and employers organizations. In some countries it is progressively becoming more inclusive extending to other groups in society such as consumers, the unemployed, NGOs and academics, in order to achieve a more broad-based consensus and greater social cohesion. For instance, academics have played an increasingly important role in social dialogue in high-level consultations in Japan and in a variety of tripartite institutions—including the National Wages Council in Singapore—while South Africa created the National Economic Development and Labour Advisory Council with representation for youth and the unemployed, among others.

Cordova (ILO, 1984) developed a typology of agreements based on consultations, which seek to provide a voluntary system of principles guiding the functional development of labour–management relations, leaving questions of substance.

Framework Agreements

They aim at establishing the so-called rules of the game and seek to institutionalize the various levels of interactions between parties.

Codes of Conduct, etc.

These deal primarily with the behaviour of parties in respect of their interactions and do not contain substantial provisions. They aim at establishing specific rules for limited purpose (for example, recognition of trade unions, declaration of strikes or lock-outs, etc.).

Standards of a Substantive Nature

These fix the basic minimum or outer standards or standards of direct and general application that must be taken into account for subsequent agreements on minimum wages, social security, conditions of employment, etc. They are like collective bargaining agreements, but at the national level of negotiation.

Macroeconomic Trade-Offs

These combine industrial relations and non-industrial relations elements as a means of alleviating or diminishing macroeconomic crises. Usually, such tripartite approaches include fiscal measures, like increased public investments and social security benefits to secure wage moderation. The package of trade-offs is intended to lower the level of unemployment and the wage increase.

Joint or Tripartite Statements

These do not imply concrete agreements but merely express intentions or urge negotiators to follow certain procedural steps or to accept some substantive approach. They are social accords or pacts or procedures delineating a possible action in the interests of the parties concerned and for the benefit of society at large.

Many Asian countries have institutions for social dialogue which received an impetus from the ILO's Asian-Pacific Project On Tripartism (APPOT) in the early 1990s. However, most of these institutions are merely ornamental in nature. There is no dearth of tripartite codes of practice in Asian countries; India, Indonesia and the Philippines have produced several of them. But utopian principles enunciated in these codes have largely remained on paper. For, being voluntary in nature, non-compliance usually has, little or no consequences. The ILO (1999) document prepared for the Asian Regional Consultation as a follow-up to the Social Summit lists several new initiatives, many of which unfortunately remain without substance. The Tripartite Commission of the Republic of Korea produced a social accord, which was immediately translated into law. However, the law soon became controversial and produced widespread industrial unrest. In India, the bipartite committee which was set up in the wake of discussions at the tripartite Indian Labour Conference in 1996 to review labour laws became an abortive exercise due to the polarization between employers and workers. Sri Lanka's National Workers' Charter was a non-starter. Few countries—Australia, Japan, and Singapore, for instance—have tripartite involvement in substantial aspects.

During the 1980s and 1990s new forms of social concertation came into vogue to deal with social and labour issues in the context of regionalization and globalization. The labour component of the North American Treaty between the USA, Canada and Mexico, OECD initiatives on employment and the agreement on Social Policy attached to the Treaty of Maastricht, and the European Community directives are examples of regional initiatives. Initiatives on the social clause and the ILO declaration on fundamental principles are examples of international concertation. The most effective ones, however, are the initiatives at the industry level, which provide for the enforcement of labour standards through social labelling and social support. At the national level, even pro-labour governments were unable to do much in the areas of employment and social protection as the experiences of Australia and Poland reveal. Social dialogue that ignores ground-level realities and contextual factors merely remain pipe dreams. Also, the higher the level at which consensus is sought, the more abstract is its content.

INSTRUMENTS FOR SOCIAL CONSENSUS IN THE REFORM PROCESS

ILO Convention No. 144 provides the basis for establishing and encouraging social consensus through tripartite and bipartite consultations. Many countries, including India, have ratified ILO Convention No. 144, but not ILO Convention Nos. 87 and 98 concerning the freedom of association and the right to collective bargaining. The non-ratification of these conventions could cast doubts on the fairness and genuineness of the consensus process.

Trebilcock (1994) reviewed social dialogue arrangements in different countries during the reform process. The study found that in some countries, there is form without substance. The special tripartite committee set up in India during the post-reform process is a classic example of this. In many countries—like Mexico for instance—the social dialogue partners have unequal power and in yet others—Argentina, for instance—direct lobbying is preferred to tripartite consultation. In Australia, for a while, the unions and the government excluded employers from social dialogue. In Sweden, employers opted out of tripartite dialogue because it was considered futile. Countries which have had a tradition of tripartism—the Scandinavian and some West European countries, for instance—are switching to bipartism in times of adjustment. Countries, which have not had a tradition of tripartism—Vietnam, for instance—are trying to establish tripartite fora to deal with the issues emanating from economic transition.

The components of the structural adjustment programme (SAP) during the reform process cover several aspects of the governance of the economy and the enterprises within it. Policy changes usually concern finance, tax, foreign exchange, international trade, industrial licensing, competition, changes in labour policies, removal of subsidies, etc. Agricultural reforms, particularly land reforms, however, have remained taboo in most countries. On social and labour matters, the crucial issue in almost all countries is the law and procedure relating to the protection of retrenched/dismissed workers. Legal rules and agreements governing wages, working conditions, forms of employment, etc., are usually sought to be revised in countries which seek to or are made to adjust. For the workers, this is a key aspect of 'job security' and for the employers, a major element of 'freedom' or the 'right to manage'. Typically, employers focus on product markets and unions harp on labour markets. The labour market impact is a function of the interaction between product market and labour market forces. In quite a few situations, industry and product market characteristics strengthen employers and weaken or make unions vulnerable. In others, both are left with limited choices/options and defenceless, vulnerable or endangered.

Social dialogue during the reform process poses deep dilemmas for both unions and employers. Competition, privatization, technological change, mergers, acquisitions and various forms of adjustment and/or restructuring bring about changes in the dynamics of unions and industrial relations at the enterprise level. They also impinge on diverse groups of workforce in diverse ways. The resultant divisive influence may pit one group of workers against another and one union against another. Certain groups of workers and certain unions may lose and others benefit. For instance, some adjustment measures may have adverse effects on unskilled workers while skilled workers may benefit. In cases where both groups of workers are represented by different unions, the impact of such adjustment would be perceived differently by different unions.

Similarly, employers also face dilemmas. Take, for instance, devaluation. Manufacturers who produce goods with a high import content and cater primarily to domestic demand usually oppose devaluation since it would push their costs up. But predominantly export-oriented manufacturing units and a section of those who deal in foreign trade welcome it. When it comes to liberalization, local employers typically prefer domestic liberalization occurring first and globalization or competition across borders only after a while so that the intervening time can be used to prepare a level playing field.

SAPs usually entail major paradigm shifts in the governance of the economy, the management of enterprises and policies concerning labour, labour markets and labour market institutions. Resistance to reforms needed for adjustment is common to most, if not all, countries. The only way the resistance can be dealt with in a sustainable manner is by caring for the concerns of all those involved and/or affected by the changes. Change should be seen as beneficial and worthwhile by all the social partners rather than by one group or a few groups only. This requires consultation and cooperation within a group and among groups of each constituency (that is labour and unions, management and employers and governments, centre and state at the bipartite and tripartite levels). It means vertical consultation within a constituency should both precede and follow horizontal consultation between or among different constituencies/social partners.

SAPs also involve huge political risks. Broad-based political support and coalitions need to be worked out. Generally, employers have been more supportive of reforms than have trade unions (Venkata Ratnam 1993). But in many cases, even employers' organizations that initially endorsed SAPs began to circumspect as they experienced some of the adverse effects of adjustment. Political support for SAPs is possible when all concerned see that the gains outweigh the pains during the transition and in the long term as well. Economic crises and other pressures for restructuring at the enterprise level have resulted in greater consultations to develop cooperative attitudes and approaches.

SOCIAL DIALOGUE ON EMPLOYMENT AND SOCIAL PROTECTION

In the globalizing economy, unemployment has become a global concern, with the exception of a few countries, which face labour shortages. It is not unusual to find countries with mounting unemployment problems facing critical skill shortages. Intercountry differences are quite sharp within and across regions as well as within sub-regions such as South-East Asia.

Recession, oil price shocks, technological change and debt crisis has reduced the employment intensity in manufacturing, and, to an extent even in the services sector. As an ILO report (1995) argues, 'Anxieties over the issue of job creation have surfaced against a backdrop of profound change in the global economy . . . the social costs of implementing major economic reforms in order to increase international competitiveness and hence reap the gains from globalization are high'. The basic conclusion of this report that, while globalization generates problems such as these, the potential benefits far outweigh the costs' does not, however, find favour with most developing countries because the costs may not necessarily be borne by those who benefit.

Since the oil price shock of the 1970s, collective bargaining at the national, industry and enterprise levels has responded to the challenges of recession, unemployment and inflation. With the result, that in several industrialized market economies, there have been concession agreements that have recognized, among other things, a trade-off between jobs and wages and that have been based on an understanding of various facets of employment policy, including job creation, redundancy and counter-redundancy measures. From these agreements, several institutional structures have emerged that enable vocational training, placement and other income support measures. In recent years, developing countries reeling under mounting debt and foreign exchange crises have had to initiate similar measures to cope with adjustment pressures.

As Cordova (1984) puts it:

> Given the magnitude of the . . . crisis it should not come as a surprise that an increasing number of countries stepped up tripartite approaches. They probably realized that adequate responses to the crisis escaped the capabilities of a single actor or could easily be undermined by any of the others.
>
> A more important development related to the conclusion of tripartite agreements in countries where there was almost no tradition of national basic agreements . . . Ireland, Spain and Italy during early 1980s . . . The importance of these experiences lies in the fact that neither idiosyncratic factors, nor the structure of collective bargaining, nor the orientation of the trade union movement seemed to favour the conclusion of tripartite or bipartite national agreements. Yet, faced with a critical unemployment and inflationary situation, governments, employers and unions saw fit to agree on a series of trade-offs intended to weather the crisis.

Reviewing about 400 agreements in 20 OECD countries during the late 1970s to early 1980s, Cordova further writes:

> A common denominator of tripartite approaches was the recognition of the need to combine industrial relations and non-industrial relations elements as a means of alleviating or diminishing the crisis. As a rule fiscal measures, social security benefits, increased public investments and improvements in the provision of social security were offered to workers and employers in order to secure wage moderation. The package of trade-offs was expected to lower the level of unemployment and avoid price increases.

LEVELS OF CONSULTATION

The main purpose of tripartite or bipartite consultations on employment aspects is three-fold: (a) participate in the evolution of employment policy to create more, better and productive jobs; (b) initiate policy framework and participate in the implementation and/or monitoring measures for active labour market intervention methods aimed at developing institutions and mechanisms to facilitate the creation of skills, job search and placement facilities; and, (c) develop policies and approaches to offset as far as possible any negative consequences of total or partial closure, workforce reductions, wage losses, etc. Tripartite and/or bipartite consultations may take place at any or all of the levels discussed below.

International

ILO Recommendation No. 122 on Employment Policy lists the possible actions employers and workers and their organizations can take in the field. ILO Recommendation No. 166 on Termination of Employment at Employer Initiative also lists a series of measures that can be taken to avert or minimize the adverse effects on employment of economic, technological and structural changes.

In the context of structural changes, the ILO has organized several tripartite consultations in various regions to deliberate on employment and related issues. Also, at the regional level, the Organization for Economic Cooperation and Development (OECD), the European Commission and the Association of the South East Asian Nations (ASEAN), for instance, have taken a variety of initiatives concerning employment issues. The Social Charter of the European Union and the proceedings of the ASEAN Labour Ministers' Conferences, too, are valuable examples of consultation and cooperation at the regional level on matters relating to employment.

National

Depending upon the economic situation and employment scenario different notions prevail in different countries. In some of the East and South-East Asian countries where unemployment was not a problem (till the recent Asian crises) and which have faced labour shortages, the predominant notion is that jobs are *acquired* through skills and competence. In other countries, particularly of South Asia, the dominant notion is that jobs are *inherited* as property. And, laws, collective bargaining and other methods are used to perpetuate that notion and jobs are virtually *imposed* through a network of rules. In Malaysia, for instance, labour adjustment is considered a prerogative of the management while in South Asia labour adjustment usually requires prior consent of the government. In some countries, jobs are available by choice, in others, where labour shortages persist, the local population usually shuns dirty, dangerous, drudgerous and dead-end jobs. The Malays in Malaysia, for instance, do not like to work in plantations. In other countries, particularly some of the communist and/or socialist Countries, forced labour was the only way to guarantee jobs for all. Between these two extremes, there are situations, as in India, where the poor cannot remain unemployed and hence underemployment at below-subsistence levels is a pervasive phenomenon. In India, therefore, the proportion of the poor is higher among the employed rather than among the unemployed.

The National Tripartite Consultative Mechanisms (NTCMs) in several countries have employment as a major item on their agenda and some have even created separate tripartite institutions specifically to address related issues.

Australia gave statutory recognition to tripartite consultation on industrial relations and other labour and employment matters in 1977 and its Social Accord statement of 1983 explicitly called for tripartite consultative mechanisms in various fields including general economic planning, prices and income policy, occupational health and safety, industrial policy, etc. The Australian Trade Union Council concluded that the creation of wealth is a prerequisite for its distribution. The tripartite National Board of Employment, Education and Training (NBEET) that it has set up is an example of an integrated approach to the full range of education, training and employment issues. It recognizes the need to develop a more skilled and educated labour force to facilitate the restructuring of the economy through greater equity of access to education and training at all levels.

In Belgium, for instance, Beaupain notes (in Trebilcock et al., 1994), there is virtually daily contact between the social partners and the government departments concerned, as well as with officials of regional bodies on general employment policy as well as on specific measures including union management discussions and employment regulation. The management committee of the National Employment Office (office national de l'emploi-ONEm), with an equal representation of union and employers' organizations, is meant to implement legislation on employment, find employment for job seekers and provide for vocational training. The restructuring of federal regional responsibilities meant that unemployment was to be tackled at the national level, vocational training at the level of the community and placement of jobseekers at the level of the region. The tripartite consultation has adopted itself to the reform of government structures and Belgium reportedly pursues an extremely active employment policy. As Beaupain notes,

> This has found expression at many levels, with incentives to withdraw from the labour market (early retirement, aids to career interruption, reduction of labour costs), lower social insurance contributions for employers who engage the young or the long-term unemployed, as well as general wage moderation, the development of alternating or sandwich training courses for young workers, the introduction of greater flexibility in working conditions, and the possibility for the employed to accept part-time employment while retaining their entitlement to (partial) employment compensation.

The measures have yielded results in as much as Belgium's unemployment rate is lower than the average for the European Community.

One of the features of the interoccupational central agreement between employers and workers organizations in 1988 was the creation of an employment fund with contribution equivalent to 0.18 per cent of gross wages for 1989 and 1990. The fund was

> to support high-risk groups of job seekers, primarily among young persons with only partial compulsory schooling, unemployed unskilled workers and the long-term unemployed. Exemption from this contribution was foreseen for sectors and firms whose efforts in 1989 and 1990, on behalf of three groups through collective agreements in the firms and sectors in question, were considered equivalent by the minister of employment and labour.

In the 1990 agreement, valid for 1991–1992, the canvas of the scheme was expanded and the contributions raised to 0.25 per cent of gross wages. Both Singapore and Malaysia have a Skills Development Fund with contributions from employers and the government.

Italy is a rare example where there have been tripartite agreements to make way for legislation that is necessary to introduce flexibility in a rigid system, which Treu catalogues (in Trebilcock et al., 1994): partial liberalization of the hiring system (Act 83 of 1983 and Act 56 of 1987) in general, and particularly for hiring young workers under education contracts and as apprentices, greater use of fixed-term contracts (Act 56 of 1987, which subjects it to collective bargaining as to numbers and situations in which such contracts may be used); and re-regulation of part-time work in order to make it more convenient (Act 863 of 1984).

Treu also notes that national tripartite agreements in Italy

> established a series of measures directed at stimulating job growth, particularly for the more vulnerable sectors of the labour force: young people in the first instance and then, to a lesser extent, women. The major feature of these agreements was the introduction of education contracts, which covered over 120,000 young persons in less than a decade. The early problems of implementation were sought to be overcome through monitoring by social partners and/or the tripartite commission at a decentralized level. There are agreements on relocating workers displaced by the restructuring process, which provide among other things, income maintenance assistance and preferential procedures for external labour mobility. Italy also introduced a system whereby the employer is paid a contribution for each new employee hired.

During the 1980s, the Philippines had a tripartite declaration on employment policy. There is no dearth of tripartite declarations in Asia, but the problem in several cases is the gap between precept and practice. Even when such declarations have led to legislative initiatives, problems have been encountered at the implementation stage. The difficulties encountered in the recent tripartite initiatives in Korea to change labour laws to reduce employment protection and the Sri Lankan initiative for a National Labour Charter illustrate this.

REFORM PROCESS AND SOCIAL DIALOGUE—THE CASE OF INDIA

Some of the mechanisms India has established to promote consultation and cooperation at the national level are:

Indian Labour Conference
Standing Labour Conference
Special Tripartite Committee (set up in 1991 following structural adjustment reforms)
Industrial Committees
State Labour Advisory Boards
Statutory Welfare Funds

There are 44 tripartite committees at the national level. Additionally, in the public sector, there is a national-level bipartite machinery in select core industries like banking, coal, oil, port, transport and steel. Such bipartite arrangements also exist at the industry-cum-region level in jute, engineering, plantations, textiles, etc., which are predominantly in the private sector.

There is a plethora of measures which, though appropriate, are not very effective. They have served only to raise the standard of living of workers in the organized sector, which accounts for less than 10 per cent of the total workforce in the country.

Since structural reforms were introduced in 1991 and to date, the Indian Labour Conference (ILC) has met only twice. A Special Tripartite Committee (STC) constituted to focus on social and labour issues arising out of structural changes met 11 times from 1991 to date, while six tripartite industrial committees were either set up or reconstituted. All of them met at least once till 1999 while some met as many as four times. Additionally, as a follow-up of one of the conclusions reached in the 30th Session of the ILC in September 1992, the government set up a standing advisory committee in the Planning Commission consisting of representatives of the Government of India, central trade union organizations and two organizations working in the unorganized sector besides two experts. Significantly, this 18-member committee does not have any employer representation. Despite resistance from the Council of Indian Employers, the ministry of labour has also given additional seats in the ILC to the fast-growing Confederation of Indian Industry (CII). The CII represents Indian employers on the ILC independent of the Council of Indian Employers, which has three constituents, namely, the All India Employers' Organization and Employers' Federation of India representing the private sector and the Standing Conference on Public Enterprises representing the public sector. The empowered authority set up in the Ministry of Industry to oversee the functioning of the new social security net has, however, accorded representation to both employers' and workers' organizations.

The government has also set up a number of committees to review policies concerning industrial restructuring, industrial sickness, the financial and insurance sectors, the investigation into stock market allegations about sugar, and the disinvestment in the public sector besides setting up a joint parliamentary committee to probe into the stock scam. The trade unions have, however, vigorously opposed the reports on the financial and insurance sectors as well as the report on legal and institutional reforms to deal with industrial sickness and public sector disinvestments.

The tripartite process got a boost following the announcement of macroeconomic reforms for structural changes in the economy. While the first three meetings took place within 15 months, the fourth one was almost a year after the third (Table 6.1). But, the year 1994 was hectic with five STC meetings, several TIC meetings and several rounds of consultations on two major sick units, viz., the NTC mills and IISCO. It is perhaps more than a coincidence that the government was eager to give labour a sense of importance in 1994, which happened to witness the campaigning for at least three rounds of elections for state assemblies. Afterwards, these committees—both STC and TICs—met less frequently.

The following were some of the major conclusions of the STC regarding the broad principles for guiding tripartite consultations:

- The major problems in India are unemployment, poverty and inflation. The concerted efforts of all sections of people, the industry, government, management, trade unions and workers is required to meet the crisis.
- No action should be initiated that may affect the interests of workers adversely.

TABLE 6.1 Composition of and Attendance at Special Tripartite and Industrial Committee Meetings, December 1991–April 1999

	Central Govt		State Govts/	Emp-	Work-	Total	Date of
	MOL	Others	UTs	loyers	ers		Meetings
Indian Labour Conference	1	19	32	30	30	112	Sep. 1995
							Jan. 1995
							Nov. 1995
							Dec. 1996
							Dec. 1997
							April 1999
Special Tripartite Committee	**1**	**4**	–	**10**	**10**	**25**	
	6	1	–	7	13	27	21.12.91
							20.01.92
	9	8	–	9	16	42	04.05.93
	12	2	6	9	5	34	16.03.94
	6	12	–	3	17	38	30.03.94
	9	13	–	2	14	38	09.04.94
	6	9	–	5	19	39	09.05.94
	6	10	–	3	13	32	16.08.94
							11.04.95
							1996
							13.6.98
Industrial Committees:							
1. Cotton Textiles	**1**	**1**	**11**	**12**	**12**	**37**	
	11	6	9	16	12	54	21.02.92
	–	–	–	–	–	–	09.02.94
	–	–	–	–	–	–	31.05.94
2. Chemicals	**1**	**4**	**6**	**12**	**12**	**35**	
	13	6	5	12	12	48	21.04.92
	8	7	6	21	17	59	04.02.94
3. Engineering	**1**	**4**	**8**	**11**	**11**	**35**	
	–	–	–	–	–	–	18.08.92
	–	–	–	–	–	–	04.02.94
	–	–	–	–	–	–	14.02.94
	–	–	–	–	–	–	30.11.94
4. Electricity	**1**	**1**	**9**	**10**	**10**	**31**	13.11.92
5. Jute	**2**	**4**	**4**	**12**	**12**	**34**	
	12	7	2	7	8	36	03.04.92
	12	7	2	8	7	36	05.02.94
6. Road Transport	**1**	**1**	**6**	**7**	**7**	**22**	
	12	2	6	9	5	34	13.03.93

Note: Figures in **bold** indicate composition. Other figures indicate attendance.

- Profit is no indicator of efficiency and loss is no barometer of inefficiency.
- Labour is not opposed to modernization. Rather, it is against retrenchment, but agreeable to retraining and redeployment.
- Parliament has amended the Sick Industrial Companies (Special Provisions) Act which permits public sector enterprises too to be referred to the Bureau of Industrial and Financial Reconstruction (BIFR) for a decision on revival, closure, etc. The labour side of the Committee feels that a convention should be developed whereby the BIFR will await the results of the STC.
- In industries such as cotton textiles, chemicals, electricity, engineering, jute, and road transport where sickness is rampant, TICs should be revived or be constituted if none have existed for those industries.
- Public enterprises were classified into four categories to consider their future:
  1. Units which are currently viable, but likely to become sick in the future.
  2. Units which are already sick, but can be salvaged with appropriate remedial and timely action.
  3. Units which are chronically sick and which require radical treatment.
  4. Units which are sick, but their current working can be made profitable with no cash loss to begin with, provided their past liabilities are appropriately taken care of or are not allowed to act as a drag, and the dues to labour are paid.
- It was agreed that a unit referred to the BIFR would be first discussed in the tripartite committee. The views of the committee would be incorporated in the respective notes for the Group of Ministers (GOM)/Cabinet by the concerned administrative ministry which would seek direction of the GOM/Cabinet about the stand to be taken by the government before the BIFR. However, there have been instances where individual cases were referred to the BIFR even before an STC or the concerned TIC could discuss and express its views, and, the time that was given to workers to present their alternative proposals had expired. The government, however, feels that parallel processes of reference to the BIFR and a simultaneous discussion in STC are not mutually contradictory, and that they are both meant to deal with matters expeditiously,

not prejudge issues. It is possible that the government also may explain away its lack of a clear stand or policy on such matters with the argument that it is open to any idea that is acceptable to all parties concerned provided it is possible and feasible as well.

The government can take decisions when it really wants to. On other occasions, it can avoid taking decisions and blame it on the lack of consensus among the other social partners, namely, the organizations of workers and employers.

Tripartite Initiative in Select Cases

National Textiles Corporation: Several tripartite meetings were held between 1991 and 1999 exclusively to discuss the case of one of the corporations, the National Textile Corporation Limited (NTC). Set up in April 1968, NTC owns and runs 119 mills besides 15 taken-over mills. The government acquired the mills to protect employment but did little to modernize the old and obsolete plant and equipment. Between 1984 and 1998 employment in NTC mills declined from 0.25 million to 0.12 million. Three-fourths of this reduction occurred before the government announced reforms for structural changes in the economy.

The government, as employer, realized that workers alone were not responsible for the present chronic sickness while trade unions considered the workers not responsible (at all?). The accumulated loss of NTC mills by 1998 was over Rs 30,000 million. The government had so far been reimbursing a substantial part of the cash losses providing interest subsidy and wages of workers. It has, however, denied wage revision for workers in loss-making public sector units since 1992 to date.

In August 1992, the cabinet approved the NTC turnaround strategy. The main features of this strategy were outright closure of 14 mills, merger of 18 mills, modernization of 55 mills and rationalization of 79,982 workers/officers through the Voluntary Retirement Scheme (VRS). The financial implications of this package at that time were Rs 5,327.80 million for modernization and Rs 6,890 million for VRS. A total of 33,000 workers availed of the VRS and Rs 2,450 million was paid to them. But due to resistance from such groups, the matter was placed before the STC. The committee constituted a sub-committee under the chairmanship of the minister of state for textiles. The textile research associations (TRAs) framed revised proposals based on mill-by-mill studies at the instance of the sub-committee. These are still to be acted upon.

In March 1994 the case of NTC mills was discussed in two exclusive meetings of the special tripartite body. The secretary (textiles), Government of India, stated that if the revised proposal of TRAs was accepted by the STC, the ministry would refer the matter to the cabinet for a decision otherwise there would be no option but to go back to the BIFR. The trade union members were of the view that since the sub-committee had accepted the revised proposal of the TRAs, the government too should accept it and treat it as a guideline. While some trade union leaders wanted an expeditious decision at the meeting on 16 March 1994, at the next meeting, on 30 March 1994, several trade union representatives suggested that more time be given to discuss the matter at the unit level. Pending unanimity, the discussions remained inconclusive. Later, there was pressure to go ahead with modernization by selling surplus land. At this stage, there is now confusion whether the government has the title to the land and whether the proceeds from the sale of land in one mill or subsidiary can be used for modernization of another mill or subsidiary. Subsequently, several formal and informal meetings have been held. The 1999–2000 budget has no provision for revival of NTC mills. All portents indicate that closure of the NTC mills is imminent.

Indian Iron and Steel Company: Among the steel plants set up in the private sector long before India's Independence, one was the Indian Iron and Steel Company (IISCO). It was taken over by the government in the early 1970s and made a subsidiary of the Steel Authority of India (SAIL) in 1978. The company has remained sick since the mid-1960s to date even though in the last two years it reported cash profits amidst allegations of financial window dressing. The accumulated loss of IISCO was Rs 8,160 million on 31 March 1993 as against its net worth of Rs 3,880 million. Beginning 1989, several attempts were made to modernize IISCO but these did not fructify because of political tangles. There was even a collective agreement on 11 June 1989 between the management of IISCO and 18 unions on modernization of the plant. The agreement provided, among others, for retraining and redeployment, and a VRS for contract workers. This was the only instance in India where recognized unions and management have negotiated a VRS for contract workers. It is apt to mention here that in some central public sector undertakings, *badli* (substitute) workers were retained even though surplus, because the management thought that it could not extend the VRS to their (substitute) labour. Proposals to privatize the company also met with stiff opposition. The unions hotly contended the findings of an expert committee.

Trade unions initially proposed in 1994 that they would contribute 50 per cent of the equity and run the unit jointly in cooperation with the SAIL management which, they expected, would hold the remaining 50 per cent equity. A representative of the private sector employers' organizations said that workers should be given 51 per cent equity so that they could be asked to take on full responsibility and leadership roles in modernization. About 9,000 workers of IISCO reportedly bought shares in the company when SAIL shares were disinvested in March 1994. In May 1994 it was agreed that workers would prepare an alternative viable modernization plan on the basis of their offer of holding 50 per cent shares in IISCO and submit it to SAIL by 30 June 1994. But the unions subsequently backed out on the pretext that they would make a commitment only after assessing the feasibility report for modernization prepared by SAIL. IISCO did not hold any formal meeting with the SAIL management on this issue. The chairman of SAIL also said that there was no issue to be discussed with the unions and that some of the points raised by the unions needed to be discussed at the highest level, meaning perhaps the ministry and cabinet levels.

During the early phase of reforms the ministry of steel had prepared a bill for privatization, but did not pursue it in the wake of resistance from trade unions and the recommendations of the STC. In September 1998, the board of directors of SAIL decided to divest IISCO along with two other loss-making units. While this was approved by the government, the actual disinvestment is yet to take place.

Tripartite Initiative on Select Issues

Here we discuss, synoptically, the outcomes of tripartite deliberations on select issues like the National Renewal Fund (NRF), reference of sick units to the BIFR, the rationalization of workforce and the resultant contradictions of tripartite deliberations on these, and related subjects like public sector disinvestment, worker ownership and worker cooperatives.

National Renewal Fund: One of the initiatives of the central government to provide a social security net in India, the National Renewal Fund (NRF) does not have social security benefits for unemployment. There are, of course, some central and state-level schemes for employment generation for the unemployed.

The ministry of labour, it is understood, did not show interest in the concept mooted by the ministry of finance since some senior officials in the ministry of labour at that time felt that it should not be a party to oversee the exit of the employed, even if it was through the VRS route. The ministry of industry, which then had officials at the helm of affairs who vigorously supported the package of reforms that was unfolding, readily agreed to be the nodal agency operating the NRF. Significantly, to date, the Director General of Employment and Training (DGET) in the ministry of labour has not played any role, even in respect to training and retraining, except provide some information on the vocational training institutions the ministry runs.

The setting up of the NRF caused a certain amount of apprehension among trade unions. They initially rejected even the concept paper on the subject because they felt it did not reflect their views and related mainly to retrenchment compensation. Despite the assurance of the finance minister, the major thrust of the NRF was on funding voluntary retirement. The data on the performance of NRF during 1992–99 (see Table 4.15) speaks for itself.

Some government officials responsible for administering the NRF consider the fund to be a useful institution. The nodal agency is not too keen to involve the other related ministries, particularly the Ministry of Labour which seems to want to maintain a distance from rather than be an active partner in the activities of the NRF. For retraining and redeployment to be the major objectives, the DGET in the Ministry of Labour should play a more active role. Only those organizations who have the resources, facilities and expertise to offer vocational technical transfer should be vested with the responsibility of training and retraining. Financial assistance in such cases should be linked to the absorption of trainees in relevant areas rather than the actual numbers trained.

A conference on NRF recommended that training should be imparted free to retrenched people while those covered by the VRS could be asked to part-finance it if they want it for alternative sources of livelihood. It can also not be assumed that all those who opt for VRS need training. The emphasis on retraining and redeployment also raises other issues in the context of widespread unemployment. According to press reports (see Editorial in *Indian Express*, 18 February 1995), the Kerala State Public Service Commission received 200,000 applications for 16 office jobs in the clerical (non-executive) cadre. With pervasive downsizing and casualization of the organized sector jobs, this problem has only been exacerbated.

Significantly, the tripartite committee on vocational training has not met in the post-structural adjustment period even though training and retraining have been of prime concern. In 1997, a proposal of the labour ministry at the tripartite fora for setting up a skills development fund met with stiff resistance from employers' organizations. As noted in Chapter 4, the employers' argument was that if the government administers the fund, the money collected from them would be spent on staff salaries rather than on providing skill training.

Board of Industrial and Financial Reconstruction (BIFR)

The Board of Industrial and Finance Reconstruction (BIFR) was set up as a quasi-judicial body to recommend the revival or closure of sick units referred to it. The unions initially argued against this and wanted the matter to be referred first to the STC or TIC for a decision. They later reconciled with the government's decision that a reference to the BIFR cannot be avoided, but the views of the STC would be placed before the BIFR for the latter's consideration.

The unions were apprehensive that the reference of a unit to the BIFR would adversely affect the unit's creditworthiness and create for it problems in raising funds from financial institutions/banks for its day-to-day working, thus leading to a deterioration of its condition. The matter was examined by the Department of Economic Affairs in consultation with the Industrial Development Bank of India which has reported that a mere reference of a unit to the BIFR in itself should not affect its creditworthiness. Normally, financial institutions and banks undertake holding on operations of sick industrial units in their portfolio, pending the formulation of a rehabilitation package by the BIFR unless the viability of the unit is in serious doubt.

During 1998 and 1999 the BIFR ordered the closure of six central public sector enterprises. In the year 2000, the government announced its decision to close some of these. It had to, however, backtrack in the face of stiff opposition from some of its coalition partners.

The establishment of public sector units is a political decision. Their sickness, too, is often caused by political decisions. Again, the decision to refer such units to the BIFR is a political decision. Similarly, not to accept the decision of the BIFR is also a political decision.

Rationalization of the Workforce: In 1957, the ILC called for modernization without retrenchment. The same was reiterated at some of the meetings of the STC in 1992. However, in several STC and TIC meetings, and in almost every case referred to the BIFR, the need for the rationalization of the workforce has been emphasized even though unions have argued that retraining, not retrenchment is acceptable if workforce rationalization is not accomplished through VRS.

The heavy incidence of overstaffing in public enterprises is one of several reasons for their sickness. The agenda notes circulated in various STC and TIC meetings give glaring estimates of overstaffing. Estimates on surplus, too, are bargained in the political process as discussions on Eastern Coalfields Limited and UCO Bank, among others, reveal.

In some STC meetings trade unions have insisted that there should not be any retrenchment at all. But the employers' side has observed that some retrenchment was inevitable as a result of the modernization and the closure of units which could not be revived at all. In certain TICs, engineering and textiles, some unions agreed that workforce rationalization would be necessary to revive sick units. For dealing with cases of individual enterprises and in bipartite agreements for their revival—for instance, in Indian Drugs and Pharmaceuticals (IDPL)—40 out of 44 unions agreed for a reduction of workforce as a precondition for revival. Unions have accepted and signed agreements providing for the reduction of a certain percentage of the workforce during the process of the revival of sick units.

Contradictions

Trade unions have opposed NRF and retrenchment. But, in several cases, they have agreed that funds should be made available from the

NRF for payment of terminal dues, including payment under VRS, and for labour adjustments.

The STC, at its second meeting on 20 January 1995, noted that some public enterprises were sick and had problems concerning working capital. The government had stopped financing them, resulting in workers not being given work, but being paid wages. There were no funds even to buy raw materials. In all such cases it noted that if the enterprise did not currently account for a cash loss, the government should provide the necessary finance for the day-to-day working of the units. It is not clear whether the government subscribed to this view, but there are instances (IDPLs Muzaffarnagar unit, for instance) where workers were paid wages, but the unit remained virtually closed since it defaulted on paying its energy bill due to a paucity of funds. Similarly, some NTC mills (public sector) were closed for several months, but workers continued to receive wages. In some private sector mills, superannuated workers continue to be on the payroll because of the inability of the management to pay them their statutory dues.

Further, there are cases where workers are not allowed to seek voluntary retirement or the VRS is withdrawn for want of funds even though the problem of surplus labour persists in such organizations. Trade unions have argued, in STC and TIC meetings, that the government should release grants to clear terminal benefits, including VRS benefits. In a few other units, the gratuity was not paid and the workers went to court. Both public and private sector jute mills in West Bengal defaulted on provident fund accounts, but only the private sector mill owners/managers were arrested while the public sector ones were spared.

In 1998, the government first increased the retirement age from 58 to 60 years for those employed in the civil service and government. Soon after, it announced a liberal VRS. It then announced another VRS that promised up to five year's salary to workers in cash-starved sick public sector companies should they choose to leave the services of the company voluntarily, thus facilitating its closure. In some sick public sector companies, when the ministers concerned have assured workers that the units will not be closed, they have stopped applying for the VRS, insisting on job security and pay revision regardless of the viability of the company.

Public Sector Disinvestment

The general principles or mechanisms for public sector disinvestment have never been discussed at length in STC meetings. Workers' organizations have, however, been vociferously opposing public sector disinvestment while private sector employers have been calling for disinvestment of up to 51 per cent. Workers, on the contrary, have generally responded very positively to the issue of shares to them in profitable public sector undertakings. In several organizations, particularly profitable ones in the petroleum ministry, the unions have fought for and got higher allocations of shares on preferential and concessional terms during the last three years. Bank employees have also responded very favourably to the share issue, despite suggestions to the contrary by a section of the workers' organizations. Employees unions have been arguing that workers be given 51 per cent share in companies which they want to run.

The Disinvestment Commission, appointed in 1996, submitted reports on a piece-meal basis, on the companies referred to it. Since the commission is advisory in nature, most of the recommendations have not been implemented. In the wake of the change in government, the Disinvestment Commission has been replaced by a Department of Disinvestment. However, the government has announced the disinvestment of shares of profitable companies of up to even 75 per cent of the equity in some cases. It has also announced its decision to close nine sick public sector units, but has backtracked on account of political pressures. When its disinvestment targets have not been met, it has asked public enterprises to buy back their own shares. When the companies have protested, it has favoured cross-holding of shares. The government's stance to allow some profit earning public sector firms to acquire other public sector firms put up for disinvestments has caused avoidable misunderstanding.

The public sector officers' association has recently formed an association of employee shareholders to protect the interests of minority shareholders. This forum can use the judicial system to stall controversial decisions affecting the interests of employees and employee shareholders.

Workers' Cooperative

In India there have been quite a few instances (West Bengal alone boasts of more than 25 cases), in the jute, textile and engineering industries particularly, where workers have taken over sick units and turned them around. Initially, in one of the earliest STC meetings when the workers' representatives expressed their willingness to run sick units if the government waived existing loans, the finance minister promptly endorsed the view. But this was somehow not minuted in the records of the meeting. In any case, workers' response to taking over sick public sector units has generally been lukewarm. Workers and their unions are not to blame for this. Banks and financial institutions are sceptical about the workers' ability to manage sick units in spite of evidence in some cases—such as Kamani Tubes Limited in Mumbai (Maharashtra), Jaipur Metals and Electricals in Jaipur (Rajasthan) and the New Central Jute Mills in Calcutta (West Bengal)—where workers employed management professionals in turnaround efforts.

As discussed earlier, workers' representatives had proposed to take 50 per cent of the equity base in IISCO and run it in cooperation with SAIL management. But, later, they offered a less than 5 per cent share of the equity. In NTC mills alone, only four proposals have been received from three states but even these have not been pursued by any of the social partners. The unions' view is that, 'taking over of units by workers' cooperatives is feasible, but the problem is availability of funds'. Even public sector banks do not feel confident that trade unions can really takeover and turnaround sick units and therefore deny assistance to proposals from trade unions.

Performance, Pitfalls and Prescriptions

Performance/Achievements: The World Employment Report, 1998–99 (ILO, 1998) observes that,

> India's economic performance has fluctuated in the 1990s due to both economic liberalization and weather. Although the trend growth rate has been higher than earlier, it has not been sufficient or sustained for long enough to reduce significantly the existing high levels of underemployment and to absorb new job seekers productively.

Chapter 4 reviewed the performance of Indian economy during the 1980s. The outcome of structural changes in India has been mixed and one is unclear about what the future holds due to a variety of reasons, including apprehensions about political stability, the role of the rain god in determining the prospects of agriculture, and a decline in the value of rupee vis-à-vis the US dollar. On balance, the economy has shown positive signs on various counts, including growth rate, inflation, employment, and foreign exchange reserves.

The current scenario calls for a higher degree of cohesion and consultation between the central and state governments. State governments now have a greater role to play in adopting policies at the state level that seek to balance growth with equity. Unfortunately, in most states, tripartite consultations are either weak or non-starters.

The 34th Session of the ILC, held in December 1997, took note of the diminishing role and importance of tripartism even at the central level. Earlier that year, the government took the decision to rationalize the number of tripartite committees from 54 to about 30 by reducing and combining subjects.

Workers' organizations have, so far, been able to prevent the closure of sick central public sector undertakings. The ministry of industry considered eight units as potentially unviable and recommended their closure. The BIFR recommended closure of at least five of these eight companies. The government did not act upon these recommendations, despite repeated announcements about their closure. This is partly because in respect of one unit the case was pending before the West Bengal High Court and largely because it was perceived to be a politically risky move.

Pitfalls:
1. The role of the government, particularly in the present context, seems to be diminishing. This is reflected, rather unfortunately, in social and labour matters too. Given the fact that in most developing countries tripartism thrives largely on the whims and fancies of the government, a reduced role for the government may also mean a reduced role for tripartism, leading, ultimately, to the atrophy of the latter.
2. Economic reforms in India have evolved not out of social consensus but as a consequence of the conditions attached to IMF loans. This has made it difficult to forge a consensus on the content and direction of reforms.
3. Labour being in the concurrent list of the Constitution of India, on several aspects of social and labour matters state governments

have either exclusive or concurrent jurisdiction. ILC, with its total strength of 112 members has one representative each from the country's twenty-five states and seven union territories besides 20 from the central government and 30 each representing employers and workers. But the STC has no state government and union territory representation (Table 6.1). In the six industrial committees, however, there is some representation for certain states, not all. Such representation is not based solely on the importance of the industry to a state; road transport and electricity, for instance, are important to all states while jute and cotton textiles may not be. Thus, the states and union territories have largely been left out of the special tripartite consultation process at the national level in the context of structural adjustments.

4. Significantly, again, none of the states and union territories have found it worthwhile or practicable to institute similar structures and processes to initiate a social dialogue on issues of their respective concerns. The gap in interaction between the centre and the states is critical for at least two major reasons: First, there is widespread realization that the central and state governments are not moving in the same direction or at a similar pace in pursuing the so-called reform policies. This is more glaring when the party in power is different from the one at the centre, with the possible exception, ironically though, of West Bengal, a marxist communist stronghold but now vigorously pursuing market-oriented policies. Second, there is an east–west divide marked by a disproportionately large flow of investments in the west and relatively huge job losses in the east, where fresh investments are meagre. If unchecked, this might exacerbate the existing regional imbalances and escalate social tensions due to poverty, unemployment and deprivation. A leading French novelist, who visited India in February 1999 to release his second book on India, asserted that if the current trends are not checked, the country which produced a non-violent Gandhi to liberate India from the colonial rule, may give birth to a violent Gandhi in the 21st century to liberate India from economic and social injustice.

5. Several state governments do not have any policy on industrial restructuring or industrial sickness; only a few have announced liberal packages for sick units. Generally, they are ambivalent about making commitments and apathetic when it comes to implementation.

6. A vote, albeit negative perhaps, in favour of market forces may well mean that the labour ministry is pushed further lower in the pecking order even as the economic ministries—particularly finance and, to an extent, industry—become the centrifugal forces, making the rest of the government dance to their tune.
7. In most cases, the recommendations of the STC and TIC have to be followed up by the concerned ministries/departments or the organizations under them. Most often action involves policy issues the consideration of which entails interministerial consultation before decision by the competent authority or authorities. There are several instances in which the minister for labour has given a particular assurance to trade union leaders—whether it involved an issue of dearness allowance, the rehabilitation of sick units or the retraining and redeployment of affected persons—but the bureaucrats in the administrative or economic ministries have made contradictory statements or delayed action. This has affected the credibility of both the minister and the ministry (of labour) and their ability to effectively represent even the central government viewpoint.
8. The differences between the administrative ministries and the supposedly autonomous regulatory authorities are also being addressed publicly through the media. All this manifests the growing unease and difficulties in arriving at consensus on policy within the government itself. In such a situation, reaching a wider social consensus becomes an even more arduous task.
9. Political risks make decision making on social and labour issues inconclusive. Hence, tripartite consultations run the risk of being merely ritualistic.
10. In structural adjustments that emphasise the primacy of market forces, shifts occur along the following lines: macro to micro orientation in economic planning; centralized to decentralized collective bargaining; collective, solidaristic, parity-based collective bargaining contracts to individual contracts that stress disparity under euphemisms of merit and efficacy; representative to direct participation or workers' involvement/empowerment; communications through unions to direct communications with individual employees, etc. If caution is not exercised such developments could lead to a transition from tripartism to bipartism and from bipartism to individual contractual relations. If this were to

occur, consultations—tripartite or bipartite—can become a casualty, resulting in a laissez-faire or free-for-all situation.

Prescriptions to Strengthen Social Dialogue

1. The government which has, all along, been playing the role of an unequal among equals in social dialogue, needs to approach the subject with an open mind, and review policies to mitigate the adverse impacts of its prior decisions.
2. The government at the centre can do with better coordination among the various concerned ministries. As a representative of the workers' organization pointed out about the TIC on electricity generation and distribution, the deliberations would have been meaningful had the power minister been present. There are numerous such instances, which point not only to lack of coordination, but also to the fact that the related ministries are either pulling in different directions or are deliberately biding time.
3. In a federal set up, there is a need for dialogue and understanding among the various concerned ministries in the central government and between the central and state governments. Lack of consistency in the policies and attitudes of the central and state governments can have adverse effects on the legitimate interests of the government and public besides those of workers and employers.
4. Tripartite consultations will merely perpetuate the tyranny of the minority, unless social dialogue includes groups such as the unorganized sector and consumer organizations. For broad-basing: (i) social dialogue needs to incorporate social partners beyond the organized/formal sector. It should represent a wider cross-section of society and must include groups which are 'socially excluded' from the developmental process. The National Economic Development and Labour Advisory Council (NEDLAC) in South Africa, for instance, comprises, besides government, workers' and employers' organizations in the formal sector, interest groups such as women, academics, the unemployed, and NGOs, (ii) social dialogue should occur at both the macro and the micro levels. It should expand not only in the realm of industrial relations and labour market issues, but also in wider issues involving labour's participation in the development of social policy and the national macroeconomic agenda. The policies of

international financial institutions, public policies on economic liberalization at the national level and the external pressures of globalization and competitiveness, for instance, are impinging heavily on labour markets and industrial relations, (iii) social dialogue should cover both planning and implementation rather than be restricted, as in the case of structural adjustment programmes, to implemention. Ownership of social programmes is critical for social participation. Otherwise, attempts to promote social dialogue would be considered *fait accompli* measures.

5. A western social scientist once observed that Indians are power mongers. Indians in the audience objected to this, saying that they had been invaded many times over the centuries, but that they had not invaded others. The social scientist clarified what he had meant by his statement: Indians want to influence but not be influenced by others. The chief executive of an MNC concurred with this, saying that in India any issue will evoke emotive discussion, arguments and counterarguments. Tripartite meetings have become veritable exercises in loquacious verbosity. There is little transparency and virtually no mutual trust. There is no sense of equality or commonality.

6. Interdependence among social partners is desirable. Overdependence, however, is a sign of weakness and insecurity and reflects a concern for political survival rather than for preserving and pursuing the wider public interest. The social partners, particularly the government, should develop a shared vision and pursue it boldly and vigorously.

7. Tripartite consultations at the national, regional, state and sectoral levels should be strengthened with bipartite consultations at the enterprise and plant levels. Significantly, some TICs have made specific recommendations in this respect.

8. For tripartism to succeed, the social partners should desist from actions which perpetuate politicized polarization. Instead, the approach should be to focus on issues, not individuals, safeguard interests rather than take positions, invent creative and multiple options to a problem rather than be saddled with either/or solutions, reach agreements rather than score points over others, share credit for problem solving rather than deny or grab credit and deal with functional conflict and avoid dysfunctional frictions.

Major Portents

Organized labour is beginning to distrust political parties which, as observed earlier, tend to oppose 'new economic policies' while in opposition and follow them when they are in power. Often desperate times need desperate solutions. Governments acting under the pressure of debt and exchange crises are unable to fulfill the promises they make under political compulsions. As Talcot Parsons, a renowned sociologist, once observed, human beings in every civilization have two contradictory pursuits: pattern maintenance and adaptation to change. While changes/reforms/adjustment are a continuous process and usually resisted for their negative or uncertain fallouts, they become more objectionable for political reasons when they are carried out under the label of 'structural adjustment' or under IMF/World Bank prescriptions. There is little realization that the borrower has to heed the lenders' advice and lose its sovereignty, be it an individual household or a nation that fails to balance the domestic budget with domestic means.

Organized labour is not able to provide credible alternative strategies to economic reforms pursued by the government, particularly when dissatisfaction with the provision of public services/utilities is higher than the distrust they may have of market forces. Economic reforms are carried out on a negative vote despite the lack of consensus and the concern about social and economic consequences. Governments are damned if they do not undertake 'reforms' and damned if they do. Hence, the need for caution. Further, political instability and the lack of a popular mandate weakens the resolve—whatever its direction—of the government.

The major issues are employment and social protection. There is a fear that with globalization, labour is becoming a redundant resource. The impact on numbers and quality is varied. In India, for instance, reforms have generated more jobs than they have displaced. Available estimates put the impact of job loss at four million if reforms go full speed. In the telecom sector alone, about five million jobs were generated in the past decade through ISD/STD telephone booths in the 500,000 odd villages in India, while teleworking is expected to generate another one million jobs by 2008. However, well-paying, secure and low-productive (low-value adding) jobs in the organized sector are being replaced by low-paying, more insecure and highly productive jobs mostly in the unorganized/self-employed segment. Most countries with an ongoing reform process do not have credible systems of compensation or social security for those affected. The key issue then is to put in place such systems to deal with the huge problem of a redundant/obsolete workforce at minimal social cost.

Economic development should be the means and human development the goal. The Asian Development Bank (ADB, 1998) asserts that without an initial skills base, no amount of new high-technology imports will ensure sustained development. Along with the investment in human resources, which provides the social infrastructure, the role of investment in physical infrastructure to provide energy, roads, transportation and modern telecommunication systems cannot be ignored.

REFERENCES

ADB (1998). *Asian Development Report*. Manila: ADB.
Cordova, E. (1984). *Collective Bargaining: A Response to Crisis*. Geneva: ILO.
ILO (1995). *World Employment Report*. Geneva: ILO.
ILO (1998). *World Employment Report*. Geneva: ILO.
ILO (1999). *Towards Full Employment*. Bangkok: ILO.
Trebilcock, A. (1994). *Social Dialogue*. Geneva: ILO.
Venkata Ratnam, C.S. (1993). *Structural Adjustment Reforms and Employers*. Geneva: ILO (Mimeo).

SEVEN

The Labour Adjustment Process

Adjustment is adaptation to change. In the present context of liberalization, privatization and globalization firms are following two main approaches to deal with adjustment: cost-based competitiveness and value addition as the source of competitiveness. The former approach is inevitably leading to a higher incidence of job loss than the latter. The greatest challenge today is to ensure that, overall, more jobs are created than are displaced. Otherwise the result will be jobless growth or more growth with less jobs. This means economic growth will be at the expense of human welfare. Competitiveness of enterprises and economy will become the means to social progress if attention is paid, both at the macro and micro levels, to action in three areas: human resource development, labour market flexibility and labour standards.

Human resource development should focus on preparing people to cope with the challenges of adjustment.

> The growing gap between technology and skills reemphasizes the importance of flexible training, which includes enterprise based training and continuous education. Human resource development and the creation of a highly skilled and flexible workforce are especially important in a global economy because these enable enterprises and nations to remain competitive (ILO, 1997).

When employment security is on the decline, training holds the future for employability. To those who have exceptional difficulties in securing training and employability, income security measures through appropriate social safety nets can become a viable option. Workers skills, qualifications and attitudes are becoming important criteria in the location of firms. Low unit labour costs are an important consideration in attracting investment and generating more jobs, thus contributing to the reduction of unemployment and poverty.

Labour market flexibility and deregulation are controversial subjects. Aspects relating to labour market flexibility were discussed in the earlier chapter. If deregulation results in the dismantling of existing regulations and social protection, it is cause for grave concern. Competitiveness should not become an excuse for lowering labour standards. In this context, the ILO Declaration on Fundamental Principles, 1998 is considered an important milestone. It identifies seven core conventions whose application will be monitored vigorously even if member-countries have not ratified them. These core conventions relate to the following aspects: freedom of association, collective bargaining, elimination of child labour and forced labour, non-discrimination, and equal remuneration. The new vision of the ILO (1999) concerning Decent Work has four core dimensions that are of critical concern for human resource development: rights at work, enterprise promotion for employment growth, social protection and social dialogue.

SOCIALLY RESPONSIBLE RESTRUCTURING

Adjustment measures inevitably lead to the restructuring of businesses, occurring on a widespread scale throughout the world. Whatever be the driving force for restructuring—growth, maturity, decline, merger, acquisition, alliances; changes in ownership, technology, products, processes, materials, customer preferences, etc.—the short-term implication for employees is downsizing. Starcher (1999) identifies the following five paradoxes facing businesses in this context:

1. There is increasing evidence that those practices which provide more meaningful work and a higher quality of life in the workplace have a very direct impact on profits through increased productivity,

greater innovation, higher quality and reliability, and more skilful and committed people at all levels. Yet, current management practices do not reflect this finding. In fact, there is evidence which indicates that some practices may be moving in exactly the opposite direction.

2. We read that human and social capital are becoming all important in the post-industrial economy. Human capital includes intelligence, values, technical knowledge, experience, creativity, a network of contacts, corporate memory, as well as professional skills and experience. Nearly all corporate codes of ethics or conduct state that 'people are our most important assets.' Yet management actions often destroy the human tissue of their own organizations as they downsize, reduce training budgets, and divest whole 'communities' within their group.

3. Research shows that employee satisfaction translates into customer satisfaction. Employee motivation and loyalty are closely related to customer loyalty, and the most profitable customers are the long-term loyal ones. Yet many companies still treat their employees as costs. The human side of downsizing is often carried out in a way that results in the morale, motivation, loyalty, creativity, and productivity of employees suffering.

4. Surveys indicate that almost all large companies have downsized and many of them have downsized several times. Yet these same surveys show that fewer than one in four downsizings really achieve their objectives of reducing costs, increasing productivity, and improving quality and customer service.

5. Numerous studies have shown that over one-half of mergers and acquisitions do not achieve their objectives. Often the only beneficiaries are the shareholders of the company being acquired who cash in on over-inflated valuation, while acquiring companies realize very limited added value. Yet 1998 saw more mergers and acquisitions than any other year in history and 1999 maintained this pace.

In view of the above, enterprises need to seek adjustment and undertake restructuring only when it is essential rather than as a fad or for ushering in change just for the sake of it. When restructuring leads to downsizing, the hidden costs of downsizing should be assessed and particular attention paid to information sharing, two-way communication and consultation. There is a need to generate ownership among the people in the organization for the changes proposed. Negotiated changes and flexibility (Ozaki, 1999) are easier to implement than unilateral dictates from the management through office circulars. As the case studies in the volume suggest, the process makes all the difference in terms of whether change will be acceptable, regardless of its consequences.

HUMAN RESOURCE OBSOLESCENCE AND RESPONSIBLE DOWNSIZING

Human obsolescence related to the aging process—be it physical ability or alertness of the sensory organs—is something that cannot be avoided, only delayed. This is a natural phenomenon. The subject of discussion here, however, concerns such obsolescence caused, expedited and exacerbated by human failure. Our focus is human obsolescence which is man-made, not biological.

Even as the unemployment problem in certain parts of the world is causing economic risks, social tensions and political uncertainties, the winds of liberalization and globalization are forcing firms everywhere to produce and deliver superior quality products/services at low cost. Doing more with less has become the norm. With the domination of market forces and economic pressures, social and political considerations are becoming relatively less important. With equity giving way to efficiency, development is becoming customer oriented, but not human-centred. Corporate success, in today's scheme of things, requires human sacrifice. Progressive reduction in workforce is one of the stated goals of Human Resource (HR) departments of several companies in transition. Lean manning is considered an important element of human resource strategy of several companies on the growth path. Technological progress is accelerating human obsolescence particularly in contexts where skills development is not a life-long pursuit.

Reasons for Workforce Adjustment

The possible reasons for human resource obsolescence could be both external and internal.

External Reasons:
- Structural and other changes in the economy/enterprise
- Rapid advances in technology
- Product/process obsolescence
- Materials substitution (jute to plastics, for instance)
- Chronic sickness/corporate failures
- Decline in employment elasticity due to automation of routine skills.

Internal Reasons:
- Improper/inadequate human resource planning
- Wrong selection/recruitment/placement
- Inadequate training
- Inadequate/improper motivation/reward systems
- Substitution of labour with capital

Approaches to Deal with Human Resource Obsolescence

1. The approaches could be several. But every approach must incorporate marketable skills on a continuing basis. Learning should become a life-long pursuit. Individuals must own a greater share of the responsibility and the willingness to acquire multiple skills.
2. Worker flexibility must be combined with employment security. Develop a multi-skilled, adaptive and willing workforce to ensure internal changes in work practices/hours with external (worker mobility across functions/locations, etc.), numerical (size not rigid), and functional flexibility (ability to perform several tasks as needed).
3. Job specifications should be reviewed at regular intervals to make skill requirements reflect the current and future needs. For example, a paper manufacturer in South India observed that, 'In the past workmen without much qualification were appointed on account of a commitment with the union to employ the son of a workman who retires/dies. The educational level of the workman was often not satisfactory.' That lack of basic education on the part of the workman is a negative factor. This was realized and has been impressed upon the trade union, and SSLC (10 years of schooling) has now been stipulated as the minimum qualification. Similarly, at the supervisory and other levels, qualified

personnel have been inducted. In another case, a new clause was incorporated in the appointment letter: 'Company requires the employees to acquire new skills and you shall participate in such skill learning schemes. On successful acquisition and application of new skills, you shall be entitled to additional remuneration as per scheme. You shall also be placed on a job different from that for which you have been employed.'

4. Employment practices perpetuate and exacerbate obsolescence. Several Indian organizations follow the practice of employing an heir of a deceased/retired employee, usually regardless of qualifications, and at a time when the organization is switching to or adapting modern, state-of-art technologies. The possible way to deal positively with obsolescence is to stipulate realistic job specifications and review them as the job content changes. It is also necessary to provide opportunities for existing employees to acquire new qualifications and skills.

5. Downsizing and job reduction should be the last resort in economies where unemployment is high. It is irrational to talk about human resource development and yet have as a goal 'the progressive reduction of manpower'.

6. Entrepreneurship, self-employment and livelihood programmes including entrepreneurship and outplacement are all fine ideas. But one needs to be careful in prescribing entrepreneurship as a source of livelihood for the redundant and for unemployables. These, one must add at the cost of repetition, must be preceded by necessary and adequate training and appropriate follow-up systems services.

7. Much has been made about the so-called legal hurdles' in the form of various clauses in the Industrial Disputes Act. Permission for lay-off, retrenchment and closure have been considered elusive. But data confirms that in certain states the government has adopted a case-by-case approach. In Tamil Nadu, for example, during 1988–93 employers were granted permission in 40 per cent of the cases while another 40 per cent were rejected and the rest 20 per cent, still undecided. The ILO Convention No. 158 on Termination of Employment at Employer initiative (Annexure 1) suggests that technical, economic and structural factors constitute valid reasons for the termination of employment. In India, strangely, retrenchment is easy if there is a transfer of ownership,

even within the family, but not so in the event of a firm's imminent bankruptcy. The public policy should insist on notice and higher compensation, but not on prior permission.
8. Companies consider voluntary retirements as one option for labour adjustments. Voluntary retirements need to be really voluntary. The only way employers can avoid voluntary retirements for employees in categories found surplus is through the proper identification and targeting of schemes. Simultaneously, organizations need to initiate action to reassess the workflow and work norms: otherwise the work of the people who leave the organization will either suffer or get contracted out.

Measures to Avert/Minimize Job Losses

In addition to the above, several measures can be considered to avert/minimize job loss. There is need for caution, though. Restrictions on hiring, for instance, if continued over several years, may have unintended consequences and dysfunctionalities in terms of critical skill gaps at a much later date.

1. Restrictions on hiring
2. Spreading reductions over time
3. Internal transfers
4. Training and retraining
5. Voluntary early retirement
6. Income protection
7. Restriction of overtime
8. Entrepreneurship
9. Extra shift/extended work week if demand is not a constraint
10. Counselling and outplacement
11. Reduction of normal hours of work
12. Priority of rehiring

Protection from Obsolescence

Where obsolescence is inevitable, protection would be in the form of an insurance. In India, the traditional joint Hindu family system has afforded a measure of security against job and income loss. Public expenditure on social security is meagre and insufficient at about 4 per cent. In Scandinavian countries, particularly Sweden, the social security provisions (as legislated in the Swedish Act of 1985) have been so good that liberal compensation roughly equalling the salary is provided. Thus, in the short run, the adverse effects of job loss in monetary terms are negligible.

How should one provide for and who should pay for protection from obsolescence are key questions in developing countries where social security nets are virtually absent. The capacity to provide social protection depends on the health of the economy and rates of inflation and unemployment. If the economy is in a poor state of health and the rates of inflation and unemployment are high, the country cannot provide much social protection. Idealism needs to be tempered with pragmatism. Obsolescence in some sectors can be protected through subsidies from other sectors. But when obsolescence becomes a widespread phenomenon, subsidies cannot be sustained without surgery.

Protecting Existing Jobs

The easy way of dealing with obsolescence seems to be to not recognize it as a problem. The following questions must be asked:

1. Are we protecting productive jobs? If not, does it not lead to the frittering away of productive resources for unproductive purposes?
2. What does obsolescence cost, relative to new job creation?
3. How does it affect the fresh entrants into the labour market?
4. What will the social costs of protection and non-protection of existing jobs be?

Case Studies

British Steel: As part of massive restructuring, British Steel had to close several plants, phase out/disinvest non-core operations, and lay-off or retrench several persons. Nearly 100,000 jobs were eliminated. The adverse effect of job losses was significant in certain areas where British Steel was a major employer in the community. To mitigate the negative effects and to facilitate rejuvenation of industrial activity in the region/community, British Steel had set up a separate corporation for active labour market interventions in terms of special investments to create jobs. It had conducted hinterland surveys for assessing job creation/livelihood programmes using local resources/ opportunities, provided training and other inputs to encourage enterprise creation and helped boost job opportunities in an otherwise depressed area.

Japan Railways: In the wake of the privatization of Japan National Railways, too, nearly 93,000 jobs were considered redundant. It was agreed that 32,000 workers, even though redundant, would continue to be employed by the six new firms created as a result of privatization. 41,000 workers were transferred to a reserve pool, called 'kyukokutetsu' for three years to be retrained. The remaining 20,000 were expected to retire voluntarily between October 1985 and April 1987. The Japan National Railway Reconstruction Supervisory Committee created for administering the privatization programme assessed the manpower requirements not only of Japan Railways but also looked at ways of preventing human obsolescence.

Two-way communication and information sharing between employers and workers' representatives and the general climate of mutual trust in labour–management relations have facilitated mutual cooperation particularly in fighting human obsolescence. There are several examples of how labour and management have made common cause in fighting the problem through a less contentious strategy of training and retraining (Gladstone and Ozaki, 1991).

In Sweden, the Development Agreement of 1982 between unions and employers at national level states that both parties will collaborate in introducing new technology and in training for change (Jones, 1990). In Denmark, the Danish Employers Confederation (DA) and the Federation of Trade Unions (LO) delegated 'joint-decision-making powers on basics for employee training' to newly established technology committees (SLB). In the Federal Republic of Germany, the workers' council is involved in 'who is to get what kind of training'. At UMMI, a joint venture of Toyota and General Motors in California (USA), joint training initiatives by the labour and management produced an interesting role reversal: the management assumes the task of ensuring 'workers decent wages, job security and participation in decision-making' while 'labour accepts its responsibility for promoting productivity and growth'. A somewhat different approach to union involvement in training can be noticed in Singapore. The Singapore National Trade Union Congress (SNTUC) took the initiative to provide training to those affected by industrial restructuring in the wake of the management's unwillingness to train multi-skilled workers due to its fear of losing them to other employees.

In India, there is a welcome realization about the need for labour–management cooperation in training in the context of modernization and restructuring. The example that readily comes to mind is the 1989 agreement between the unions and management with respect to modernization of the Indian Iron and Steel Company, Burnpur. The agreement outlines, among other measures, action plans for retraining and redeployment of affected workers. There is also considerable innovation in the attitudes of the management and unions in several organizations in tackling the resistance to computers and spreading computer literacy. In contrast, the agreement between bankman's unions and Indian Banks' Association (representing 58 banks including public, private and foreign banks) signed an agreement in October 1993 providing for limited computerization: one per cent of the branches can be computerized in a year if a bank has less than 500 branches, and so on. For this the bank staff (non-executives) would get an increment. The agreement provides, thus, for full computerization in Indian banks (effectively it means the public sector banks because all foreign and new private sector banks anyway have state-of-the-art computer facilities) over the next 150 years! Little wonder that Mrs Joan Robinson once observed that India is so diverse that whatever you say the opposite is equally true.

Financing Training to Avert/Mitigate the Problem of Obsolescence

Innovative schemes exist to finance training and retraining for redeployment so as to avoid or minimize the adverse effects of human obsolescence.

In Sweden, the government declared that 10 per cent (the rate may vary, depending on profits) of profit over SwKr 0.5 million (about US$ 0.1 million) in all companies must be set aside, tax-free, in the so-called Renewal Funds for being spent on training and R&D as agreed between the companies, the unions and the government. Volvo, for instance, was financing 75 per cent of an ambitious training programme from this source.

In both Singapore and Malaysia, the state has created a Skills Development Fund. Malaysia enacted the Human Development Act in 1992 whereby employers contribute 1.5 per cent of their wage bill to the Skills Development Fund and the government provides a matching contribution.

In India, schemes like the Textile Workers' Rehabilitation Fund (TWRF) attempted to provide some income support to affected persons. As elsewhere, here too the implementation was ineffective. The National Renewal Fund (NRF) was established during 1991–92 to facilitate, among other things, the retraining and redeployment of employees affected by structural adjustment reforms and enterprise restructuring. Unfortunately, the NRF has virtually become the National Retrenchment Fund as the Fund has been utilized mainly to finance voluntary retirements—about 90,000 between 1991 and 1994 through the NRF and another 90,000 through company-funded schemes. Only about 1,000 have been retrained and barely 100 found jobs in skills related to areas in which they were retrained. As a concept the NRF is good, but its implementation is faulty. It needs more coordination with the ministry of labour and the active involvement of the social partners. The retraining efforts hardly took off.

It must be added that retraining costs less than retrenchment. Training even redundant employees in marketable skills and outplacement services (including counselling) offer opportunities to deal with workforce obsolescence and redundancy in a labour-friendly manner. Here, of course, the attitudes of managements count. One public sector firm in India admitted that it costs less to retrain than to retrench and invested in retraining. Another public sector firm in India, however, did not want the redundant workers who took voluntary retirement to return to the company for retraining because it thought that such people would be a bad influence.

CONCLUSION

Management philosophy and attitudes can make a vast difference. One view is that obsolescence is inevitable. The other view holds that obsolescence is partly avoidable and partly unavoidable, therefore the thinking is: let us do our best to minimize/avert the adverse effects on the people in our organization. Manmade obsolescence needs the ingenuity of homo sapiens to fight against it. Let those in charge of managing people think as if they are the ones affected when considering how to deal with human obsolescence. Let them and let us all stop worrying about the problem and start thinking about a solution. For every problem there is more than one solution. However, let not anxiety lead to a situation whereby the solution to the problem itself is the cause for a hundred other problems.

REFERENCES

Gladstone, Alan and Muneto Ozaki (eds) (1991). *Labour Management Cooperation in Training and in Technological and Other Changes.* Geneva: International Labour Office.
International Labour Organisation (1992). *World Labour Report.* Geneva: ILO.
International Labour Organisation (1997). *ILO Enterprise Forum, Geneva, 1996— Summary of Proceedings.* Geneva.
International Labour Organisation (1999a). *Decent Work.* Geneva.
International Labour Organisation (1999b). *Enterprise Forum, Geneva, 199-A New Spirit of Enterprise: Articles and Cases.* Geneva.
Jones, H.G. (1990). 'The Job Cycle: A Positive Approach'. *Future.* October. pp. 843–861.
Klingel, Sally and Ann Martin (1988). *A Fighting Chance.* ILR Press, New York State School of Industrial Relations, Cornell University.
Ozaki, M. (1999). *Negotiating Flexibility.* Geneva: ILO.
Sengupta, N.K. and C.S. Venkata Ratnam (1994). *Report on the Workshop on National Renewal Fund.* New Delhi: IMI. Mimeo.
Social and Labour Bulletin (SLB) (1981). Geneva: ILO. No. 2. pp. 133–134.
Starcher, G. (1999). *Socially Responsible Enterprise Restructuring.* Geneva: ILO (1999b). *Enterprise Forum.* 1999. op. cit.
Venkata Ratnam, C.S. (1991). *Role of Employers' Organisation in Privatisation.* Geneva: ILO Bureau for Employers Activities. Mimeo
Venkata Ratnam, C.S. (1992). *Managing People.* New Delhi: Global Business Press. pp. 84–95.

ANNEXURE I

Tripartite Consultations for Job Maintenance and Job Creation

TERMINATION OF EMPLOYMENT AT THE INITIATIVE OF THE EMPLOYER

The articles contained in ILO Convention No. 158 and Recommendation No. 166 should guide the policy and practice on the subject.

Justification for Termination

The employment of a worker shall not be terminated unless there is a valid reason for such termination connected with the capacity or conduct of the worker or based on the operational requirements of the undertaking, establishment or service (Article 4). Economic, technological, structural or reasons of a similar nature may constitute valid reasons for termination of employment, but the burden of proof is on the employer (Article 9).

The following inter alia, shall not constitute valid reasons for termination (Article 5):

(a) Union membership or participation in union activities outside working hours or, with the consent of the employer, within working hours.
(b) Seeking office, as, or acting or having acted in the capacity of a workers' representative.
(c) The filing of a complaint or the participation in proceedings against an employer involving alleged violation of laws or regulations or recourse to competent administrative authorities.
(d) Race, colour, sex, marital status, family responsibilities, pregnancy, religion, political opinion, national extraction or social origin.
(e) Absence from work during maternity leave.
(f) Temporary absence from work because of illness or injury (Article 6).

PROCEDURES

Prior to or at the Time of Termination

The employment of a worker shall not be terminated for reasons related to the worker's conduct or performance before he is provided an opportunity to defend himself against the allegations made, unless the employer can not reasonably be expected to provide this opportunity (Article 7).

Appeal

A worker who considers that his employment has been unjustifiably terminated shall be entitled to appeal against that termination to an impartial body, such as a court, labour tribunal, etc. Remedies for unjust termination may include, consistent with national law and practice, proposal for reinstatement of the worker or adequate compensation or such other relief as may be deemed appropriate (Article 10).

Notice

A worker whose employment is to be terminated shall be entitled to a reasonable period of notice or compensation in lieu thereof unless he is guilty of serious misconduct, that is, misconduct of such a nature that it would be unreasonable to require the employer to continue his employment during the notice period.

A worker whose employment has been terminated shall be entitled, in accordance with national law and practice, to:

(a) A severance allowance or other separation benefits, based on length of service and the level of wages, and paid directly by the employer or by a fund constituted by employers' contributions; or
(b) benefits from unemployment insurance or assistance or other forms of social security; or
(c) a combination of such allowance and benefits.

Consultation with Workers' Representatives

When the employer contemplates terminations for reasons of an economic, technological, structural or similar nature, the employer shall provide concerned workers representatives in good time with relevant information including the reasons for the termination contemplated, the number and categories of workers likely to be affected and the period over which the terminations are intended to be carried out. The employer shall also, in accordance with national practice, give workers representatives opportunity for consultation on measures to be taken to minimize or avert the adverse effects of terminations contemplated.

Measures to Avoid Termination

ILO Recommendation No. 166 suggests the following measures to avert or minimize terminations of employment for reasons of an economic, technological, structural or similar nature:

- Restriction of hiring
- Spreading of the workforce reduction over a certain period of time to permit natural reduction of the workforce
- Internal transfers
- Training and retraining
- Voluntary early retirement with appropriate income protection
- Restriction of overtime
- Reduction of normal hours of work
- Priority of rehiring within given period of time if qualifications meet job specifications

Eight

Aligning Labour Policy with Economic Policies and Industrialization Strategies

The stark reality about India's labour policy during the past 50 years has been that it has covered only a small fraction (less than 8 per cent) of the labour force. It has a long way to go in protecting the vulnerable, maintaining harmony and ensuring productivity. Neither labour policy nor labour law has kept pace with the changes in society and the economy. For good governance what is required is a firmness to defend traditional values and promote change with a dual focus on both equity and efficiency.

KEY CONCERNS

The manifestos of the major political parties in the 1998 General Elections had consensus in the thrust, though not in the tone, regarding their concerns about labour. Broadly, these can be listed as under:

- Job protection and employment creation
- Extending legal protection to the unorganized sector
- Some promised improvement in living standards while others talked about linking wages to productivity

- Vocational training and skills development
- Trade union recognition through secret ballot
- Workers' participation in management at all levels, while some mentioned workers' takeover of sick units through cooperatives and worker ownership
- Industrial sickness and attendant problems
- Social security benefits, including pension

The agenda of the government should therefore cover, as a basic minimum, the concerns of the pre-poll 'political consensus'. It should also include some other issues, which are not necessarily populist. These are:

- A paradigm shift in the labour policy environment
- The aligning of labour policy with economic policy
- Labour law reform
- Competitive labour policies at the state level
- The reviewing of the link between the Parliament, the judiciary and the bureaucracy

Paradigm Shift in the Labour Policy Environment

The processes of liberalization, privatization and globalization mean that the government's role in social and labour matters has to change, not diminish. Paradigm shifts in the government's role and attitude to labour should reflect the following:

1. The content and purpose of labour policy and labour law should focus on facilitation rather than regulation, proaction and reaction, and on the creation of harmonious relations conducive to social and economic development rather than dispute resolution. A decline in the role of the state in economic activity need not necessarily lead to a decline in its regulatory/supervisory role in labour and industrial relations matters. In fact, when the private sector becomes the engine of growth, the state may need to play a much stronger role in ensuring a balance between the rights of both labour and management.
2. Labour policy should focus more broadly on the entire labour force. It should be developmental, not regulatory. There should be a decisive shift towards proactive labour market intervention,

with the major thrust on the development of skills and attitudes conducive to building a cohesive and productive work culture. Labour policy must be more closely aligned to changes in industrial and other policies. It should provide the stimulus for rather than shun job creation.
3. Globalization is leading to decentralized industrial relations. There is a need to create and strengthen institutions/mechanisms for information sharing, consultation, communication and consensus development at the enterprise/firm level.
4. The labour market is characterized by dualism: an illiterate, unskilled, unorganized, unprotected and mute majority of the workforce existing side by side with a literate, skilled, organized, protected and vocal minority. Political unions, acting in unison with the state, may force it to pursue labour market policies based on political considerations rather than on considerations of labour and product market characteristics. The resultant distortions are contrary to the declared goals of equity and efficiency and may even precipitate state and market failures. The state should therefore broad-base the scope of labour policy and labour legislation to cover the unorganized sector in a more-substantive manner than is currently being done.
5. The state should give up its negative function and assume a positive one of promoting sound labour–management relations. Statistics on strikes and lockouts do not always reflect the actual state of industrial relations either at the firm, industry, state or national level. Here, the state can provide mediation and arbitration services. It can also acknowledge the semi-public status of labour market parties, but in democratic tripartite structures.
6. Hitherto, the need for public sector enterprises to be model employers has been stressed. Now, with growing competition in the context of globalization, there is a need for them to be model performers as well.
7. Sustaining growth and fostering competitive labour markets are critical to ensuring job and income security. The demand for jobs does not depend on the supply of labour. There is a need for a fundamental change in employment and income security measures. The concept of bankruptcy is not accepted in India where jobs are treated as property with attendant hereditary rights in some employment contexts. Employment flexibility,

recruitment, transfer, promotion, work assignment, workforce adjustment, etc., need to be considered dispassionately with due regard to both employment and social stability as well as to business imperatives, if any. Job security at any cost, regardless of the viability of the enterprise which provides the job in the first instance, can lead to a counterproductive work culture. It should be the obligation of the state to eradicate poverty and to end unemployment through the creation of productive jobs which do not sacrifice the basics of the quality of life. Here, labour-intensive industrialization strategies are appropriate and the options should be different in existing vis-à-vis new businesses. During the transition period, foreign investment may lead to jobless growth. Therefore, parallel domestic/public investments should target areas where the job potential is high.

8. The state should, therefore, ensure a wider social dialogue for broad-based social consensus and social cohesion. Tripartism cannot survive without state patronage. Despite the long tradition of tripartite consultation, in the past quarter century it has atrophied due to the weak and unrepresentative character of the three social partners. Traditionally, tripartism is restricted to consultations among the government and organizations of workers and employers in the organized sector. There is a need to extend the scope to other sections of society including the unemployed, unorganized and even consumers. In South Africa, the establishment of the National Economic Development Labour Advisory Council merits attention for possible lessons. Academicians should be associated with tripartite bodies. While the government has already taken initiatives to rationalize and restructure tripartite committees, there is a further need to reform the way in which tripartite meetings are conducted. They focus on the draft proposals concerning the agenda and follow the double-discussion procedure in considering ILO conventions. Ministries other than the labour ministry also need to take an active interest in such consultations.

9. There is a growing concern that globalization benefits few but effects many in negative ways. The commitment to rural labour, women labour, child labour, bonded labour, and labour in the unorganized sector has, so far, been largely rhetorical.

10. The state also has an obligation to make social justice an integral part of developmental planning. Exhortations like 'sacrifice today for a better tomorrow' will not hold much water in societies where the rich continue to get richer and the poor poorer. As Reich (1995) cautioned, 'Persistent unemployment/underemployment, declining wages and living standards undermine the moral fabric of capital democracy . . . . In a democracy, people will vote for economic dynamism only if they have a fair chance of benefiting from it.'

Aligning Labour Policy with Economic Policy

Fifty years ago, in the newly independent and industrializing India, the state avowed its commitment to the welfare of workers. The politically controlled economic system required politically oriented economic action by workers. An influential section of the union movement tacitly endorsed the state's preference for adjudication rather than articulating the need for promoting collective bargaining.

In today's world, the policies of protection, self-reliance and import subsistence are giving way to policies of competition with a view to integrating the national with the global economy and boosting foreign investment and exports. To catch up with other industrialized countries, India needs to attract capital, cut costs and enhance competitiveness. In the sphere of labour, this means a new alignment between industrialization policies and industrial relations policies.

Towards this end, labour policy should stress on: (i) the observance of a minimal number of core/basic labour standards; (ii) free trade unions and collective bargaining; (iii) workplace institutions capable of internalizing enforcement of labour standards/government regulations and effecting changes at the micro level smoothly; (iv) investment in education and training; (v) bringing the entire labour force under the purview of minimal, but effective—rational and rationalized—regulatory/administrative norms; (vi) proactive labour market policies that provide building skills/competencies, reduce/eliminate the existing mismatch between acquired and required skills, facilitate information and counselling facilities for employment; and, (vii) a culture of non-interference by one party in the affairs of the other.

Labour market flexibility is a factor, not *the* factor that influences the flow of foreign direct investment. The minimum that foreign investors expect is: (a) a clear enunciation of the rights and responsibilities of employers and workers/unions; (b) an unambiguous and easily understandable legal and institutional framework; (c) predictable arrangements concerning union recognition, collective bargaining, skills development, flexibility and workforce adjustment; (d) well-defined, clear-cut and time-bound procedures for grievance redressal; and, (e) an administrative and judicial system that can be trusted for its transparency, integrity, expediency, efficiency and accountability.

Competitive Labour Policies at the State Level

Labour is in the concurrent list under Article 246 of the Constitution of India. Given the trend towards the accentuation of regional disparities, state governments may consider the pros and cons of competitive labour policies with a view to inducing investment and encouraging job creation. Presently, states can and do make a difference in areas like trade union registration, recognition, minimum wage laws, defining or redefining limits or granting exemptions concerning the applicability of certain legislations, etc. The labour bureaucracy can also make a difference in matters ranging from inspections and penalties to adjudication and even the use of force (deployment of the police, for instance).

Since 1991 to date, several state governments have made far-reaching changes in their policies. For instance, Uttar Pradesh, requires the labour inspector to obtain prior permission of the labour commissioner or labour minister; Rajasthan has granted exemption to several firms; and both Rajasthan and Andhra Pradesh have simplified several forms with regard to labour inspection. Orissa and West Bengal have introduced secret ballot. Maharashtra proposed a new legislation in the mid-1990s—the Maharashtra Industrial Relations Act to replace the existing Bombay Industrial Relations Act and Prevention of Unfair Labour Practices Act; and Kerala announced radical moves in labour policies as part of its 1994 industrial policy.

The desirability, possibility and feasibility of competitive labour policies merits serious consideration. The implications of industrial relations pertaining to centre–state relations, particularly public sector undertakings, also needs careful review.

Labour Law Reform

In a global economy, labour law as an autonomous subject stands at a crossroad. Some judges feel compelled to interpret law not on the basis of the text of the clauses, but in the light of the preamble to that particular piece of legislation and more importantly, the Indian Constitution itself. Therefore, the 'new economic policies' may sometimes be interpreted as being inconsistent with the Indian Constitution. Elsewhere in the world, there is another view gaining ground: the social vision of labour law which went with the old-established institutions and practices has come under challenge to change and risks irrelevance. The current scenario requires striking a balance between these two extreme viewpoints.

There is a perception that the existing laws give virtual veto power to the unions in the organized sector to block changes like improvement in plant and machinery, the rationalization of manpower, and growth of productivity. Further, there is a perception that labour legislation has paved the way for a multiplicity of unions, the growth of intra- and inter-union rivalry, the exacerbation of industrial strife and the excessive intervention by the state in industrial relations.

There are as many as 165 legislations—both central and state—that address themselves to various aspects relating to labour. But more laws mean less when implementation is thinly spread out. Even minimum wage laws have meant little when the wages fixed are low and implementation lax. Study groups of the National Commission on Labour and the National Labour Law Association (NLLA) prepared draft labour codes in 1969 and 1994 respectively. The Commission on Labour Standards appointed by the Government of India, in its report submitted in 1995, almost entirely endorsed the NLLA's Draft Labour Code. It suggested a few changes: initiate a national debate or wider consultation on the Draft Labour Code through Project LARGE (Legal Adjustment Reforms for Globalising Economy) and simplify the law without further delay.

Labour law reform is not easy. The Korean experience confirms this. When the economy was doing well, the organized labour put up bitter struggles against the new Korean law which was enacted to make, among other things, workforce adjustment easy. In the wake of the Korean economic crisis, however, a tripartite agreement provided for the very changes that were opposed just a year earlier. Several economies in transition (notably China and Vietnam) and those undertaking structural adjustment (many in Africa and Latin America) have been able to rewrite labour law without much friction.

The Government of India has appointed the Second National Commission on Labour (1999) to address itself to the issue of aligning labour policy and labour laws with the contemporary concerns of product markets. The contrast between the terms of reference of the first and the second national commissions on labour (Table 8.1) points to the stark shift in emphasis from the labour market (First National Commission on Labour) to the product market (Second National Commission on Labour) and a palpable concern for a separate simplified approach (one umbrella legislation) for the unorganized sector.

TABLE 8.1 **Terms of Reference of the First and the Second NCL**

Terms of Reference of the First National Commission on Labour (1966)	Terms of Reference of the Second National Commission on Labour (1999)
1. To review the changes in conditions of labour since Independence and to report on existing conditions of labour.	(a) To suggest rationalization of existing laws relating to labour in the organized sector.
2. To review the existing legislative and other provisions intended to protect the interests of labour, to assess their working and to advise how far these provisions serve to implement the Directive Principles of State Policy in the Constitution on labour matters and the national objective of establishing a socialist society and achieving planned economic development.	(b) To suggest an 'umbrella' legislation for ensuring a minimum level of protection to the workers in the unorganized sector.
	While drafting the framework for the above, the Commission may take into account the following:
3. To study and report in particular on:	(i) Follow up implications of the recommendations made by the Commission set up in May, 1998 for review of various administrative laws governing the industry.
(i) The levels of workers' earnings, the provisions relating to wages, the need for fixation of minimum wages including a national minimum wage, the means of increasing productivity, including the provision of incentives to workers.	(ii) The emerging economic environment involving rapid technological changes, requiring response in terms of change in methods, timings and conditions of work in industry, trade and services, globalization of economy, liberalization of trade and industry and emphasis on international competitiveness
(ii) The standard of living and the health, efficiency, safety,	

(Contd.)

Terms of Reference of the First National Commission on Labour (1966)	Terms of Reference of the Second National Commission on Labour (1999)
welfare, housing, training and education of workers and the existing arrangements for administration of labour welfare, both at the centre and in the states. (iii) The existing arrangements for social security. (iv) The state of relations between employers and workers and the role of trade unions and employers' organizations in promoting healthy industrial relations and the interest of the nation. (v) The labour laws and voluntary arrangements like the code of discipline, joint management councils, voluntary arbitration and wage boards and the machinery at the centre and in the states for their enforcement. (vi) Measures for improving conditions of rural labour and other categories of unorganized labour. (vii) Existing arrangements for labour intelligence and research; and to make recommendations on the above matters.	and the need for bringing the existing laws in tune with the future labour market needs and demands. (iii) The minimum level of labour protection and welfare measures and the basic institutional framework for ensuring the same, in the manner which is conducive to a flexible labour market and adjustments necessary for furthering technological change and economic growth. (iv) Improving the effectiveness of measures relating to social security, occupational health and safety, minimum wages and linkages of wages with productivity and in particular the safeguards and facilities required for women and handicapped persons in employment.

The major thrust of changes in labour laws should be along the following lines:

- It would be expedient to have fewer laws but ensure better enforcement. It would be still more expedient and equitable to have one labour code instead of numerous legislations, as China and Vietnam did in the mid-1990s. The nature and extent of protection for labour has little to do with the number of laws.
- Multiple definitions should be eliminated across different legislations. Wages, for instance, are defined in a dozen ways in as many legislations. The legal distinction between worker, workman and other worker is exclusionary, and unless otherwise

defined perpetuates discriminatory practices and confusion. Dictionary meanings should be considered adequate. The Labour Code can cover all working people rather than have variations in limitation concerning numbers employed, amount of wages/salaries drawn, etc.

- There should be one national minimum wage act for all occupations rather than separate ones for select notified industries/occupations. It should be made easy to understand, simple to administer and effective to enforce.
- Several amendments to the Trade Unions Act suggested earlier by bipartite committees and incorporated subsequently in a bill prepared by the ministry of labour do not serve any useful purpose. They do, however, perpetrate distrust among unions and create strife. Japan and Denmark do not have trade union acts. In Japan, the union movement is consolidated and multiplicity reduced without legal intervention. Denmark is a country with one of the highest rates of unionization.
- Almost all political parties and many unions favour secret ballot. But it would be prudent to review the experiences of Andhra Pradesh, Orissa and West Bengal before taking any action, since the experience so far suggest that the present conditions are not conducive to secret ballot. It has led to anti-establishment votes and to the destabilization of recognized unions, causing strife in industrial relations and resultant litigation.
- The provisions of the Industrial Disputes Act should be reviewed while preparing the Labour Code. Legislations in some South-East Asian countries as well as China and Vietnam offer valuable insights. In the wake of structural changes and liberalization, more than 100 developing countries and transitional economies have reformed their labour law. The three most important changes in legislation, which are necessary in the Indian context also, are as follows: (a) Employment can be secure only so long as the enterprise where employment is held is secure and viable. According to ILO Convention No. 168, the termination of employment at the initiative of the employer can be valid if structural, technical, economic and other changes so require. Workforce adjustment as per business needs is imperative. Notice, consultation, and compensation provisions can and should be tightened. The requirement of prior permission of the government

should be dispensed with in matters concerning lay-off, retrenchment and closure; (b) Section 9-A, concerning notice of change, should be amended. Notice is required and consultation is to be encouraged, but the employer should have the responsibility, if not the right, to make changes necessary to maintain and improve competitiveness; (c) As in the Malaysian legislation which forbids bargaining in respect of recruitment, transfer, promotion, work assignment and workforce adjustment, in India, too, collective bargaining should be encouraged on aspects other than the above.

- The industrial relations machinery should be made independent as recommended by the National Commission on Labour.
- Some studies point out that job protection laws impede job creation. Increase in the price of labour and its relative inflexibility have also been found responsible for the stagnation of job opportunities. These studies have also found that job loss was less with adjustment than without it. It is necessary to investigate the technological determinedness of employment decisions, employment effects of adjustment vis-à-vis non-adjustment and consequences of job creation on further job creation and claims of the unemployed and fresh entrants to the job market. The cost of job protection and its effects on job creation require careful analysis. The ILO–South Asian Multidisciplinary Team's study drew attention to the need to shift the focus from job protection to income protection.
- A skills development fund and a tripartite national wages council should be set up.

Reviewing the Link between the Parliament, the Judiciary and the Executive

The process of the integration of the Indian economy with the global economy started seven years ago. Some say it started much before that. Political manifestos, however, do not realize the need for a linkage between the industrialization strategy and industrial relations strategy. The apparent contradiction with the preamble to the Indian Constitution—which still retains the magic phrase, 'socialist democracy'—leaves the field wide open for a variety of interpretations by the judiciary. There is a need to reassess the roles of the Parliament, the judiciary and the bureaucracy.

Since Justice Krishna Iyer gave his interpretation of the definition of industry in the Bangalore Sewerage Company case, there have been couple of other landmark judgements on the subject which have reversed and re-reversed the Bengal Sewerage judgement. When the Supreme Court declared that P&T was not an industry, but a sovereign activity under the state, P&T officials refused to appear before the conciliation machinery of the central government with regard to the disposal of certain grievances of their employees.

Some judgements of the Supreme Court have the effect of prescribing legislation. For instance, in the case of Food Corporation of India concerning the representative union, the Supreme Court mandated that the matter be settled through secret ballot and even prescribed the procedure for conducting it. Similarly, in many cases relating to child labour, environment and sexual harassment, the judgements have prescribed dos and don'ts.

There have been judgements in recent years which have upset the organized labour while those concerning unorganized labour including contract labour have generally gladdened the hearts of the workers.

Our labour bureaucracy is caught between these two extremes. 'Labour policy in future will be market friendly', a high-ranking official of the labour ministry assured the audience at a conference on globalization. The labour leader present on the podium demurred, 'If labour policy is not labour friendly what kind of a labour policy is it?'

'I am the labour commissioner, not the management commissioner,' was the stern reply of a labour commissioner to an industrialist who was pleading his case about the rigidities in the labour market of the country.

The labour bureaucracy has, however, enormous powers. It can stall the will of the Parliament through delays or a notification in the gazette. For instance, the amendment to Section 9c of the Industrial Disputes Act in 1982 has not been notified to date. In another case, though electronics is not notified for the purposes of the Minimum Wages Act in one state, a labour inspector who found a lathe machine in a unit chose to classify the unit as an engineering industry and applied the Minimum Wages Act to it.

It is important that all the three wings—the Parliament, the judiciary and the bureaucracy—function in harmony and unison without compromising on the rationale of their respective roles.

CONCLUSION

Labour policy should concern itself with the entire labour force. Till not too long ago, the labour policy in India had addressed itself mostly to the 8 per cent labour force in the organized sector. Even salaried workers constitute only a fraction (about 15 per cent) of the total labour force in the country. It is time greater attention was paid to the issues confronting the workforce in the unorganized sector. A credible mechanism for providing literacy and vocational skills training to all aspirants in the labour market, together with a support mechanism for basic health and social security, are imperative. Further, workplace industrial relations systems should be put in place that facilitate change, promote flexibility and prepare the workforce to be able, adaptive and attuned to respond to the challenges of change.

REFERENCES

Debroy, B (1997). 'Labour Market Reform'. Policy Paper No. 22 prepared for Project LARGE (Legal Adjustments and Reforms for Globalising the Economy). New Delhi: Allied Publishers.

Kuruvilla, S. and C.S. Venkata Ratnam (1996). 'Economic Development and Industrial Relations: The Case of South Asia and Southeast Asia'. *Industrial Relations Journal.* 27(1), pp. 9-23.

ILO-SAAT (1996). *India: Economic Reforms and Labour Policies.* New Delhi: ILO-SAAT and UNDP.

Japan Institute of Labour (1996). 'Industrial Relations and Labour Law in Changing Asian Economies'. Proceedings of the 1996 Asian Regional Conference on Industrial Relations. Tokyo: Japan.

Reich, R. (1995). Address to the delegates of the 10th World Congress of International Industrial Relations Association. Washington DC: IRRA. May 31-June 4.

Venkata Ratnam, C.S. (1997). 'Competitive Labour Policies in Indian States'. Working Paper prepared for Project LARGE. New Delhi: Allied Publishers.

Venkata Ratnam, C.S. (1997). 'The Role of the State in Industrial Relations in the Era of Globalisation'. Paper presented at the subregional tripartite meeting on Globalisation and Transformation of Industrial Relations in South Asia at New Delhi during 15-17, 1997. New Delhi: ILO-South Asia Multidisciplinary Advisory Team (Mimeo).

NINE

Judicial Activism*

Even as the pressure on the reform of labour law, labour administration and labour judiciary mounts in the wake of the challenges of liberalization and globalization, the response of the judiciary to some of the vexing social issues in the context of employment offers new challenges and responsibilities for different interest groups. So far the discussions and debates have focused on the challenges of the 1990s and beyond. They cover issues relating to structural adjustment problems, corporate governance, and the efficiency of labour and management for enhancing competitiveness.

Building on the discussion in the previous chapter, we focus on the challenges posed by judicial activism and the implications thereof. We also consider the relative importance of citizenship/consumer rights and human/social rights of workers and their unions. The second part of the chapter presents a summary of the judgements handed down in six cases and raises the key questions that the judgements leave open for discussion.

Law making is a complex exercise. The original bill may have been well drafted and properly vetted by the Law Commission. When it is tabled for discussion in the Parliament, several interest groups

---

*Paper presented at the seminar on Impact of Recent Judgements on Employees, Employers and Consumers organised by the Indian Industrial Relations Association and National Labour Law Association at New Delhi in October 1998.

press for amendments of all sorts. Democratic decision making often entails accommodating conflicting views and making compromises with the result that by the time the original bill comes out of the Parliament as an act, it loses its original shape and sharpness.

Judges are human beings and carry human frailties with them. Being humans, they have their own inclinations and ideological persuasions. Not surprisingly, some judges deem it their privilege to pass judgements based on the intent (preamble) rather than the content (clauses/text) of the law. This gives them the power to extend the scope of the law and stretch its inerpretation through a creative display of mastery over the language. Judges are not ordinary mortals to be swayed by practical considerations. Some of them are powered by the ideals they believe in and the idealism they cherish. Therefore, while the affected parties may label them pro-labour or pro-capital, the judgements *per se* cannot normally be faulted. In labour law, judges are not bound by the precedent effect even though employers/ managers are.

The need for judicial activism arises when the judiciary comes face to face with legislative arbitrariness or executive (bureaucracy) abuses. When justice is elusive elsewhere, the judiciary takes it upon itself to 'award' social justice by offering creative interpretations and innovative solutions to vexing issues. Unfortunately, however, when judges interpret the law in a manner that an influential section of the Parliament considers not palatable, it has not lost the opportunity to amend the law to make judgements redundant. For instance, there have been many such examples in the evolution of the Industrial Disputes Act—particularly provisions concerning closure, lay-off and retrenchment—since 1947. It is sad, though, that both the Parliament and the judiciary consider it necessary to periodically and frequently assert their supremacy through such shadowboxing.

The bureaucracy is a wonderful animal with its weird ways of working. As a former finance minister said, India's progress will have to wait till its politicians learn to say no and its bureaucrats learn to say yes (in a real sense). In quite a few cases, both employers and workers have been unhappy with the final form of a particular piece of legislation. For instance, consider the case of the early 1980s amendments to the Industrial Disputes Act inserting Chapter VB on grievance redressal, which the Parliament had already enacted. In order to stall the implementation the bureaucracy simply did not notify the enactment in the Official Gazette. The matter is stalled and will be till either the bureaucracy or the Parliament intervenes.

Governments and employers often consider that judgements in specific cases apply only to the parties in the cases concerned. They do not seem to realize the value of the underlying principles to parties in similar situations on subsequent occasions. It is also a matter of concern that smaller benches of the Supreme Court sometimes give judgements that set aside verdicts given earlier in similar cases by larger benches of the Supreme Court. This undermines the binding nature of the verdicts of the larger benches and manifests a growing trend towards judicial indiscipline.

IMPLICATIONS OF JUDGE-MADE LAW ON EMPLOYERS AND WORKERS

Sometimes the situations can be tricky and complex: workers may be lawless, employers may consider themselves above the law and judges may think they are the law. Not infrequently, conflict is perceived or created between issues such as morality, legality, humanity, economic-sense, political wisdom and fiscal prudence. Employers and workers have been affected by judicial activism, public interest litigation and consumer courts both positively and negatively.

Both employers and workers have been affected by some judgements. For instance the decisions on public interest litigation on environmental matters such as the closure of polluting industries and the prohibition of mining activities in forest areas have been resisted by both the parties. In one case involving the closure/shifting of factories in Agra to prevent the pollution they supposedly caused to the Taj Mahal, one of the seven wonders in the world, both employers and workers, rallied holding placards which said, '*Taj hamara shan hai, Udyog hamara jan hai*' (Taj is our pride, but industry is our livelihood).

The need for judicial activism arises when managements are insensitive to workers' demands, workers are apathetic to consumers interests, trade unions are ignorant about the imperatives of making business units viable to keep jobs and incomes secure, and bureaucrats aid and abet politicians in treating workers as vote banks.

Examples of Judgements which Make Employers Happy	Examples of Judgements which Make Workers Happy
Imposition of fine on trade union leaders for indulging in arson, loss of company property, etc.	Regularization of casual/contract labour. Absorption of contract labour as regular labour when the system of contract labour is abolished.
Ruling that a strike has not only to be legal, but also justified; Application of the norm of no work no pay in the case of strikes and for those who do union work as against company work.	Striking off of the contents of service conditions and standing orders in matters like treating unauthorised absence for over a week as abandonment of employment.
Restrictions on protest demonstrations, political bundhs, etc.	Requirement of a notice of change when the Voluntary Retirement Scheme is introduced because work done by more people will now be required to be done by fewer people.
Decision of the Karnataka High Court upholding the dismissal of the president of the employees' association of a public sector establishment for having criticized its chairman in the media and for having made a representation to the Governor.	Ruling of the Supreme Court that the service of employees in an organization cannot be terminated arbitrarily and abruptly by giving notice of one or three months or pay in lieu of notice.
Decision that in the case of accidents by a bus or lorry, the compensation payable to the victims should be recovered from the earnings of drivers.	Abolition of child labour in hazardous industries.

THE RELATIVE IMPORTANCE OF CITIZEN/ CONSUMER RIGHTS AND SOCIAL/HUMAN RIGHTS OF WORKERS

In the post-liberalization era of globalization, the consumer is no more a mere king on paper. The Consumer Protection Act, 1986 and the redressal forum created thereunder have given him/her rights that threaten to subordinate the rights of workers and their unions. In several judgements, both consumer courts and civil courts are telling workers and their unions that rights are theirs only if in exercising them they do not step on the rights of others. The right to agitation by disgruntled workers cannot affect the liberties and freedoms of citizens. Political bundhs and protests should not paralyze civic life or interrupt or impede others from carrying on their activities. The workers' rights to collective bargaining was taken away from insurance workers in the early 1980s itself when it was found that the agreement between management workers in the Life Insurance Corporation was prejudicial to the interests of the policyholders. Telecom unions in Orissa and Mathadi workers in Mumbai have been asked to pay damages for causing loss to the consumer. In the latter case the workers were fighting for minimum wages and the consumer in question happened to be one of the largest business houses in the country. Courts are fixing responsibility not only on organizations but also on individual employees/unions or association leaders/activists. In rare cases, they are also empowering employers to recover money from the sacred provident fund money. Public sector workers in many parts of the world have been fighting a losing battle in opposing the privatization of public utilities. The wrath of dissatisfied customers of such public utilities typically includes a significant proportion of union members themselves (of course from other sectors)!

Labour law, in a layman's perception, is codified common sense. It cannot change customs and practices if it does not adapt itself to the changing times. There are certain aspects/principles that may be universal and lasting in their appeal. There are others, which need adaptation. Continuity and change should be the theme. Overemphasizing one cause over the other may eventually prove counterproductive. The purpose of law should be to achieve a delicate balance between conflicting and competing claims. It can be neither pro-labour nor pro-capital; it should be pro-people and pro-humanity. In a market economy, law can and should be used as a brake to ensure that it does not become amoral. By the same token, there should be some alignment with evolving public goals and preferences so that the planned shifts are swift enough. As an important public institution, the role of the judiciary in a civil society which is still maturing is paramount. Given the dismal state of social and human development in the country and the pathetic employment conditions for a majority of the workforce, the scales of justice may have to tilt in favour of the vulnerable and weaker sections of the society despite the pressures of competitiveness. This means a dualism in the attitudes of the Parliament, judiciary and bureaucracy that manifests a more concentrated attention on improving the working and living conditions of the unorganized sections of labour.

REVIEW OF JUDGEMENTS IN SELECT CASES

Let us now review and discuss the judgements pronounced in seven select cases.[1]

I. Employment in Hazardous and Polluted Industries

Case: M.C. Mehta vs Union of India 1987 and subsequent cases, including the Supreme Court decisions on the Delhi's hazardous/heavy industries' relocation case.

The Supreme Court ordered the closure or shifting/relocation of 168 industries from Delhi by 30 November 1996. (This order was subsequently modified on 31 December 1996.) The government was asked to facilitate the allotment of alternative sites, etc. The judgement lists the rights and benefits of workers employed in these units. It envisages alternative employment with no adverse change in terms and conditions. The retrenched workers, if any, should be paid compensation in terms of Section 25 F(b) and additional compensation over and above this. In several other states too courts have ordered the closure/relocation of thousands of hazardous and polluting industries. In many such cases, the workers affected are to be treated as being under active employment between the dates of the closure and restarting. In another decision on aqua-culture farming, the Supreme Court ordered, on 11 December 1996, the winding-up/destruction of aqua-culture farms operating within 500 metres of the high tide line of coastal states and awarded six years wages as compensation to the affected workmen, payable by the concerned employers.

The judgement defined employers' liabilities/obligations and workers' rights concerning the regulation of hazardous processes under the Factories Act, 1948. In several other cases, the Supreme Court has offered relief to affected workers. Consider the 1984 Bhopal tragedy concerning the gas leak at the Union Carbide factory. The relief provided has not reached the affected persons till date (December 2000). An ILO Convention has given workers the right to leave the workplace if they consider it potentially unsafe.

---

[1] This section has benefited from the notes and comments of Prof. S.C. Srivastava, Professor of Law, Kurukshetra University and Secretary General of the National Labour Law Association.

II. Contract Labour

Case: *Air India vs United Labour Union and Others (Supreme Court of India, 6 December 1996)*

If work is considered perennial as per the provisions of the Contract Labour (Regulation and Abolition) Act, 1970, contract labour should be prohibited and abolished. The judgement in question held the view that the principal employer is under statutory obligation to absorb contract labour, who are affected by such abolition, as regular employees from the day on which the contract labour system in the establishment, for the work which they were doing, gets abolished. The date of engagement of such labour will be the criteria to determine their seniority. Excess workforce, if any, can be retrenched, as per the legal provisions under the Industrial Disputes Act on the principle of 'last come, first go' subject to reappointment as and when vacancies arise. In this case, the Supreme Court upheld the judgement of the Bombay High Court.

The Supreme Court of India observed that there is no express provision in the Act for the absorption of employees whose contract labour system had been abolished. Yet, it was not the intention of the legislation to be oblivious to the interests of the affected workers. Air India was, therefore, asked to abolish the contract labour system for sweeping, cleaning, dusting and watching the building and absorb the workers affected on its abolition as regular employees. During 1996–98, there were several such judgements involving several thousand workers in canteen, cleaning, security, loading and unloading operations etc., mostly in public enterprises owned and managed by the state.

Employers consider it essential to have a contract labour system to be able to maintain flexibility and enhance competitiveness in the context of globalization. They do not pay attention to the neglect of human resources and the social dimensions of contract labour. They do not explain the rationale for the duality in recruitment standards in terms of education/skill background, training, experience, safety record, etc. of regular, full-time workers and contract labourers. Typically the contract labourer is less educated and skilled, undertrained, overworked, underpaid and more prone to accidents than the regular/full-time employee. How is the exploitation of contract labour to be minimized or mitigated? What difference, if any, does the distinction between 'contract of' and 'contract for labour' make in considering the issue of continuance or abolition/prohibition of contract labour? Does the contract labour system manifest a failed human resource/industrial relations system in that the contract labour, relative to regular labour, is often less educated, less trained, overworked and underpaid, more prone to accidents and highly vulnerable to exploitation? Are there alternatives to the prohibition/abolition of contract labour? These and other issues require further consideration.

III. Child Labour

Case: *M.C. Mehta vs State of Tamil Nadu and Others (Supreme Court of India, 10 December 1996)*

This public interest litigation highlights the magnitude of the problem of child labour in India.

In a landmark judgement the Supreme Court ordered the elimination of child labour and listed the obligations of the state and employer thus: (state to provide) compulsory education of children affected by the judgement and (employer to provide and state to ensure) alternative employment for adult members of the family whose child is in employment in a factory or a mine or in other hazardous work, in lieu of child. State to create a child labour rehabilitation-cum-welfare fund and employer and state to deposit a sum of Rs 20,000 and Rs 5000 respectively for each child employed in contravention of the provisions of the Child Labour (Prohibition & Regulation) Act, 1986. The parent/guardian of the concerned child would be paid monthly interest of the deposit of Rs 25,000. Employment to adult member and payment of deposit in the name of the child would cease if the child were not sent for education.

This judgement lists the obligations of the state and the employer, but not those of the parents, trade unions and other interest groups in society in dealing with child labour.

IV. Sexual Harassment at Workplace

Case: *Visakha & Others vs State of Rajasthan (Supreme Court of India, 13 August 1997)*

The Supreme Court upheld the writ petition, brought as a class action by certain social activists and NGOs, concerning the fundamental rights of working women with particular reference to the evil of sexual harassment of women at workplaces. In the absence of a law and based on the contents of international conventions and norms, the Supreme Court issued directions, in the course of its judgements, formulating guidelines and norms which would be binding and enforceable in law until suitable legislation is enacted.

The Supreme Court directives cover the following aspects: (1) Duty of the employer or other responsible persons in workplaces and other institutions; (2) Definition of sexual harassment; (3) Preventive steps to be taken by employers or persons in charge of the workplace, whether in the public or private sector; (4) Action under criminal proceedings; (5) Provision for disciplinary action; (6) Establishing a compliant mechanism, complaints committee, etc. The directions also deal with third-party harassment, workers' initiative and the need for raising awareness.

The judgement is welcome. Given the problems in proving harassment, should the Court have also held that the accused be treated as guilty until he/she is proven innocent? Would it then have opened the floodgate for frivolous complaints. Is the definition of harassment too wide as to have implications for office romance? How are the harassers and harassed to be tackled during/after the investigations? What are the obligations of the employers in the case of third-party harassment (of employees by customers, outside the company premises, for instance)? Whether and how is the proportionality of the offence and the punishment to be decided?

V. Consumer Dispute Over Sudden, Illegal Strikes

Case 1: *Common Cause vs Union of India and Others (National Consumer Disputes Redressal Commission, New Delhi, 9 May 1996)*

Common Cause, an NGO, filed a case under the Consumer Protection Act, 1986 seeking action against both Air India and the erring group of members of its staff for disrupting a large number of flights due to a sudden strike resorted to by members of the Indian Flight Engineers' Association. Even though there is no contract between the consumers and the Indian Flight Engineers' Association, the Consumer Protection Act holds the service providers (including staff and trade union) responsible for the hardship and loss to passengers. Section 18 of the

Trade Unions Act is not a bar to the filing of complaints against trade unions under the Consumer Protection Act.

This verdict of the commission stressed that persons employed on salary in an organization which is rendering a service for a consideration are equally accountable under the provisions of the Consumer Protection Act, 1986 along with the management of the said organization even though there was no privity of contract between the person hiring/availing the service (consumer) and the concerned employee. In several other consumer cases, the trade union has been held liable and asked to pay damages.

While the commission did not inflict any punishment on the airline or the association and no compensation was awarded to the petitioner in this case, the following observations were made in the judgement:

> . . . we also think it necessary to administer a strong word of caution that in case similar instances of disruption of services by illegal strikes or agitations come to the notice of this Commission, in future on the part of the employees of any organization rendering service to the public for consideration or any association or union of such employees, we will be dealing with the matter in a very strict manner and will have no hesitation to award proper compensation to the consumer who are thereby affected and aggrieved. If however, the disruption in service is the consequence of a strike or agitation legally launched in conformity with the provisions of the law governing industrial and labour relations the employees or their unions, no proceedings under the Consumer Protection Act can be instituted against the employees or their Associations/Unions.
>
> . . . Henceforth whenever a strike notice is served by any section of employees or their Trade Union . . . and the strike appears to be imminent, the Airlines shall insert a publication in all the leading newspapers of the country informing the public about the possibility of there being a strike so that the consumers may not be taken by surprise by the strike but may be enabled to make such alternative arrangements as are possible so as to mitigate the hardship that is otherwise bound to be caused to them.

Consumer courts have jurisdiction over breach of commercial contracts. In exercising their jurisdiction, consumer courts seem to hold employment contracts subordinate to commercial contracts if the former are created to fulfil the commercial contracts in question. Do the provisions/judgements under the Consumer Protection Act abridge/impinge on Section 18 of the Trade Unions Act? Can the employer make a recovery from the concerned employees' provident fund, etc. in order to pay the compensation under awards by the consumer redressal forum? What, if any, are the implications for employment relations if the consumer courts entertain complaints under the Consumer Protection Act, 1986 made by an employee–consumer? Can the standing offers prevent the employer from making employees file complaints as consumers?

Case 2: Bharat Kumar K. Palicha and Another vs State of Kerala and Others (Kerala High Court, 1997)

The petition seeks the relief of a declaration that the calling for and the holding of what has come to be known as 'bundh' is unconstitutional and is hence illegal. The petitioners consider that the bundh entails an exhortation to violence and physically restraining or preventing others who are citizens of the country from doing/attending to their work. Any citizen who does not participate in the bundh is (often) physically prevented, attacked, harassed or even threatened with dire consequences. It causes disruption to civic life (through stoppage of transportation, forced closure of shops/establishments, etc.), can lead to violence and violates Article 21 of the Constitution of India in that there is deprivation of personal liberty and even a threat to life.

The question is framed thus: It may be true that political parties and organizers have a right to call for non-cooperation or a general strike as a form of protest against what they believe to be either an erroneous policy or exploitation. But when exercise of such a right infracts the fundamental right of another citizen who is equally entitled to exercise his rights, the question is whether the right of the political party extends the right of violating the right of another citizen.

In an earlier case (Railway Board vs Niranjan Singh, 1996), the Supreme Court held that

> The fact that the citizens of this country have freedom of speech, freedom to assemble peacefully and freedom to form associations or unions does not mean that they can exercise those freedoms in whatever place they please. The exercise of those freedoms will come to an end as soon as the right of someone

else to hold his property intervenes. Such a limitation is inherent in the exercise of those rights.

The Kerala High Court held that

This Court has sufficient jurisdiction to declare that the calling of a 'bundh' and the holding of it is unconstitutional especially since, it is undoubted, that the holding of 'bundhs' are not in the interests of the Nation by leading to national loss of production . . . the State can't shirk its responsibility of taking steps to recoup and of recouping the loss from the sponsors and organizers of such bundhs. We think that these aspects justify our intervention under Article 226 of the Constitution.

The Court finally held that 'the calling for a bundh by any association, organization or political party and the enforcing of that call by it is illegal and unconstitutional. We direct the state and its officials, including the law enforcement agencies, to do all that is necessary to give effect to this'.

The exercise of one's right should not clash with others' rights. In several court cases, the right to protest by agitating workers is questioned if the striking/agitating workers' rights clash with the rights of willing workers and customers who want their work to be carried on without interruption or intimidation. In some instances, the courts have ordered police protection for willing workers/customers. There seem to be inherent restrictions to the rights of workers' and employers' in employment/industrial relations.

VI. Notice of Change Required for Introducing Voluntary Retirement Scheme[2]

Case: KEC International Ltd. vs Kamani Employees Union & Others (Bombay High Court, 17 April 1998)

Justice F.I. Rebello of the Bombay High Court held that the income tax approved voluntary retirement scheme (VRS) results in the reduction of posts and hence attracts Section 9-A read with Item 11 of the IVth Schedule of the Industrial Disputes Act. This judgement, when appealed, was admitted by a division bench of the Bombay

---

[2] See: Rajen Mehrotra (1998). 'Notice of Change—A Must for Voluntary Retirement Scheme? Impact of Bomaby High Court Decision in KEC International Case'. *Current Law Reporter.* July 1998. pp. 3–10.

High Court on 22 June 1998 which stayed the operative part of the judgement.

Justice Rebello held that: (a) the preamble of the notice for the VRS by the petitioner mentions that there was a need for the company to continuously upgrade the quality of products. Hence item 10 of Schedule IV of the Industrial Disputes Act can be attracted, subject to the material that comes on record finally, (b) once the approval is taken under the Income Tax Act the scheme of VRS may necessarily result in a decrease in the existing strength of workers. Therefore, prima facie it must result in the reduction of posts. Hence VRS would be covered by item 11 of the IV Schedule of the Industrial Disputes Act, (c) those workmen who have accepted VRS but have encashed the compensation cheque have been distinguished from workmen who have accepted VRS but have not encashed the compensation cheque. In the latter category, the complaint of violation of Section 9-A of the Industrial Disputes Act is maintainable.

Any VRS scheme should be based on the principle that it is for organizational restructuring and only those whose jobs have become redundant should be given the opportunity to apply. If this principle is accepted, then when employees leave under the VRS scheme, there would be a need for work reorganization based, usually, on the principle of work simplification. Thus it will affect the work content/norms of the remaining workers and attract the provision of notice of change under the Industrial Disputes Act, 1947. While this part of the judgement is founded on logic, the other aspects dealing with the case require examination. The merits of the case should not depend on whether the VRS scheme is with or without income tax exemption. Similarly, the employees' rights should cease once they receive the compensation cheque for voluntary separation in response to their own request. It should not have made any difference depending on whether or not they have encashed it.

VII. Service Contracts and Standing Orders

Case: *Uptron India Ltd vs Shammi Bhan & Others (Supreme Court, 1998)*

Primarily service rules and regulations, standing orders or contracts of employment govern the law of employer–employee relationship. In the above case, the Supreme Court considered that clause 17(g) of the certified standing orders of the company providing that 'the services of a workman are liable to automatic termination if he overstays on leave without permission for more than seven days' was bad and violative of the principles of natural justice as 'it does not purport to provide an opportunity of hearing to the employee whose services are treated to have come to an end automatically'.

In several earlier judgements, the Supreme Court held that the termination of a service of a workman, under a specific clause in the standing orders, for the overstaying of leave period without prior explanation amounted to 'retrenchment' under Section 2(oo) of the Industrial Disputes Act. One-sided contracts, taking advantage of the unfavourable labour market conditions, have rightly been decided in favour of the affected employees in many cases.

QUO VADIS?

Judicial processes are subject to axiomatic and vexatious delays. As Upendra Baxi once remarked, 'If justice delayed is justice denied, justice hurried is justice buried.'

It is difficult to get judgements. It is even more difficult to get them implemented or complied with. Courts can deliver judgements and take the concerned party to task for contempt of court if it comes to their notice that its judgements have not been respected. The judicial system does not have the apparatus to enforce its verdicts and take action when they are not complied with. After the decisions of the Kerala High Court and the Supreme Court, several political parties have continued to give calls for hartals and bundhs in complete disregard of the said judgements.

The courts can do little if the affected party does not complain because of the change in circumstances as was seen in the *Raptokas Bret* case. Even in the Kamani case on VRS, the judgement of the single judge bench was stayed by a two judge bench and later, both the union and the employer reached an out of court settlement. As a result, the company was able to implement VRS without issuing a notice of change. We are thus witnessing not only judicial activism and judicial indiscipline, but also judicial ineptness. Are we heading for judicial anarchy? Quo vaids?

TEN

India and International Labour Standards*

The International Labour Organization (ILO) has played a significant role in promoting international labour standards. India is a founder member of the ILO and has contributed to the codification of its standards. It has, in turn, benefited from these standards in developing its own legal and institutional framework on social and labour aspects. In recent years, efforts have been made to link the standards to world trade through social clauses through the World Trade Organization (WTO) and company codes and consumer boycotts are seeking to achieve the same purpose through social labelling. Here we discuss the relevant aspects with reference to India.

INTERNATIONAL LABOUR STANDARDS

The conventions adopted by the ILO constitute the international labour standards. Their purpose is to maintain certain basic minimum

---

* This is a substantially revised version of a paper presented at the 41st annual conference of the Indian Society of Labour Economics at the University of Hyderabad in December 1998 and published in the *Indian Journal of Labour Economics*, December 1998 issue.

standards, worldwide. As a means of reconciling globalization and social justice, efforts are being made to link international trade with a social clause system so that developing countries do not enjoy the benefits of trade liberalization on the basis of comparatively low labour costs. There is sound justification for international labour standards. Normatively, their desirability is not in doubt. The controversy, however, is about the means of their enforcement, particularly the arguments concerning the attempted linkage between certain core labour standards and international standards. Thus, the question is not whether international labour standards should be implemented. The question is whether the countries and companies that continue to pursue competitive advantage through the violation of fundamental rights should be punished through some sort of linkage with trade. Employers in several developed countries and unions, governments and employers in several developing countries have been resisting any formal linkage between labour standards and trade.

While producers in developed countries seem to seek to benefit by exploiting cheap labour in developing countries, workers in developed countries feel that if developing countries are allowed the comparative advantage of cheap labour it may affect the jobs of workers in their own countries. Therefore the linkage of the social clause to trade is considered by social partners in developing countries as an effort of governments and workers in developed countries to deprive the developing countries of this advantage. In the words of Ernesto Zedillo, Mexico's president, some developed countries are 'determined to save developing countries from development'.

The developed countries' arguments are based on the realization that 'poverty anywhere is a danger to prosperity everywhere'. There is also concern about the race to the bottom spurred by the notion that, 'If you don't raise your standards, we may have to lower ours.' Social dumping could cause job losses in developed countries. Visa restrictions for Indian software professionals going to the US have made American companies in California consider shifting base to India if their problems in accessing skilled manpower persist.

However, given the abysmally low share of manufactured/value-added export from developing countries to developed countries, there could be no net employment threat to developed countries from developing countries to warrant any fear of the race to the bottom.

The conclusion of the Uruguay Round of trade liberalization resulted in the General Agreement on Trade and Tariffs giving way to the establishment of the WTO in 1995. The World Social Summit at Copenhagen in 1995 committed itself 'to promoting the goal of full employment as a basic priority of our economic and social policies, and to enabling all men and women to attain secure and sustainable livelihoods through freely chosen productive employment and work'. To this end the summit reiterated the need to promote respect for the seven ILO conventions including those on equal remuneration and non-discrimination, the freedom of association, the right to organize and bargain collectively and the prohibition of forced and child labour. The Delhi Declaration of January 1995 at the Fifth Labour Ministers' Conference of Non-Aligned and Other Developing Countries expressed deep concern about the efforts to link international trade and enforcement of labour standards through the imposition of the social clause. The Singapore Declaration of December 1996 at the WTO Ministerial Conference in Singapore pledged its commitment to the observance of internationally recognized core labour standards, but conceded that the ILO was the competent body to determine and promote these standards. The trade ministers also agreed that labour standards should not be used for protectionist purposes and that the comparative advantage of the low-wage developing countries should not be questioned. In 1997, the International Labour Conference of the 113 member-states of the Non-Aligned Movement and five Observer States including China stressed the need to ratify core labour standards. It sought from the ILO and the world community technical assistance and the promotion of economic development for achieving higher standards of social justice. It further suggested that 'instead of a trade-related mechanism, like social labelling which basically legitimizes the social clause, the ILO should provide proactive help to developing countries facing protectionist pressures in the context of labour standards'. The ILO took the initiative in 1998 by adopting the Fundamental Principles Declaration (discussed later) and in 1999, Convention No. 182 concerning immediate action to end the worst forms of child labour. A number of developing countries still tried to push the WTO to ensure respect for core labour standards and proposed to establish a working forum on trade, globalization, development and labour issues at the third Ministerial Conference in Seattle in October 1999. Suspicions were roused when the American

Federation of Labour and Congress of Industrial Organizations (AFL-CIO) pledged support to Al Gore in the US Presidential elections in 2000 and US President Bill Clinton in an interview to a newspaper in Seattle said that trade sanctions should be used to enforce core labour standards. The WTO and Geneva summits also took place in 2000. These events highlighted the negative social impact of globalization.

Fundamental differences persist on the subject within and between developed and developing countries. While employers in several developed countries including two world bodies of employers, namely, the International Organization of Employers (IOE) and the International Chamber of Commerce (ICC), endorse the view that labour standards be kept within the domain of ILO supervision, governments in most developed countries and a few developing countries and the International Confederation of Free Trade Unions (ICFTU) insist on trade sanctions as the means to improve labour standards. Governments, employers and trade unions in most developing countries, however, continue to mistrust the real motives behind such a linkage.

The real problem is that trade is neither free nor fair. There is concern among several developing countries that the WTO agreement provides for the free movement of capital and products from developed countries to developing countries, but does not provide for the mobility of labour (which the developing countries have in surplus) or for easy access to technology. Further, while low wages may constitute a comparative economic advantage, there is also a comparative social disadvantage. The question is whether labour standards across countries in different stages of development can be harmonized when on most other parameters there is no realistic basis for comparison, leave alone any advantage. In the absence of credible evidence on a fairer distribution of the benefits of trade among nations, the consensus on the linkage between labour standards and trade remains elusive.

Although trade unions in South Asia have declared that they have not been content with the level of compliance with labour standards, several of them have been afraid that linking labour standards with trade would further hurt them. Therefore, most of them have adopted a dual strategy: oppose linkage of trade with labour standards at the international level; nationally, continue to put pressure on the respective governments to improve labour standards.

FUTURE OF INTERNATIONAL LABOUR STANDARDS

The desire to strike is blocked by the reluctance to wound. The future of international labour standards is caught up in the parallel but contradictory processes of globalization and regionalization, the divide between the north and the south, the relative supremacy of the ILO and the WTO, and the diverse pressures within and among social partners about the desirability of harmonizing labour standards vs deregulating labour markets. Then there are definitional problems. For instance, the US now recognizes child labour as forced labour. Many developing countries may not share this view.

Although usually seen as an issue of developing and transition economies, harmonizing core labour standards within developing countries could be a contentious and difficult task (Block and Roberts, 1998). Regional agreements such as the North American Free Trade Agreement (NAFTA) do provide for the compliance by the three member-states, the US, Canada and Mexico of their domestic regulations. However, this minimalist approach in the separate agreement on labour aspects rules out any scope for the homogenization of labour standards (Adams and Singh, 1996).

Governments and workers' unions in many developed countries are in favour of a linkage between core labour standards and international trade. But, all of them have aggressively sought the modification of trade agreements. Governments and employers' organizations in several developing countries consider any such linkage undesirable. Trade unions in many developing countries are still caught in the cold war divisions of the eastern and western block international trade union federations, trapped in an ideological dilemma.

Griesgraber and Gunter (1997) find that the reduction of tariff barriers on a world scale makes the weaker economies vulnerable to the power of transnational corporations, and often leads to greater impoverishment of the already-poor countries and peoples. Hoe (1995) stresses the need to protect workers' rights but considers that trade-related international labour standards may constitute hidden trade barriers. Maskus (1997) concludes that the potential economic impact of international labour standards, especially economic competitive advantage, could be counter-productive.

Much of the controversy about linkage between core labour standards and trade is over the difficulties in harmonization across countries at drastically different stages of economic development. Considering the fact that by 1993 there were at least 68 regional trading agreements (Kirmani, 1994), it is difficult to conceive of and operationalize a global policy unless some integration takes place among them. Labour standards in the growing Asian economies and the 1997 crisis have been the subject of major discussions and have taken away part of the glitter and shine from the past success of the export-led growth strategies of these economies. In some of these countries, economic growth did eventually lead to social development and improvement in labour standards. While organizations like the Organisation for Economic Cooperation and Development (OECD) and ICFTU are keen to push and foster core labour standards, the Asean-Pacific Economic Cooperation (APEC) feels that trade, investment and development will lead to improvement in labour standards. In countries which have faced crises and chaos, a steep decline in basic labour standards was witnessed during periods of such crises, reform and recovery.

In developing and new industrializing countries the dominant notion is that labour standards improve only when economies and job opportunities grow. The link between economic growth and labour standards may be less than proportionate, that is, while labour standards may not improve at the same pace or rate as economies grow, the fall in labour standards would be more steep than the pace or rate of decline in economic growth. In countries where economies achieve sustained growth rates, concerted efforts to improve labour standards could run concurrent with the deregulation of labour markets. Both could, in such a situation, be complementary and not contradictory.

There are some situations where there is a trade off between one set of labour standards and another. For instance, published research shows that several non-union firms pay more wages to keep unions away. The freedom of association may be missing, but freedom from want is achieved to a certain extent through higher wages. The general belief is that higher wages could mean greater exploitation. Research, however, suggests that the contrary could also be true. Firms which use the inducement strategy (incentive payments, etc.) may achieve higher productivity, but those which follow the involvement strategy achieve better returns on investment. In the former, the emphasis is merely on doing more in less time, while in the latter it is doing more with less resources by creatively engaging workers through suggestion schemes, two-way communication, small group activities, quality control circles, etc.

ILO DECLARATION ON FUNDAMENTAL PRINCIPLES AND ITS FOLLOW-UP (1998)

On 18 June 1998, at its 86th session, the International Labour Conference adopted the Declaration on Fundamental Principles. The declaration reiterates the binding nature of the Philadelphia declaration and requires compliance of the core conventions covering the following aspects even by those countries that have not ratified the relevant conventions:

(a) Freedom of association (No. 87) and the effective recognition of the right to collective bargaining (No. 98).
(b) The elimination of all forms of forced or compulsory labour (Nos. 29 and 105). In 1999, the ILO adopted Convention No. 182 concerning Immediate Action for the Abolition of the Worst Forms of Child Labour. This became the eighth core convention.
(c) The effective abolition of child labour (No. 138).
(d) The elimination of discrimination in respect of employment and occupation (Nos. 100 and 111).

All member countries of the ILO are required to submit a report on their progress in implementing the principles enshrined in the above conventions. The ILO, in turn, will prepare a report each year on one of the above four categories of fundamental principles and rights. The report will be based on the information gathered and assessed in accordance with established procedures. In the case of member-states that have not ratified the fundamental conventions, the report will be based on the findings of the annual follow-up. In the case of member countries which have ratified these conventions, the report will be dealt in accordance with Article 22 of the ILO Constitution.

The above declaration does not, however, favour linking international labour standards with trade.

FROM INTERNATIONAL LABOUR STANDARDS TO CORPORATE CODES

International labour standards have proved effective and useful in formulating national policies, legislation and practices on diverse social and labour aspects: ILO conventions and recommendations cover issues ranging from tripartite consultations at the national level to communications and grievance procedures of undertakings; wages, working hours, leave, holidays to occupational safety and health; non-discrimination to affirmative action for the aged, disabled, women and other vulnerable groups; labour markets, labour law, labour administration, human resource development, etc. The ILO conventions and recommendations are not binding in these matters, except when a state ratifies the concerned convention's and/or reiterates the relevant principles in national legislation.

The US government is known to use a variety of instruments/mechanisms to enforce international labour standards (Samford, 1996). These include the Caribbean Basin Initiative (CBI), the Generalized System of Preferences, Section 301 of the Trade Act, 1974 (referred to as Super Clause 301), extraterritorial application of the US labour law, voluntary corporate codes of conduct, and the North American Agreement on Labour Corporation (NAALC), the labour-side accord of the NAFTA.

Currently, several NGOs and corporations are making efforts at disseminating information about products and companies that do not involve child labour to consumers through what is now known as 'social labelling' (US Department of Labour, 1987). In addition to creating a child-labour-free production environment, some have even provided or funded schools for child labourers and employment or welfare benefits for their parents. Social labelling is mainly prevalent in the export segment of four industries, viz., hand-knotted carpets, garments, leather products and tea.

The main child labour labelling programmes for carpets are: Rugmark, Kaleen, STEP, and Care & Fair. Rugmark and Kaleen are product labels fixed to individual carpets. STEP and Care & Fair are company certification programmes. Participating companies use the labels for advertising and marketing purposes.

A private, voluntary certification programme that provides market-driven incentives for carpet manufacturers to produce without child labour, the Rugmark Foundation was established in India in 1994 and expanded to Nepal in 1995. Under this programme, individuals and companies in the carpet industry are organized to stop the use of child labour. It has independent, professional and international credible monitoring and certification systems for carpets manufactured without the use of child labour. The affected children have been rehabilitated through education. As of May 1997, the Indian Rugmark Foundation had certified the export of about 636,000 labelled carpets from 164 licensed producers/exporters. The programme is monitored and enforced through an elaborate system of license approval, random inspections and carpet tracking. It has conducted 1754 unannounced visits to licensee facilities, found 143 children illegally working at looms and put them in two schools that it has helped establish.

The Carpet Export Promotion Council (CEPC), set up by the ministry of textiles, Government of India, as a quasi-government body, established the Kaleen labelling programme in India in June 1995. It is funded partly through government grants and partly through subscription income from industry members. An independent agency conducts inspections and the Development Commissioner conducts periodic reviews. All registered exporters pay a fee for child welfare activities. As on May 1997, 572,000 Kaleen labels had been issued to 219 CEPC members, roughly 10 per cent of the total membership.

The STEP and Care & Fair programmes, initiated by Swiss and German NGOs respectively, are essentially company certification programmes. These programmes require suppliers in India and elsewhere to honour the terms of the demands and code of conduct which includes the elimination of child and bonded labourers, and contributing to the health and education programmes of carpet workers and their families.

Among the other labelling programmes, is Reebok International Limited in the soccer ball industry. By an agreement between the company and the exporters in Pakistan in association with the Federation of International Football Association and the International Labour Organization, the soccer balls produced for Reebok bear the label 'Guarantee: Manufactured without child labour'. The major elements of the programme are: reorganizing all production in a new facility under one room where children below 15 years of age are prohibited to enter or work; external monitoring to ensure that children are not entering the workplace and that soccer ball panels are leaving the factory for stitching; and support for the education/vocational training of children in the region.

The 'Fair Trade' labelling called the TRANSFAIR seal in the tea industry is another example. Its objectives are: to ensure the payment of a fair price, which covers production costs plus a fair trade premium that flows to the actual producers; the participation of the actual producers in decisions regarding use of the fair trade premium; the provision for advance payment; and the promotion of a long-term relationship between producers and importers.

The avowed aim of 'fair trade' labelling in tea is to 'promote producers in the Third World' who are at a disadvantage under the current trading conditions and help them achieve independence and equality. The additional price paid for the tea produced under conditions complying with the core labour standards is used directly for the improvement of the living conditions of the tea pickers, the plantation workers and the smallholders.

Social labelling programmes are still voluntary and thrive on actual or potential consumer boycott threats. There is a growing awareness and acceptance of these programmes, the costs of which are often borne by the exporters and the importers themselves. Consumers in developed countries are also reportedly willing to pay a higher price for such labels, particularly under company certification programmes. There is an ongoing effort to cover the subcontracting arrangements as well under these programmes.

In addition to the labelling programmes, two kinds of code of conduct are being popularized by the countries of the North. These concern: (a) actual labour standards: what people are paid, how jobs are designed, the levels of safety, etc.; (b) formal policies which purport to shape corporate conduct in certain ways. These are fundamental conditions which apply universally across workplaces. At the national level, the US government announced a set of model business principles in 1995. These cover fair employment practices envisaged under the 1998 ILO Declaration as Fundamental Principles: (a) avoidance of child and forced labour; (b) avoidance of discrimination based on race, gender, national origin or religious beliefs; and (c) respect for the right of association and the right to organization and collective bargaining. Ironically, the US has ratified only one of the eight core conventions of the ILO.

The International Organization of Employers (IOE, 1997) expressed the following misgivings about labelling campaigns: that they address only a small section of the child labour employed in export markets, without going to the heart of the problem; that they act as a 'quick fix' to the problem of child labour by appealing to the 'feel good' sensibilities of consumers; that they do not guarantee non-employment of child labour by virtue of the label; and that they may sometimes lead to producers being penalized even though they may not have employed child labourers.

THE CASE OF INDIA

As a founder member and one of 10 countries of chief industrial importance, India holds a non-elective seat in the governing body of the ILO. India has ratified 38 of the 182 conventions (Annexure 10.1).

The ILO has influenced India and vice versa. A tripartite committee on ILO conventions oversees aspects relating to international labour standards, proposals concerning new conventions/ratification of old conventions, compliance of the provisions in the ratified conventions, etc. For several years, the committee was dormant but has now been activated once again. Like in most other countries, the ILO conventions and recommendations have played a significant role in India as regards the legal framework on wages, working conditions, welfare, social security, protection of the vulnerable sections of society, human resource development, equality, non-discrimination, etc. India has also received technical cooperation and assistance from ILO to establish several institutions and to strengthen labour inspection and administration.

The Constitution of India and its labour legislation upholds all the fundamental principles envisaged in the eight 'core' international labour standards (see Annexure 10.2). India has also ratified three of the eight core conventions that constitute the fundamental principles. It is also likely to ratify two more of the remaining five core conventions: Convention No. 105 concerning the abolition of forced labour and Convention No. 182 concerning immediate action to end the worst forms of child labour. India's record in this regard is better than that of the US, which has ratified only one of the seven core conventions. Among the Western European countries, France and Germany have ratified all the core conventions. Though some South Asian countries have ratified more core conventions than India, it can be said with certainty that the Indian record is at par with, if not better than, its neighbouring countries (Annexure 10.3).

India is actively considering the ratification of Convention No. 105 concerning the abolition of forced labour. India has not ratified Convention Nos. 87 and 98 concerning the freedom of association and right to collective bargaining due to 'technical difficulties' involving trade union rights for civil servants. This, however, is not a major hurdle because the government can always exempt certain services while ratifying the concerned conventions. The real intention seems to be, as former Chief Labour Commissioner of the Government of India, S. Nath (1997) opines, 'These conventions have not been ratified by India because the policy of the government has been to restrict the freedom of association to only manual workers (by defining them as workmen) and exclude supervisory and managerial workers. The other interest of the government is not to allow the right of collective bargaining even to industrial workers in government's departmental undertakings like the Railways, Post and Telecommunications, Central Public Works Department, etc. The government, on the basis of the Pay Commission's recommendations and not through collective bargaining, decides their pay, etc.'

There are certain restrictions on the formation of federations in the telecom sector. In 1981, the right to collective bargaining was taken away from the insurance sector workers when it was found that collusion between the unions and the employers (public sector) was undermining the interests of the policy holders. Since then, insurance workers engage in consultations, but their pay revisions are notified unilaterally by the concerned Government department.

India's record in respecting the freedom of association and collective bargaining is much better than that of many other countries in the region, which have ratified either one or both conventions. Mere ratification, however, cannot guarantee the achievement of the underlying objectives. It has to be backed by a strong political will and legislative framework as also by effective vigilance by the other social partners such as NGOs and consumer groups. But these considerations cannot be a justification for non-ratification. India ratified Convention No. 11 concerning the Right of Association (1921) for agricultural workers way back in 1923. The Union Ministry of Labour in association with the National Labour Institute, set up by it in the 1970s, has organized several workshops and rural camps to facilitate the organization of rural workers. Still, given the huge social inequities both in terms of caste and land distribution, the density of unionization among rural workers is negligible.

India has a long way to go before it can comply with the core labour standards. Its large workforce in the informal sector (92 per cent) would be content even if the minimum standards in national legislation—not international labour standards—were the maximum. In the slate industry in one of the Indian states, a trade union leader, an influential political party and district government officials wanted to help workers secure minimum wages. Duly encouraged, the workers went on strike for three days. The employers, who had multiple businesses, did not feel the heat and therefore did not show any eagerness to end the strike. On the fourth day, the workers agreed to return to work. The employers agreed to take the workers back, after further reducing their wages as a token of punishment for their (the workers) temerity. In another case, a young and committed Indian Administrative Service officer in the state labour ministry was not amused with the flourishing dollar-earning trade of tobacco merchants who were getting away with paying less than the minimum wages to their poor, non-unionized labour. He computed the difference in the wages payable as per law and the wages actually paid to the workers and got the difference paid to the workers under supervision by him and his staff. After the payments were made, he (the labour commissioner) and his staff left. Soon after, hired *goondas* of the employers took back the money from the workers with the warning that if the workers reported the matter they would lose their job and their families could be in danger. In a third case, a government official told the author that he personally got a bonded labourer freed from a landlord in a village in Bihar. The labourer was given money with which he bought some buffaloes. The buffaloes fell sick and died. The person sought employment in the village to eke out a living. However, the concerned landlord warned the villagers not to take the person into employment, as he was a troublemaker. Finally, this person had to return to bondage, this time on even harsher conditions of employment. The above-cited examples are not exceptions. They are common occurrences in many remote and rural areas. In the absence of a proper supervisory mechanism that fully understands and deals with ground realities, efforts to improve labour standards could lead to a deterioration in the labour standards.

In contrast, there are some highly organized and unionized sectors where collectively determined labour standards exceed the national and international labour standards in some aspects. During the 1920s and 1930s, the private sector steel giant Tata Iron and Steel Company, introduced a number of voluntary welfare measures long before such measures were incorporated either in national legislation or international labour standards.

In the past, some of the legislative initiatives based on ILO conventions have had the opposite effect. For instance, measures to safeguard the interests of women through maternity benefits and the restriction of employment of women in night shifts in factories and in underground mining have resulted in many employers hesitating to employ women. This should not lead to the discontinuance of maternity benefits. Giving paternity leave would perhaps restore the balance and remove the incentive for employers to employ only males. The ILO convention on night shift work was revised in the 1990s to enable the employment of women in night shift. The Government of India is pursuing, although rather half-heartedly, changes to some of the labour legislations. The administrative ministries have apparently been pressing for some of these changes. They include changes in the Factories Act to permit the employment of women in night shift, particularly in electronic units and export zones.

India is actively pursuing 14 projects to eradicate child labour in hazardous industries by 2002. The All India Organization of Employers has undertaken a project in Jalandhar (Punjab) similar to the one in Sialkot, Pakistan, concerning the abolition of child labour in the manufacture of sports goods.

India has advocated the promotion of labour standards within the framework of the ILO Constitution. It has consistently opposed proposals to link labour standards and trade through 'social labelling,' etc. The non-aligned countries summit organized by the labour minister of India at New Delhi in 1995 adopted a resolution to this effect. India played an active role in Seattle in 1999 to prevent linking trade with labour and environmental issues. All three social partners—the government, employers' organizations and national trade union centres belonging to different persuasions—are united against the linkage of international standards with trade (for statements of different social partners, see: IIRA/FES, 1996) for reasons that are articulated in most developing countries' worldwide commitment to the ILO's pillars of voluntarism, tripartism and free choice of social partners. The mandatory imposition of labour standards, by whatever name they may be called, contravenes Article 19(3) of the ILO Constitution. All social partners in India are in favour of upgrading the labour standards, but they are against linkages within the context of the WTO as it is currently constituted. They suspect that the linkage is aimed at putting artificial barriers against competition and, in the words of the Mexican President, 'saving India and other developing countries from development'. Also, the concern for improving labour standards should be more holistic and encompass the entire working class rather than the microscopic minority engaged in production for exports.

Under Article 236 of the Constitution of India, labour is in the concurrent list. Since liberalization there has been a tendency among some state governments to pursue competitive labour policies with a view to attracting investments and creating jobs. The Constitution Review Committee appointed by the Government of India in 2000 should examine this aspect, given the need for a unified law on matters which fall within the ambit of the eight core labour standards under the 1998 ILO Declaration on Fundamental Principles.

A national consultation on international labour standards where several NGOs and national trade union centres participated made a proposal with the following components (CEC, 1996):

1. Reject labour rights–WTO linkage.
2. Uphold the principles of universal labour rights and the need for evolving structures to monitor the enforcement of labour rights.
3. Set up a UN Labour Rights Commission as an alternative.
4. Establish, at the national level, a powerful National Labour Rights Commission to monitor and enforce labour rights.

The 1998 ILO Declaration on Fundamental Principles and Rights at Work, and its follow-up, substantially addresses the central issue. So long as the ILO takes time to make its instruments yield the desired results and resistance to the WTO continues to build up, initiatives at the industry level through social labelling and at the community level through consumer boycotts will apply the kind of pressure that apex inter-governmental and international organizations are ill-equipped to exert.

REFERENCES

Adams, R.J. and P. Singh (1996). 'Early Experience with NAFTA's Labour Side Accord'. *Comparative Labour Law Journal.* 18(2), pp. 161.

Block, R.N. and K. Roberts (1998). 'Ranking Labour Standards Across Countries: A Case Study of the United States and Canada'. Proceedings of the 11th World Congress—Developing Competitiveness and Social Justice: The Interplay Between Institutions and Social Partners. Bologna: International Industrial Relations Association.

Centre for Education and Communication (CEC) (1996). *Labour, Environment and Globalization: Social Clause in Multilateral Trade Agreements—A Southern Response,* New Delhi: CEC.

Elliot, E.A. (1998). 'International Labour Standards and Trade: What Should be Done?' J.J. Schott (ed). *Launching New Global Talks—An Action Agenda.* Washington DC : Institute for International Economics, pp. 165-177.

Griesgraber, J.M. and B.C. Gunter (1997). *World Trade: Towards Fair and Free Trade in the 21st Century.* London: Pluto Press (Rethinking Bretton Woods Series No. 5).

Hoe, L.A. (1995). 'Human Rights, International Labour Standards and Trade in a Globalised Economy: An Assessment of the Economic, Moral and Political Dimensions'. Dissertation. Birmingham: University of Birmingham.

Indian Industrial Relations Association and Friedrich Ebert Foundation (IIRA/FES) (1996). *Social Clause in Trade—Trade Union Perspective.* New Delhi: IIRA/FES.

International Organization of Employers (1997). *Employers Handbook on Child Labour: A Guide for Taking Action.* Geneva: IOE in collaboration with Bureau for Employers Activities and the International Programme on the Elimination of Child Labour, ILO.

Kirmani, N. (1994). *International Trade Policies: The Uruguay Round and Beyond.* Washington DC: International Monetary Fund.

Kyloh, R. (ed) (1998). *Mastering the Challenge of Globalisation: Towards a Trade Union Agenda.* Geneva: ILO Bureau for Workers Activities.

Maskus, K.E. (1997). *Should Core Labour Standards Be Imposed Through International Trade Policy?* Washington DC: World Bank (Development Research Group).

Mitchell, D.J.B. (1998). 'Emergence of Convergence? General Report on Forum 5: Bargaining Globally: Labour–Management Relations in a Multinational Context'. *International Trade Agreements and Social Clauses.* Volume 3. Proceedings of the 11th World Congress—Developing Competitiveness and Social Justice: The Interplay Between Institutions and Social Partners. Bologna: International Industrial Relations Association.

Sajhau, Jean-Paul (1997). *Business Ethics in the Textile, Clothing and Footwear (TCF) Industries: Codes of Conduct.* Geneva: ILO.

Samford, C. (1996). 'Strange Idea: The North American Agreement on Labour Cooperation and Other U.S. Approaches to Enforcing International Labour Standards'. Senior Honours Thesis submitted to the New York State School of Industrial Labour Relations, Cornell University. Ithaca, N.Y.: Cornell University.

Nath, S. (1997). *Labour Policy and Economic Reforms—India, 1991-1996: A Study in the Context of Industrial Restructuring.* New Delhi: (Mimeo.), pp. 35.

Trebilcock, A (1998). *What Future for Social Clause.* Proceedings of the 11th World Congress—Developing Competitiveness and Social Justice: The Interplay Between Institutions and Social Partners. Bologna: International Industrial Relations Association.

Treu, T. (1998). *Keynote Address. Volume 1.* Proceedings of the 11th World Congress—Developing Competitiveness and Social Justice: The Interplay between Institutions and Social Partners. Bologna: International Industrial Relations Association.

US Department of Labour (1997). *By the Sweat and Toil of Children. Volume IV: Consumer Labels and Child Labour.* Washington DC: Bureau of International Labour Affairs, US Department of Labour.

V.V. Giri National Labour Institute (1998). *Child Labour in the Sports Goods Industry—Jalandhar: A Case Study Sponsored by the Federation of Indian Chambers of Commerce and Industry and International Labour Office--International Programme for Elimination of Child Labour.* New Delhi: V.V. Giri National Labour Institute.

ANNEXURE 10.1

ILO Conventions Ratified by the Government of India

Sl. No.	Number, Title and Year of Adoption by the ILO	Date of Ratification by India
1	1. Hours of Work (Industry) Convention, 1919	14.07.1921
2*	2. Unemployment Convention, 1919	14.07.1921
3	4. Night Work (Women) Convention, 1919	14.07.1921
4	5. Minimum Age (Industry) Convention, 1919	09.09.1955
5	6. Night Work of Young Persons (Industry) Convention, 1919	14.07.1921
6	11. Right of Association (Agriculture) Convention, 1921	11.05.1923
7	14. Weekly Rest (Industry) Convention, 1921	11.05.1923
8	15. Minimum Age (Trimmers and Stokers) Convention, 1921	22.11.1922
9	16. Medical Examination of Young Persons (Sea) Convention, 1921	20.11.1922
10	18. Workmen's Compensation (Occupational Diseases) Convention, 1925	30.09.1927
11	19. Equality of Treatment (Accident Compensation) Convention, 1925	30.09.1927
12	21. Inspection of Emigrants Convention, 1926	14.01.1928
13	22. Seamen's Articles of Agreement Convention, 1926	31.10.1932
14	26. Minimum Wage-fixing Machinery Convention, 1928	10.01.1955
15	27. Marking of Weight (Packages Transported by Vessels) Convention, 1929	07.09.1931
16	29. Forced Labour Convention, 1930	20.11.1954
17	32. Protection Against Accidents (Dockers) Convention (Revised), 1934	13.01.1964
18@	41. Night Work (Women) Convention (Revised), 1934	25.03.1938
19	42. Workmen's Compensation (Occupational Diseases) Convention (Revised), 1934	13.01.1964
20	45. Underground Work (Women) Convention, 1935	25.03.1938
21	80. Final Articles Revision Convention, 1948	17.11.1947
22**	81. Labour Inspection Convention, 1947	07.04.1949
23	88. Employment Services Convention, 1948	24.06.1959
24	89. Night Work (Women) Convention (Revised), 1948	27.02.1950
25	90. Night Work of Young Persons (Industry) Convention (Revised), 1948	27.02.1950
26	100. Equal Remuneration Convention, 1951	25.09.1958

(Contd.)

Sl. No.	Number, Title and Year of Adoption by the ILO	Date of Ratification by India
27	107. Indigenous and Tribal Population Convention, 1957	29.09.1958
28	111. Discrimination (Employment & Occupation) Convention, 1958	03.06.1960
29#	116. Final Articles Revision Convention, 1961	21.06.1962
30#	118. Equality of Treatment (Social Security)	19.08.1964
31@@	123. Minimum Age (Underground Work) Convention, 1965	20.03.1975
32	115. Radiation Protection Convention, 1960	17.11.1975
33	141. Rural Workers' Organization Convention, 1975	18.08.1977
34	144. Tripartite Consultation (International Labour Standards) Convention, 1976	27.02.1978
35	136. Benzene Convention, 1971	11.06.1991
36#	160. Labour Statistics Convention, 1985	01.04.1992
37	147. Merchant Shipping (Minimum Standards) Convention, 1976	26.09.1996
38	122. Employment Policy	1999

Source: Government of India (Ministry of Labour) (1998). *Annual Report 1997-98.* New Delhi, pp. 179–80.

* Later denounced. The Convention requires, *inter alia*, furnishing of statistics concerning unemployment every three months, which is considered not practicable.
@ Convention denounced as a result of ratification of Convention No. 89.
** Excluding Part II.
@@ Branches (a) to (c), (e) and (g) covered.
\# Article 8 of Part II.

ANNEXURE 10.2

Components of Social Clause and Indian Legislation

Social Clause Aspect	Indian Constitution/Legislation
Freedom of Association and Right to Collective Bargaining (Convention Nos. 87 and 98 respectively).	Freedom of Association is guaranteed as a fundamental right in the Indian Constitution. The Trade Union Act, 1926 meets with part of the objectives of Convention Nos. 87 and 98. Both conventions have, however, not been ratified by the Government of India.

(Contd.)

Social Clause Aspect	Indian Constitution/Legislation
Forced Labour Convention, 1930 and Abolition of Forced Labour Convention, 1953 (Convention Nos. #29 and 105). These provide for progressive abolition of forced labour in all its forms. Convention No. 182 concerning Immediate Action to End the Worst Forms of Child Labour.	Article 23 of the Constitution and the Bonded Labour System (Abolition) Act, 1976. India has ratified Convention No. #29, not 105. India is moving towards ratifying Convention Nos. 105 and 182.
Equal Remuneration Convention, 1951 (Convention No. 100). Its purpose is to eliminate sex-based discrimination in remuneration and provide for equal remuneration, to both men and women, for work of equal value. The four underlying bases for determination of work of equal value are: skills, efforts, responsibility and working conditions.	The Constitution upholds the principle of equality between men and women. The Equal Remuneration Act, 1926 seeks to provide for equal remuneration to men and women.
Discrimination (Employment and Occupation) Convention, 1958 (Convention No. 111). It covers any discrimination, exclusion or preference '... which has the effect of nullifying or impairing equality of treatment' and which can be the result of not only legislation but also of existing factual positions or practices.	The Constitution upholds equality, denounces discrimination and encourages preferential treatment to disadvantaged groups in society. Convention No. 111 has been ratified.
Minimum Age Convention, 1973 (Convention No. 138). It provides that minimum wage for employment should ordinarily be 15 and raised to 18 in dangerous occupations.	The Child Labour (Prohibition and Regulation) Act, 1986 bans employment of children below the age of 14. In several laws the minimum age is variously defined. Employment of children in certain heavy and hazardous industries (Schedule A, part 3) is prohibited by law and the government is taking steps to enforce it strictly. Several court judgements under public interest litigation actively support the prohibition and regulation of child labour.

Annexure 10.3

Ratification of Core Conventions in Select Countries

Country	Convention No.							
	29	87	98	100	105	111	138	182
Australia	*	*	*	*	*	*		
Bangladesh	*	*	*		*	*		
Canada		*		*	*	*		
China				*				
Germany	*	*	*	*	*	*	*	
France	*	*	*	*	*	*	*	
India	*			*		*		
Japan	*	*	*	*				
Nepal	*		*	*	*			
Pakistan	*	*	*		*	*		
Sri Lanka	*		*					
UK	*	*	*	*	*			
USA					*			

Eleven

New Paradigms in Employment Relations*

This chapter reviews the new paradigms in employment relations in the formal, modern sectors of the Indian economy. Labour laws, trade unions and industrial relations have perhaps not been such a major limiting factor in the modern sectors of the economy as, for instance, they were in traditional manufacturing. It is assumed that: (a) the conditions of employment in the modern sectors are generally better than the minimal provided under various labour laws; (b) a larger proportion of employers in the modern sectors have been technically qualified professionals belonging to a middle-class background and been employees themselves before they became entrepreneurs; and (c) a relatively larger proportion of modern, high-tech firms are somehow 'union-free'. These assumptions need further verification and do not by themselves adequately explain why the aspects that undoubtedly have a significant bearing on the new paradigms have not been considered.

Work and employment relations being a reflection of the developments in the wider society, the politico-socio-cultural and

---

* An earlier version of this chapter was presented at the Industrial Relations Conference of the Council of Indian Employers in Bangalore in 1996 and published in *Indian Journal of Industrial Relations*, 32(2), October 1996, 153–178.

techno-legal environment should, ideally, provide the backdrop for any meaningful discussion. In this chapter, however, the political, cultural and legal aspects have not been tackled in much detail.

So far, societies have graduated from being predominantly agricultural to being industrial to being post-industrial or service and high-tech economies. This transition and transformation has resulted in a shift from (a) land to money to information in terms of wealth base; (b) muscle to machine-tending skills to mind in the dominant use of human skills/energy; (c) one-sided dependence to interdependence to independence in employment relations; (d) emphasis on fear to paternalism to fairness in motivational approaches; (e) direction and control to inducement (carrot and stick) to consensus and commitment in the principles and philosophy of managing people at work.

TABLE 11.1 Shifting Focus in the Realm of Work

Aspect	Traditional Agriculture	Early/Traditional Industry	Post-Industrial Service/High-tech
Wealth	Land	Money	Mind/Information
Skill/Effort	Brawn/Muscle	Machine-tending	Brain/Mind Attitude and Ability Matter, not just Skill
Management Philosophy	Unilateral	Pluralistic	Egalitarian
Management Style	Autocratic	Paternalistic	Collegial
Employment Context	Master–Servant	Employer–Employee	Partners
Relationship	One-sided Dependence	Interdependence	Mutuality and Independence
Communication	Top-down	Two-way	Transparent
Motivation	Fear	Favour	Fairness
Performance Appraisal	Information Confidential, Boss	Formal, One-way	Formal, Open, Participative Appraisals
Control	Direction and Control	Inducement	Consensus/Commitment

Since the economy is fairly diverse, the future trends would reflect the heterogeneity of workplace contexts. As Stern (1993) has observed, 'In India we have the diversity of Europe and the unity of a continent.' Some parts of Indian society are still predominantly rural/agricultural in character, some dominated by traditional manufacturing, while the remaining comprise the high-tech manufacturing and modern services sector. Therefore, the emerging picture about the world of work, even if it is changing rapidly, appears static to some and dynamic to others. Given the vast diversity of the country, the picture at the macro level is vastly heterogeneous. Here there are changes in eight broad areas: (i) market, (ii) work, (iii) technology, (iv) worker, (v) work organization, (vi) skills, (vii) compensation, and (viii) workplace governance.

CHANGES IN THE MARKET

In the emerging economic scenario, the market-place is witnessing six interrelated changes: (i) plan to market (World Bank, 1996), (ii) import-substitution to export-oriented growth (Kuruvilla and Venkata Ratnam, 1996), (iii) protection to competition (Das, 1996), (iv) sellers' to buyers' market, (v) producer to consumer orientation, and (vi) swadeshi to videshi. Survival in the market-place depends on low-cost, high-quality products/services; zero-defect, on-time delivery; exceeding, not just meeting, customers' expectations; and innovation.

A section of employers holds the view that though the market-place has changed, the regulatory environment and the relevant government policies on social and labour issues have not. It is futile to expect others—'others' may include the government or, for that matter, trade unions—to solve the problems of the management of a company. If a management analyzes a problem positively, it will find one or more ways to solve it. Also, state governments today are far more responsive than before (Venkata Ratnam, 1996d). They are aware that to remain in power they need to attract investment and create jobs. Towards this end, for example, labour inspection has been eased or centralized. In some states, 40 per cent of applications for change of work practices, lay-off, retrenchment or closure during 1988–1993 were approved by the Tamil Nadu government; in another 40 per cent, it favoured workers/unions; and as regards the remaining 20 per cent, the government is yet to make up its mind (Government of India, 1995).

The laws are framed such that even though closure and retrenchment are difficult, the retrenching of workers in times of sale or transfer of business is not. But courts have upheld: the levying of a fine of Rs 100,000 each on several workers/union leaders for arson during strike; the no-work, no-pay principle, mandating strikes to be not only legal but justified (without specifying the criteria for the justification); denying the customary practice of paid honorary jobs for full-time trade union activists.

Unions too are cooperating. Quite a few firms have been closed through the VRS route, and many restructured through heavy downsizing. An average of a 10 to 20 per cent reduction in workforce has taken place in several firms since the early 1980s. Some have reduced their workforce to one-third or even less during the 1990s. Unions have signed a number of concessions and cooperative agreements that may well be considered suicide pacts.

In India, companies like Arvind Mills, Infosys, Ranbaxy, Sundaram Fasteners, and TI Cycles have changed their market strategy not just to adjust to the changes, but to become major global players in their respective areas (Das, 1996). Sundaram Fasteners won a five-year contract competing with 12 foreign companies in a global bid for supplying radiator caps to all General Motors plants worldwide: 'Against a standard reject rate of 150 parts per million, it has achieved six parts per million and never missed a delivery in the last two years. It requires a long-term vision, identifying products which have a long shelf life, avoiding the temptation for wild diversification and focusing on not only cost but also value, quality, timeliness and innovation.'

The positive response to changes in market is not uniform, though. For instance, while the domestic pharmaceutical sector is buoyant, the domestic white goods sector and electronics industry (hardware) is not equally robust. Overall, however, there is a resurgence of confidence even though there is concern in several quarters about local brands in many sectors being replaced by foreign ones. Critics of the market have several questions:

- Why should potato chips be allowed to come in with micro chips?
- Why is competitiveness not possible without downsizing?
- Why can't economic development be achieved without ecological destruction?
- Why is there a craze for 'having' (material culture) rather than 'being'?

CHANGING NATURE OF WORK

Work is becoming increasingly technology driven and is impacting on both content and contexts. Based on the concrete experience of many workplaces, the following scenario is representative of the changing nature of work. It must be added, though, that the change is more true of modern, high-tech workplaces than of agriculture and agro-based or traditional manufacturing:

- Robotized workplaces (assembly operations)
- Unmanned workstations (power plants)
- Officeless work (journalists in the newspaper industry or sales professionals)
- Open 24 hours, 365 days a year (be it a factory, bank or a restaurant)
- Contract for work → contract of work
- Employed worker → independent contractor
- Dependent/interdependent → independent worker
- Permanent → temporary
- Office → home
- Fixed → flexible hours of work
- Jobs as property → jobs for prosperity
- Lifetime employment → lifetime employability
- Single task/single career → multiple tasks/multiple careers
- Individual → team
- Functional → cross-functional
- Ladders → loops
- Managers → facilitators
- Fordist-Taylorism → Neo-Fordist Toyotaism
- Sequenced/Segmented approach → parallel/circular work organization
- Autonomous hierarchies → interdependent partnerships
- Employee as a servant → employee as a partner/(internal) customer
- Loyalty → competence/competencies
- Norms → values

- Managing → leading
- Control → commitment
- Direction → empowerment

A major problem, however, is the increasing informalization of work. Short-term solutions like overtime and contract work eventually create bigger problems for the management. There are turbulent times ahead for contract work and contract labour. Hence, managements will need to deal judiciously with the problems in the area of employment relations if the solutions they seek to current problems are not to turn out to be worse than the problems themselves.

CHANGING TECHNOLOGY OF WORK

Modern technology has made the finite capacities—sight, speech, travel and effort—of humans infinite. New technologies, new materials, new processes and new methods have revolutionized the world of work.

Listed here are some ways in which the face of the factory and office are changing (Table 11.2):

TABLE 11.2 Changing Face of a Modern Factory/Office

Yesterday	Today	Tomorrow
Factory		
Putting out system	Regular premises	Work out of home
Start to finish under same roof	Make-or-buy dilemma	Outsource as much as possible
Manual machines	Electrical, mechanical	Digital, cellular
Office		
Ink Pen	Ball pen	?
Typewriter	Computer	?
Telephones	Pagers	?
Duplicator	Xerox machines	?
Telex	Fax, e-mail and internet	?
Annual filing	Electronics databases	?

CHANGING PROFILE OF WORKERS

The following changes are expected in the profile of the worker (Table 11.3):

TABLE 11.3 Changing Profile of Workers

Yesterday	Today	Tomorrow
Majority	Majority	Majority
Blue Collar	White collar	Gold collar
Illiterate workers and literate bosses	Both workers and their bosses are literate	Workers more literate than their bosses in terms of technical knowledge in their respective work areas
Workers 'low-caste' and managers 'upper-caste'	Workers and managers homogeneous	Workforce increasingly diverse
Low aspirations	Instrumental in orientation	High aspirations

Production workers comprise no more than about 15 per cent of the total workforce in today's modern, high-tech factories. Even in the defence services, hierarchy is becoming less important. In the Air Force, for instance, once the aircraft is airborne, the seniors let the juniors take charge of the control panels. In traditional cargo handling, a worker would typically aspire to become a highly skilled worker or a junior supervisor. Today, the lowest paid operator in the computer workstation at the Nhava Sheva port would say: I am already a diploma holder and have registered for a graduate diploma in engineering. After that I will do my MBA. I wish to see myself retire as general manager of this port.

MANAGING DIFFERENCES

There are three major issues in dealing with the changing demographics of the workforce: managing cerebral workers, managing expectations, and managing differences. Of these, managing differences such as the following, is the most crucial and challenging:

- Religion: Hindu, Muslim, Christian and others
- Caste: Forward, backward, most backward, Scheduled Caste/Tribe
- Language: English, Hindi, regional and other languages
- Region: North–South, East–West
- Age: Old and young workers
- Sex: Male and female. In some countries gays and lesbians too have articulated their special needs and expectations
- Intra- and international diversity

- Intersectoral diversity: Traditional and modern manufacturing, for instance
- Workforce in existing plants and greenfield sites
- Cultural integration in mergers and acquisitions

What is our attitude to workforce diversity? Is it seen as an adversity or an advantage? Do we have a choice or has diversity become imperative? Which of these issues have we already begun to address? Which of these need to be dealt with differently?

Consider, for example, the issue of reservations. Quotas for disadvantaged groups look at the demand side of the problem. Have we done enough to look at the supply side also? Do we see affirmative action as reparation for past injustice? Does affirmative action lead to reverse discrimination? Does it really entail compromise on the quality of performance? Do we see this as a political issue or a socio-economic problem?

In the years to come, women are likely to improve their presence in the total workforce and, particularly, in jobs traditionally held by males. This requires paying attention to issues like (a) balancing work–family responsibilities; (b) dual career planning; (c) taking care of the needs of the workers with family responsibilities; and, (d) creating an inclusive work environment for both men and women as colleagues and undertaking proactive, preventive measures to deal with prejudice, discrimination, stereotyping and sexual harassment.

WORK ORGANIZATION

Globalization has reduced the autonomy of the nation-state but increased the autonomy of the enterprise and exposed the latter to greater external pressures. To meet these pressures enterprises need greater flexibility. Currently, the need for firm-level flexibility is determined largely by product market conditions with little regard, if any, for labour market conditions. Technology has shortened product life-cycles and increased the uncertainty of product markets and the costs and risks of research and new product development.

New technologies in communication and transportation as well as the mobility of capital and immobility of labour are resulting in a shift away from mass production to parallel production over widely dispersed territories. As national boundaries are receding and firms are facing greater competition, they are creating activity networks internationally. These new interfirm dependencies do not necessarily conform to industrial relations structures that assume the independence of individual firms.

The ILO (1998) asserts that the various forms of organization of the production and distribution of goods for the world market often involve complex, hierarchical networks of interfirm relations. The present trends differ from those of the past in the following three ways: (i) international subcontracting has grown relative to other types of commercial relations, and trade in intermediate goods and services constitutes a growing share of total international trade, (ii) domestic subcontracting is on the rise; and (iii) commercial linkages between firms are changing intensely.

> A major share of trade and production occurs not in the market at large, within the internal and intermediate markets... Production chains are becoming, in several cases, 'buyer-driven'... These firms design and/or market, but do not make the brand-named products they order. They are part of a new breed of 'manufacturers without factories' that separate the production of goods from the design and marketing stages of the production process.

Since the 1980s, the world market for manufacturing goods, as well as product life-cycles and employment intensity have been shrinking. Some have begun to argue that the era of mass production is over and needs to be replaced with some new form such as 'flexible specialization (Piore and Sabel, 1984), 'lean production' (Womack et al. 1990) and beyond (IILS, 1993), Toyotaism (Imai, 1986) or post-Fordism (Roobeck, 1987).

Mass production is being replaced with flexible specialization. With new manufacturing methods, newer approaches to work organization are required. According to Storey (1987) the essential features of 'superior forms' of new methods of manufacturing and work organization include:

> A fuller utilisation of available work time; flexibility of work and of labour deployment; teamworking of one kind or another; just-in-time production; continued improvement, learning by doing and innovative ideas contributed by all levels of employees; the continual bearing down, and elimination of, non-value-added

activities; and workers undertaking production, inspection and maintenance functions themselves.

Enhancing competitiveness under the circumstances has focused attention not merely on the macro environment (East Asian Miracle, World Bank), but also on manufacturing itself (Hayes, et al., 1988).

New initiatives in manufacturing (Peters and Waterman, 1982; Schonberger, 1986) have a clear focus: Total Quality Management (TQM) on quality; Just in Time (JIT) on cost control; ISO on systems; and Advanced Manufacturing Technology (AMT), Cellular Manufacturing (CM), Computer-Integrated Manufacturing (CIM), Flexible Manufacturing Systems (FMS), and Lean Production (LP), on responsiveness to market demands. The strategy is to compete both on cost and quality and be responsive to market needs (Lawler, 1992).

Manufacturing methods and technologies should support such strategies. Companies are focusing on product (products which have longer life-cycles such as Denim in the case of Arvind Mills) and process (Kaizen) through advanced and integrated technologies such as computer numerically controlled (CNC) machines. AMTs offer the advantage of automation by way of low cost and high and consistent product quality. They can also cope with a wide variety of products with a minimum set-up and changeover time.

The link between manufacturing and shopfloor employees was explored by studies that focused on job content and job characteristics (Hackman and Oldham, 1980) and on a socio-technical systems approach (Trist, et al. 1963; ILO, 1979). Subsequently, several studies (Galbraith, 1977; Lawrence and Lorsch, 1969) have recognized the differences in the degree of complexity and uncertainty in production and brought in a contingency framework. They have proposed a greater devolution in decision making as the degree of uncertainty increases. To facilitate this, a series of 'softer' elements including, for example, internal customer supply chains, new ways of working and a cellular factory layout have come into vogue.

The flattening out of organizational structures, shifting from a sequential to a parallel approach, integrating of producers and customers to form a dynamic interaction and combining of the efforts of head (planning) and hand (execution) have become integral elements of the emerging systems of work organization (Table 11.4).

TABLE 11.4 **The Main Features of Traditional and Emerging Approaches to Job Design**

	Traditional Approaches	Emerging Approaches
Job content	Autonomy/Control, with skill variety, task identity, task significance and feedback	Cognitive demand, cost responsibility and interdependence
Contingency	Individual differences— growth needs strength	Organizational factors— production uncertainty
Mechanism	Motivation	Knowledge application and development

Source: T.D. Wall and P.R. Jackson (1995). 'New Manufacturing Initiatives and Shopfloor Job Design'. A. Howard (ed). *The Changing Nature of Work*. San Francisco: Jossey-Bass. p. 164.

Corresponding changes in the social side of work organization include aspects such as employee participation, teamworking, security of employment, commitment and extensive training' (Storey, 1994; 248). For example, Japan has overtaken western countries in adopting new, advanced, flexible manufacturing systems (Jaikumar, 1986; Valery, 1987). Yet, it has not abandoned Tayloristic practices and managerial control. Indeed, Storey (1987; 248) argues, 'these features are taken to new heights because employee groups are themselves engaged in seeking out "unnecessary movements" and excess labour in true Tayloristic fashion'.

As mentioned earlier, a host of non-traditional methods are noticed in workplaces worldwide which point to revolutionary changes in work organization and managing people. Workers are becoming owners and managing without supervisors. The personnel/human resource function is not only decentralized, but its responsibilities effectively devolved so that the organization no longer needs a separate personnel/human resource department. Organizations are functioning without traditional structures, separate quality boundaries, unions, personnel departments or even a complete complement of a full-time workforce. Completely unmanned work sites are becoming less rare (Flood, et al., 1996). Most such methods have still not become part of the tradition, therefore they cannot be viewed as trends. What such experiences, however, do show is that there is plenty of innovation going around.

SKILLS DEVELOPMENT

The twenty-first century belongs to those who have the skills and knowledge. In the post-liberalization/globalization era unskilled workers are either losing jobs or being pushed to the unorganized sector, where working conditions are harsh and earnings low. Skilled workers on the other hand are able to retain their jobs and improve their career and earnings.

Lifetime employment in the current and future context would mean a continuous obligation to train, retrain and redeploy employees. This also signifies a mutual obligation and commitment to technological advancement, job and work redesign, and responsibility for self-development and employee training. It also means that employees should be career resilient and career self-reliant.

The ILO (1998) observes that countries with higher and better levels of skill adjust more effectively to the challenges and opportunities of globalization because their enterprises are more flexible and better able to absorb and adapt to new technologies and work with new equipment. Skill level and workforce quality will thus increasingly provide the cutting edge in successfully competing in the global economy.

Lee and Verma (1996) argue:

> Two views can be taken of human resources, one being that they are a cost, and the other being that they are an investment. The first view translates into attempts to keep wages low and spend as little as possible on training and human resource development. The second view treats people as a source of competitive advantage. It leads firms to invest in skill development.

The paradox of skills development in India has been highlighted by two international studies in a telling manner:

1. Oxenham et al. (1990) hold the view that: India has, in effect, chosen to give more education at a higher price to a few who have already had more than the average education, rather than work for a sound education for all. The effect has been a trainable total workforce, and a flow of highly skilled people notoriously larger than the number of jobs available.

2. The World Competitiveness Report (IMD & WEF, 1994) examines the competitiveness of human resources—which is one of the 10 factors studied—based on skills, motivation, flexibility, age structure and health of the people. The criteria included in this factor include: population, employment, unemployment, educational attainment, vocational training, public expenditure on education, management quality, income levels and health facilities. According to the report, India is the least competitive of the 10 newly industrialized countries (NIEs) included in the study. The high rate of illiteracy (48 per cent as per the 1991 census), the inadequate provisions for health and the difficulty experienced in providing education and vocational training could be the major contributing factors. According to the report, the quality of skilled labour in India is good, but its proportion to the total labour force of the country too small with the result that, though the country ranked first among the 10 NIEs in terms of the quality of skilled labour, with regard to their ready availability it ranked seventh. In terms of the extent to which ongoing job training meets the requirements of a competitive economy it was ranked last.

Low literacy, a vocational bias against technical skills and an occupational preference for non-production jobs, a mismatch between skills acquired and skills required and the dearth of adequately/appropriately trained technical personnel for non-executive positions are among the major weaknesses that characterize the macro-level situation in India. The emphasis on general education and an insufficient interaction between industry and educational/training institutions has exacerbated these characteristics. Together, their role in limiting the technical and economic advancement of the country cannot be exaggerated (Venkata Ratnam, 1994).

Even a cursory review of India's vocational and technical training and education confirms that people are being prepared for tomorrow's jobs with yesterday's machines and methods. This calls for a revamp and modernization of the skills training systems. Alongside this, retraining and multi-craft training should also be stressed. Those who are unable and/or unwilling to adapt to new technologies will find that they are working harder and accomplishing less, if at all they are able to keep their jobs.

Technological and other changes and the pressures of restructuring mean a shift in the demand for skills, which are different, not always higher. Training and retraining systems for restructuring need to react quickly and flexibly. The government alone cannot fund the massive training effort called for. Hence, alternative ways of financing should be considered. Also, the systems of certification in the country are woefully inadequate. Only far greater quality assurance and cost effectiveness will ensure that the already meager investments are put to optimal use and not frittered away. The training requirements for women, the disadvantaged and vulnerable groups in society warrant special attention. With India's commitment to eliminate child labour, there is a need to arrange for the education and training of children as well as review the present systems of skills transmission in traditional crafts.

The informal/unorganized sector accounts for a major share of new job creation in the country. The small and unorganized sector accounts for a significant share of our exports. There are, however, no formal training systems designed for it. This sector attracts the failures of the formal education system and trains them to graduate into the formal sector. It is time we considered new, alternative models/systems for augmenting skills formation in this sector.

Organizations should encourage creativity and innovation. Worker education and trade union involvement in the development of basic education and skills training can play a useful role. India should develop a skills development fund and restructure the NRF in such a way that purposive retraining guarantees job placement.

Companies should ideally invest 3 per cent of their wage bill on the education and training of employees. Every employee should undergo, on an average, at least a week's education and training a year. Workers' and employers' organizations should play a more active role in influencing the formulation and implementation of proactive labour market policies.

Multinational companies often become transmission belts for modern human resource practices. Several of them are now also engaged in substantive competency analysis and competency building efforts. But these efforts have, until now, been confined largely to executives. MNCs have also been instrumental in introducing assessment centres, 360° appraisals, multimedia training and other modern methods of human resource development. Quite a few domestic firms in both the private and public sectors have been making similar efforts, albeit on a very modest scale. Greater/active involvement of the social partners is needed to give skills formation and competency building the thrust it warrants.

In sum, there are five aspects of skills development that require attention:

PRIMARY AND VOCATIONAL EDUCATION

The government should step up its investment in primary and vocational education and substantially revamp the system. In this context, the Swiss and the German models of vocational training could be examined. Employers and their organizations should also take a more active interest in shaping and supervising vocational education, while industry and academic and technical institutions should make integrated efforts, develop partnerships, share resources and improve education and training.

SKILLS DEVELOPMENT FUND

Singapore and Malaysia, for instance, have set up skills development funds with contributions from employers—a per cent (usually 1.5 per cent) of the wage bill. The collection and disbursement of funds under the scheme has been made simple by using the existing network of commercial banks. This is a macro-level initiative that India could also emulate (Kuruvilla and Chua, 2000).

RETRAINING

The National Renewal Fund (NRF) did not meet its objective. While over 80,000 opted for the VRS utilizing NRF funds, barely a 1000 people were retrained and 100 redeployed (see also Chapter 4). Several companies have clauses on redundancy and retraining. But retraining in an unemployment context would result in a situation whereby redundant workers in a family would be competing with the younger ones entering the labour market for the first time. Therefore, retraining as a solution may give rise to a new problem or not provide a complete answer to the problem of unemployment. Even so, it should be a continuous process rather than an event if human resource obsolescence due to technological, economic or other structural changes is to be minimized or averted.

MULTIPLE SKILLS/TASKS

The one-person one-skill/task concept is giving way to the one-person many skills/tasks concept. This is helpful to the organization in terms of a better utilization of people in the workplace. It also helps insure individuals against redundancy, since at least some skills are expected to remain marketable, and facilitates redeployment. There is a need to clarify the purpose of the concept and orient not only workers but supervisors and managers as well. Multiskilling requires a thorough review of work processes, assignments, appraisal and accountability and is particularly useful in assembly operations where the sequential performance of operations involves a built-in idle time.

Companies may issue passports to its employees and notify in it the skills the employee has learnt. This is deemed a method of recognition of the skills acquired by the worker. Such certification of marketable skills helps outplacement in case of redundancy.

The problem in India is not just skill, but, more importantly, attitude. As Pope John Paul II said, India's problems are two-fold: to give work to those who do not have it and to make those who have it do it. A related problem, thus, is work culture that encompasses work attitudes and work behaviours of employees at all levels.

COMPENSATION

Wages and salaries are a cost to employers and income to employees. Employers should be concerned with wage costs, not wages *per se*. The principle should be 'work smart, earn more', instead of 'work more, earn more' because physical effort has limits while smartness knows no bounds.

The system of compensation should emphasize equity, both internal and external. Pay differentials can be based on skills, effort, responsibility and conditions of work.

Wage parity is a major issue. Public policy is aimed at ensuring a sense of parity and proportionality because wide differences can create social problems. Parity is an issue whenever a pay commission or a wage board gives its recommendations or award. It is also an issue in collective bargaining. For instance, in one engineering industry the technical staff formed a separate union after pay revision because they felt that though welding was a highly rated technical trade, grass cutters were getting more pay than gas cutters. Unions in the banking sector announced a calendar of strikes because the parity between award staff and officers' wages that had existed before the pay revision was broken despite an assurance to the contrary. A committee set up to review the issue upheld the viewpoint of the award staff. In the public sector oil industry, too, there was a similar problem. Over the last two decades the difference between the lowest and the highest paid employee in the public sector has shrunk from 1:30 to 1:6 or less. Officers want the past parity to be restored while workers want to maintain the existing parity. Public sector workers are better off than their counterparts in the private sector by at least 50 per cent in terms of wages and benefits, while the reverse is the case with respect to senior managers. With the easing of restrictions on managerial remuneration there has been a phenomenal increase in disparity between the public and private sectors, particularly at senior managerial levels. Also, agreements in about 240 central public sector undertakings (CPSUs) expired on 31 December 1996; less than 10 out of the 240 CPSU's signed the agreements as of 30 September 2000. In fact, in several chronically sick central public sector undertakings, the agreements which expired on 31 December 1991 have not been renewed yet.

The sum and substance is that the compensation scene in India today is chaotic and a major crisis awaits us. Crisis presents an opportunity also to look at all relevant issues *de novo* through what Charles Handy (1990) calls, some upside down thinking.

Companies would do well to examine three types of interventions: (i) relook at performance measurement systems; (ii) develop performance-linked flexible and contingent pay and, (iii) build stake in employees as owners.

PERFORMANCE MEASUREMENT SYSTEM

There is a general perception that workers in India are productive individually but not in teams. Our performance appraisal/review systems focus on behaviour rather than performance because the latter is difficult to measure and the former, being subjective, gives ample opportunity for people to play favourites and use it for reward and punishment. In any case, the type of accountability one sees in other functions, one hardly sees in decisions concerning people. Even on a subject such as latecoming, which is a physically verifiable aspect of behaviour, managers have been known to review their decision four times in less than four hours at the cost of tremendous misunderstanding between the supervisor and the supervised (Venkata Ratnam and Srivastava, 1996). We need to relook at performance systems and make them more open and participative. It is not enough if an employee pleases his/her boss. The concept of the internal and external customer must be built into performance measurement systems. Where work is carried out in teams, team and peer appraisals are appropriate.

PERFORMANCE-LINKED PAY

This means pay is dependent on performance.
- It requires a good system of performance planning, measurement and review.
- It should not be viewed as an opportunity to reduce existing pay levels.
- Employees feel vulnerable to steep/violent fluctuations in earnings, hence, the entire pay should not be made variable. A percentage (say 70 per cent) should be fixed and the balance variable at the worker level. At the senior management level, 30 per cent could be fixed and 70 per cent variable (inclusive of commission on profits, etc.). For salespersons, a regular employees' pay could be variable by up to 30 per cent and that of commission agents up to 70 or 80 per cent.
- Individuals/Teams should be able to contribute/make a difference to the performance of work.
- Employees should not be punished for factors beyond their control.

- If teamwork is critical, team rewards must also be emphasized.
- There is no one standard model/approach/scheme to be followed.
- Pay differentials should be based on the principle of 'equal pay for work of equal value', which should take into account four parameters, handy skills, effort, responsibility and working conditions.
- The (motivational) components of performance-linked pay systems could be both financial and non-financial.
- Performance-linked pay systems should focus on both short-term and long-term performance needs. Several merit increments in a few years at the start of a career may, under certain conditions, have negative effects on performance in subsequent years. Therefore, a judicious combination of merit increments and lumpsum payments should be used.

The various types of performance-linked pay include: individual or team-based pay, incentive pay, merit increments, lumpsum payments, skill/competence-based pay, gain sharing, bonus plans, profit sharing, employee share-ownership plans, stock options and non-financial rewards.

FLEXIBLE AND CONTINGENT PAY

Currently, wages in the organized sector increase once every six or seven years and in some sectors like electronics, even faster. In most sectors, wage increases have no relevance either to individual or company/unit performance. What is needed is a gradual shift to a system that takes the people affected by the change into confidence. All rewards, including pay and employee benefits, must have behavioural objectives. These should be set and determined in consultation with the relevant target groups. Flexible and contingent (to production, productivity or profits) pay is increasingly being perceived as a logical extension of a flexible work organization. The proliferation of knowledge workers in the ranks of the workforce has also led to the concept of knowledge pay, particularly in high-tech industries. For instance, Scanlon-type flexible wage systems are common in Singapore and Malaysia. Five principles underscore international experiences in a flexible pay system:

1. Flexible pay should not be a substitute for guaranteed pay. Roughly speaking, 70 per cent of the pay should be fixed and 30 per cent kept variable. Normal pay revisions may reflect changes in the cost of living and per capita incomes in the country.
2. Pay revision should lag behind productivity improvement. The lag period should be defined.
3. The performance system should be revamped to define and measure performance.
4. Profits, the share of the workers in it and the procedure for sharing should be defined.
5. A measure of stability in workers' incomes should be provided by pooling their share in excess of the 30 per cent of their pay into a fund that can be used to pay them in lean years, and thus impart a sense of stability to them regarding their earnings.

BUILD STAKE IN WORKERS AS OWNERS

Profit sharing and stock options are also becoming the norm. Examples of state initiative in this regard can be found in France in particular and Europe in general, the latter in view of a European Commission directive. In the US and UK, employee ownership is encouraged as a tax planning device. In Pakistan and Bangladesh, apart from bonus, legally mandated welfare funds are financed through profit sharing. Even in India, a beginning was made by earmarking 5 per cent of equity issues to workers. Corporate initiatives also provide for building stake in workers as owners. We have, for instance, two examples in Bangalore: Brooke Bond in the past, and Infosys now, which have pioneered employee shareholding. Several companies in the software, services and even consumer goods and engineering industries have started employee stock option programmes. On the eve of privatization, employees are offered shares to weaken their opposition. In India, when shares were offered to bank employees the unions opposed, but the workers did not pay heed to the unions. In the public sector oil companies, the workers fought and got more shares than what the government was initially willing to offer them. Companies like Escorts promoted and gave shares to workers in their ancillaries. A number of sick companies—Jaipur Metals Electricals, Kamani Tubes and New Central Jute Mills, to name a few—achieved turnarounds through worker ownership.

Increasing competition and rising labour costs are leading employers to introduce a variety of changes in traditional compensation systems.

- Lower wage for new employees than is paid to workers currently on the payrolls, if the firm has a greenfield site. Lower wages to newcomers is usually justified on the grounds of lower contributions during the initial years when employees move up the learning curve and the differences in the two tiers of pay taper off over three years or so.
- Differential in payments to regular workers and contract/casual workers with similar skill levels doing similar jobs is increasingly causing resentment and conflict. There are quite a few instances of court judgements and collective agreements nullifying differential payments and thus reducing, if not eliminating, the incentives for employing people on a contract/casual basis.
- Lumpsum payments in lieu of merit increments in pay.
- Profit sharing and stock options are being introduced in service and high-tech industries and in software companies and will spread to traditional manufacturing industries too. In the wake of disinvestment, employee shareholding is becoming a key feature. The government now allows profit sharing in the public sector. Pay trends in the public sector set the base mark/benchmark for the private sector.
- Due to the lowering of tax rates for individuals, tax compliance is increasing in terms of executive compensation in the private sector, reflected in fewer voucher payments and an increased trend to pay benefits in cash rather than in kind. Cafeteria benefit plans are going out of fashion.
- Pension benefits are a contentious area. There is pressure on the government from trade unions to enhance pension benefits. In contrast, footloose young professionals in the software industry want immediate cash benefits rather than long-term post-retirement benefits like pension. As more and more industrial employees are covered under pension schemes, there will be increased concern about their long-term viability. When the insurance sector gets liberalized, it is possible that workers' organizations will exert pressure for greater control over workers' funds, whether it is employee shares, provident fund or pension funds.

SOME WORRISOME PROPOSITIONS

While reviewing reward systems one should check and guard against some worrisome propositions.

We now pay workers not for *output* produced, nor even for labour *input* provided, but simply for *time* spent on the job (Blinder, 1991).

Employees seek reward for work without performing.

Somebody who does something only for money is capable of doing anything for money.

We can pay for a person's needs, not for his/her greed (Mahatma Gandhi).

Whether one's pay is adequate is a relative concept and depends more on what others are receiving. A person feels unhappy when his expectations are not fulfilled. He feels unhappy even when he receives more than what he expects or deserves. For, this may create misgivings in the mind of other colleagues.

The question is not whether the organization can afford to pay more. The question is whether the organization can afford not to pay more. There ought to be a link between pay and authority/responsibility.

The productivity-linked bonus system has resulted in the paying of bonus without productivity.

There is reward for non-performance, not for performance. People are rewarded for imitation, not imagination, complying with rules rather than setting goals, and following precedents rather than taking the initiative.

Incentive schemes fail to motivate (Kohn, 1993).

It is true that people do not live by bread alone and that money is not everything. But it does come first on the list of priorities. Finally, every item of reward has a behavioural objective. Over a period, while tinkering with the reward systems, it is possible that we may lose sight of the original purpose(s). There is a possibility that B be rewarded while hoping to reward A.

(Contd)

> Further, to reduce the pressure and problem of administering an array of welfare benefits there is the danger that these be awarded in monetary terms.

WORKPLACE GOVERNANCE

The changes described in the foregoing paragraphs have a profound impact on workplace governance, particularly in three areas namely, feudal social structure, collective bargaining and workers' participation.

Feudal Social Structure

Das (1996) quotes Bagchi who is critical about the unequal and feudal social structure in India:

> As a result the owners are arrogant and the managers are servile ... In east Asia, the owner will happily sit down with an employee for a meal. It is this attitude which has helped them succeed, create universal education and without poverty. India, in contrast, is like the Philippines, which is the only failure in east Asia because it shares our feudal social structure.

The biggest hurdle to desirable changes in workplace governance is the feudal and divisive social structure in the country. Hopefully, the energetic new middle class that Das (1996) mentions will be the catalyst in making workplaces egalitarian in order that values of pluralism, equity, fairness, trust and transparency can be imbibed.

Collective Bargaining

A more radical perspective about collective bargaining was provided by Virmani (1996) who asserts that collective bargaining has failed us and therefore we must give it up. Firms are restructuring with or without union involvement through one or more of the following strategies (Shrouti and Nandkumar, 1994; also see Venkata Ratnam, 1990 and 1996b; Davala, 1995): the transfer of jobs from the bargainable category to the non-bargainable category; a ban on recruitment; the transfer of production to subcontracted units; introduction of parallel production; the transfer of permanent jobs to contract; casual and temporary workers; the introduction of voluntary retirement schemes; flexibility and productivity; automation; management proposals/demands in negotiating pay revisions; closures/sale of business; and shopfloor restructuring.

Unusual and unconventional clauses are incorporated in collective agreements. Such clauses include (Venkata Ratnam, 1996a and 1996b): age discrimination in benefits; gender discrimination in the definition of dependants; linking of most allowances, including house rent and children's education, to attendance; linking of dearness allowance to productivity; linking of canteen prices to the cost of living index; voluntary retirement schemes for contract labour; separate agreements defining the technology and usage of computers; permitting pregnant women to work before computer terminals; clauses on change of work practices, lay-off, redundancy and retraining without reference to prior administrative clearances; annulling of incentive schemes; eliminating restrictive and wasteful practices; merger of units (dock labour board with port trust, for instance); abolition of jobs and revision of work norms; subcontracting; two-tier wage systems; converting fringe benefits to cash/pension benefits; transfers, promotions, etc.; voluntary separation schemes; and concession bargaining agreements in times of crisis. Such agreements, typically the ones signed as part of revival packages approved by the Board of Industrial and Financial Reconstruction, provide for, among other things: job cuts; wage cuts; the freezing of dearness allowances; the freezing of other allowances and benefits; and the suspension of industrial action and, in some cases, even trade union rights, for a specified period.

A review of nearly 300 collective agreements signed since 1990 (Venkata Ratnam, 1996a and 1996b) reveal the following major shifts in the collective bargaining scene in India:

Centralization to Decentralization: Industry or region-cum-industry agreements may give way to firm/plant-wide agreements. This will reduce the role of employers/industry associations and central trade union organisations in collective bargaining. Such a development has already been witnessed in the engineering and cement industries.

Collective to Individual Contracts: In many industrialized market economies this is already happening. New Zealand has pioneered such a shift. Within India, several firms, particularly in Mumbai have reportedly signed individual settlements, even in the unionized worker category, either when there was a stalemate in negotiations or the recognized union lost its mass base.

Parity to Disparity in Wages/Salaries: Over the years, the disparity between officers' and workers' wages has increased in the private sector and decreased in the public sector. In the public sector, it shrank from 1:30 in the 1950s to 1:6 in the 1990s. Pay revision in the banking industry in the mid-1990s resulted in a demand by the award staff in the banking industry for the restoration of the pre-revision parity between the emoluments of staff and officers. During the 1990s and in 2000, collective agreements in CPSUs resulted in a growing disparity in wages, benefits and the allowances of employees working in different sectors/organizations.

Fixed to Cafeteria Approach in Benefits: The existing system of employee benefits discriminates in favour of employees who are old and/or have large families. Also, it does not adequately regard the individual's needs. Therefore, in the private sector and in multinational companies the cafeteria approach has already been adopted for officer cadres. With the progressive decline in the average size of employment in organizations and the virtual disappearance of blue-collar workers in many organizations, such an approach may gradually be extended even to workers.

Higher Wages for Workers and Increased Job Control to Managers: Technology is making workers deskilled, resulting in job control shifting over to managers. At least one major study of the newspaper industry in India has pointed to this development (Samaddar, 1995). This seems to have happened even in cargo handling.

Concession Bargaining Leading to a Trade-off Between, say, Jobs and Earnings/Benefits, at Least in the Short Term: As discussed earlier, typically they are part of the BIFR package for the revival of sick units.

The other shifts include: assertion of workers' rights to ascendancy in managerial rights; age/seniority-weighted benefits to attendance/skill/performance-based benefits; in-service to post-retirement employee and other social security benefits; and welfare to moneyfare (conversion of benefits into cash).

WORKERS' PARTICIPATION

Participation entails sharing information, exchanging ideas and experiences, taking decisions jointly and owning up and sharing responsibility for results. This requires mutual trust, the ability and willingness to participate and transparency in motives. In most parts of the world, participation has been reduced to three items: tea, towels and toilets (Walker, 1974). Representative participation did not take root in India because the schemes provided for the workers' participation in management, not for managers' participation in management. It suffered because there was no agreement on who to select as representatives and how to select them. It became atrophied because unions saw the fora as a possible infringement on collective bargaining rights and managers did not want to give up their right to manage. The government wanted the schemes of participation to be implemented, so meetings took place, but since these were advisory bodies, follow-up was not mandatory and, therefore, became a casualty. And, while trade unions want to start from the board level downwards, most managements insist that it should begin at the shop-floor level and move up, voluntarily, if both parties agree.

Apart from the attitudinal gap, the key problem with workers' participation in management lies in the paradoxical dilemma: as cerebral workers replace muscle workers, it becomes imperative to involve them in decision making. But, when time is a critical factor in decision making, decisions are often made and participation then sought in implementing decisions. Another problem is that workers see this as another bargaining fora or a grievance channel. There may be fears among worker leaders as to how their constituency would react should they see reason in what the management says.

Given the above limitations, in many modern workplaces, the following trends can be discerned with regard to worker participation in management:

Representative/Union → direct/employee participation
Labour-Management Committees → mixed, small group activities
Fault-finding → problem-solving approaches
Bipartite committees to discuss various issues—not just canteen, safety, etc., but also job classifications, grievances, work improvement, and so on.

NON-TRADITIONAL METHODS

In the context of Indian organizations some non-traditional developments include the following (Flood et al., 1996):

Managing without managers (small, software companies run by professionals)

Supervision without supervisors (several)

Managing without traditional structures (several companies)

Managing without traditional owners (several worker-owned companies)

Managing without unions (this is becoming common now)

Personnel management without personnel managers

Managing without quality boundaries (many companies)

Managing without a complete, full-time workforce (several companies)

Employees are not employees in all cases any longer. They are independent workers, internal customers, partners, and so on. The contract labour system may have been abolished but contract labour remain. Is there not a distinction between contract of work and contract for work? Already in some cases the distinction between an employee and an independent worker is becoming blurred. An employee has already come to be treated as an internal customer. In creative organizations, employees walk in with assignments and walk out with assignments. They do not want to remain wage labour or salaried employees. They want to be partners, getting royalty rather than just a salary or a rightful share in the profits.

In some places, in fact, these concepts are already in operation and showing significant results. Admittedly, they have not become a tradition yet, but they do have the potential to. With these non-traditional methods, the traditional personnel function is undergoing a transformation. Many organizations have created separate human resource units/departments to give a special thrust to the neglected developmental role of personnel. More importantly, there is a decisive trend towards not only greater decentralization but also greater devolution of personnel/human resource functions back to the line manager. Simultaneously, human resource issues are becoming an integral part of business strategy. This is in recognition of the fact that if the business of business is business, then the business of personnel should also be business.

WORK AND EMPLOYMENT RELATIONS IN THE FUTURE

Work and employment relations are in a state of flux and transformation (Pettinger, 1999). Among the factors that have contributed to this are advanced technology, the forces of liberalization, privatization and globalization, the pressures of mergers and acquisitions, the ever-increasing diversity in the workplace and cross-cultural interactions, the influence of the media, increased consciousness about democratization and human/trade union/worker rights, the growing experience and knowledge about the values, attitudes and behaviour of people, growing competition and a rise in the expectations of the new workforce.

During the twentieth century, there was a shift from the Taylorist Fordist systems of division of labour, with mono skills, multiple job classifications and pyramidical levels/layers in the organization to Toyotaism based on lean production with multiple tasks/skills, fewer job classifications and flatter, slimmer downsized/right-sized organizations. This trend has continued into the new millennium, but with a caveat: 'beyond lean production'. Routine, repetitive and middlemen activities are either automated, robotized or being reeingineered through the application of advanced information technology. The cost-plus attitude is being replaced by strategies based on cost cutting and value addition to provide the competitive edge to companies. The work and workplace are being revamped continuously and rapidly. In this scenario, those who learn fast and are adept at adapting to the rapid changes will survive the threat of jobless growth and income insecurity.

Managements will cease to enjoy the elitist position that James Burnham visualized in the 1930s. With the reduction of hierarchies, individual managers will have less power over other people, but acquire a wider span of control. Revolutionary developments in information technology are not only making middle-level managers redundant; they are making it mandatory to learn and use information technology to measure and control performance.

The following shifts are taking place in employment relations:

- Shift in the power base from land/capital to knowledge
- Shift in the use of human energy from muscle to mind, brawn to brain
- From top-down to transparent two-way communication
- From fear to favour to fairness as the basis of motivation
- From leadership based on direction and control to one based on consensus and commitment
- High expectations of both workers and organizations. Flexible/adaptive work organization, continuous training in skills and attitudes, say and stake for employees who are becoming critical and indispensable
- The new collectives at the workplace will not be trade unions, but semi-autonomous work teams. New workplaces are replacing close supervision with leaders who are coaches, mentors and facilitators
- Improving labour standards and fostering ethical behaviour are becoming business imperatives.

DIVERSE FORMS OF EMPLOYMENT

The forms of employment are diverse indeed:

- Full-time employees
- Part-time employees
- Home workers
- Casual/Contingent/Badli/Substitute workers
- Contract workers
- Migrant intra- and inter-country workers
- Foreign workers
- Tele-workers
- Apprentices who are not workers but perform work while learning it
- Bonded labour
- Child labour
- Displaced workers
- Disabled workers
- Rationalized workers

- Self-employed workers, etc.

  The major concerns are:

- The already thin employment in the organized sector is becoming thinner. The number of jobs in the sector (31 million plus) are less than the number of people waiting for jobs in that sector as evidenced by the registrations in the employment exchanges (around 40 million).
- The new forms of work appear to be less paying and less secure while being more drudgerous and dangerous.
- There is a shift away from lifelong employment to lifelong employability and a consequential shift in emphasis from job security to income security.
- There is a need for proactive labour market policies in areas such as job search, skills inventory, the matching of demand and supply, information dissemination and counselling.

DOWNSIZING

Downsizing is occurring on a large-scale in many big firms. Though the estimates of surplus labour in the organized sector vary between 20 and 30 per cent, some large firms are known to have reduced their workforce by over 50 per cent in the last 10 years while a considerable number are planning to reduce it by third in the next five years. Unless new investments lead to the net addition to jobs in the organized sector—which did not happen in the 1990s—employment in this sector will shrink further over the next few years.

The effects of downsizing are not confined to laid-off workers; they extend even to those who remain in the organization. Dealing with the resultant morale and motivation issues requires a carefully designed strategy whereby employees are taken into confidence and all efforts made to minimize or avert the adverse effects on people in line with the recommendations of the ILO on the termination of employment in the employer's initiative.

In the past, firms believed in upsizing, that the big fish swallowed the small fish. Now they feel that the fast fish edge the slow fish out. It is worth considering whether in the past upsizing did not upgrade organizations and whether downsizing is now leading to downgrading.

In the Indian public sector, downsizing through the VRS has created vested interests. It offers incentives to those who want to leave early, but has not contributed much—in most cases—to the reduction of personnel costs as the posts that these VRS retirees occupied have not been subsequently abolished, particularly in managerial rungs.

The warning is equally clear at the macro level: In 1987 the UNDP declared that 'Economic development should be the means and social development should be the goal.' In 1999 the ILO stressed that 'Principles of the rights at work provide the ground rules and the framework for development; employment and incomes are the way in which production and output are translated into effective demand and decent standards of living. Social protection ensures human security and civil inclusion, and enables economic reform.'

FLEXIBLE WORK AND CONTINGENT WORKFORCE

In the past, many large companies in the private and public sectors encouraged lifetime employment. This is no longer so. In the past people stayed with a company in a single job/career. The new workforce is by and large aggressive, ambitious, footloose and loyal to themselves with the result that today neither are companies loyal to their employees nor employees loyal to their companies. Yet, today's organizations are expected to become learning organizations and build a customer base. But with high employee turnover, it is difficult for them to accumulate knowledge and become learning organizations.

Mere commercial contract encourages an instrumental orientation. Companies which fail to create a psychological contract will not be able to involve workers and get their commitment to work creatively and to their full capacity. Workers who are not loyal to their employers cannot be expected to build a loyal customer base. Hence, an employment contract with weak attachments on either side can have potentially counterproductive effects if either party pursues and persists in seeking an unfair advantage.

Contract work is increasing. Companies generally do not pay the same degree of attention to the recruitment, training and safety, wages, and productivity of contractual workers as they do with their regular employees. Often, when courts order companies to regularize contract workers, they start raising questions about qualifications, experience and suitability. But such arguments are not credible because they were not raised when the particular contract labour was hired in the first instance.

There have been questions about whether the contract is for work or of work. In either case the ultimate tests are the business and dependency tests. On both counts companies usually stand exposed because of the way in which contracts are structured/implemented. Also, when contracting out becomes a source of exploitation of cheap labour and an aggrieved party goes to court, such arrangements are questioned by the judiciary.

There are instances of new employment contracts, based on notions of a contingent workforce, which are a crude reminder of the earlier, old putting out system when trades distributed raw materials and tools to home workers, who would undertake the assigned tasks and bring back the finished products to the traders. Today's producers without factories are akin to such traders. In some cases workers/trade union leaders are turning out to be major labour contractors. In yet other cases, production decisions are left entirely to workers who organize themselves without a foreman or a contractor.

Companies need to draw a line on how much temporary help and contract employment to use and what implicit or explicit continuity to offer employees. The short-term economic and long-term economic and social consequences of new employment practices need to be evaluated carefully. Unfortunately in India we do not have empirical and longitudinal databases and hence we tend to rely on hunches, hindsight and anecdotal case histories/experiences. In view of that, it is important to formulate well-thought-out and comprehensive approaches to outsourcing and job security.

ENTERPRISE FLEXIBILITY

Firms maintain flexibility through organizing their production in diverse ways and through strategic decisions such as the following:

- Parallel production
- Outsourcing
- Lease licence manufacturing

- Franchising
- Employment of contingent workforce
- Shifting workforce from contract of employment/work to contract for work, etc.

These measures significantly reduce the number of regular employees needed and considerably increase the management's leverage over workers and their unions in times of industrial strife.

LABOUR FLEXIBILITY

Flexible practices in labour utilization should not increase the rigidity for labour. According to the labour law in several South-East Asian countries, the rights to recruit, reward, transfer, motivate, assign work and adjust the workforce are considered managerial rights. In India, however, these are the subject of collective bargaining. The applicability of several labour laws increases with the increase in the size of employment. This serves as a disincentive, and managements tend to reduce employment below certain threshold limits so as to not come under the purview of labour laws. This has, along with other factors, contributed significantly to an increase in capital intensity and a decrease in labour intensity in several industries.

Firms seek labour flexibility on one or more of the following counts:

- Numerical flexibility (size of workforce)
- Skill flexibility (composition of workforce)
- Functional flexibility (job enrichment/job enlargement)
- Locational flexibility (transfer/mobility)
- Time flexibility (flexi time)
- Pay flexibility (flexi pay)

REFERENCES

Blinder, A. (1991). *Paying for Performance*. Washington DC: Brookings Institution.
Das, G. (1996). 'A Million Reformers Now'. *Business World* (Calcutta). 27 December 1995-January 1996.
Davala, S. (1995). *Labour Strategies of Multinational Corporations in India*. New Delhi: Friedrich Ebert Stiftung.
Dayal, I. (1996). *Successful Applications of HRD: Case Studies of Indian Organisations*. New Delhi: New Concept.
Galbraith, J. (1977). *Organisation Design*. Reading, MA: Addison-Wesley.
Government of India (1995). *Economic Survey* 1999-2000; CSO, National Accounts Statistics, 1997-98 Advance Estimate. New Delhi: Government of India.
Flood, P.C. et al. (1996). *Managing without Traditional Methods: International Innovations in Human Resource Management*. Wokingham: Addison-Wesley.
Hackman, J.R. and G.R. Oldham (1980). *Work Design*. Reading, MA: Addison-Wesley.
Handy, C. (1990). *The Age of Unreason*. Cambridge, MA: Harvard Business School Press.
Hayes, R.H. et al. (1988). *Dynamic Manufacturing: Creating the Learning Organisation*. New York: Macmillan.
Howard, A. (1995). *The Changing Nature of Work*. San Francisco: Jossey-Bass.
IILS (1993). *Lean Production and Beyond*. Geneva: IILS.
ILO (1979). *New Forms of Work Organisation*. Vol. 2. Geneva: ILO.
ILO (1998). *World Labour Report*, 197-198. Geneva: ILO.
ILO (1999). *Decent Work*. Geneva: ILO.
Imai, M. (1986). *Kaizen: The Key to Japan's Competitive Success*. New York: McGraw-Hill.
IMD and World Economic Forum (1994). *World Competitiveness Report*. Geneva: IMD and World Economic Forum.
Jaikumar, R. (1986). 'Post-industrial Manufacturing'. *Harvard Business Review*. November-December, pp. 69-76.
Kohn, Alfie (1993). 'Why Incentive Plans cannot Work'. *Harvard Business Review*. Vol. 71(5), September-October. pp. 54-63.
Kuruvilla, S. and C.S. Venkata Ratnam (1996). 'Economic Development and Industrial Relations in South and Southeast Asia: Past Trends and Future Developments'. Paper presented at the IIRA 10th World Congress at Washington DC. 31 May-4 June 1995. *Industrial Relations Journal* (UK). 27(1), March, pp. 9-23.
Kuruvilla, S. and Douglas Chua (2000). 'How Do Nations Build Skills'. *Global Business Review* 1(1).
Lawler, E.E., III (1992). *The Ultimate Advantage: Creating the High Involvement Organisation*. San Francisco: Jossey-Bass.
Lawrence, P. and J. Lorsch (1969). *Organisation and Environment*. Irwin: Home-wood.
Lee, J.S. and A. Verma (eds) (1996). *Changing Employment Relations in Asian Pacific Countries*. Taipei: Chung-Hua Institution for Economic Research.
Locke, R. et al. (1995). *Employment Relations in a Changing World Economy*. Boston: MIT Press.
Majchrzak, A. (1988). *The Human Side of Factory Automation*. San Franscisco: Jossey-Bass.
Oxenham, J. et al. (1990). 'Improving the Quality of Education in Developing Countries', in K. Griffin and J. Knight (eds), *Human Development and the International Development Strategy for the 1990s*. London: Macmillan in association with the United Nations. pp. 101-127.

Peters, T.J. and R.H. Waterman (1982). *In Search of Excellence: Lessons from America's Best-run Companies*. New York: Harper.
Pettinger, R. (1999). *Employee Relations: A Guide to Policy and Practice in the Workplace*. Longon: Kogan Page.
Piore, M. and C. Sable (1984). *The Second Industrial Decade*. New York: Basic Books.
Roobeck, A. (1987). 'The Crisis in Fordism and the Rise of a New Technology Paradigm' *Futures*, Vol. 19, No. 2, pp. 129-154.
Samaddar, R. (1995). *Workers and Automation*. New Delhi: Sage Publications.
Schonberger, R.J. (1986). *World Class Manufacturing: The Lessons of Simplicity Applied*. New York: The Free Press.
Shimada, H. (1993). 'Japanese Management of Auto Production in the United States: An Overview of "Human Technology"', in IILS, *Lean Production and Beyond*. Geneva: IILS.
Shrouti, A. and Nandkumar (1994). *New Economic Policy, Changing Management Strategies—Impact on Workers And Trade Unions*. New Delhi: Friedrich Ebert Stiftung.
Stern, R.W. (1993). *Changing Asia*. Cambridge: Cambridge University Press.
Storey, J. (ed) (1987). *New Wave Manufacturing Strategies: Organisational and Human Resource Management Dimensions*. London: Paul Chapman.
Thurman, J. et al. (1993). *On Business and Work*. Geneva: ILO.
Trist, E.L. et al. (1963). *Organisational Choice*. London: Tavistock.
Valery, N. (1987). 'Factory of the Future'. *The Economist*. 30 May, pp. 1-18.
Venkata Ratnam, C.S. (1990). *Unusual Collective Agreements*. New Delhi: Global Business Press.
Venkata Ratnam, C.S. (1994). 'Skills Development in Medium and Large Scale Firms in India'. Paper presented at the 1994 Asian Regional Conference on Human Resource Management and Economic Development in Asia organised by Japan Institute of Labour and Japan Industrial Relations Research Association, 17-18 March 1994, Tokyo, Japan. Tokyo: Japan Labour Institute.
Venkata Ratnam, C.S. (1996a). 'Welfare or Moneyfare: Collective Bargaining and Social Security'. A Project of the UNDP/Centre for Development Studies, Trivandrum. New Delhi: International Management Institute (Mimeo).
Venkata Ratnam, C.S. (1996b). 'Restructuring Agreements'. A Project of the Planning Commission. New Delhi: International Management Institute (Mimeo).
Venkata Ratnam, C.S. (1996c). 'Future of Indian Trade Unions'. New Delhi: International Confederation of Free Trade Unions, Asia-Pacific Region (South Asia office) (Mimeo).
Venkata Ratnam, C.S. (ed) (1996d). *Industrial Relations in Indian States*. New Delhi: Global Business Press (forthcoming).
Venkata Ratnam, C.S. and B.K. Srivastava (1996). *Personnel Management/Human Resources*. New Delhi: Tata McGraw-Hill (6th reprint).
Virmani, B.R. (1996). 'Redefining Industrial Relations'. *Indian Journal of Industrial Relations*. 31(2), October 1995, pp. 153-177.
Verma, A. (1995). *Employment Relations in a Growing Economy*. London: Routledge.
Walker, K. (1974). 'Workers Participation in Management'. *IILS Bulletin*. Geneva.
Womack, J.P., D.L. James and D. Roos (1990). *The Machine that Changed the World*. New York: Rawson Associates.
World Bank (1995). *East Asian Miracle*. Washington DC: World Bank.
World Bank (1996). *World Development Report*. Washington DC: Oxford University Press and World Bank.

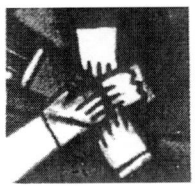

Author Index

Adams, R.J. 128, 285
ADB (Asian Development Bank). 156, 162, 176, 238
Agiletta, M. 79
Ahluwalia, I.J. 16
AIMA (All India Management Association). 162
APO (Asian Productivity Organization) 41

Babu, V. 134
Bamber, G. 79
Baru, S. 158, 159, 160
Begin, J. 121
Bengal Chamber of Commerce 149
Bhagwati, J. 133
Bhanoji Rao, V.V. 134
Bhatt, B.J. 112
Bhattacharya, B.B. 133
Blinder, A. 323
Block, R.N. 285
Blyton, P. 94
Bronstein, A.S. 80

Campbell, D. 99
Chandler, A.E. 87

Chellaiah, R.J. 134
Chew, R. 110
Chew, S.B. 110
Chiang, T.B. 115
Chibber, P. 141
Chua, D. 316
CMIE, 20, 24, 25
Collier, D. 85
Collier, R.B. 85
Cordova, E. 209

Das, G. 304, 305, 324
Davala, S. 21, 32, 33, 61, 324
De, N.R. 72
Debroy, B. 133
Delhi Science Forum. 166
Deyo, F.B. 85, 110
Drekker, 85
Dreze, J. 132
Dunlop, J.T. 30

Edgren, G. 79
Egorov, V. 79, 89
Erickson, C. 110, 129

Fallon, P.R. 21, 154
Fashoyin, T. 94

Flood, P.C. 312, 328
Fong, P.E. 84
Freeman, R.B. 92, 96–7
Frenkel, S. 91, 128
Frensen, J. 22

Galbraith, J.K. 93, 311
Gangopadhyay, S. 149
Ghemawat, P. 141
Gladstone, A. 247
Government of India, 87, 304
Goyal, S.K. 22
Grace, E.123
Griesgraber, J.M. 285
Guha, B.P. 150, 134
Guntur, P.C. 285
Gupta, S.P. 50
Gupte, V. 150

Hackman, J.R. 311
Hakeem, M.A. 153
Hashim, S.R. 155
Hayes, R.H. 311
Hoe, L.A. 285
Huff, W. G.
Hyman, R. 82, 90

ICFTU (International Confederation of Free Trade Unions) 99
ICFTU-APRO (International Confederation of Free Trade Unions–Asian Pacific Regional Office) 57, 90
IILS (International Institute for Labour Studies) 80, 310
IIRA/FES 295
ILO (International Labour Organization) 32, 77, 79, 80, 89, 90, 93, 96–7, 122, 134, 151, 154, 160, 164–5, 167, 169–70, 209, 213–14, 231, 239–40, 310–11, 313
ILO-APPOT (International Labour Organization–Asian Pacific Project on Tripartism) 37, 57
Imai, M. 310
IMD (International Institute for Management Development) 71
IOE (International Orgn of Employers) 291

Jaikumar, R. 312
Jalan, B.P. 164
Johri, C.K. 149
Jones, H.G. 247
Joshi, V. 134

Kapila, U. 134
Katz, H.C. 118, 122
Kaufman, B.E. 76
Kennedy, V.D. 30
Kerr, C. 78
Kochan, T.A. 27, 79, 80, 85, 92, 100
Kohn, Alfie. 323
Kumar, N. 61
Kuruvilla, S. 77, 82, 108–14, 118–9, 124, 127, 129, 149, 304, 316

Lansburry, A. 85
Lawler, 311
Lawrence, P. 311
Lazonick, A.E. 87
Lee, J.S. 313
Lee, M.L. 117
Little, I.M.D. 134
Locke, R.M. 83, 85
Lorsch, P. 311
Lucas, R.E.B. 21, 154

Madrid, J.C.K. 86
Markensten, K. 61
Maskus, K.E. 285
Mathur, A. 22, 72
Mathur, K. 38
Majumdar, S.K. 179
Mazumdar, D., 179
Marshal, A. 179
Masilamani, S. 171
Mehrotra, R. 278
Miller, E.L.112

Nandkumar, 324
Nath, S. 34, 292
NCL (National Commission on Labour) 195
NLLA (National Labour Law Association) 96

Offreneo, R. 115, 121
Oldham, 311
Oxenham, J. 313
Ozaki, M. 79, 93, 242, 247

Pagnucco, A. 114, 119
Park, Y.D. 117
Patibandla, M. 141
Pechanski, V. 79
Peters, T.J. 311
Pettinger, R. 329
Piore, M. 79, 85, 310

Ramaswamy, E.A. 22, 32-3, 72, 119
Rao, S.L. 134
Rasaiah, R. 108, 123
Reddy, Y.R.K. 119
Reich, R. 98
Roberts, K. 285
Roobeck, A. 310

Sabel, C. 79, 310
Schonberger, R.J. 311
Schregle, J. 77, 99
Sen, A. 132, 133
Sen, R. 87
Sengenber, W. 99
Sengupta, A.K. 33, 72
Sengupta, N.K. 134
Sharma, B. 48, 124, 127
Sheth, N.R. 28, 32, 38
Shrouti, A. 324
Singh, 285
Smith, A.E. 83
Standing, G. 90
Starcher, G. 240
Stern, 303
Storey, J. 310, 312
Sziraczi, G. 90

Taira, K. 87, 89
Thirkel, J. 89
Thomson, A. 85
Tolliday, S. 83
Towers, B. 78
Trebilcock, A. 92, 211, 218
Trist, E.L. 311
Tsuru, T. 90
Tulpule, B 61
Turnbull, P. 76
Turner, L. 118

UNDP (United Nations Development Project) 71, 106, 165
US Department of Labour 288

Vaid, K.N. 23
Valery, N. 312
Venkata Ratnam, C.S. 23, 28, 52, 77, 79, 82, 88-90, 93, 111, 114, 121, 153, 155, 304, 314, 324-5
Verma, A. 23, 90, 124, 127, 313
Virmani, B.R. 324

Wadhwa, C.D. 149, 177
Wadhwa, W. 134, 149
Walker, K. 41, 327
Warner, R. 85
Waterman, R.H. 311
WEF (World Economic Forum) 71
Weiler, P.C. 90
Whitley, 26
Workers' Solidarity Centre 21
World Bank 78, 93, 97-8, 106, 134, 167, 304, 311

Zapata, F. 78
Zeitlin, J. 83

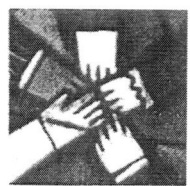

Subject Index

Balance of payments 135–6
BIFR (Board of Industrial and Financial reconstruction Corporation) 217–8, 224

Central Government finances 142
Code of Conduct 115–6
Collective bargaining
  concessions 69, 326
  decentralized 79, 93, 325
  duration 45
  enterprise level 43, 92
  individualization of contracts 81, 325–6
  levels 43
  pay revision 53
  productivity 45, 113
  structures 114–5
  subjects 46
  trade-offs 79, 93
  unions 62
Communication 95
Compensation
  See: Wages
Consumer courts 56

Debt 135–6, 161

Decentralization
  collective bargaining
  workplace flexibility 122
Democracy and development 17, 161
Department of Public Enterprise 53
Disinvestment
  See Privatization

East Asian economic crisis 82
Education and training
  See: Skills development
Employee shares/stock options 64–5, 320–1
Employers' organizations 89, 100
Employment 147–8, 154–5
Exchange rates 138
Exchange reserves 135
Export oriented policies 8, 100, 108–111
Export Processing Zones 67, 86–7, 100

Five Year Plans 14
Flexibility 80, 81, 117–8, 240, 243, 332–4
Foreign investment 140–1

Globalization 89, 100–1
Governance 157–8, 169

Subject Index **341**

Government Role 79, 86-7, 107, 128-9
   union power 118
Grievance redressal 95

High performance workplaces 77

Import substitution/industrialization strategy/policies 108-11
Industrial relations
   adversarial 82
   centre-state relations 18
   contextual factors 84
   diverse trends 81-2
   economic development 104, 107-11
   human resource policies 79-81, 127
   industrialization policy 15-6, 18, 48-9, 77,
   macro level policies 127
   transformation 98
Inequality 156
Inflation 148
International labour standards
   See: Social clause

Job security 96, 124, 163, 175, 245-8
Judicial activism 267-80

Labour
   competitiveness 152
   law reforms 50-1, 53, 95-6, 168, 184-97, 260-4
   policy 255-9
   productivity 16, 149
Labour management relations
   See: Industrial relations
Lean production 81
Liberalization 45-8, 89, 100-1
Lock-outs 148, 153-4

Mixed economy 77
Multinational Corporations 58-73

National Renewal Fund 57, 226-7, 249
Need-based minimum wage 38-9
Non-governmental organizations, 87, 100

Pension 53-4
Poverty 148, 155-6, 164
Privatization 63-7, 144-6, 158, 160, 163-4, 166, 168, 170, 230-1
Productivity 149

Redeployment 57
Regional economic blocks 126-7
Regional imbalances 182-4
Retraining 57

Sickness 173
Skills development 77, 85, 97, 110, 123-4, 169, 217-8, 239, 313-7
Social Accord 92
Social clause 99, 126, 281-7
Social dialogue
   See: Tripartism
Social exclusion 92
Social labelling 87, 288-91, 299-301
Social pacts 92
Social safety nets 56-7, 150-1
Social security 96, 148, 150
State government finances 143
Strikes
   incidence of 124-5, 148-9, 153-4
   right to 117
Suicide pacts 93

Tariff structure 139-40
Trade unions
   cyber unionism 91
   declining 120-1
   federations 115-6
   fragmentation 121
   movement 89-90
   recognition 42-3, 185-8
   response to changes 94, 99-100, 169-74
   role 100
Tripartism 36-8, 55-6, 66, 71, 92, 208-38

Unemployment 147-8

Voluntary retirement 58

Wages
　cheap labour 95
　contingent compensation 85, 317–21
　controls 48–9
　flexible 123
　minimum wages 148, 91–3
　policies 61
Washington Consensus package 132
Workers' cooperative 230–1
Workers' participation in Management 38–42, 86, 122–3, 127
Workforce
　new generation 94
Workplace changes 85, 118–9, 303, 306–12
Works committees 38, 327
World Trade Organization 84, 126, 162

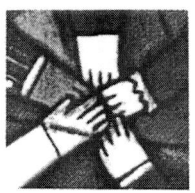

About the Author

C.S. Venkata Ratnam is Professor of Human Resource Management and Industrial Relations at the International Management Institute, New Delhi. Earlier he was on the faculty of the Administrative Staff College of India, Hyderabad, and Andhra University, Waltair. Professor Venkata Ratnam has been a consultant to several organizations in India and abroad including the International Labour Organization, Geneva, the Asian Productivity Organization, Tokyo, and the International Confederation of Free Trade Unions, Singapore. He is the Founder-Secretary of the Indian Industrial Relations Association and editor of the journal *Global Business Review*. Among his previous publications are *Unusual Collective Agreements, Managing People, Industrial Relations in Indian Industry* (edited) and *Industrial Relations in Indian States* (edited).